AMERICA'S
INTERE!
POST-COLD WAR WORLD
ISSUES AND DILEMMAS

AMERICA'S NATIONAL INTEREST IN A POST-COLD WAR WORLD
ISSUES AND DILEMMAS

ALVIN Z. RUBINSTEIN
University of Pennsylvania

McGRAW-HILL, INC.

New York   St. Louis   San Francisco   Auckland   Bogotá   Caracas
Lisbon   London   Madrid   Mexico City   Milan   Montreal   New Delhi
San Juan   Singapore   Sydney   Tokyo   Toronto

AMERICA'S NATIONAL INTEREST IN A POST-COLD WAR WORLD
ISSUES AND DILEMMAS

Copyright © 1994 by McGraw-Hill, Inc. All rights reserved.
Printed in the United States of America. Except as permitted under the
United States Copyright Act of 1976, no part of this publication may be
reproduced or distributed in any form or by any means, or stored in a data
base or retrieval system, without the prior written permission of the
publisher.

 This book is printed on recycled, acid-free paper containing
10% postconsumer waste.

2 3 4 5 6 7 8 9 0 DOH DOH 9 0 9 8 7 6 5 4

ISBN 0-07-054162-0

This book was set in Melior by Better Graphics, Inc.
The editors were Peter Labella and Fred H. Burns;
the production supervisor was Denise L. Puryear.
The cover was designed by Rafael Hernandez.
R. R. Donnelley & Sons Company was printer and binder.

Library of Congress Cataloging-in-Publication Data

America's national interest in a post-cold war world: issues and
    dilemmas / [edited by] Alvin Z. Rubinstein.
        p.   cm.
    Includes bibliographical references.
    ISBN 0-07-054162-0
    1. United States—Foreign relations—1989-   I. Rubinstein, Alvin
Z.
E840.A638   1994
327.73—dc20   93-33417

ABOUT THE EDITOR

Alvin Z. Rubinstein is professor of political science at the University of Pennsylvania. He is also a senior fellow of the Foreign Policy Research Institute, a private think-tank in Philadelphia. He is the author of many publications. Among his books are the following: *Soviet Foreign Policy Since World War II*; *Red Star on the Nile*; *Soviet Policy toward Turkey, Iran, and Afghanistan*; *Yugoslavia and the Nonaligned World*; and *Moscow's Third World Strategy*, which received the Shulman Prize of the American Association for the Advancement of Slavic Studies.

Dr. Rubinstein has also edited and co-edited ten other books. The recent such edited works are *Russia and America: From Rivalry to Reconciliation*; *The Arab-Israeli Conflict: Perspectives*; and *Anti-Americanism in the Third World*. In addition, he has more than 100 articles in scholarly journals to his credit.

In pursuing his various research interests, Dr. Rubinstein has been awarded fellowships and grants from a number of sources. These include the Rockefeller Foundation; the Guggenheim Foundation; the Ford Foundation; the Earhart Foundation; the Social Science Research Council; and NATO. He has been a visiting professor at the University of Virginia, Lehigh University, and the American University in Cairo. He has been a visiting fellow of Clare Hall at the University of Cambridge, and a visiting associate of St. Anthony's College of Oxford University. He has traveled and lectured widely in Russia, the Middle East, South Asia, and Western Europe. On various occasions he lectured for the U.S. Information Agency in various posts abroad.

**To Frankie
Whose Questions Prompted
This Exploration**

CONTENTS

PREFACE

"There is scarce truth enough alive to make societies secure."

William Shakespeare
Measure for Measure

U.S. foreign policy is at a crossroads. The bipolar world that dominated international relations between 1945 and 1991 is changing into an asymmetrically ordered multipolar world. Cold War challenges are being replaced by new ones. And in this new environment, the United States is increasingly constrained by growing domestic concerns and budgetary limitations from pursuing the freewheeling internationalist policy of the past. Containment worked and helped defeat the former Soviet Union. A new strategy that can attract the support of the American people has yet to emerge. What should be its aims? What are the key threats it must cope with? What options are available to U.S. leaders? What considerations—political, moral, strategic, economic—should determine the choice of options?

This collection of essays was prepared to introduce students to the evolving issues and policy dilemmas facing American foreign policy in the decade ahead and to encourage an examination of the difficult choices that must be made. It is not a survey of theory or theorists, but an exploration of policy imperatives. The readings were selected with the following objectives in mind: first, to set forth succinctly but informatively the key issues of U.S. foreign policy; second, to juxtapose for discussion diverse interpretations which involve substantially different policy responses; and third, to challenge students to identify what concrete policies they would recommend to the leadership— and to justify these recommendations in terms of America's national interest. In each instance the material was chosen also for qualities that will hopefully engage the student's interest—readability and relevance to the contemporary challenges in a rethinking of America's aims and priorities.

The editor's introductory essay to each chapter seeks to place the readings in a political–diplomatic perspective and to draw attention to their saliences. Taken together, these essays and the readings are intended to present a coherent and comprehensive exploration of the key issues that face U.S. leaders. Many foreign policy problems cannot be included because of considerations of space: for example, defining deterrence in a post-Cold War world; dealing with rogue regimes; restoring industrial competitiveness without undermining the principle of free trade; forging closer ties to Latin America; fostering regional settlements in the Middle East, Southern Africa, Southern Asia, and Eastern Europe; reconciling internationally recognized boundaries of established nation-states with the mounting pressure of ethno-linguistic groups for autonomy or independence; and enhancing the role of international law. The list goes on, but practical needs draw the line at what can fruitfully be encompassed in one volume.

This book is divided into six parts. In Part One the first chapter discusses the origins, dynamics, and continuing utility of the nation-state even in an era of technological and economic transformation; and the second chapter explores the meaning and viability of the concept of balance of power, which is perhaps the most enduring explanation for the behavior of nation-states in international relations. Part Two examines three factors that established the framework within which U.S. foreign policy developed at different periods in its history. Chapter 3 introduces the notion of the national interest and offers three different perspectives which illustrate the difficulties inherent in distinguishing "essential" interests from those that are merely "important," and in agreeing on what criteria should guide the actions of policymakers. Chapter 4 grapples with the moral dimensions of foreign policy. Are there universal moral principles that should shape a nation's behavior? What if they conflict with the national interest? For example, during the Cold War, the desire to avoid nuclear war took precedence, for the most part, over the concern for human rights. On what grounds are such choices to be made? Chapter 5 considers what circumstances should determine whether recourse to the use of force is necessary for protecting vital national interests. When to intervene, on whose behalf, and for what purpose(s) are problems that increasingly beset American leaders. Yet, until we decide what comprises the "national interest" there will be difficulty in agreeing on the roles to be played by ethical principles and military force in U.S. policy. All are interrelated elements in the search for a coherent strategy.

Part Three looks at several problems in which there is an inextricable linkage between domestic considerations and foreign policy implications. Not only are these perplexing situations growing in importance, but solutions to them cannot long be deferred without seriously affecting the future of American society. Chapter 6 examines the dilemmas involved in the fight against drugs; Chapter 7, the issue of illegal immigration; and chapter 8, America's adaptation to a rapidly changing world economy.

Part Four explores the nature of U.S. alliances and alignments in an altered world. Chapter 9 presents contrasting views of what NATO and East Asia mean for the United States. Chapter 10 offers a general and still highly tentative outline of what the U.S. approach should be to Russia. Chapter 11 provides two competing overviews of the United States' involvement and interests in the Middle East. U.S. policy toward the much-publicized conflicts in the Arab-Israeli and Persian Gulf sectors of the Middle East is not detailed, but both essays put forth a thoughtful rationale for what should guide U.S. policymakers in the area.

Part Five deals with two functional problem areas: nuclear proliferation, particularly in the Middle East and South Asia, with proposals for controlling its spread; and attempts to enhance the importance of the United Nations' role in crisis management and peacekeeping, with what these imply for the United States.

Finally, Part Six offers a number of perspectives on what the United States should do as it gropes for a coherent national strategy that will take us into the next century. There are no easy answers, only alternatives based on very different assumptions and objectives. Until a follow-up national strategy to the policy of containment is formulated and adopted by the President and the Congress, and accepted by the country at large as suitable for the future, there will be a need for continuing debate on the issues presented here.

The post-Cold War world is unlike any that we have heretofore known. New thinking means, at a minimum, redefinition of jaded labels such as left and right, (neo)liberal and (neo) conservative, even radical and reactionary. The complexity of foreign policy concerns demands clarification of basic policy assumptions.

I appreciate the many and profound ways in which the threads of foreign policy issues are part of the larger fabric that defines our sense of what America is and should be. But policymakers generally react to concrete and pressing issues. Focusing on them is a way of identifying and analyzing the principal priorities that have commanded the attention of successive generations of U.S. leaders. Further, introducing students to foreign policy through the study of key issues compels them to seek their own ways to integrate political, moral, economic, and strategic concerns; and to relate previous American policy to the unfolding new agendas.

It is a pleasure to express my appreciation to the authors and institutions whose thoughtful writings are represented here: grateful acknowledgment is made to the publishers whose permission to reprint specific material is indicated in a footnote at the beginning of each reading, and to Robin Stoehr, for her support. I also want to express my appreciation for the helpful comments of those who reviewed the manuscript for this text: Joseph Lepgold, Georgetown University; Frederic Pearson, Wayne State University; Phil Shively, University of Minnesota; and Vladimir Wozniuk, Western New England College.

Alvin Z. Rubinstein

AMERICA'S NATIONAL INTEREST IN A POST-COLD WAR WORLD
ISSUES AND DILEMMAS

PART ONE

AMERICA IN A WORLD OF NATION-STATES

CHAPTER 1

The Systemic Context

The United States is part of an international system made up of nation-states. Its foreign policy proceeds on the premise that agreements, to be effective, must ultimately be concluded with the governments of other sovereign states. This determines the approach to dealing with friends or foes, functional or humanitarian problems, and regional organizations and the United Nations.

A relatively new political-territorial unit, the nation-state dates from about the middle of the sixteenth century, though the 1648 Treaty of Westphalia is usually cited to symbolize its formal beginning. Out of this development came concepts that are central to the way in which we think about foreign policy: "Sovereignty," the supremacy of a political leadership within its own territory; "territoriality," the inviolability of a nation within internationally recognized boundaries; equality of nations in international law; balance of power, a mode of seeking security in an imperfect world; and the notion of the national interest. Leslie Lipson (Reading 1) explains the circumstances that shaped the creation of the nation-state and the dominant characteristics that shaped its behavior.

As with all previous historical political-territorial units—the family, tribe, city-state, centralized empire—the nation-state evolved in response to the quest for security,

for protection against external threats. Integral to this concern were also the aims of promoting domestic stability and preserving order. The nation-state appeared in Western Europe because of a fortuitous combination of circumstances: navigational discoveries that extended the mobility of Portuguese, Spanish, English, French, and Dutch seapower; advances in military technology that quickly gave Western rulers the edge over those in other regions of the world; the Protestant Reformation, which fostered the rise of capitalism and an economic "take-off" in the West; and adventurous, ambitious leaders, eager for gold and goods. The consequent period of expansion led to the conquest of stagnating feudal imperial systems in Central and South America, Central Asia and the Indian subcontinent, China, and Africa. In the centuries that followed Westphalia, the Western states expanded and dominated the world. Their drive, military power, and economic vitality made them seem invincible, but they, too, became afflicted with the same kinds of weaknesses that had undermined the regimes over which they had triumphed in the eighteenth and nineteenth centuries. Two world wars, communal strife on a global scale, led to the decline of some countries, but not to a different international system.

In time, the nation-state system may be supplanted by new ideas and institutions.

But that era is yet in the future. The multinational corporations, the global revolutions in communications, and the permeability of the nation-state to everything from popular culture to financial markets affect structure, processes, and values in every country. Still, the expectations in the 1970s and 1980s of attendant radical political changes have proved to be premature at best, perhaps even unrealistically utopian: interdependence has not yet transcended nationalism; integration and regionalism have not ended national egoism and narrow self-interest; cooperation has not rendered conflict obsolete; and looming ecological problems have not significantly restructured national priorities or elite thinking.

The ideals of the Western political order have been globalized. They inspired former colonial areas to strive for their freedom and to establish themselves as independent nation-states. The number of nation-states has more than tripled since the end of the Second World War, and the list keeps growing. In 1991, for example, Ethiopia toppled its pro-Soviet dictator and ushered in a government that has accepted the prospect of the province of Eritrea's declaring itself an independent country (as it did in April 1993). Even more dramatically, the abortive attempt in August to overthrow then-President Mikhail Gorbachev accelerated secessionist movements throughout the Soviet Union: in September, the Soviet parliament recognized the independence of Estonia, Latvia, and Lithuania (the Baltic states that, 51 years earlier, had been forcibly incorporated into the Soviet Union, as a result of a deal between Stalin and Hitler); and in December, the Soviet Union itself was dissolved, and the remaining twelve constituent union-republics became independent and members of the United Nations (the Russian Federation assumed the seat in the Security Council formerly held by the USSR). In 1992 Yugoslavia fell apart. Thus far, the new nations of Croatia, Slovenia, Macedonia, and Bosnia-Herzegovina have emerged from the ethno-linguistic mosaic that was created in 1919 out of the ruins of the Austro-Hungarian empire. The Czech and Slovak Federated Republic arranged a peaceful political divorce, which went into effect on January 1, 1993. Ethnic tensions and nationalist fervor may bring further fragmentation.

The prospects of most of these new nation-states are bleak. Few have politically unified elites and most are not economically viable, but nationalism has superseded concerns over economic vulnerability. Security is an even more daunting problem. In an age of high-tech weapons and fast-moving powerful armies, small states with indefensible borders and restive minorities have little prospect of repelling determined invaders. Kuwait was fortunate: the United States mobilized an international coalition on its behalf to reverse Iraq's aggression; Bosnia-Herzegovina is a different matter. Notwithstanding all of this, self-determination, historical memory, cultural cohesiveness and distinctiveness, and the appeal of independent nationhood add up to a potent force.

Hedley Bull's brief for the nation-state's remaining the key political-territorial actor in international relations is a healthy corrective to formulations that look beyond the existing state system to nascent alternatives (Reading 2). While acknowledging the state's shortcomings, he notes its growing prominence. He lauds the progress toward regional cooperation and integration, but points out that it does not signify the surrender of sovereignty or the end of national loyalties, or of a national commitment to retaining the nation-state as an independent political entity. His stress on the positive functions of the nation-state in maintaining a stable international order and a framework for lasting coexistence is both perceptive and paradoxical. He postulates the inevitability of rivalry in the state system, but then, in a surprisingly hopeful perspective, insists that states are not always antithetical to one another's interests and that they may be edging toward the rudiments of some kind of international society, with a core community of interests between greater and lesser powers evolving over time.

The nation-state system has a number of implications for U.S. foreign policy in a post-Cold War world. First, the United States needs a differentiated policy. It cannot be all things to 183 other nations and additional assorted ethnic groups seeking independence. It cannot serve as the world's policeman—it no longer has the surplus resources, financial wherewithal, overwhelming deployable military power, or domestic support for such a role. With communism discredited and the Soviet Union a historical memory, there is no ideological-military adversary requiring a mass mobilization of the American people against a global threat.

In the very nature of coming to terms with a changing international situation, the United States must make important policy choices. Some nations—and issues—matter more than others. What are the priorities and how do we determine them?

Second, the multiplicity of states has increased the difficulties of maintaining friendly relations between them, but the danger of global war has virtually disappeared. The concept of security needs to be rethought. With the collapse of the Soviet Union came a sharply diminished possibility of nuclear or conventional war in Europe. Looking ahead, Russia is less a military threat than an economic problem. Where, then, are the security threats to U.S. interests likely to come from? Rivalry is an integral element of the state system and tension between states are inevitable, but conflict is not. All of this has far-reaching implications for national strategy, traditional alliances, and defense expenditures.

Third, although a great power, indeed still the world's strongest, the United States is less capable of affecting regional and global alignments and developments, or the domestic behavior of nations, than at any time since 1945. It finds itself with fewer instruments to influence a world of more numerous, independent-minded actors. Beset by complex and troublesome problems, it lacks the freedom of action and diplomatic maneuver which an earlier generation of leaders enjoyed. To cite but one example, the United States invaded Panama in December 1989 to overthrow the dictatorship of Manuel Noriega and restore a democratic system. This mission was accomplished, but despite U.S. assistance there was not the melioration of Panama's endemic problems, as had been widely expected by the Panamanians. If the United States cannot reverse the pattern of economic inequality, poverty, corruption, weak leadership and complacent oligarchies, and lack of law and order in a relatively compliant client state, what can it expect to accomplish elsewhere? Lacking the resources or, at any rate, the willingness to assume a greater burden to help other countries, what should U.S. policy be toward the more than 100 impoverished less developed countries?

Fourth, the United States needs to come to terms with resurgent nationalism. In most instances, such manifestations do not threaten vital U.S. interests, yet they elicit mixtures of concern, censure, and sympa-thy. Under what circumstances and to what extent should the United States support the efforts of newly established states to find security and develop stable societies?

1.   Nation-States and the Evolution of the Modern State System

Leslie Lipson

The Crisis of the Nation-State.   There is no unit of government that has conformed with consistency to its own ideal. The system of classical Greece, with its principle of autonomy for each urban-rural cluster, negated the possibility of wider union either through a free combination of states or through imperial subjection to one. Efforts of the former kind were not long enduring; and efforts of the latter description, though repeatedly made, provoked opposition and war. Rome, which commenced its political history as a city-state like the rest, was the one which did succeed in the policy of imperial conquest, thereby eliminating the city-state as an independent unit and substituting for it the new unit of a widespread empire. But even Rome could not command the world, and the unity and peace that were her ideals arrived at their bounds to the north and east. A similar story was repeated in the Middle Ages, when the dream of a universal order was pursued by Papacy and Holy Roman Empire alike. In practice, however, neither in the secular sphere nor the spiritual was universality achieved. Each of these three experiments was an endeavor to provide a structure within which men could build their welfare in safety. Each lasted for as long as it was able to fulfill that need, and collapsed when it could no longer do so.

SOURCE: Leslie Lipson. *The Great Issues of Politics: An Introduction to Political Science*, Englewood Cliffs, NJ: Prentice-Hall, 1954, pp. 350–361, excerpts. Footnotes deleted. © 1954, renewed 1982. Reprinted by permission of Prentice Hall, Englewood Cliffs, New Jersey.

In this respect, the history of the nation-state is identical with that of its predecessors. The nation-state emerged at a time when it was more capable than the medieval system of supplying humanity with security and well-being. But this unit of government, like the rest, has failed to apply its own ideal, with the result that it is now decaying or even dying. Our contemporary world is in the throes of a major transition from the out-moded nation-state to some new unit. Thus seen in historical perspective, the age in which we live is comparable to the readjustment that occurred between the breakdown of the *Polis* and the rise of the Roman Empire, or between the fall of Rome and the emergence of the medieval order, or between the collapse of the latter and the founding of the nation-state. Once again, a fresh attempt is being made to discover the territorial unit best adapted under twentieth-century conditions to furnish men with their basic political needs. Since modern internationalism, however, is a reaction to the declining adequacy of nationalism, the threads of the discussion must be picked up at the point where the last chapter left off. What failings has the nation-state revealed? Is there a superior alternative in sight?

Despite the strivings of states to build nations and of nations to organize states, a perfect correspondence has not been everywhere achieved between nationality and statehood. The world still abounds with instances of people united by a common culture, language, and religion, who are striving toward a national consciousness and seeking to formalize it in a state of their own. Such aspirations are especially noticeable nowadays in the colonial dependencies of imperial powers. Conversely, there are cases aplenty of states that have continued to include in their jurisdiction a subject people who are unincorporated in the national body politic. In some countries those subjects are a minority; in others, South Africa, for example, they are the majority. These are facts that require an explanation. If the nation-state was in vogue and set the fashion for over four centuries, why has there been so imperfect a correlation between statehood and nationality?

Imperialism and Sea Power. The answer—which is a product partly of historical timing and partly of economic and military factors combining in a political result—is most revealing. It must not be forgotten that, when the nation-state was born, there came simultaneously into the world its twin —sea-powered imperialism. How inseparably these were connected is plainly written in the annals of Spain, Portugal, England, France, and the Netherlands. Of course, the practice of imperialism, which can be defined as the forcible subjection of a community to alien rule, was no novelty. Nor was the employment of sea-power, as the Athenians, Phoenicians, Norsemen, and Venetians, may bear witness. What was new, however, was the expansion of political power upon an oceanic scale. The discovery that the earth was round and could be circumnavigated was quickly put to a use that challenged comparison with Rome. The peoples of western Europe first mapped the world; then with gunpowder, galleons, and gumption, they partitioned it. . . .

The success of imperialism, however, and its duration for four centuries, involved the nation-state in a fundamental inconsistency. Depending on the angle from which it is viewed, this unit of government can be considered the opposite of either localism or internationalism. Both of the latter principles were characteristic of the medieval period, one receiving theoretical lip-service and the other reflecting more accurately the realities of social organization. Since the nation-state marked a rejection of the system immediately preceding, nei-

ther local nor international influence was tolerable to its architects. . . .

As in other respects, the doctrine that was the maid-of-all-work for the nation-state—the theory of sovereignty—here, too, was enlisted into service. Sovereignty was construed to mean that the government of the nation-state, supreme within its own jurisdiction over local bodies and churches, acknowledged no political or legal superior beyond its territorial boundaries. "My dogs," as Queen Elizabeth I of England once phrased it, "shall wear no collars but mine own." Authority, allegiance, and law were to be the exclusive monopoly of the nation-state, and, as such, were not articles for import across national frontiers. Were they, however, articles for export? There precisely lay the inconsistency. The nation-state, whatever its professions, acted upon a double standard. Both in external and internal affairs it claimed to be a law unto itself. Limitations upon its freedom of action diminished its sovereignty and consequently were inadmissible. But, though unwilling to submit to control from outside, it professed to see no wrong in subjecting others to its will. The practice of imperialism violated the principle of sovereignty by denying to others the very freedom on which the nationalist insisted. In effect, throughout the entire era of the nation-state, there never was a time when the political ordering of mankind conformed consistently to the idea of having a number of separate units of government, each self-contained. Imperialism meant a division of the human race into élite peoples who ruled, and whose nationality could find outlets for expression, and subject peoples whose national aspirations must be suppressed. Hence imperialism negated the first premise from which the nation-state proceeded. Therefore it is no accident that the twins, which were born together have lived in perennial conflict, in this century are dying together.

This combination of nationalism with imperialism and the ensuing dilemma produced an economic counterpart. During the sixteenth, seventeenth, and eighteenth centuries—that is, before the philosophy of laissez faire became prevalent—prosperity was sought by methods that exactly applied political concepts to economics. The politics of nationalism were matched by the economics of nationalism, which was the essence of the mercantile system; and, correspondingly, political imperialism was yoked to economic imperialism. Colonies, considered the "possessions" of the imperial power, were organized to supply it with raw materials and precious metals, as they were also to import its manufactures and carry on their commerce in its ships. This is not to deny that additional motives influenced the settlement or acquisition of colonies. The desire of dissident minorities to emigrate; the strategic quest for bases, ports of call, and defensible frontiers; the work of missionaries who preached the Christian gospel—many a magnet, besides trade, attracted nations to plant their flag on distant shores. But that the single most important factor in empire-building was the economic, can hardly be denied. Through imperialism the nation-state could grow more prosperous—or so it was hoped.

From the standpoint of security an empire might be judged as much of a liability as an asset. It was true that the treasure which some colonies yielded could be used to build more warships and pay more troops that would then defend the mother-country and also keep subjects more surely in subjection. But, situated across the oceans, colonies were remote and exposed. They might prove hard to defend against an invading rival or to hold against a rebellion. Furthermore, when the imperial power was itself in danger of attack on its home terrain, less force could be spared for garrisons abroad. By spreading its resources thin, the imperialist nation-state held out many hostages to fortune. It was therefore vulnerable to either amputation at the extremities or attack at the heart. The latter alternative was, of course, the primary concern of nation-statesmen, since colonies were of no avail if the motherland were insecure. Hence in every case the organization of the nation-state passed through a phase of expansion and consolidation, wherein the purpose was to arrive, if possible, at a defensible frontier. . . .

Anarchy Among Nations. The nation-state was now hopelessly caught in a tangle of contradic-

tions. As if it were not already difficult enough to make the boundaries of state and nation co-extensive, it now became abundantly plain that the territorial unit chosen for military purposes was completely at variance with the area appropriate to economics. Protection was organized to run along national lines; prosperity, to run across them. The task of organizing a unit wherein the needs of nationality, security, and prosperity would harmoniously coincide was well-nigh impossible, and the situation was rendered more chaotic by the competition between states for the same objectives. An area that a state considered strategically necessary for its own protection might be inhabited by people whom its neighbor regarded as belonging to its own nationality. Valuable economic resources that lay in the borderland between two states would be sought by both. Thus Alsace-Lorraine, the Low Countries, the Brenner Pass and the Trentino, Bohemia, the Polish Corridor, Suez and Panama, all these and others became foci for international rivalries and scenes of conflict.

Under such circumstances, it is not surprising that the nation-state became less and less capable of providing for the minimal needs of protection and order. Even at its best, though it maintained order within its own territory and minimized, without eliminating, the possibility of civil war, it could not guarantee that international relations would be peacefully conducted. The very doctrine of sovereignty meant juxtaposing internal stability with external anarchy. In all essentials, therefore, the history of the nation-state merely repeated (with a change of scale, because the unit was larger) the earlier experience of the city-state. International relations were like inter-*polis* relations, and the old drama was re-enacted in modern dress. Nation-states, like city-states before them, were small, medium-sized, or big. If small, their only chance of survival was to accept protection from the biggest power nearby, or, if they lay between rival powers, to announce their neutrality and trust it would be respected. Medium-sized states could also serve as buffers to keep their larger neighbors from one another's throats. They might, however, be induced to enter into systems of alliances since their support or opposition could have some effect on the balance of power. Their riskiest policy, of course, was to be afflicted with delusions of grandeur and dress in big power costume without having the chest to fill it, as has been true of Italy.

The major states themselves took up the script where Athens, Corinth, Sparta, and Thebes left off. Each in turn strove for leadership. Each was destined to strut and fret its hour upon the stage— Spain, Austria, France, Britain, and Germany. All had their periods of ascendancy. None could perpetuate its domination, because new challengers arose against every champion. The net result was that throughout a period of more than four centuries the nation-state system was incapable of securing a lasting peace. Major convulsions recurred with frightening regularity—the Thirty Years' War (1618-1648), the War of the League of Augsburg (1688-1697), the War of the Spanish Succession (1701-1713), the Wars of the French Revolution (1793-1815), World War I (1914-1918), and World War II (1939-1945). These were interspersed with more limited conflicts, so that scarcely a decade went by without an outbreak of hostilities somewhere. Indeed, the history of any important country contains testimony to prove that the establishment of a nation-state gives no assurance that its citizens will escape the horrors of war. . . .

Collective Insecurity. There is abundant evidence to confirm the fact that the nation-state is no longer able to provide protection and prosperity within its own borders. In the first half of the twentieth century two wars occurred whose world-wide scale of operations was without precedent in history. Together they demonstrated that the anarchy of the nation-state system breeds an insecurity that is contagious and allows few to isolate themselves from its effects. The fears, suspicions, and distrust of nation for nation cause each to maintain what armaments it can afford, and their costliness is a drain upon economies that otherwise could make more progress in the arts of peace. For other than

military reasons, these same economies have become interdependent, which renders them vulnerable to world-wide movements over which no single nation has control. To this truth the depression of the early 1930's bore witness. As a plague that sweeps across political frontiers, the same malady struck at one country after another producing the same symptoms: falling prices, lowered purchasing power, rising unemployment, reduced revenues from taxation, unbalanced budgets, bankruptcies, bank failures, and default on debts. Prosperity, as well as peace, had become indivisible.

This world-wide succession of events in a thirty-year period—war, depression, and war again— offered the clearest proof that an international society was emerging for which the nation-state was an unsuitable unit of government. Not only in trade and commerce, but in cultural contacts and the movement of ideas, communication between peoples had become easier and more rapid. Just as in the fifteenth and sixteenth centuries, therefore, a national order could not predominate unless the localism of the medieval system was abandoned, so in the twentieth century an international order could not prevail if politics were conducted through national channels. For, in paradoxical fashion, the determination to build security within the borders of the nation-state contributed to insecurity all around. States were severally behaving like individuals who place their reliance on self-protection and carry weapons on their person instead of resorting to public agencies such as police and courts. That system, as imagined by Hobbes or as practiced under frontier conditions, can be productive only of general disorder, which is precisely what happened in the world of nation-states. The efforts of each to build its own protection one-nationwide ultimately brought little protection to anybody. What is more, the particularism of nation-states defeated any possibility of a political development from the protection of each to an order embracing all.

2.   The State's Positive Role in World Affairs

Hedley Bull

We are constantly being told, at least in the Western world, that the state (and along with it, the
system of states) is an obstacle to the achievement
of a viable world order. First, the state is said to be
an obstacle to peace and security: while the world
continues to be organized politically as a system of
states, war will remain endemic—a condition of
affairs that could be tolerated before the advent
of nuclear weapons but can be no longer. Second,
the state is said to stand in the way of the promotion of economic and social justice in world society. It is the sovereign state that enables the rich
peoples of the world to consume their greedy,
mammoth portions of the world's resources, while
refusing transfers to poor countries; and it is the
sovereign state, again, that makes it possible for the
squalid and corrupt governments of many poor
(and some not so poor) countries to ignore the basic
needs of their own citizens and to violate their
human rights. Third, the state is held to be a barrier
to man's grappling effectively with the problem of
living in harmony with his environment. The connected issues of the control of the world's population, the production and distribution of food, the
utilization of the world's resources, and the conservation of the natural environment, it is said, have to
be tackled on a global basis, and this is prevented
by the division of mankind into states.

Those who see the problem of world order as one
of getting "beyond the state" (or the sovereign state
or the nation-state) are not necessarily agreed as to
what form of universal political organization
should replace the system of states, or what combination of suprastate, substate, or transstate actors
should deprive the state of its role. But they all feel

SOURCE: Hedley Bull, "The State's Positive Role in
World Affairs," *Daedalus*, vol. 108, no. 4, Fall 1979, pp.
111–122, excerpts. Footnotes deleted. Reprinted by permission of *Daedalus*, Journal of the American Academy
of Arts and Sciences, from the issue entitled, "The State,"
Fall 1979; Vol. 108, No. 4.

that there is some basic contradiction between, on
the one hand, the unity or interconnectedness of
the global economy, the global society, the global
polity, and, on the other, the system under which
each state claims exclusive jurisdiction over a particular area of the earth's surface and of the human
population. Thus political economists tell us that
we must transcend the state in order to manage
"the economics of interdependence," lawyers
sound the clarion call of an advance "from international law to world law," and political scientists
speak of the need to disavow the "states-centric
paradigm." The term "statist" is applied in a new,
pejorative sense to describe those unable to free
themselves from the bad old ways.

No doubt the system of sovereign states, when
compared with other forms of universal political
organization that have existed in the past or might
come to exist in the future (e.g., a world government, a neo-medieval order in which there is no
central authority but in which states are not "sovereign," or an order composed of geographically isolated or autarchic communities) does have its own
particular disadvantages. But the attack on the state
is misconceived.

In the first place it seems likely that the state,
whether we approve of it or not, is here to stay. If
this is so, the argument that we can advance the
cause of world order only by getting "beyond the
state" is a counsel of despair, at all events if it
means that we have to begin by abolishing or sub-
verting the state, rather than that there is a need to
build upon it. Of course, the state is not the only
important actor on the stage of world politics: non-
state groups and movements of various kinds play a
role, as do individual persons. There never was a
time in the history of the modern international
system when this was otherwise: in eighteenth and
nineteenth century Europe, too, states shared the
stage with chartered companies, revolutionary and
counterrevolutionary political parties, and national

liberation movements. Indeed, it is difficult to believe that anyone ever asserted the "states-centric"
view of international politics that is today so knowingly rejected by those who seek to emphasize the
role of "the new international actors." What was
widely asserted about European international relations from the time of Vattel in the mid-eighteenth
century until the end of the First World War was
the *legal fiction* of a political universe that consisted of states alone, the doctrine that only states had
rights and duties in international law. But assertion
of such a doctrine does not imply that the actual
course of international political events can be understood in terms of this fiction rather than in
terms of the actions of actual persons and groups of
persons, such as are set out in any history of the
period.

It is sometimes suggested that in recent decades
"other actors" have increased their role in world
politics at the expense of that of the state, but even
this—although it may be so—is difficult to establish conclusively because of the impossibility of
reducing the question to quantitative terms. It is
true that international governmental and non-
governmental organizations have multiplied visi-
bly, that multinational corporations have had a
dramatic impact on the world economy, and that
vast new networks of contact and intercourse have
grown up at the transnational level. But the state's
role in world politics has been growing dramatically also.

There has been a geographical spreading of the
state, from Europe outward. Two centuries ago
most of the non-European world lay beyond the
boundaries of any sovereign state, in the sphere of
the Islamic system or of Oriental empires or of
tribal societies. Today the sovereign state is established throughout the world. No doubt the multi-
plication of states—the United Nations began with
51 member states and now has 178—has been accompanied by an increase in heterogeneity among
them. There has been a certain debasing of the
currency of statehood as a consequence of the
growth of ministates and microstates, and many
of the non-European ones—to which Michael
Oakeshott contemptuously refers as "imitation

states"—are imperfectly established and unlike the
originals in important respects. But for the first
time the sovereign state is the common political
form experienced by the whole of mankind.

At the same time the role of the state in world
affairs has expanded functionally. Whereas a few
decades ago states in their dealings with one another confined themselves to diplomatic and strategic issues and allowed economic, social, and
ideological relations among peoples to be determined for the most part by the private sector, today
the state has extended its tentacles in such a way as
to deprive businessmen and bankers, labor organizations and sporting teams, churches and political
parties of the standing as international actors independent of state control that they once enjoyed. It
has been said that the growth of transnational relations has deprived traditional interstate politics of
its previous autonomy. But what is rather the case
is that the growth of state involvement in trade, in
exchange and payments, in the control of migration, and in science and culture and international
sporting events has brought an end to the autonomy of transnational relations.

It is difficult to see evidence of the decline of the
sovereign state in the various movements for the
regional integration of states that have developed
in the post-1945 world, such as the European Economic Community, the Organization of African
Unity, the Organization of American States, or the
Association of South East Asian Nations. It is not
merely that the EEC, which provides the most impressive example of progress toward a goal of regional integration, has not in fact undermined the
sovereignty of its member states in the sense of
their legal independence of external control. Nor is
it merely that the very considerable achievements
of the Community in promoting peace, reconciliation, prosperity, and cooperation in Western Europe have depended more upon intergovernmental
cooperation than on Community institutions bypassing the constituent states. It is that the movement for European integration has been led from
the beginning by the conception that the end goal
of the process is the creation of a European super-
state, a continental United States of Europe—a con-

ception that only confirms the continuing vitality of "statist" premises.

Nor is there much evidence of any threat to the state as an institution in the attempts—sometimes successful, sometimes not—of nationalist separatist groups to bring about the disintegration of existing states, as in Nigeria, Pakistan, Yugoslavia, Canada, the United Kingdom, or Iraq, to name only a few. For if we ask what have been the goals of the separatist Biafrans, East Bengalis, Croats, Quebecois, Scots, or Kurds, the answer is that they have been trying to create new states. While the regional integrationists seek to reduce the number of states in the world, and the nationalist separatists seek to increase it, both are as committed as the defendants of existing states to the continuation of the state as an institution. It might be thought that a serious challenge to the position of the state lies in the tendency of Socialist and Third World states to accord rights and duties in international law to nations that are not states; and that, in particular, national liberation movements—most notably, the Palestine Liberation Organization—have achieved a degree of recognition in the United Nations and elsewhere that in some way sounds the death knell of the state, or at all events brings to an end its claims to a privileged position among political groups in the world today. But again, what we have to notice is that the thinking both of the national liberation groups and of the states that lend support to them is confined within statist logic. What national liberation movements seek to do is to capture control of existing states (as in the case of the PLO or the FLN in Algeria), to create new states (as in Eritrea or Nagaland), or to change the boundaries of states (as in Ireland). In seeking recognition of their claims in international society, the starting point of their argument is the principle that nations ought to be states, and the strongest card they have to play is that they represent nations that seek to be states.

It is not a matter for celebration that regional integrationists and nationalist disintegrationists are as unable as they appear to be to think beyond the old confines of the states-system. There are other ways in which their aspirations might be satisfied than by seeking to control sovereign states.

One may imagine, for example, that a regional integration movement, like that in the countries of the European Community, might seek to undermine the sovereignty of its member states, yet at the same time stop short of transferring this sovereignty to any regional authority. If they were to bring about a situation in which authorities existed both at the national and at the European level, but no one such authority claimed supremacy over the others in terms of superior jurisdiction or its claims on the loyalties of individual persons, the sovereign state would have been transcended. Similarly, one may imagine that if nationalist separatist groups were content to reject the sovereignty of the states to which they are at present subject, but at the same time refrained from advancing any claims to sovereign statehood themselves, some genuine innovation in the structure of the world political system might take place. . . .

In the second place, those who say that what we have to do is get "beyond the states-system" forget that war, economic injustice, and ecological mismanagement have deeper causes than those embodied in any particular form of universal political organization. The states-system we have today is indeed associated with violent conflict and insecurity, with economic and social inequality and misery on a vast scale, and with failures of every kind to live in harmony with our environment. But this is no reason to assume that a world government, a neo-medieval order of overlapping sovereignties and jurisdictions, a system of isolated or semi-isolated communities, or any other alternative global order we might imagine would not be associated with these things also. Violence, economic injustice, and disharmony between man and nature have a longer history than the modern states-system. The causes that lead to them will be operative, and our need to work against them imperative, whatever the political structure of the world.

Let us take, for example, the central "world order goal" of peace. It is true that the states-system gives rise to its own peculiar dangers of war, such as those that have been stressed by exponents of "the international anarchy" (C. Lowes Dickinson), "the great illusion" (Norman Angell), "the arms race" (Philip Noel-Baker), or "the old game, now forever discredited, of the balance of power" (Woodrow Wilson). It is true that war is endemic in the present states-system, not in the sense that it is made "inevitable" (particular wars are avoidable, and even war in general is inevitable only in the sense of being statistically probable), but in the sense that it is institutionalized, that it is a built-in feature of our arrangements and expectations. We may agree also that nuclear weapons and other advanced military technology have made this state of affairs intolerable, if it was not so before.

But the idea that if states are abolished, war will be abolished, rests simply on the verbal confusion between war in the broad sense of armed conflict between political groups and war in the narrow sense of armed conflict between sovereign states. Armed conflicts, including nuclear ones, will not be less terrible because they are conducted among groups other than states, or called police actions or civil uprisings. The causes of war lie ultimately in the existence of weapons and armed forces and the will of political groups to use them rather than accept defeat. Some forms of universal political organization may offer better prospects than others that these causes can be controlled, but none is exempt from their operation.

Of course, it is possible to imagine a world government or other alternative form of universal political organization from which war, economic injustice, and ecological mismanagement have been banished. But so is it possible to imagine a states-system so reformed that it has these utopian features: a world of separate states disciplined by the arts of peace, cooperating in the implementation of an agreed universal standard of human welfare and respectful of a globally agreed environmental code. It is a perfectly legitimate exercise to compare these different utopias and to consider whether some are more feasible than others. What is not acceptable—but what critics of the states-system commonly do—is to compare a utopian vision of a world central authority, or of whatever

other alternative universal political order they favor, with the states-system, not in a utopian form but as it exists now.

In the third place, the critics neglect to take account of the positive functions that the state and the states-system have fulfilled in relation to world order in the past. The modern state—as a government supreme over a particular territory and population—has provided order on a local scale. To the extent that Europe, and at a later stage other continents, were covered by states that actually maintained their authority and were not constantly breaking down as a result of internal or external conflicts, local areas of order have been sustained by states over vast areas of the world. Most of our experience of order in modern times derives from these local areas of order established by the authority of states; and the chief meaning that we have been able to give to the concept of world order before very recent times is that it has been simply the sum of the local areas of order provided collectively by states.

States, moreover, have cooperated with one another in maintaining a structure of interstate, or international, order in which they confirm one another's domestic authority and preserve a framework of coexistence. For all the conflict and violence that have arisen out of their contact and intercourse with one another, they have formed not only an international system, but also a rudimentary international society. They have sensed common interests in preserving the framework of coexistence that limits and restrains the rivalry among them; they have evolved rules of the road that translate these common interests into specific guides to conduct; and they have cooperated in working common institutions such as international law, the diplomatic system, and the conventions of war that facilitate observance of the rules. Experts on "the international anarchy" will tell us, and rightly so, how precarious and imperfect this inherited structure of international order is, and exponents of "spaceship earth" will show how inadequate it is to meet the needs of the present time. But it does represent the form of universal political order that has actually existed in modern history, and if we are to talk of extending the scope of order in world affairs, we need first to understand the conditions under which there is any order at all. The critics of the states-system contrast it with the more perfect world order they would like to see; but the historical alternative to it was more ubiquitous violence and disorder.

We associate states with war: they have claimed, and still claim, a legal right to resort to it and to require individual citizens to wage it in their name. They dispose of most of the arms and armed forces with which it is waged, and notwithstanding the large role played in modern war by civil factions of one kind or another and by so-called barbarian powers beyond the confines of European international society, states have been the principal political groups actually engaged in war. But if we compare war among modern states with other historical violence or with future violence that we can readily enough imagine, we have to note that, with all its horrors, it has embodied a certain normative regime, without which violence has been and might be more horrible still.

Thus states when they go to war have recognized a need to provide one another and international society at large with an explanation in terms of a common doctrine of just causes of war, at the heart of which there has always been the notion that a war is just if it is fought in self-defense. No doubt there is great ambiguity and much disagreement about the meaning of this rule; other causes have been thought to be just in addition to that of self-defense. It is only in this century that limitations on the right of a state to go to war have been clearly expressed in legal terms, and the limitations are in any case observed more in the breach than in observance. Yet the conception that resort to war requires an explanation in terms of rules acknowledged on both sides is a mark of the existence at least of a rudimentary society; it imparts some element of stability to the expectations independent political communities can have about one another's behavior. Where—as in the encounter between political communities that do not belong to a common states-system or international society—war can be begun without any feeling of a need for an explanation, or the explanation felt to be necessary

derives from rules accepted on one side only and not on the other—as in Europe's belief in its civilizing mission, or the Mongols' belief in the Mandate of Heaven, or in the conception of a crusade or holy war—no such element of stability can be achieved. . . .

We associate states not only with war but also with sovereignty—which in internal affairs connotes supremacy, the supreme jurisdiction of the state over citizens and territory, and in external affairs connotes independence, freedom from external control. The claims of the state to a right of external sovereignty or independence are sometimes taken to imply rejection of all moral or legal authority other than that of the state, and indeed such claims have sometimes been put forward in its name. When they are (as by Hegel or Treitschke), they are a menace to international order. A state's rights to sovereignty, however, are not asserted against the international legal order but conferred by it (from which it follows that they can be qualified by it, and even taken away). A state's right to sovereignty or independence is not a "natural right," analogous to the rights of individuals in Locke's state of nature: it is a right enjoyed to the extent that it is recognized to exist by other states. So far from it being the case that the sovereignty of the state is something antithetical to international order, it is the foundation of the whole edifice.

The order provided by the states-system, founded upon the exchange of recognition of sovereignty, is rightly said to be inferior to that provided within a properly functioning modern state. Within the states-system there is still no authoritative legislature, empowered to make laws, amend and rescind them in accordance with the will of the community; no independent judicial authority to which the impartial interpretation and application of the laws is entrusted; no central authority commanding a monopoly of force to ensure that the law will prevail. It is this perception of the contrast between the more perfect order enjoyed by individual persons in domestic political systems and the less perfect order enjoyed by states in international society that provides the impulse behind the desire to create a central world authority that will reproduce the conditions of domestic society on a universal scale. The states-system does, however, provide an imperfect and rudimentary form of order that holds anarchy at bay. It provides external support to the internal order created by states in areas where their writs run. And it maintains among states a regime of mutual tolerance and forbearance that limits conflict, sustains intercourse, and provides the conditions in which cooperation can grow.

The case for the states-system as it has operated in the past is that it is the form of universal political organization most able to provide minimum order in a political society in which there is not a consensus broad enough to sustain acceptance of a common government, but in which there is a consensus that can sustain the coexistence of a plurality of separate governments. When independent political communities have little or no intercourse with one another—as between European communities and pre-Columbian American communities, or between the former and China before the nineteenth century—a states-system is not necessary. Where such intercourse exists but consists of almost unmitigated hostility, as between Europe and Islam during much of the history of their encounter, a states-system is not possible. But in relation to European political society from, say, the sixteenth to the early twentieth centuries, a strong argument was put forward to the effect that the attempt to create strong central authorities, or to restore and develop the central authorities that had existed in the past, would lead only to division and disorder; whereas there could be fashioned—out of the surviving rules and practices inherited from Christendom and the new body of precedent emerging from the experience of secular Europe—a decentralized form of interstate society. The question now is how far this argument is still valid in relation to the decentralized interstate society of today, now expanded to encompass the whole globe and inevitably diluted and modified in the process.

Today, order in world affairs still depends vitally upon the positive role of the state. It is true that the framework of mere coexistence, of what is sometimes called "minimum world order," inherited from the European states-system, is no longer by itself adequate. The involvement of states in eco-nomic, social, cultural, and communications matters has led us to judge the international political system by standards which it would not have occurred to a nineteenth century European to apply. We now expect the states-system not only to enable independent political communities to coexist, but also to facilitate the management of the world economy, the eradication of poverty, the promotion of racial equality and women's rights, the raising of literacy and labor standards, and so on. All of this points to a universal political system that can promote "optimum world order," a system that can sustain not only coexistence but cooperation in the pursuit of a vast array of shared goals.

If one believed that states were inherently incapable of cooperation with one another and were condemned—as on the Hobbesian theory—to exist permanently in a state of war, there would be no escape from the conclusion that the requirements of world order in our time and the continued existence of states are in contradiction of one another. In fact, states can and do cooperate with one another both on a regional and on a global basis. So far is it from being the case that states are antithetical to the need that we recognize to inculcate a greater sense of unity in human society, that it is upon the states-system that our hopes for the latter, at least in the short run, must principally depend. It is the system of states that is at present the only political expression of the unity of mankind, and it is to cooperation among states, in the United Nations and elsewhere, that we have chiefly to look if we are to preserve such sense of common human interests as there may be, to extend it, and to translate it into concrete actions. We do not live in a world in which states are prepared to act as agents of the international community, taking their instructions from the UN or some such body; but we do have to restore the element of consensus among states, without which appeals for a sense of "spaceship earth" are voices crying in the wilderness.

In the fourth place, there is no consensus in the world behind the program of Western solidarists or global centralists for "transcending the states-system." In the Socialist countries and among the countries of the Third World there is no echo of these views. From the perspective of the two weaker sections of the world political system, the globalist doctrine is the ideology of the dominant Western powers. The barriers of state sovereignty that are to be swept away, they suspect, are the barriers that they, the weaker countries, have set up against Western penetration: the barriers that protect Socialist countries from capitalism and Third World countries from imperialism. The outlook of the Western globalist does indeed express, among other things, an exuberant desire to reshape the world that is born of confidence that the economic and technological power to accomplish it lies at hand. One senses in it a feeling of impatience that the political and legal obstacles ("ethnocentric nationalism," "the absurd political architecture of the world," "the obsolete doctrine of state sovereignty") cannot be brushed aside. It is also notable that the prescriptions they put forward for restructuring the world, high-minded though they are, derive wholly from the liberal, social-democratic, and internationalist traditions of the West, and take no account of the values entertained in other parts of the world, with which compromises may have to be reached. . . .

Among the Third World countries the idea that we must all now bend our efforts to get "beyond the state" is so alien to recent experience as to be almost unintelligible. Because they did not have states that were strong enough to withstand European or Western aggression, the African, Asian, and Oceanic peoples, as they see it, were subject to domination, exploration, and humiliation. It is by gaining control of states that they have been able to take charge of their own destiny. It is by the use of state power, by claiming the rights due to them as states, that they have been able to resist foreign military interference, to protect their economic interests by excluding or controlling multinational corporations, expropriating foreign assets, planning the development of their economies, and bargaining to improve the terms of trade. It is by insisting upon their privileges of sovereignty that they are able to defend their newly won independence against the foreign tutelage implicit in such phrases as "basic human needs," "the international protection of human rights," or (more sinister still) "humanitarian intervention.". . .

Finally, those in the West who disparage the states-system underestimate the special interests the Western countries themselves have in its preservation and development. We have noted that distrust of the state and the states-system appears to flourish especially in Western societies. A number of factors account for this. The liberal or individualist political tradition, so much more deeply rooted in the West than elsewhere, has always insisted that the rights of states are subordinate to those of the human beings that compose them. Loyalties that compete with loyalty to the state—allegiances to class or ethnic group or race or religious sect—can be openly proclaimed and cultivated in Western societies and often cannot be elsewhere. Moreover, it is only in the West that it has been possible to assume that if the barriers separating states were abolished, it would be our way of life and not some other that would be universally enthroned.

It is the last point that is the crucial one. We in the West have not had—to the same degree as the Socialist countries and the Third World—a sense of dependence on the structure of the states-system. We assume that if the division of the world into separate states were to come to an end, and a global economy, society, and polity were allowed to grow up, it would be our economies, our ways of doing things, our social customs and ideas and conceptions of human rights, the forces of modernization that we represent, that would prevail. On the one hand, we have not had the feeling of vulnerability to "nonstate actors" shaping us from outside that Socialist countries have about Western libertarian ideas, or that developing countries have about Western-based multinational corporations, or that Islamic countries have about atheistic materialism. On the other hand, we have believed that our impact on the rest of the world does not depend merely on the exercise of state power. Our ways of doing things attract the peoples of Socialist countries even without efforts by our governments to promote them, and the withdrawal of Western governors, garrisons, and gunboats from the Third World countries has not brought the processes of Westernization at work in these countries to an end.

Questions for Discussion

1. Why the nation-state system? What are its characteristics? How has it changed?
2. Why has the nation-state persisted as the key political actor in international relations? What are its strengths? its weaknesses?
3. Discuss the case for the position that the nation-state system promotes international stability. What is the obverse of this argument?
4. Is the state system detrimental to the fashioning of global security?
5. What alternatives are there to the nation-state? Discuss their pros and cons.
6. Can the nation-state cope with the emerging set of transnational problems?
7. In what ways does the nation-state system affect U.S. foreign policy and the choices it faces?
8. Is the nation-state an outgrowth of nationalism, or is it reinforced by nationalism?

Selected Bibliography

CAMILLERI, JOSEPH A., AND JIM FALK. *The End of Sovereignty? The Politics of a Shrinking and Fragmenting World.* Aldershot, Hants, U.K.: Edward Elgar, 1992.

DAVIDSON, BASIL. *The Black Man's Burden: Africa and the Curse of the Nation-State.* New York: Times Books/Random House, 1992.

HERZ, JOHN. *International Politics in the Atomic Age.* New York: Columbia University Press, 1959.

HINSLEY, F. H. *Power and the Pursuit of Peace: Theory and Practice in the History of Relations Between States.* Cambridge: Cambridge University Press, 1963.

JACKSON, ROBERT H. *Quasi-states: Sovereignty, International Relations and the Third World.* Cambridge: Cambridge University Press, 1991.

MANNING, CHARLES A.W. *The Nature of International Society.* New York: Wiley, 1962.

MORGENTHAU, HANS J. *Politics Among Nations: The Struggle for Power and Peace,* 4th ed. New York: Knopf, 1966.

NYE, JOSEPH S., and ROBERT O. KEOHANE (EDS.), *Transnational Relations and World Politics.* Cambridge: Harvard University Press, 1972.

OHMAE, KENICHI. *The Borderless World.* New York: HarperCollins, 1990.

ROSECRANCE, RICHARD. *The Rise of the Trading State.* New York: Basic Books, 1985.

SMITH, ANTHONY D.S. *Nationalism in the Twentieth Century.* New York: New York University Press, 1979.

WENDT, HENRY. *Global Embrace: Corporate Challenges in a Transnational World.* New York: Harper Collins, 1993.

CHAPTER 2

Playing the Game of Nations

Since the dawn of time, leaders have sought to protect their communities by aligning themselves in accordance with the adage, "the enemy of my enemy is my friend." Perceptions of threat prompt adaptations and new alignments, even if these be, as they often are, with former adversaries. In politics, nothing is forever. It is survival of the group that is the transcendent value.

At the heart of shifting political alignments are ongoing assessments of power relationships. Social psychologists tell us that any relationship—parent-child, owner-employee, teacher-student—entails calculations of power. Regardless of the level at which it is operating, the political process involves the quest for power. In foreign policy, it can be summarized by the six W's: Who gets what, when, where, why, and with what means? Abundant theories have attempted to explain why leaders choose certain options as protection against a perceived threat. The study of foreign policy and international relations has expanded enormously, especially since the end of the Second World War. Sparked by the advent of the Cold War between the United States and the Soviet Union, it produced a veritable cottage industry of analyses seeking to explain the behavior of the inscrutable Soviet leaders.

However sophisticated and strongly rooted in empirical data, theories have been inadequate in explaining actual historical cases or in allowing us to predict, with some degree of confidence, the behavior of nation-states in the international system. Too many unanticipated occurrences confirm that reality is more complex than the most elaborate theory or model trying to explain it.

Viewed in historical perspective, the balance of power theory proves to be a seminal starting point for any understanding of the alignments that political leaders make to defend their interests. Its modern intellectual lineage dates back to Niccolo Machiavelli (1469–1527) and the precepts for retaining power that he prescribed for his patron. His classic, *The Prince*, rejected Plato's belief that "the good" was knowable and realizable, arguing instead that man is not perfectible and that the evil in him necessitates the constraints inherent in political communities. To function effectively, a ruler must concern himself with the accumulation and organization of power. Only in this way can he assure his perpetuation in the office and protect his political community from external enemies. By addressing himself to the baseness in man, the ruler could, through cunning, ruthlessness, and strength, persevere. In foreign affairs, he must always prepare for the worst from neighbors and rivals, approach treaties and agreements as tactical moves rather than permanent commitments, and be willing to

security
dilemma

use force to achieve his ends. Successive thinkers have merely embellished Machiavelli's treatise.

Thus, balance of power theory remains perhaps the most dependable guide to understanding the alignments that nations make to enhance their security. Its durability is testament to its adaptability, general explanatory value, and utilitarian applicability. Balance of power theory attempts to explain and systematize the coalitions and alliances of nations. According to the theory, if any nation, or combination of nations, seeks to expand, other states will organize against them in the interests of self-preservation and security. From this premise, various questions arise: Does the balance of power lead to situations of equilibrium or do its practitioners seek a margin of superiority by entering into a particular coalition? What kind of balance is most stable, a two power balance (bipolar world) or a complex balance (multipolar world)? Why does the balance of power invariably break down? Does balance of power theory operate with nuclear states?

Arnold Wolfers offers a far-ranging examination of the concept in relation to American foreign policy after World War II (Reading 3). His extolling of the theory's utility rests on the assumption that America's aims of security and stability define its essentially status quo orientation in the international system. The analysis critically assesses the role of ideology and of nuclear weapons, correctly concluding that both tend to be much overrated as determinants of foreign policy. As Wolfers explains, the term "balance of power" can be used in different ways: to mean a general distribution of power in the international system, an equilibrium or a distribution of power

between two rivals or coalitions, an outcome of coalition-building, or a goal for enhancing security. It may also refer to the balance of power in a particular region, where one country or group of countries seeks to avoid domination by a regional hegemon. The term has many nuances.

Finally, Wolfers mentions, but does not develop, the connections between balance of power considerations and nuclear deterrence. For deterrence—either nuclear or nonnuclear—to operate, three conditions are necessary, according to Hedley Bull. Country A (let us say by way of example, the United States) must convey a threat to retaliate against country B (for instance, Russia or China); in such circumstances, country B must have the capability to "undertake the course of action from which the deterrer wishes it to desist"; and country B (the country threatened with punishment) must believe that country A (the country making the retaliatory threat) "has the capacity and the will to carry it out, and decides for this reason that the course of action it would otherwise follow is not worthwhile."[1]

The aim of deterrence, like the aim of balance of power politics, is to prevent war. But deterrence is only part of the general conception of balance of power. If it should fail, then the latter would be expected to bring into operation the alignment of military power that would defeat the aggressor.

The world was multipolar from the sixteenth century until 1945. A system of changing constellations essentially reflected balance of power considerations: rulers changed partners in response to varied com-

[1] Hedley Bull, *The Anarchical Society: A Study of Order in World Politics.* New York: Columbia University Press, 1977, pp. 118–119.

binations of external and domestic pressures. In the sixteenth century, Spain's power and expansion caused other countries to coalesce against it; in the seventeenth and early eighteenth centuries, France was deemed the biggest threat in Europe; at the end of the nineteenth and early twentieth centuries, France and Britain, historic enemies for centuries, had become firm allies against a Germany that twice came close to establishing its hegemony on the European continent. America's response was, in balance of power terms, a reaction to Germany's drive to overturn the existing international order and institutionalize its military-strategic preeminence over all of Europe.

After the end of the Second World War, for 46 years, from 1945 to 1991, the world was bipolar. Dominated by the United States and the Soviet Union, this bipolar world avoided a big war, but allowed, even fostered, local wars in peripheral areas. However, with the end of the Cold War and the ensuing U.S.-Russian reconciliation, Third World clients lost their strategic significance and their license to pursue regional ambitions. The dissolution of the Soviet Union at the end of December 1991 dramatically confirmed what cooperation in the 1990–1991 Gulf crisis had already suggested, namely, that the Cold War, and with it the bipolar era, was over.

The post-Cold War system is unlike any that we have heretofore known. In some ways it resembles that of the 1920s: the absence of a serious military threat to any of the major powers; the lack of a defining ideological adversary; uncertainty in Europe, the Far East, and the Middle East in the wake of collapsed empires; and the impulse to look inward to domestic problems and politics at the expense of foreign policy. Long-established alignments are in disarray. The condi-

tions that forged their unity and cooperation in time of war and Cold War no longer hold. All of this makes for ambivalence in once predictable relationships.

The passing of bipolarity has ushered in a transitional, acentric world composed of independent, asymmetrically equipped nations vying for advantage. Acentrism epitomizes the new diffusion of power. Influential actors are emerging—Japan, China, Germany, the European Community—but they still lack the proper mix of political will and economic and military strength required for a role as a world power, or even as a regional hegemon. The United States, although the world's most powerful country, finds its influence limited. A straitened economic condition circumscribes the political leverage that should be the concomitant of a military superpower. But even when the United States was an unsparing patron to clients in the Third World, even then its power was nigh impossible to translate into influence, into persuading seemingly dependent governments to accede to its wishes.

Although Stanley Hoffmann wrote his essay at a time when the Soviet Union still existed, his assessment of the political ramifications of the term "diffusion" may have even greater salience now (Reading 4). He sees the irreversible weakening of the once-unchallenged role of the nation-state, and with it a very different kind of prognosis for traditional balance of power politics. In his view, nation-states no longer make the key decisions about the world economy; they do not monopolize finance, production, and communications; their economic well-being is hostage to the cooperation of other actors; and they cannot achieve their economic goals by national means alone. Beyond the economic realm, this has far-reaching implications for security, for alliances, and for potential conflicts. Inevitably, he suggests, the United States will have to adapt its policies to a world of diffused power.

If balance of power considerations have a diminished role to play in U.S. foreign policy, the reasons are to be found in the mutual reinforcement of three strong factors. Two have been noted above, namely, the absence of a serious military threat to the United States or any of the other great powers, and the accelerating interdependency of nations, under the impact of technological change and the growing permeability of ideas, information, and investment. A third factor is the trend toward a kind of democratization of foreign policy decisionmaking. Foreign policy is still made by a relatively small number of individuals, but—and this is an important development—increasingly, ruling elites need to fashion a broad consensus behind their policies. As we move into an international era in which democratic societies are becoming more numerous, consensus is crucial for abrupt reversals of alignment or policy, particularly if the use of force is involved. Even in nondemocratic systems, the ruling elites have to show greater sensitivity for the mood and attitudes of their subjects. The ruler or a small cabal cannot practice traditional balance of power politics, with its amoral, non-ideological, cynical, often bewildering turnabouts, with the same impunity as before.

3.   The Balance of Power in Theory and Practice

Arnold Wolfers

For an inquiry into the manner in which the balance of power concept can serve to elucidate the current problems of American policy or even guide American decision-makers, it is necessary first to examine the age-old debate among theorists on the meaning of the term as well as the debate on the international phenomena to which the term can be usefully applied. As happens frequently, much confusion arises from the fact that the "balance of power" means different things to different people. There is agreement only that, when used in the discussion of international relations, the term refers somehow to the distribution of power among nations. But in some instances, it is used as synonymous with the general distribution of power. In other instances, it is intended to imply the superi-ority of one country over another—a surplus of power on one side comparable to the balance on the credit side of a bookkeeping account. Finally, and more frequently, balance is taken to mean equilibrium, as when the scales are even on an instrument for weighing.

In order to cut the semantic knot from the start, I shall choose, arbitrarily perhaps, the last meaning and shall speak of the balance of power as implying an equilibrium or a distribution of power between two opponents in which neither side has attained a position of superiority or supremacy. Such a definition points to the opposite of hegemony or domination. To make such a distinction between balanced and unbalanced power does not suggest that there is any sure way of measuring and comparing the relative power of nations and, thus, of deciding how great the unbalance or how close the balance is. Even the extent of a nation's military power, which is only part of its over-all power, can only be tested in war, but such a test means that the balance

SOURCE: Arnold Wolfers, "The Balance of Power in Theory and Practice," *Naval War College Review*, vol. XI, no. 5, January 1959, pp. 1–19, excerpts. Reprinted by permission.

of power process has failed in its purpose of preserving the peace. However, it makes sense to speak of an existing balance of power—or of a fair approximation of such a balance—whenever there are indications that two opposing nations, or blocs of nations, are being deterred from putting their opponents' total power to the test. In peacetime, one can speak of a balance of "mutual deterrence" which today, when nuclear power is involved, has been called a "balance of terror." It presupposes that according to their respective estimates the other side possesses not less than equal power.

With this definition of the balance of power in mind, one can inquire into theories on the chances or merits of an equilibrium of power among adversaries and on the process by which such equilibrium is established, preserved or upset. I shall distinguish and discuss four theories—three of long standing, one of recent vintage—and inquire into their significance for contemporary foreign policy. One theory regards the balance of power as the ideal distribution of power; a second considers it the automatic outcome of developments inherent in the multistate system; to a third, the balance of power represents a goal of foreign policy which some policy-makers find useful to pursue; according to a fourth theory of mid-twentieth century origin, it has become an obsolete notion, which can be misleading to anyone concerned with contemporary international affairs.

Very few people in this country can be persuaded, I presume, to take seriously the kind of glorification of balanced power among adversaries that often found expression in earlier centuries. While the idea of "checks and balances," intimately associated with the American Constitution, is still considered a valuable device in domestic affairs, equilibrium on the world stage arouses grave misgivings because it implies . . . each side holding the other in check. Such a concept could hardly be more remote from our ideals of the kind of world in which we would wish to live. At best, then, a balance of power between . . . two main opponents . . . may be the least objectionable or evil distribution of power presently attainable. . . .

Strong current predilections run in the direction of what is called "collective security." This theory assumes that the peace of the world depends not on having the power of all nations balanced and checked by the power of others, but on the contrary, on making overwhelming power available to those who are ready to oppose potential aggressor nations or to punish actual aggressors. By the rules of collective security, the peace-loving nations of the world cannot have too much power since they can be expected never to abuse their superior power position. The stronger they are, collectively, the better their chances of deterring or, if necessary, of punishing potential violators of the peace. On this premise, the ideal situation is one in which the "defenders of the peace and law of the world community" enjoy unchallengeable hegemony.

Without being able to do justice, here, to the arguments in favor and against collective security which fill the pages of a long series of articles and books, I cannot refrain from pointing to some recent events that have cast doubts on the ideal of hegemony for the "peace-loving nations."

In World War II the Soviet Union, an ally of the West in its struggle against the "aggressor nations" of the Axis coalition, became labelled as one of the "peace-loving" nations. It was therefore assumed that there was no need for concern about the postwar distribution of power between the Soviet Union and its Western Allies. In fact, President Roosevelt was incensed when Churchill raised the old bogie of the balance of power to warn against a strategy that would place Vienna under the control of the Soviet Union. Moreover, implicit in the Allied demand for unconditional surrender was the desire that Germany and Japan should be impotent after their defeat, in spite of the fact that the complete elimination of their power was bound to have an unbalancing effect in Eurasia. In its efforts to prevent a no longer "peace-loving" Soviet Union from dominating the entire "world island" of Eurasia, the United States has since discovered how costly and dangerous indifference to the distribution of power can prove.

The Suez crisis of 1956 struck another and more serious blow at the notion that some nations can be classified as falling regularly into the category of peace-loving countries and, therefore, can be assumed to need no external checks and balances. Two of the chief pillars of the United Nations collective security system, Britain and France, and democratic Israel turned up on the side of aggression. . . . There may be some validity, then, to the proposition that, from the point of view of preserving the peace—though not necessarily from the point of view of promoting justice—a balance of power that places restraint on every nation is more advantageous in the long run than the hegemony even of those deemed peace-loving at a given time.

It has been said that equilibrium was never really regarded as an ideal, even by those statesmen who have been its foremost verbal champions. The British, in particular, have been accused of hypocrisy for advocating the balance of power as a universally beneficial principle, when they have derived unique benefits from its observance. It is pointed out that Britain was seeking an equilibrium between her continental rivals, not between herself and her potential enemies. Britain could then assume the role of the "balancer" with all the advantages of that position.

But preference for equilibrium need not be a mere rationalization of national interest. In fact, it is deeply rooted in what today would be called conservative thought. Characteristic of such thought, which found its classical expression in the writings of Machiavelli and Hobbes, is a pessimistic view of human nature. It sustains Lord Acton's expectation that "power corrupts and absolute power corrupts absolutely." Men with a conservative bent of mind need find nothing shocking, therefore, in the suggestion that all nations, including their own, should be restrained by counter power. They will thereby be spared many temptations as well as being prevented from abusing their power.

The suggestion that all nations need the restraint of the balance of power does not mean that the same amount of power is required to deter an aggressive would-be empire builder or megalomaniac dictator from initiating violence as is required to prevent a satisfied nation, especially a democratic nation that operates under strong internal restraints, from seeking to cash in on the weaknesses of others. In any "balance of deterrence," different estimates of the power distribution and variations in the willingness to take risks have to be taken into account. A fanatical government bent on conquest will tend to overestimate its own power

and underestimate that of its "decadent" opponents. Nobody could seriously praise a balance of power, therefore, except on the assumption that it is of a kind that promises to place effective restraints even on the least self-restrained of the parties. . . .

For the exponents of the second theory of balance of power, the controversy between those who contend that the balance of power is a good thing and those who condemn it makes no sense. They say that equilibrium of power is not a matter of choice; instead, it tends to result from a competition for power among nations that is inherent in the multistate system. In this view, a mechanism is at work, similar to the "invisible hand" operating in a market economy that tends to produce an equilibrium between supply and demand. Theorists have construed a model of a multistate system, in which equilibrium automatically results without the assistance of deliberate choice in favor of equilibrium by the actors. While today such a model is not regarded as more than an abstract initial working hypothesis, the conditions existing in the 19th century gave it the character of a rather striking portrait of reality. After the end of Napoleon's Continental hegemony, world power came to be distributed among five or six major European nations. All of them were jealous of their relative power positions, all keenly aware of any change in the distribution of power, and all eager to prevent any one of the others from stepping into the shoes of Napoleonic France. Therefore, in order to render impossible or to defeat any incipient hegemony, two or more powers could be counted upon to line up almost intuitively against any ascending power that threatened to become their superior. In their game of power politics, they were united by their common interest in not allowing the balance to be tipped against them. Competition for allies and competition in armaments were the chief instruments of a balancing process in which the realities of European power politics came close to resembling an automatic balancing system.

However, even in that period, the flaws in the expectation that an equilibrium of mutual deterrence would actually come about without deliberate and intelligent efforts on the part of governments were only too visible. Again and again, a country which believed it had attained a position of superiority struck out against its rivals, or another country which feared an increasingly adverse balance initiated war before the balance had tilted too far against it. In such instances, war was the instrument by which break-down of equilibrium was overcome or prevented, a method of adjustment hardly comparable with the relatively smooth-working price mechanism of the market economy. Innumerable historical cases could be cited to show the extent to which the success of the balancing process depended on the choices made by statesmen of the countries involved. British statesmen were faced with a momentous choice when prior to the outbreak of war in 1914, they had to decide whether or not to give full British backing to France and Russia as a means of deterring the Central Powers. There was no automatism in operation to prevent them from making the wrong choice. Similarly, when three years later Germany had hegemony almost within her grasp, there was nothing automatic about the decision of the United States to enter on the side of the hard-pressed Allies; in fact, by resuming unrestricted submarine warfare early in 1917, Germany was largely responsible for speeding up a decision that might have been reached too late to right the balance of power.

While it makes little sense, then, to use the term "automatic" in a literal way, as if human choices and errors have no effect upon the process of establishing or upsetting a state of equilibrium, there is nevertheless a significant element of truth in the theory of "automatism," and one that is valid even today. If it is correct to assume that any government in its senses will be deeply concerned with the relative power position of hostile countries, one is justified in concluding that efforts, to keep in step with such opponents in the competition for power, or even to outdo them, will almost certainly be forthcoming. If almost all nations react in this way, a tendency towards equilibrium follows as a consequence—it comes into play if both sides aim at equilibrium, but it also operates if the more aggressive side strives for superiority, thereby provoking his opponent to match his moves. In the latter case, which is the most frequent, it makes some sense to say that there are forces at work behind the backs of

the human actors that seem to push them in the direction of balanced power irrespective of their preferences.

It is also worth noting, particularly in the light of recent events, how nations seem to be drawn into the balancing process almost without conscious choice or deliberation. The policy of the United States since World War II offers a particularly striking illustration. Despite its long-established policy of resisting all pressures and temptations toward involvement in the peace-time balancing of power, the United States reversed its traditional stand without hesitation when in 1946 no other country was in a position to contain the ascending Soviet Empire and to restrain it with at least equal counterpower. . . .

Some weak countries seek safety by getting on the band wagon of an ascending power in the hope that they might somehow escape complete subjugation once their powerful "friend" has gained supremacy. We can also point to countries which are so absorbed with their internal affairs or which ignore considerations of national power that we must regard as purely accidental the effects their policies may exert on the distribution of power, whether helping to preserve or upset the balance. With due respect, then, for anything the "invisible hand" may do to induce a trend towards power equilibrium, it may generally be concluded that more insight can be expected from a theory that places the emphasis on the effects of human intentions and actions.

The question is whether, as a matter of expediency, nations, under certain circumstances, do or should make power equilibrium rather than power superiority the target of their efforts. If equilibrium is, in fact, their objective, they must assume that it is a practical policy which can serve the best interests of their country. Frequently, one would suppose, the intention will be to achieve superiority until the competitive race proves it to be unattainable. Then equilibrium—or stalemate as it is often called today—may become the accepted goal. Both sides, in fact, may come to realize that a superiority is leading nowhere except to exhaustion, and agree, tacitly at least, to settle for the less ambitious and less costly goal of balanced power. Such a realization has been the rationale of most attempts to bring about disarmament through agreement, although the success of such attempts has been quite exceptional.

Frequently, as indicated earlier, when governments make the balance of power their aim, what they desire to bring about is a balance between the power of other nations that will place their country in the enviable position of a "balancer." Countries too weak to become active balancers are usually hopeful that an equilibrium will be established between their stronger neighbors, but they can do little to promote it. Up to 1914, the United States was one of the passive beneficiaries of the balance of power which Britain did so much to maintain on the Continent. Today, the United States stands out as the country that can do most to keep other nations, especially those within the free world, in a state of equilibrium. Not a few American moves have been directed towards this goal. The United States is interested in the maintenance of the peace between its many non-Communist friends and allies. It acts true to the traditions of the state system, therefore, when seeking, for instance, to keep Israel and its Arab neighbors in a condition approximating balanced power.

The connection continually drawn here between equilibrium and the preservation of peace is significant. It points to the fact that even at a time when collective security exerts much appeal, mutual deterrence through balanced power is still regarded, in some circumstances at least, as the safest practical device for the preservation of peace. This is particularly true in cases in which neither of two rivals can be trusted to want peace more than what it may hope to achieve by resorting to force. If, from the point of view of peace, it is desirable that both rivals be held in check, it is an advantage to third powers to have the rivals check each other by their own means and efforts. . . .

Status quo powers are those states which seek to preserve the established order or which have renounced the use of force as a method of changing that order. Presumably, therefore, they can achieve their objective of deterring or stopping their opponent only if they possess defensive counterpower no less than equal to the power of their opponent.

Success does not require superiority of power.

Although the United States may be thoroughly dissatisfied with a world order in which some countries suffer under partition, bondage as satellites, or despotism, it nevertheless qualifies as a status quo power because it has renounced the use of force as a means of remedying the iniquities of the status quo. Therefore, acceptance of power equilibrium as the goal of American policy does not mean that the United States has sacrificed its defensive objective, but only that it has forfeited the greater security that status quo powers can obtain from a position of superior power.

The other category of nations—the so-called "revisionist" countries, those bent on changing the status quo, if necessary by force—are in a less favorable position. They can resign themselves to a policy of balanced power only in despair, since they are well aware that only with rare exceptions can the established order be seriously modified without the threat or use of a force so preponderant that it will overcome the resistance of the opposing side. Thus, for these states to give up pursuit of superior power in favor of balanced power means, in effect, their renunciation of their ultimate national goal: a substantial change in the existing world order. . . .

If a country is able to give convincing evidence of seeking only equilibrium, it will not usually be suspected of aggressive intentions, since it is obvious that the attainment of its relatively modest power goal can give it defensive capabilities at best. Its attitude, therefore, will tend to appeal to all friends and allies that belong in the category of status quo powers, though it will disappoint its "revisionist" friends. There is a chance, too, that the more modest power goal will have some effect on the behavior of the opposing side—in this case on the Soviet Union. If the Soviets feel secure from threats of external aggression and, at the same time, are suffering from the heavy burden of the arms race, they too may resign themselves . . . to the continuation of the status quo and to the maintenance of a mere balance of power. Although we do not want to make too much of a virtue of necessity, the acceptance by the United States of the balance of power as the avowed goal of policy may have certain other advantages. Such a policy will remove unfounded public expectations of future superiority and eliminate temptations to conduct policy as if the United States could soon expect to impose its will on an inferior opponent.

This suggestion—that the United States might do well to make a reasonable balance of power . . . a target of its foreign policy and the standard by which to measure its efforts in the power field—runs counter to the last of the theories mentioned earlier. The whole notion of a balancing of power policy, according to the exponents of this theory, has been rendered obsolete by the emergence of new forces that have radically changed the conditions of international politics. While, in former times, the balance may have been a condition both of peace and of the continued independence of many nations, it has ceased, they say, to be a practiced goal today, because of the impact of a number of new factors with which statesmen did not formerly have to contend.

One of these factors, strongly emphasized at the close of World War II, was the rise of the United States to a leading position in world politics. Many argued that the newcomer was little fitted for the task of playing the balancing game. Was it possible to expect that a country so little accustomed to, or inclined towards, power calculations in foreign affairs would be able to switch sides from former friends to former enemies if such a move were necessary for the restoration of the world balance of power? Would the United States agree to "entangling" itself in alliances? The record of American policies since World War II has laid these misgivings to rest and has thoroughly disproved the alleged ineptitude of the United States in the matter of the balancing of power process. With a speed that came as a shock even to many Europeans supposedly reared in the traditions of the power game, America's enemies of World War II became her military allies, and soon the United States was to emerge as the center of a peace-time alliance system of unprecedented breadth. Statesmen in Washington became quickly aware of the need for establishing and maintaining a balance between the power of the East and the West. Concepts such as containment and deterrence, which soon became the catchwords of the day, pointed to equilib-

rium as a minimum American objective. Therefore, it may be suggested that, rather than confirming the theory of obsolescence, this first factor demonstrates the continuing primacy of balancing-of-power considerations.

A second new factor, the so-called "bipolarity" of the postwar world, was thought to be of even greater consequence. After all, the so-called balance of power system of the 19th century rested on the simultaneous existence of five or six major powers. Now only two were left, while the remaining lesser powers were able to throw so little into the scales against a potential ascending state that their influence could be discounted. Here, too, however, experience in the era of the two superpowers has merely added weight to the contention that whenever there is more than one sovereign power in the world, the balancing process will begin to operate. Even had it been true that all significant power was to remain vested in the USA and the USSR, as it was at the close of World War II, their competition in armaments and in economic development could have led to a balance of power between them which might have been maintained by their efforts alone. But the condition of the extreme bipolarity of 1945 has been steadily on the decline as other centers of not inconsiderable power have arisen or reasserted themselves in many parts of the world. As the situation stands today, these lesser powers could, if they wanted, throw their weight to one side or another and significantly affect the distribution of power between the two main opposing camps. Moreover, regional balancing of power is under way among some of the lesser countries: for instance, between the Arab countries and Israel, or between Pakistan and India. Neither bipolarity nor the rise of new states, then, has resulted in the disappearance of traditional policies of power. On the contrary, one of the striking characteristics of the present situation is the manner in which some of the new states, which one might have expected would be preoccupied with their thorny internal problems, have come to throw their weight around in the world balancing process. . . .

A third novelty which has rightly attracted attention is the ideological note that has been introduced into the world's major power struggle. Some observers predicted that ideological affinities and antagonisms would become so strong that nations would become unwilling, whatever the requirements of the balancing process, to leave the camp of their ideological preference. If this had occurred, the distribution of power in the world would have been at the mercy of ideological competition. Ideological appeals have, undoubtedly, affected the orientation of some countries toward East or West, but in such cases one cannot necessarily say that efforts to establish a balance of power have ceased. Indeed, whenever ideological power has shown a tendency to gain the upper hand over other forms of power, competition between East and West does not disappear but is transferred to the field of ideology, propaganda and subversion. . . .

Ideology has not, however, come to reign supreme. There have been instances of recent date to show that the "blood" of military power considerations can still run thicker than the "water" of ideological sympathy. As mentioned earlier, Communist Yugoslavia lined up with the West when it felt threatened by Soviet military superiority, and countries with no Communist bias like Nasser's Egypt have taken full advantage of opportunities to swing toward the Soviet side when, for reasons of national interest, they wished to weaken or restrain the Western camp. If ideology interferes with the relatively smooth functioning of the traditional balancing process, it is most likely to do so by blinding ideologically fanatical leaders and elites to threats emanating from the camp of their ideological preference. When statesmen jeopardize national security interests in this way, one can speak of a kind of "ideological stickiness" which may lead to alignments that run counter to the requirements of equilibrium.

Finally, there is the new factor of nuclear weapons. The question has been raised whether the conditions of the nuclear age, with its weapons of unprecedent destructiveness and its revolutionary developments in weapons technology, does not defeat all efforts at rational power calculation and comparison. If it does, governments would be unable to establish any particular world power distribution or to know even approximately whether equilibrium exists at any given time. Thus, it would be hopeless to attempt to rely on the balance

of power for the security of their countries or for the preservation of peace.

No one can deny that the art of estimating power—one's own and that of an adversary—which has been the source of many tragic errors even in prenuclear days, has been immensely complicated by the introduction of even new and untried instruments of war. Yet, despite this new element of uncertainty, there has probably never been a time in which more efforts have been exerted towards estimating comparative military power, strategic nuclear striking power included. All the talk of a stalemate on the strategic plane would be meaningless if these estimates had become a matter of sheer guesswork. It must be remembered, in this connection, that in time of peace it is the balance of mutual deterrence that is important, and deterrence rests not on the *actual* relative strengths of the two sides—which only war can reveal—but on what governments *believe to be* the existing distribution of power. In fact, the more both sides overestimate the relative power position of their opponent, the more likely it is that they will be deterred from using their power. Since the chief danger has always been an underestimation of enemy strength and determination, the advent of nuclear weapons has had the effect of buttressing the deterrent value of the balancing process. Even a megalomaniac will not easily discount enemy nuclear retaliatory power, provided it is creditable to him that his opponent will use that power to counter his moves. If credible, the threat of retaliation with less than equal nuclear force may suffice for deterrence provided the lesser force is enough to cause unacceptably great damage. The problem, today, therefore, is not so much equality of nuclear power, but the difficulty of creating equilibrium on other levels, so that one is ready to meet various types of attack and can convince an opponent that his attacks will actually be met. . . .

One may conclude, then, that the nuclear factor, while unable to end the balancing of power process or to rob it of its former functions, merely adds to the difficulties of manipulating the process in such a way that a reasonable degree of equilibrium can be attained, preserved and ascertained.

One last remark about the alleged obsolescence of the balance of power and balancing process is necessary. Those who accept the obsolescence theory must have asked themselves what alternative course is open to nations in the present era. An organization like the United Nations, despite its provisions for collective security, cannot put the balancing process to rest because it leaves all coercive power in the hands of its members. There can be only one alternative—the elimination of all military power from the control of individual nations, which, if it occurred, would obviously relieve governments of the need to concern themselves with the world distribution of power among nations. With the monopoly of military power by a single world authority, and only with such a monopoly, international power politics itself—and with it the whole balancing of power process—would disappear. Nations, even if embroiled in conflict with one another, would have no more reason to worry about the power position of other nations than a Rhode Island or an Oklahoma about the power of larger and potentially more powerful neighboring States of the Union. Unfortunately for those who would like to see such a world authority established, it must be said that there is not the slightest

chance of its establishment in the foreseeable future. Can anyone imagine the United States or the Soviet Union, for that matter, subordinating themselves voluntarily to an authority over which their chief opponent might come to exercise supreme control? If they did, they would make themselves as impotent as is any State in the Union compared to the Federal Government. If ever the two superpowers had enough confidence in each other not to mind being ruled by a world authority which was controlled by the other, there would be no need for such a world authority anymore! Under such ideal conditions of mutual confidence, the two together could, and probably would, rule supreme in the world, but one must add that their chances of preserving their mutual confidence and of agreeing on the use of their power would be greater if they preserved a high degree of equilibrium between themselves. . . . Under these circumstances the balance of power, while far from ideal, suggests itself as an acceptable and practical substitute for the supremacy in the world that the United States with all its potential power cannot presently hope to attain for itself.

4.   Diffusion of Power in a Post-Cold War World
Stanley Hoffmann

A convenient starting place is the phenomenon often referred to as the diffusion of power, and the perspective provided by the long-dominant theory of international affairs, Realism. That theory looks at the international system as a milieu in which states compete, seek to increase their power, try to prevent the rise of rivals or hegemons through uni-

SOURCE: Stanley Hoffmann, "Reconsiderations: A New World and Its Troubles," in Nicholas X. Rizopoulos (ed.), *Sea-Changes: American Foreign Policy in a World Transformed.* New York: Council on Foreign Relations Press, 1990, pp. 277–286; 289–291, excerpts. Footnotes deleted. Reprinted by permission of the Council on Foreign Relations.

lateral moves as well as through balances of power, and depend for their survival and success above all on military might and the economic underpinning of it.

From that perspective, power has been largely concentrated, since 1945, in two "poles," the United States and the Soviet Union. The "diffusion of power" means that this will no longer be the case. But where has power gone? Here, we must make an important distinction: between two arenas that exist, or "games" that go on, simultaneously. One is the traditional strategic-diplomatic arena, which corresponds to the Realists' analysis, with its emphasis on the actors' quest for relative gains, or (in the case of great powers thirsting for total security) absolute gains in a zero-sum contest. The other is the modern arena of economic interdependence, in which state actors are interested in relative gains, to be sure, but within a world economy, whose continuing growth is in their common interest, and in which my gains may well require that you make some yourself. The stakes are clearly not the same: physical security, the control of territory in one case; market shares, the creation and expansion of wealth in the other. Nor are the necessary ingredients and possible uses of power the same.

In the strategic-diplomatic arena, we have moved from bipolarity to a much more complex and unprecedented situation. Here, the main actors are still the states; it is in this realm that the United Nations and the various regional organizations have been least effective. . . . The United States will remain the most important player in terms of global military power, and the United States and the Soviet Union will keep the capacity to destroy the planet several times over. But the Soviet Union's economic weakness and political turbulence have reduced its ability and will to be a worldwide challenger; and the number of active players has increased and will increase some more, because of the proliferation of military technologies—nuclear and conventional. A return to bipolarity would require a new Soviet-American confrontation; but the condition of the Soviet Union makes this highly unlikely in the foreseeable future. Neither a success of perestroika, a period of revolutionary turbulence and disintegration, nor a repressive regime attempting to reimpose order and control is a good candidate for a return to global ambitions. Security concerns and balances are most likely to be regional than global; and while the United States, because of its military preeminence and its capacity to project might abroad, might see itself as the "sun" at the center of the solar system, there is no obvious need for the "planets" to turn around it in such a fragmented system—now that the somewhat artificial and never totally effective unity imposed by the Cold War is waning. In this system, nuclear states and states with an abundance of conventional forces will be the powers of importance in each region. Besides states, the only significant actors in

this realm will be private individuals in the business of arms sales.

The picture is quite different in the arena of economic interdependence. Here, the term "diffusion" is both misleading and imprecise. It is misleading insofar as it conceals the emergence of the new "international business civilization,". . . —a worldwide phenomenon spreading out from the industrialized nations of North America, Western Europe, and East Asia. Diffusion of power suggests dispersion, whereas this "supranational capitalism" of banks and enterprises is to a large extent both concentrated in its origin (a limited, although slowly growing, number of countries) and a unifying force, at least because it does not respect borders, particularities, and traditions. Indeed, as Heilbroner points out, it is this force that periodically rearranges the distribution of economic and political power.

The term "diffusion" is imprecise because it lumps together a variety of phenomena. One is the fact that many key decisions about the world economy are made not in the political realm of states, but by private agents—investors, corporations, firms, banks, speculators, merchants, mafias— either without much control by state authorities or with enough influence to manipulate them. Another fact, which results in part from the previous one—but to which state, trade, business, and fiscal policies contribute as well—is the internationalization or multinationalization of production, finance, and communications. A third one is the mutual entanglement of state economic capabilities, either in the form of "pooled sovereignties" (as in the European Economic Community or EEC) or in the form of states whose power is each other's hostage (as in the U.S.-Japan relationship). A fourth is the inability of many states to reach their national economic objectives by national means alone. . . .

Present-day Western Europe shows all four phenomena at work. They amount to a decomposition of sovereignty, the ability of the state to command and control that may still exist in the traditional arena. Thus, diffusion here means not only, as in that arena, that the field of major state actors is becoming more crowded, but two other things as well. First, in contrast to the situation in the strategic-diplomatic domain, there are serious rivals for the United States: the losers of World War II, who became the main beneficiaries of American protection during the Cold War, Japan and Germany (or an EEC in which Germany will be the principal actor). Second, all the state actors, in different degrees, are exposed to the vicissitudes of a global market they do not control.

International politics today is not the preserve of states and businesses: we have to move beyond, or rather under, the two arenas or stages where actors play. The diffusion of power has a third and quite different dimension, which, like the emergence and eminence of the sphere of economic interdependence, moves us far away from the Realist analysis of international politics. Realism reduces world affairs to a game played, in Raymond Aron's words, by diplomats and soldiers on behalf of statesmen. Today, we note a worldwide trend (uneven, to be sure, like the "international business civilization")—a trend so messy that there is no adequate term for it. "Democratization" is not quite right, because it brings to mind the spread of representative systems based on consent; in fact, despite recent surges, their triumph is far from universal. "Populism" would be better, were it not for the word's baggage of connotations derived from peasant and farmers' movements in nineteenth century Europe and America. Maybe demands for "people power," or for "citizens' say," is the best approximation: the information revolution so many of the authors of this volume mention does, on balance, make the control of people's minds and moves by governments more difficult, and it is popular demands and pressures that set much of the agenda of the governments' foreign policies. The notion, inseparable from Realism, that this agenda is "objectively" set by the map of geography and by the map of alignments dictated by the "security dilemma" is obsolete. The agendas are either dictated by domestic imperatives or delicate attempts at reconciling these with external constraints.

This third form of diffusion of power is important above all for explaining a shift in stakes, or state preferences and goals, that many of the contributors mention. It is a shift away from traditional goals of conquest, control, and coercion. The de-

cline in the utility of force, stressed here by a . . . realist Realist, Robert Tucker (who for so long had firmly remained in the camp of traditional power analysis), would not have occurred if it had not been for the three factors that were central to Kant's philosophy of history and ethics of foreign policy: the increasing destructiveness of war; the attractions of "greed," or commerce, that is, economic issues to which force is not relevant; and the rise of popular participation. The last raises domestic obstacles to the pursuit of imperial policies, and it also fosters mass resistance among the victims of such policies, which force is often unable to crush. It is a shift toward those economic stakes that are likely to bring to the nation or to its citizens the wealth and welfare people aspire to—which means that the control of market shares is more important, in a world where firms are endlessly mobile, than that of territory, and that access to resources and markets through trade and investment is seen as far more effective and sensible than access through force.

If the diffusion of power is a first way of apprehending the sea-change, a second and perhaps more fruitful one is to look at the world in terms of a contest not between two domineering states, but between three levels. There is the global level, where the "world business civilization" operates, with its own logic and instruments, outlined here by Strange and Heilbroner. There are the states, which try to exploit this logic and its carriers in order to increase their countries' wealth, or to increase their power and influence over others (since wealth is more than ever a source of power); but the states are, with respect to the world capitalist system, in a doubly uncomfortable position. On the one hand, they are still engaged in another "game": the traditional one, of security fears, calculations, and contests, whose logic is that of Thucydides, not Adam Smith. On the other, they are trying to prevent the logic of world capitalism from depriving them of financial, monetary, and fiscal autonomy and from magnifying the differences between rich and poor states, as well as between modern sectors, fully integrated in the global economy, and backward ones. Thus, the world economy is not their single obsession, and they are ambivalent about it.

Moreover, they are besieged by more than the uncontrollable forces—private, at home and abroad, as well as public, in the form of foreign trading and investing states, abroad—of a world economy that is only partly denationalized. They are also under pressure from the third level, that of the people.

The people, to be sure, count on their state to play the game of wealth effectively, and want the benefits of growth that the economy dangles before their eyes. But the global requirements of efficiency are not those of equity, and wealth for the nation and for some of its members may be very different from welfare for most. Participation, equity, and wealth: people want all three, but often they can have only two of these, and sometimes none at all. To keep the engines of growth working, there is often a need, in the advanced countries, to attract immigrants as manpower. All of this exposes the state to a double danger. When its political and economic system leads to poverty and stagnation, there is a risk of rebellion, or of such pressure from below that the system collapses (consider the end of the Stalinist system in the 1980s); but when the state's participation in the global economy leads to inflation, unemployment, growing inequalities, or an "invasion" of inassimilable aliens, a populist backlash is always to be feared. . . .

These are, of course, broad trends described with broad brush strokes. In today's Japan, national homogeneity has been carefully preserved, and the people appear still satisfied with the strategy, aimed at national wealth rather than individual welfare, that has been selected, in the world economy, by the governments they have confirmed in power for so many years. In China, the regime still—but for how long—seems to have the power to keep demands for economic change compatible with the preservation of a bureaucratic and authoritarian system of command. But there is yet a third way of looking at the global dynamics at work: a simultaneous movement of unification and fragmentation. The capitalist economic system tends to unify the world by internationalizing and integrating the markets of goods and capital, and by creating a sort of world elite of managers, private and public. Still there is a fragmentation of the world

into states, with the trappings of sovereignty, including currencies, armies, and national rules and welfare systems for labor: formal fragmentation, if you like—the kind for which Marx, who saw states as mere façades concealing class relations, had little understanding. And there is another kind of fragmentation that he grasped extremely well in his analysis of world capitalism: the substantive one. It results both from the dynamics of the global market, which tends often to exacerbate inequality both among and within states . . . and from the dissatisfaction of many people with "their" state, precisely because, for ethnic, religious, or ideological reasons, they do not recognize it as theirs, or else because the government has failed to feed, employ, enrich, or protect them, and thus has broken the bonds of consent.

One reason for offering this rather abstract picture is to point out that a post–Cold War world will be anything but harmonious. We are entering a new phase of history. It is assuredly not the "end of history," a silly notion based on a series of mistaken assumptions (that the death of communism means the definitive triumph of Western liberalism, the end of ideology, and the coming of a "boring" era of material concerns and unheroic squabbles); it is a period in which the discrepancy between the formal organization of the world into states and the realities of power, which do not resemble those of any past international system, will create formidable contradictions and difficulties. . . .

First, there is a huge array of possible "traditional" quarrels, in a world where there is at least still one ideology of violent conflict—Islamic fundamentalism—and where the disappearance or decay of secular ideologies leaves nationalism, over much of the planet, as the only glue of loyalty. The Arab-Israeli conflict, Kashmir, and Cyprus are daily reminders of gloomy forms of permanence. Evidence of the declining utility of force for the superpowers and for other major actors, such as the nations of Western Europe and Japan, may not deter those for whom passion overruns cost-benefit analysis, and those for whom force seems the only alternative to despair, humiliation, or destruction. If one remembers that the increased economic capabilities of smaller states . . . allow them to buy or build formidable modern arsenals and to make themselves largely independent of arms shipments by fickle superpowers—and if one believes, as Tucker and I do, that the latter, no longer chasing each other all over the world, may play less of a moderating role in such regional conflicts now that their potential as triggers of a superpower collision has vanished—there is then no reason to expect that the traditional arena of world politics will be empty or boring—except, perhaps, strangely and happily enough, in Europe, prophets of recurrent doom notwithstanding.

Second, the realm of interdependence will also breed conflicts that could be serious. As Kahler says, elites depend on popular satisfaction for their survival in power, and the disruptions and distributional conflicts the "world business civilization" may bring with it could "cause some states to define their security requirements more broadly rather than less," or to divert domestic turbulence toward conflict abroad. Among the advanced countries, the different strategies chosen by the main players in the quest for market shares and wealth may become incompatible if they lead to permanent imbalances. This is already the message of the so-called revisionists who point out that the Japanese brand of neomercantilism—which subordinates the interests of consumers to those of producers, entails a deliberate and long-term strategy aimed at gaining the lead in advanced technologies, and results in a "continued displacement of industrial sectors and the shift of technological capability toward Japan"—may not be reconcilable with America's consumer orientation, lack of industrial policy, and lesser "ability to adapt quickly to changing circumstances." Conflicts over trade and industrial policy ultimately involve as stakes both the power of states, since wealth is a component of power (even though the uses of economic power are often constrained or capable of boomeranging), and the fate of labor at home. Without the restraining force exerted by the Cold War, and by the need of Western Europeans and Japanese for American protection, such conflicts could become acute.

The potential for trouble, not between the "North" and "South," but between the advanced countries and certain groups of less-developed ones, is equally serious. It is often said that the poorer among the latter cannot cause much harm, whatever they do. This may be true, in cases other than oil, if harm is defined in purely economic terms. But radical anti-Western ideologies could turn fiercely against the institutions and agents of Western capitalism; also, the weakness and heterogeneity of some of these states, and the pressure of increasing populations, may well lead to violent regional conflicts, as well as to formidable quarrels over immigration and refuge to and expulsions from the richer countries. Two of the problems that have become urgent, drugs and the environment, could all too easily lead to confrontations between advanced states eager to protect their health and their future, and states such as those of South America that need to cultivate drugs, or to forgo strict protection of the environment, in order to develop.

Third, the conflicts between state and people must be taken seriously, too—not only because popular or populist attacks on ill-constituted states and unacceptable governments, or governmental attempts to divert such attacks, could lead to interstate troubles, but also because the victory of "people power" is neither a guarantee of moderate behavior abroad nor at all guaranteed. Popular victories can trample over minority rights and create nationalist explosions. Conversely, democratic revolutions may wilt if the winners get bogged down in party squabbles and parochial issues, or else caught between the "demands" of the world business civilization and domestic discontent, and replaced by authoritarian or military rulers. This, in turn, may be bad, both for regional peace and for the cause of human rights. . . .

It is therefore, to use Richard N. Gardner's terms, for a "comeback of liberal internationalism" that one must plead. Each person may have his or her own favorite blueprint, but the main directions are clear. Among the advanced countries the main tasks will be, first, the establishment of a new security system in Europe, which will probably be a mix of a much-reformed NATO no longer dominated by the United States, a Western European defense organization, and an organization set by the Conference on Security and Cooperation in Europe (CSCE); second, an agreement among the main suppliers of arms and advanced technologies to restrict such sales drastically, to strengthen the nuclear nonproliferation regime, and to establish regional arms limitation and conflict resolution regimes; third, a deal to redistribute power—now still largely in the hands of the United States—among the main actors in the international financial and economic organizations, the United States, Japan, and the EEC.

The end of the Cold War and of the straitjacket of worldwide East-West security concerns should allow the advanced countries to concentrate their efforts on social, economic, and political conditions in an increasingly diversified "South." Both ecological imperatives and the issue of the population pressure of the poor and the refugees require a set of bargains, thanks to which ample resources will, through multilateral assistance and with the participation of the leading private firms, be made available to the developing countries, in exchange for commitments on environmental protection, health care, energy efficiency, agricultural productivity, and human rights. The demands on the resources of the richer states—caught between the needs and expectations of their own people and the fear of external chaos—will be both so large and so conflicting that organizations for regional and global cooperation will have to be strengthened, through guaranteed revenues, the creation of independent secretariats, and frequent high-level meetings.

Robert Tucker asks whether a world without a central threat and a hegemon will be able to create order. It is not certain. What is proposed here is very much a halfway house: not a world government for which states and peoples are unprepared (and that the managers of the world business civilization would not like), but a new experiment in polycentric steering, in which the three major economic powers—plus the Soviet Union if it overcomes its problems, and perhaps China once it

begins to turn its potential into effective power (something that would require drastic political changes)—would form a central steering group, and in which regional powers would play comparable roles in their areas. Nothing like this has ever been tried—but then, the hidden theme of this essay has been the advent of discontinuity in international affairs.

Two big question marks remain. First, will a development of multilateral diplomacy and institutions not merely add a layer to the three—the global market, the states, the people—that exist already, and simply add cooperative inefficiency to market inequities, state erosion, and popular discontent? Will it help global unification or make for more fragmentation (including, now, among international and regional agencies)? The risk exists; the example of the EEC shows that where the will can be found, the danger can be overcome. Second, will the United States be willing to commit itself, and sufficient resources, to such a path? The answer could be yes, on two conditions: if adequate leadership can at last be provided—leadership that would understand and explain that, as Kahler puts it, "unilateral American action is likely to be less effective, and the workings of an untrammeled market . . . less desirable than . . . international collaboration"; and if domestic reform to provide for the underpinnings of power is undertaken. Without such reform, popular turbulence and resentments against competitors will mount. To be sure, such reform will require fiscal sacrifices, and while it absorbs attention and funds, America's own contributions to the needs of others might remain limited. But none of America's problems at home or abroad can be solved if "people power" is equated with no new taxes; and in the immediate future, one of the welcome effects of the diffusion of power is the ability of Western Europe and Japan (already the largest donor of foreign aid) to play a larger role.

The world after the Cold War will not resemble any world of the past. From a "structural" point of view—the distribution of capabilities—it will be multipolar. But the poles will have different currencies of power—military (the Soviets), economic and financial (Japan and Germany), demographic (China and India), military and economic (the United States)—and different productivities of power—demographic power is more a liability than an asset, the utility of military might is reduced, only economic power is fully useful because it is the capacity to influence others by bringing them the very goods they crave. Moreover, each of these poles will be, at least to some extent, mired in a world economy that limits its freedom of action. What we do not know is what relations are going to develop among these actors, what institutional links they will set up to manage their relations with one another, and their relations with the rest of the world, in a context of vigilant, demanding, and often turbulently mobilized masses. The fate of this new world will depend on the ability of the "poles" to cooperate enough in order to prevent or moderate conflicts—including regional ones, and to correct those imbalances of the world economy that would otherwise induce some states, or their publics, to pull away from or to disrupt the momentum of interdependence. Above all, it will depend on domestic currents that remain highly difficult to predict. Since foreign policy today is so largely shaped by domestic demands and expectations, the most dangerous remaining tension, and the most difficult to overcome, is that between the global dimension of the issues that foreign policy will have to deal with and the fact that political life remains, at best, limited to the horizons of the state and is, often, even challenging the unity, the borders, and the effectiveness of the state.

The world is like a bus whose driver—the global economy—is not in full control of the engine and is himself out of control, in which children—the people—are tempted to step on either the brake or the gas pedal, and adults—the states—are worried passengers. A league of passengers may not be enough to keep the bus on the road, but there is no better solution yet.

Questions for Discussion

1. Are there any "rules of the international game of nations," or is anarchy the prevailing mode of operation?
2. What is meant by the balance of power?
3. What are some variations on this concept? For example, distinguish between its practice in a bipolar world and a multipolar world.
4. How has the balance of power changed in the twentieth century?
5. How has balance of power considerations influenced U.S. foreign policy?
6. Have nuclear weapons changed the relevance of balance of power considerations?
7. What changes in the international system have operated to diminish the utility of the balance of power as a determinant of U.S. foreign policy?

Selected Bibliography

BRIDGE, F.R., AND ROGER BULLEN. *The Great Powers and the European States System.* London: Longman, 1980.

BULL, HEDLEY. *The Anarchical Society: A Study of Order in World Politics.* New York: Columbia University Press, 1977.

CENTRE FOR ARAB UNITY STUDIES. *The Future of the Arab Nation: Challenges and Options.* London: Routledge, 1991.

CRABB, CECIL V., JR. *Nations in a Multipolar World.* New York: Harper & Row, 1968.

GADDIS, JOHN L. *The Long Peace.* New York: Oxford University Press, 1987.

GALLOIS, PIERRE. *The Balance of Terror.* Boston: Houghton Mifflin, 1961.

GRAY, COLIN S. *War, Peace, and Victory: Strategy and Statecraft for the Next Century.* New York: Simon and Schuster, 1990.

GULICK, EDWARD V. *Europe's Classical Balance of Power.* Ithaca: Cornell University Press, 1955.

KAPLAN, MORTON A. *Systems and Process in International Relations.* New York: Wiley, 1957.

LEBOW, RICHARD NED, AND BARRY S. STRAUSS (EDS.). *Hegemonic Rivalry: From Thucydides to the Nuclear Age.* Boulder: Westview, 1991.

PETTMAN, RALPH. *International Politics: Balance of Power, Balance of Productivity, Balance of Ideologies.* Harlow: Longman, 1991.

WIGHT, MARTIN. *Systems of State.* Leicester: Leicester University Press, 1977.

PART TWO

DETERMINING THE NATIONAL INTEREST

CHAPTER 3

Perspectives on the National Interest

The national interest is a term subject to infinitely elastic interpretation. It rests on no established foreign policy criteria with which to evaluate problems and has no invariable political ends. In practice, it is what each administration says it is. It is something out of *Alice in Wonderland*, as when Humpty-Dumpty told Alice, "When I use a word, it means just what I choose it to mean, nothing more, nothing less." "The question is," Alice replied, "whether you *can* make words mean so many different things." In 1848, Viscount Palmerston, England's Foreign Secretary, declared, "We have no eternal allies and we have no perpetual enemies. [Only] our interests are eternal and perpetual, and these interests it is our duty to follow." Machiavellian in the focus on his country's preservation and well-being, he left obscure precisely what those interests were and the circumstances under which they might have to be secured by the use of force.

The Founding Fathers of the United States of America were children of the Enlightenment. The Age of Reason bred distrust of the rule of men as opposed to the rule of law, and it led them to establish a government of limited powers to ensure against tyranny and to foster the pursuit of liberty, tranquility, and happiness. Although focused on the internal task of fashioning a viable republic, they understood that America could not isolate itself completely from the rest of the world, that foreign policy was a means of helping to safeguard the new experiment in the New World. Hans J. Morgenthau examines the underlying assumptions of what he calls "the Federalist conception of the American national interest in foreign affairs" and contrasts it with the Wilsonian conception which took hold and has competed with it ever since the early twentieth century (Reading 5).

The Federalist conception of the national interest prevailed throughout most of the nineteenth century. There were differences among the men responsible for giving substantive and specific content to the general principles they all tended to share— Alexander Hamilton versus Thomas Jefferson and James Monroe versus John Quincy Adams, to mention a few. But they had in common a belief in the uniqueness of the American republic and in the need to practice balance of power politics. George Washington's farewell address of 1796 provided firm guidelines: keep out of Europe's dynastic quarrels, "the causes of which are essentially foreign to us," avoid entangling alliances, but, if necessary, consider "temporary alliances for extraordinary emergencies." The threads of continuity in the Federalist fabric held up extraordinarily well for more than a century, though at times modifications in the basic pattern were made. By way of illustration, two developments may be noted.

In the interest of gaining Napoleon's recognition of the U.S.'s claims to West Florida against Spain's, President Jefferson refused to assist in any way the struggle of the people of Santo Domingo, who had successfully revolted against Spain in 1805 and who two years later resisted France's attempt to subjugate them. Jefferson's quest for control of Florida—an early expression of the "manifest destiny" that would drive American expansion across the continent—induced him to accommodate to the brutality of a dictator he despised and whose ambitions he knew might some day threaten the security of the United States.

In December 1823, President James Monroe, who was sympathetic to the efforts of Spain's South American colonies to gain independence, joined with Great Britain to stymie efforts of the Holy Alliance (Austria-Hungary, Russia, Prussia) to prop up Spanish rule. Monroe understood that only by enlisting the deterrent capability of Britain's formidable navy could he forestall the Holy Alliance's projection of power into the Western Hemisphere. The ensuing "Monroe Doctrine," which enhanced U.S. security by discouraging European powers from fishing in the potentially rich political waters of the hemisphere, rested on the willingness of Britain throughout much of the nineteenth century to commit its naval power to such an end.

Monroe's action was a reversal of a position previously enunciated by his Secretary of State: on July 4, 1821, John Quincy Adams had used the occasion to reaffirm the enduring validity of George Washington's injunction against a policy of intervention and to caution the country against becoming involved in overseas crusades with inveterate power-seekers of Europe. He declared that wherever "the standard of freedom and Independence has been or shall be unfurled," there will America's "heart, her benedictions and her prayers be. But she

goes not abroad, in search of monsters to destroy. She is the well-wisher to the freedom and independence of all. She is the champion and vindicator only of her own." Adams argued that once America enlisted "under other banners than her own, were they even the banners of foreign Independence, she would involve herself beyond the power of extrication, in all the wars of interest and intrigue, of individual avarice, envy, and ambition, which assume the colors and usurp the standard of freedom":

> The fundamental maxims of her policy would insensibly change from *liberty* to *force*. The frontlet upon her brow would no longer beam with the ineffable splendor of Freedom and Independence; but in its stead would soon be substituted an Imperial Diadem, flashing in false and tarnished luster the murky radiation of dominion and power. She might become the dictatress of the world. She would be no longer the ruler of her own spirit.

This is as eloquent a counter to the premises of Wilsonianism as one is likely to come across.

The continuing debate over national interest is joined by Irving Kristol (Reading 6) and Alan Tonelson (Reading 7). In both resonate the tension between the pull of the Federalist focus on tending to our own interests and the tug of a Wilsonian internationalism that has globalized America's involvement. Both authors come with very different premises and recommendations; but they agree on certain courses of action. Kristol, more than Tonelson, accepts the inevitability of adopting a doublestandard in determining which issues and countries matter more, whereas Tonelson's insistence on a coherent, integrated approach to the world has an almost Wilsonian cast to it.

In a pluralist society like the United States, varied interpretations of the national interest are inevitable. Different groups are motivated by different policy aims: "National interest to one may well be national lack of interest to another. In fact, it may be concluded that the conception of national interest which prevails at any one time is no more than an amalgam of varying policy motivations which tend to pass for a 'national' interest as long as the groups holding these opinions continue to rule."[1]

The determination of the U.S. national interest in three major instances that ended in a heavy commitment of military forces was the ad hoc response of Presidents whose earlier pronouncements and policies gave no indication that they would act as they did. In none of the three instances were there established policy criteria that could have given the leadership of the aggressor nation pause before proceeding as it did; and in none was there any searching policy review by the Congress prior to the President's decision to involve the United States in a significant way.

When North Korean forces invaded South Korea in late June 1950, President Harry S Truman acted immediately to come to its aid, even though six months earlier his Secretary of State, Dean Acheson, had defined vital U.S. interests in Asia as extending from Alaska to Japan and southward, deliberately excluding South Korea. Why was it that what was of no strategic importance in January became a vital interest in June? According to Professor Ernest May, "It is hard for people in government to sit down and say that a certain country is or is

not vital apart from exact circumstances that lie in the future. Moreover, it is always difficult to take any particular piece of property and say we couldn't live without it. Its importance usually stems from its being seen in a particular context as part of a chain of possible events."[2] For Truman, confronted with a Soviet military challenge in Germany, a newly established Communist regime in China, and the vulnerability and strategic importance of Japan, the North Korean attack seemed a possible prelude to a Soviet-orchestrated campaign of expansion.

John F. Kennedy's extension of the military involvement in Vietnam, by contrast, had less to commend it: there was no threat to a vital U.S. interest, no essential resources or American stake was at risk, and no direct Soviet or Chinese hand was in evidence. Vietnam became an American tragedy, and no brief comment can do justice to the question of how the United States came to be in that quagmire. I would suggest that it began as a small move by Kennedy to recoup domestic prestige lost as a consequence of his mistake in sanctioning the use of Cuban exiles in April 1961 to attempt an overthrow of Fidel Castro. Although the plan had been devised by the CIA during the Eisenhower administration, President Dwight D. Eisenhower had refused to give a green light for the operation. His administration talked tough about "rolling back communism," but he did not allow ideological motivations or emotional sentiments to cloud his judgment about what the national interest was, nor would he commit military personnel without a clear purpose. Moreover, Kennedy misread Khrushchev, exaggerating Soviet intentions in the Third

[1] Ernest B. Haas. "The Balance of Power as a Guide to Policy-making," *The Journal of Politics*, vol. 15, August 1953, p. 383.

[2] As cited in Leslie H. Gelb. "When Is a Foreign Interest 'Vital'?," *The New York Times*, August 8, 1983.

World. He interpreted a speech Nikita Khrushchev had made in early January 1961 calling for support of "national liberation movements" (that is, insurgencies seeking to topple pro-Western governments) as meaning that the USSR was preparing to push the pace of revolution throughout the Third World. Such was not the case, despite Khrushchev's reckless attempt in the fall of 1962 to implant nuclear missiles in Cuba, where Moscow had already committed 20,000 troops to uphold the internationally recognized Castro regime. After Kennedy was assassinated, Lyndon Johnson became obsessed by Vietnam, and it was he who committed 500,000 troops to a grueling, costly war in a marginal part of the world. His motivations remain obscure, but, a monumental egoist, he often asserted that he would not be the first President to lose a war. Where in all of this lay the national interest is, in retrospect, difficult to ascertain.

Finally, when Iraq invaded Kuwait in August 1990, President George Bush mobilized an international coalition under the imprimatur of the United Nations and used force to reverse Saddam Hussein's aggression. Since the end of the Gulf War information has come to light that the Bush administration had chosen not to see what it did not want to believe. In its fundamental hostility to Iran, it had pandered to Saddam Hussein, hoping to moderate his conduct by assorted carrots. It had arranged U.S.-government-guaranteed loans, overlooked Saddam's bellicose speeches and military buildup (conventional and nuclear), and completely misinterpreted his intentions toward Kuwait. In the continual dispute between the Department of Defense, which objected strongly to the sale of advanced technology and components to Iraq, and the Department of Commerce, which sought to increase trade to help offset the balance of trade deficit, the administration had tilted toward commerce. As matters developed, after Saddam Hussein's defeat it became known that Iraq's military equipment was formidable and it was closer to acquiring a nuclear capability than U.S. intelligence had thought. Happily, Iraq's military leadership, led by Saddam Hussein himself, was inept and consistently outmaneuvered by the U.S.-led forces.

These examples highlight the salience of the subjective factor in the determination of the national interest. This process involves a complex and not always predictable interaction between the President and his advisers, between the Executive and Legislative branches of government, between government officials and the lobbyists of various pressure groups, between officials and nongovernmental groups (academic, business, labor, church, etc.), and between government and the media.

In evaluating diverse interpretations of what constitutes the national interest, a number of questions may be asked:

1. Is there a sense of priorities, since not all interests can be adjudged as vital?
2. Has the process of deciding on a course of action been exposed to a broadly based discussion of policy options and implications?
3. Is there a complementarity between commitments, on the one hand, and capabilities and support in the country at large, on the other?
4. Are the criteria for the decisions precisely stated and sound?

5.   What Is the National Interest of the United States?

Hans J. Morgenthau

One of the greatest of American statesmen, Woodrow Wilson, gave a speech at Mobile, Alabama in which he declared, "It is a very perilous thing to determine the foreign policy of a nation in the terms of material interest. It not only is unfair to those with whom you are dealing, but it is degrading as regards your own actions." Woodrow Wilson, in thus speaking, echoed an opinion which was widespread in his time. Some decades earlier, Gladstone had propounded in Great Britain a similar philosophy in opposition to the policies of Disraeli. Few would be bold enough today to express in so uncompromising terms their disparagement of the national interest. Even so, we have still to cope with a philosophy, very much alive in our midst, which, while it recognizes the national interest and its importance, defines it in terms which take the heart out of the concept and out of the policies intended to support it.

From the very beginning of American history, two irreconcilable philosophies have struggled for predominance over the American mind. One prevailed during the Federalist period of American foreign policy, that is to say, roughly the first decade of American history, and its outstanding representative was Alexander Hamilton. The other conception of the national interest of the United States seems to be the exact opposite of that of the Federalist, and is represented by any number of individuals and policies in recent American history. Woodrow Wilson is the outstanding exponent of it.

THE FEDERALIST CONCEPTION

The Federalist conception of the American interest in foreign affairs was based on three presupposi-

SOURCE: Hans J. Morgenthau. "What Is the National Interest of the United States?", *The Annals of the American Academy of Political and Social Science*, vol. 282, July 1952, pp. 1–7, excerpts. Reprinted with permission.

tions. The first was that the interest of the United States in international affairs was fundamentally different from those interests which European nations traditionally pursued. The Farewell Address of Washington is a clear example of this presupposition: the idea that the United States was an experiment in government unique in its essential aspects and that one of the main purposes of American foreign policy was to protect this experiment against encroachments by the traditional ways of the European nations.

This purpose leads to the second presupposition of the Federalist conception of foreign policy, and that is what one might call the isolation of the United States. However, this conception was not similar to that which was propounded by the isolationists of the 1920's and 1930's and is still being defended to a certain extent by the neoisolationists of today. They believe that there exists something like an natural isolation of the United States from the rest of the world, an isolation which can best be preserved by abstention from an active foreign policy and by retreat into what is now called the "continental fortress" of the United States. The Founding Fathers had a clear conception of the relationship between the isolation of the United States from the affairs of Europe and an active foreign policy to be pursued by the United States. With the Founding Fathers, the isolation of the United States was not a gift of nature to be preserved by doing nothing. It was rather the result of an intelligent and deliberate foreign policy to be achieved by hard thinking and hard work.

The third presupposition of the Federalists was that, in order to make the United States immune from foreign interference and, more particularly, from being drawn into the squabbles of Europe, its foreign policy had to be a policy of the balance of power. Men like Alexander Hamilton, John Adams, and even John Quincy Adams realized that the isolation of the United States was a mere function of the balance of power in Europe. They realized that only as long as the most powerful European nations were pitted against each other, unable therefore to cross the Atlantic for adventures in the Western Hemisphere, was the United States safe from European intervention and from being drawn into the conflicts of Europe.

THE NEWER CONCEPTION

The other conception of the national interest of the United States has developed since the Spanish-American War. In both its manifestations, it denies the intimate connection between the isolation, that is the security, of the United States in the Western Hemisphere and a discriminating active foreign policy with regard to the other nations of the world.

I implied that there are two manifestations of that conception. One may be called isolationism pure and simple, that is to say, not only a retreat from intervention in the affairs of other continents, but a retreat from an active foreign policy altogether. The other manifestation may be called isolationism turned inside out. It is unlimited, world-embracing interventionism. It is a policy which makes no distinction between the interests of the United States and the interests of other nations, and within the interests of the United States it refuses to recognize a hierarchy of objectives. For instance, it is in favor of collective security as a matter of principle, and hence feels constrained to intervene whenever the security of any nation, regardless of its relation to the concrete interests of the United States, is endangered.

This radical isolationism on the one hand and this radical interventionism on the other are two different manifestations of the self-same underlying philosophy of foreign policy that identifies the national interest of the United States with some worth-while conception of human welfare and certain abstract principles of universal morality. Both derive from a misunderstanding of the Federalist position. They share the Federalist concern about the United States' becoming involved in the conflicts of Europe, but they misunderstand the rationale of that concern.

For the Federalists, the ultimate objective of American policy, domestic and international, was the integrity of the American experiment; the isolation of the United States from conflicts outside the Western Hemisphere was a means to an end, to be replaced by other means if the conditions of American existence should so require. For the twentieth-century isolationists, intervention in non-American conflicts is bad in itself, never to be indulged in; for the twentieth-century interventionist, intervention is always good, never to be refrained from. Both erect the issue of isolation versus intervention into a contest between two abstract moral principles, and hence lose sight of the subordination of the issue, so brilliantly conceived and practiced by the Federalists, to the interests of the United States conceived in terms of national security and the integrity of the American experiment.

Some of you will not be surprised when I say that I have little sympathy with this new conception of the national interest of the United States, and that I firmly believe in the truth of the Federalist conception. I see in the development of American thinking and American foreign policy since the end of World War II a groping toward the rediscovery of the eternal truths of foreign policy which the Federalists discovered and which later generations tended to neglect and discard.

THE MORAL AGRUMENT

Let me make some general remarks in defense of that realistic conception of the national interest to which I adhere. Certain typical arguments are being advanced time and again against this conception. I want here only to mention two of them. One is a moral argument, the argument to which Wilson referred in the speech which I have quoted. It runs about as follows: It is something base, something immoral, for a nation to put its own interests above the interests of other nations or above the interests of humanity. From this assumption the conclusion is frequently drawn that a natural harmony exists between the interests of the United States and the interests of humanity; that, in other words, whatever the United States proposes to do and actually does in foreign policy is necessarily good not only for the United States but also for mankind.

This is not only, it seems to me, an untrue conception which flies in the face of all the experiences of history; it is also a very dangerous one. It comes dangerously close to the chauvinism of fascism and communism, which have advanced exactly the same pretenses for themselves. In practical policies, it leads of necessity either to national suicide through inaction or else to that unlimited interventionism to which I have referred above. The isolationist who has been challenged beyond endurance by the facts of experience will find it hard to resist the feeling that we should wipe from the face of the earth the nations which refuse to recognize that identity of our own interests with the interests of humanity. This philosophy, then, culminates in the policy of unconditional surrender and in the conception of wars as crusades fought for unlimited goals and waged with unlimited means.

WORLD UNITY AND WORLD DIVISION

The other argument to which I want to address myself for a moment runs about as follows: It may have been correct that in the eighteenth or nineteenth century, or in even more backward centuries, concern with the interest of a particular nation was justifiable and necessary. However, in the mid-twentieth century, the interconnectedness of the interests of all nations has become so great that no nation can really stand alone and take care of its own interests without jeopardizing those very interests.

This conception obviously appears to be quite plausible on the face of it; for it is patently true that in view of the technological revolutions in the fields of communications, transportation, and warfare, the technical preconditions for the development of an international community are today much greater than in any previous period of history. I must, however, call attention to the contrast between those technological potentialities, on the

one hand, and the moral and political reality, on the other. For while this is, technologically speaking, potentially one world, in actuality, from a moral and political point of view, never in the history of western civilization was the world, at least the politically active world, so divided as at present. . . . [1]

THE ESSENCE OF FOREIGN POLICY

In such a situation it is vain to try to draw certain political or moral conclusions from technological potentialities; for in truth the essence of foreign policy has remained what it has always been, even though its manifestations have greatly changed. As John Quincy Adams put it, "I do not recollect any change in policy; but there has been a great change in circumstances."

This is as true today as it was then, and it has been true throughout history. The basic problems of foreign policy have remained what they were in ancient Greece and what they were in the Middle Ages and in the eighteenth and nineteenth centuries. What has changed are the manifestations of those problems, the circumstances under which we must meet those perennial problems of foreign policy. It therefore follows that, despite the profound changes which have occurred in the world, it still remains true, as it has always been true, that a nation confronted with the hostile aspirations of other nations has one prime obligation—to take care of its own interests. The moral justification for this prime duty of all nations—for it is not only a moral right but also a moral obligation—arises from the fact that if this particular nation does not take care of its interests, nobody else will. Hence the counsel that we ought to subordinate our national interests to some other standard is unworthy of a nation great in human civilization. A nation which would take that counsel and act consistently

[1] Writing in 1952, Morgenthau was referring to the bipolar world of Cold War, with its two antagonistic political philosophies and antithetical political-strategic interests on the Eurasian landmass.

on it would commit suicide and become the prey and victim of other nations which know how to take care of their interests.

BASIC INTERESTS OF UNITED STATES

Let me then say a word about what, in concrete terms, the perennial national interests of the United States have been—what have, from the beginning of its history, been its unchanging interests that were pursued in different periods of history with different methods because the circumstances changed under which they had to be pursued. It seems to me that from the beginning of American history there have been two basic objectives which have determined the thoughts and actions of American statesmen.

Position in Western Hemisphere

There was, first of all, the security of the United States in the Western Hemisphere. At the very beginning of American history the situation of the United States was precarious, surrounded as it was by the outposts of great European powers; and so the security of the United States became necessarily the prime objective which American foreign policy had to pursue, the prime interest which it had to protect and promote. But even when, after the initial period, those immediate dangers passed, the United States still remained vitally concerned with its position in the Western Hemisphere. As the power of the United States grew and as it developed into predominance in the Western Hemisphere, unchallengeable from within, this concern with security was supplemented by concern with the preservation of American predominance. The Monroe Doctrine and, more particularly, the subsequent interpretations and political and military manifestations of that doctrine are the expression of this development of American concern from mere security to the safeguarding of American predominance.

European Balance of Power

This first concern leads with logical necessity to the second one, which is the maintenance of the balance of power in Europe. The United States was quick to realize that its security and predominance could not be challenged from within the Western Hemisphere. There was no nation in the Western Hemisphere, either to the north or the south, which, either alone or in combination with other American nations, could think of challenging successfully the predominant position of the United States. A danger to that position could arise only if and when an American nation would make common cause with a non-American nation for the purpose of challenging the United States. Thus the security of the United States in the Western Hemisphere was clearly recognized to depend upon conditions prevailing outside that hemisphere. Here we are again in the presence of the American concern for the maintenance of the balance of power in Europe, which is indeed the second great perennial concern of the United States in foreign affairs.

As long as there existed in Europe a multiplicity of nations of approximately equal strength, those nations had their hands full in defending themselves against their rivals on the European Continent. They had no possibility of making common cause with a Latin American nation for the purpose of challenging the predominant position of the United States in the Western Hemisphere. But if one great power would arise to a paramount position on the European Continent, such as the Germany of William II or of Hitler, or as the Soviet Union today, then such a nation, imperialistic in its policies and unchallengeable in its power from within Europe, could and was likely to embark upon adventures beyond the seas. There lay the great prize of the United States, almost irresistibly tempting to the would-be world conqueror, with all its wealth and power—and all its friendless isolation.

It is for this reason that the United States has always opposed the imperialism of those European nations which were most likely to be successful in their imperialistic designs if the United States did not oppose them. During the Napoleonic Wars, even so idealistic a statesman and thinker as Thomas Jefferson used to shift his sympathies in accordance with the shifts in the balance of power. Whenever Great Britain seemed to win over

Napoleon, he wished for the victory of Napoleon; and whenever Napoleon seemed to win over Great Britain, he thought that after all Great Britain was not so bad as he had thought her to be. Our interventions in the First and Second World Wars, whatever their moralistic and idealistic justifications may have been, had their firm basis in the national interest of the United States in seeing the balance of power in Europe preserved, or, in case of its disturbance, in seeing it restored. . . .

Those are, in necessarily brief outline, the general aspects of the national interests of the United States as I see them. I have said that no moral argument can be presented against a foreign policy which is based upon consideration of the national interest. Let me say now a word in conclusion about the intellectual and political aspects of that problem.

It seems to me that from a merely intellectual, from a rational, point of view, no nation can have a sure guide as to what it must do and what it need not do in foreign policy without accepting the national interest as that guide. One of the great weak-nesses of American foreign policy in recent decades has been its inability to follow consistently certain standards of action and judgment in its conduct of foreign affairs. We were against Italy because of its aggression against Ethiopia, but were against Franco because of his fascism. We seemed to like Mussolini because he made the trains run on time, but when he made an alliance with Hitler we did not like him any more. We did not like Stalin either; but when he was attacked by Germany and was defeating the German armies, we thought he was a somewhat uncouth democrat, essentially not so different from ourselves; and finally we turned full circle, and regard him now as the incarnation of all evil.

It seems to me this stumbling from one extreme to the other, this inability to steer a clear course in foreign affairs, undisturbed by emotional preferences, results from the lack of recognition of the national interest as the only standard for judgment and action available to a great nation if it wants to pursue a successful and rational foreign policy.

6.   Defining Our National Interest

Irving Kristol

It is very difficult for a great power—a world power—to articulate a foreign policy in the absence of an enemy worthy of the name. It is, after all, one's enemies that help define one's "national interest," in whatever form that definition might take. Without such enemies, one flounders amidst a plenitude of rather trivial, or at least marginal, options. That, it seems to me, is the condition of the United States today, as we enter the post-Cold War era . . .

But what shall we do with this victory? What do we expect of the world, what do we want of the world, what role shall we—the sole remaining world power—play in the world, in this post-Cold War era? . . .

Even to mention "national interest" as a lodestar for American foreign policy excites controversy or revulsion. The Russians know that they have been deprived of the guiding principles of Soviet foreign policy, as established by the Bolshevik Revolution. We, the victors, are naturally inclined to think that our principles have been vindicated. But if one asks what these principles are, one gets a cacophony of responses. It isn't that we didn't know what we were doing this past half-century. It's just that we had so many good reasons for doing it. And these reasons, today, reveal themselves to be not only different from one another, but incompatible.

SOURCE: Irving Kristol. "Defining the National Interest," *The National Interest*, no. 21, Fall 1990, pp. 16–25, excerpts. Reprinted with permission. © *The National Interest*, no. 21, Washington, D.C.

If one looks back at the basic principles—ideologies they may fairly be called—that have shaped American foreign policy since 1917, one can distinguish four which overlap and interweave, while always rubbing reach other the wrong way. They are, in chronological order:

1. Wilsonian liberal internationalism—a grand design for a new world order based on self-determination, nonaggression, conciliation and arbitration and "collective security" ensured by a League of Nations.
2. A chastened and revised version of liberal internationalism, wherein the same ideal informed our rhetoric while the actualities of the Cold War shaped a modestly realistic policy of "containment." With the end of the Cold War, the rhetoric has moved to a unilateral emphasis on "enhancing democracy" abroad.
3. Isolationism, of the Right and of the Left.
4. A conception of the American "national interest," vague and inarticulate, but which nevertheless leads a kind of underground existence in our thinking.

Wilsonian liberal internationalism was based on the thesis that it would be possible to create a "world community" in which nations would subordinate national interests to the sovereignty of international law, as incarnated in such institutions as the League of Nations, the World Court, and a constellation of other, more specialized institutions (such as the International Labor Organization) that would cope with specific, narrowly defined problems. The league would not only pass judgment but would have the authority to enforce its rulings through the exercise of collective action, such as sanctions, or even, if necessary, military intervention. In this vision, first elaborated two hundred years ago by Immanuel Kant, we would at last be moving toward world stability, world peace, and a "community of nations" whose shared values would make for a world order in which all nations would recognize the principles of self-determination of peoples and government by popular consent.

The popularity of this point of view is best understood as a revulsion against the nationalist excesses that produced the First World War, an especially ghastly war. But this popularity was both fragile and thin. Fragile because the spirit of nationalism, once reawakened, simply swept aside, as so many glittering cobwebs, the Wilsonian dream. Thin, because it took solid root only in the American State Department (and, to a much lesser extent, in some other foreign offices) while never being taken seriously by the overwhelming majority of the American people (or, it should be said, of any other people).

By the 1930's, this conception of American foreign policy had established itself so firmly in our State Department and in the minds of our policy-making elites—the Council on Foreign Relations being a noteworthy example—that even though the league was by now discredited for reasons of ineptitude, and the American people were moving massively into an isolationist mood, the Roosevelt administration could think of no other principles with which to fashion its foreign policy. After World War II, the United Nations replaced the League of Nations, but otherwise nothing much changed.

The post-World War II goals of American foreign policy, as officially stated, were Wilsonian. They seemed to represent the only mode of thought within which the American government has found it possible to explain its policies, and to a large degree the Cold War itself was interpreted and described in Wilsonian terms. We were the leader of "the free world," as well as of an anticommunist coalition of nations whose goal was the "containment" of communist messianism. The tensions this often involved us in turned out to be fatal. Thus, we fought a war "against aggression" in Korea, a war conducted under the aegis of the United Nations. It was also a limited, defensive war of "containment" that simply sought, at great cost, a reversion to the *status quo ante*. The American people soon made it clear that they did not like this kind of war—a fact soon forgotten (or haughtily dismissed) by our policy-makers. So we ended up fighting exactly the same kind of war in Vietnam, only this time without success. By the end of that war the American people had, in effect, disengaged themselves from any Wilsonian national purpose, while "containment" itself was tainted with the hue of defeat. Fortunately, it turned out that "containment" had done its work even while many Americans were getting weary of it.

In the years between those two wars, however, the American people and their foreign-policy-makers were—or seemed to be—largely in agreement. In a sense, American foreign policy in this period had two distinct strands—the rhetorical and the pragmatic. When President Truman announced his doctrine in 1947, he did so in familiar Wilsonian terms. The policy it inaugurated, however, was the "containment" of communist expansion through the use of American economic and military power. The American people supported this foreign policy because they despised communism as an ideology and were outraged by communist expansionism. The rhetoric they regarded as, well, just the kind of official rhetoric normally exuded by our State Department. In short, they felt involved in the Cold War *as Americans*, not as a leader of "the free world"—an abstraction that never meant much to them. Wilsonian ideals, indeed, meant nothing to them. The profound distrust that the American people felt toward the League of Nations has been transferred to the United Nations—an organization not simply futile but one that, more often than not, has exhibited a clear anti-American bias. Both Daniel Patrick Moynihan and Jeane Kirkpatrick became national heroes by giving eloquent expression to this distrust.

American policy-makers shrewdly adapted to this reality. Their liberal internationalism gradually became less international, more unilateral, even more nationalist. One heard less—and hears less today—about a community of nations living tranquilly under international law, and more about our commitment to the "enhancement of democracy around the world." As the Cold War has come to an end, this remains the dominant, official motif of American foreign policy. It has appeal not only to liberals but to many conservatives who are ideologically adrift in the post-Cold War era. From anti-communism to pro-"democratic capitalism" is a tempting move for those who wish to remain engaged in world politics.

This is, of course, a uniquely American idea, one that even our democratic allies in NATO, or out of NATO (e.g., Japan), do not share. Their conception of the Wilsonian ideal has, in any case, always been

more cynical—perhaps one should say "realistic"—than ours, in that they have never permitted their internationalism to override their specific national interests. They do believe in using international forums and international organizations to defend those interests—which is why the State Department finds them to be such faithless allies at the United Nations. None of the European democracies thinks it an important part of its foreign policy to "enhance democracy" all over the world. None of these democracies thinks of itself as "a city on a hill," as we do, having a special moral-political mission in the world, as we habitually think we do. Indeed, the very strength of this post-Cold War current of thought is its ability to tap the springs of American nationalism and American moralism, fused in a sense of *the* "American mission" or *the* "American purpose."

The inspirational rhetoric in which this foreign policy is clothed is itself so peculiarly and parochially American—no other nation talks about foreign policy this way—that one is bound to be skeptical of its viability. It may move Americans, but certainly not foreigners. Besides, it is Wilsonian enough to run into all the older Wilsonian dilemmas—dilemmas resulting from the disjunction between ideal and reality, general principles and particular issues.

For instance, there is the issue of "self-determination," a Wilsonian principle that our State Department will never, never disavow—but will ignore if convenient. We are silent about self-determination in Kashmir, but outspoken about the right to self-determination of the Palestinians on the West Bank. One picks and chooses, while "holding firm" to the principle. . . .

In any case, how do we go about "enhancing democracy" where we do have freedom of action? One now hears—revived from the intellectual dead, as it were—much talk of the importance of "economic aid." One would have thought that the myth of economic aid, as an effective adjunct to foreign policy, was by now utterly discredited. In fact, it is. We know that, except in very special, and usually temporary, circumstances, economic aid does nothing to "enhance democracy" abroad. It feeds corruption, economic inefficiency, and political irresponsibility. The evidence leading to this conclusion is so overwhelming that it cannot even be called controversial.

So why are people, who not only ought to know better but do, suddenly so enamored of the idea? The reason is obvious: they cannot think of anything else to do. They dare not contemplate, much less raise, the prospect of American military intervention and occupation to "make democracy work" in friendly countries where it is in danger of collapse—in short, to create something like an American empire with a purely ideological motive. This was never a serious possibility, and now that the Soviets have realized how futile it is, it is not and cannot be a serious option for American foreign policy.

True, one cannot object to the cluster of very small-scale programs that are being recommended to "enhance democracy" here or there or anywhere—supplying countries, for example, with "expertise" in everything from sewer construction to prenatal care. No harm in that, but no visible gain, either, so far as foreign policy is concerned.

One swift question ought to be enough to reveal the ultimate hollowness of this mode of thought: What shall we do about the Philippines? Here, after all, is a country with which we have had a long and intimate association. We understand this country better than we understand most others, and they understand us reasonably well. It also happens to be a country whose democracy we have helped establish and sustain. Nevertheless, that democracy is floundering and seems headed for disintegration. So what should we do about it? To ask the question is to provoke an echo, not an answer.

When a nation has played a leading role in world affairs for more than half a century, doing nothing comes hard.

The futility of a foreign policy whose purpose is to "enhance democracy" abroad is apparent to most Americans, and so the end of the Cold War has led to a resurgence of an isolationist temper. Among a handful of conservative thinkers this has led to a recrudescence of pre-World War II isolationism, a vein of thought streaked with nativism, chauvinism, and an unassuaged hostility to Franklin D. Roosevelt and the New Deal as well as to America's involvement in World War II, an in-

volvement they attribute to a liberal conspiracy. There is also a handful of liberals (overrepresented in Congress) whose isolationism (though they would vigorously deny the title) derives from the desire to spend the maximum amount of money on social programs at home and the minimum abroad. In general, sections of the political Left, in all countries, display this predisposition. The Left has always tended to regard foreign affairs as a wicked distraction from its noble efforts to create a "better world," beginning at home.

Though these two currents of isolationism will often coincide over specific issues of policy—such as the stationing of several hundred thousand American troops in Europe—the tenor of their thinking is radically different. Right-wing isolationism is nationalist, left-wing isolationism is antinationalist. (They violently disagree on the permissibility of flag-burning and the importance of a large military establishment.) And because of this difference, right-wing isolationists are sometimes prepared to use military force against a foreign government that engages in actions hostile to the United States, while the Left would prefer to ignore it, or make some purely symbolic gesture. (The differential responses to our [1986] bombing of Libya come to mind.) There was a time when the Right was firmly attached to the Monroe Doctrine, so that its isolationism was actually hemispheric rather than national. This is less true today, but the benign reaction of the Right to the [1989] invasion of Panama, while the Left was disconcerted, suggests that something of this traditional attitude still survives. It is also obvious in the disparity of sentiments toward Castro's Cuba.

Both right-wing and left-wing isolationism aim to exploit an instinctual isolationism, almost non-political in character, that has always pervaded American opinion. George Washington's admonition against "foreign entanglements" remains engraved in American hearts, so that every such "foreign entanglement"—World War I, World War II, Vietnam—however enthusiastically endorsed originally out of a sense of patriotism and pride, is followed by an isolationist revulsion. It was the Cold War, in which our "foreign entanglements" were understood as necessary to prevent a communist takeover of the world, that permitted our policy-makers, operating in the liberal-internationalist mode, to multiply such "entanglements," and to convince themselves that this mode of foreign policy would continue for the indefinite, perhaps permanent, future. But the end of the Cold War has changed all that. Our State Department may still believe that a strong, visible "American presence" in Europe is essential to "stability" on that continent. But it is increasingly difficult to make sense of such vague rhetoric. Our troops in Europe have been there to resist a Soviet invasion. If there is to be no invasion, why are they there? Not, one assumes, to intervene in case of "instability" in Eastern Europe, or Yugoslavia, or even the Soviet Union itself. If such intervention is necessary, surely our Western European allies can cope with it on their own. And if quarrels erupt among those allies, whose side are we to intervene on? It is the inability of our official foreign policy to cope with such direct, "naive" questions that is giving impetus to an isolationist revival, on the Right as on the Left, in the United States.

Isolationism today has a bad name, largely deserved, because some of its more prominent spokesmen, especially on the Right, evoke echoes of the 1930's—echoes of nativism and xenophobia, indifference (or worse) to nazism and fascism, broad hints of anti-Semitism. One forgets that in the 1930's there were perfectly decent spokesmen for isolationism, especially on the Left, notably Norman Thomas and the remnants of the old Progressive movement. Their case had been put eloquently by Macaulay back in 1845:

> I do not say that we ought to prefer the happiness of one particular society to the happiness of mankind; but I say that, by exerting ourselves to promote the happiness of the society with which we are most nearly connected, and with which we are best acquainted, we shall do more to promote the happiness of mankind than by busying ourselves about matters which we do not fully understand, and cannot efficiently control.

This "little England" approach to British foreign policy, though not at all unpopular, was nevertheless swept away by events, as Britain engaged in competitive empire-building in order to retain its status as a world power—indeed, at the time as *the* world power. One can predict with much confidence that a version of American isolationism will suffer the same fate. In a way, we have no real choice, any more than Britain did. A great power is responsible for what it does not do, yet is in its power to do, as for what it does. Power breeds responsibilities. Britain had no *British* reason to use its supreme naval power to suppress the international slave trade, in which the British had not been involved for many decades. Under existing international law, it didn't even have the authority to do so. Nevertheless, it used its navy for exactly that purpose, for no better reason than that such an action defined the *kind of* great power Britain would be. It was a matter of national identity, not of foreign policy in any strict sense of the term. One cannot easily divorce the foreign policy of a superpower from its very national identity.

So the United States does not really have the option of withdrawing into a "Fortress America." Not only does the degree of our integration in the world economy today make this economically impossible—our prosperity cannot be separated from the relatively unrestricted movement of goods and investments—but the American people are not about to relinquish their position as a world power. That would go against the American grain, against the sense that Americans have of their historic destiny. It would be like demanding of Americans that they be indifferent to the performance of American athletes in the Olympics—or that we hold a kind of minor-league Olympics of our own. That is psychologically unthinkable. You don't hear American sports fans chanting "We're number two!" or "We're number three!"

But if both the old and the new liberal internationalism are bankrupt, and if isolationism is a nostalgic fantasy, where does that leave American foreign policy? It is at this point that the idea of constructing a foreign policy in terms of our "national interest" gains credibility.

The notion of an American "national interest" is not a new one, and has a perfectly respectable history—until it was swamped and discredited by the liberal-international mode of thought propagated by Woodrow Wilson. Throughout the nineteenth century, the term was freely and casually used here, as it was in Europe. After all, George Washington and Alexander Hamilton and James Monroe had established its propriety, and no American thought it strange to be informed by elected officials, or by journalists and publicists, that some particular action was or was not in our national interest. After the Wilsonian revolution in American foreign policy, however, it was felt that we no longer had a national interest in having a national interest. The term and the idea were associated with either a reactionary parochial isolationism or a ruthlessly amoral *realpolitik*. Even to talk about "realism" in foreign policy was regarded as suspect—as it still is today in many circles.

It was, of course, Vietnam that dealt a mortal blow to liberal-internationalism. As has been noted, the unpopularity of the Korean War should have transmitted a warning signal that the prescribed role of the United States, as defined by our commitment to the United Nations Charter, was not something the American people felt at all comfortable with. But the intensity of the Cold War in the ensuing years, and the natural hostility of these same people to communism and communist expansionism, served to obscure this unease. After Vietnam, no president could echo John F. Kennedy's rhetoric about "our willingness to endure any sacrifice" in order to "deter aggression." Liberal internationalism remained the orthodoxy in our State Department, but the American people were leaving that church in droves.

Ironically, it was the Left, in its opposition to the Vietnam War, that breathed new life into the idea of "national interest." Much of the Left, of course, was oriented only to an anti-anticommunist foreign policy that merged into a traditional kind of left-wing isolationism. But there were scholars and writers on the Left who, seizing upon the writings of Hans J. Morgenthau and George F. Kennan, did revive the concept of the "national interest"—though, lacking the vestiges of a nationalist instinct, they didn't know quite what to do with it. It is only today, in the post-Cold War era, that some conservatives, finding anticommunism no longer a useful compass with which to orient themselves in world politics, and with the kind of nationalist

bent that has always been natural to conservatives, are trying to envisage an American foreign policy that is defined in "national interest" terms.

It is no easy task. Traditionally, national interest is defined in terms of plain military security or maintaining a "balance of power" among nations that are potential enemies or actual competitors for world status. But the United States has no reason to be concerned about its military security, so long as it retains a nuclear capability that nullifies the threat—for the moment, and one suspects for the foreseeable future as well, a minimal threat—of a hostile nuclear attack. And as the sole remaining superpower, there is no "balance" for us to worry about. True, there are theorists who would happily burden us with the mission of monitoring and maintaining a "balance of power" among *other* nations, large and small, in Europe, the Middle East, Asia, etc. This would make the United States the "world's policeman" for the status quo, or at least the world's arbiter for all changes in the status quo. Imagine the United States accepting responsibility for the fate of Kashmir and for "enforcing the peace" between India and Pakistan! We are just not going to be that kind of imperial power. Perhaps a future historian will decide we should have been. But it is not to be, because ours is a democracy and the American people violently reject any such scenario.

Where, then, do we look to find a national interest? Well, history has seen to it that we do not begin with a *tabula rasa*, and the contours of such a definition are given to us by the realities we confront. Let me suggest the following principles that can serve as guidelines:

1. It is in our national interest that no other superpower emerge whose political and social values are profoundly hostile to our own. To put it another way: We did not win the Cold War against Marxist-Leninist messianism in order to tolerate, yet again, any comparable confrontation. As things now stand, there is no visible threat of any such superpower emerging. But history has not come to an end and is still pregnant with surprise.

2. It follows that it is in our national interest that those nations which largely share our political principles and social values should be protected from those that do not. As Edmund Burke wrote more than two centuries ago:

> Nothing is so strong a tie of amity between nation and nation as correspondence in law, customs, manners and *habits* of life. They have more than the force of treaties in themselves. They are obligations written in the heart.

The United States enters the post-Cold War world with standing attachments and commitments. NATO may be an anachronism—I think it is—but we are not about to isolate ourselves from our fellow democracies in Western Europe, the Pacific, or the Middle East. Just how strong that attachment is, and how strong that commitment will be, will depend on circumstances—which, as Burke also pointed out, is the governing force in all policy-making.

3. Our relations with the other nations of the world will be decided candidly on a case-by-case basis. Now that the "Second World" has, to all intents and purposes, ceased to exist, and along with it the category of "non-aligned nations," there is no other basis on which to operate. To the degree that any of these nations has a foreign policy friendly toward us, we will surely be disposed to be friendly to it. To the degree that it displays hostility, we will reciprocate. Similarly, to the degree that any country adapts its socioeconomic-political arrangements to correspond to those prevailing in "the West," we will find it easier to be more intimate in our friendship. To the degree that it does not, our relations will be, at best, cool and correct.

There is no general formula that enables us to arrive at easy conclusions in any particular case. If there were such a formula, we could run our foreign policy by computer, feeding it such ambiguous concepts as "self-determination" or "aggression" and triumphantly announcing the results.

4. But what about the moral dimension of American foreign policy? It has always been there and, since we are an untraditional nation founded on a liberal creed, it always will be there. Have we nothing "higher" to offer the world?

Perhaps we do—though, with every passing year, I become less convinced. When some foreign political scientist or politician asks what books to read so as to discover the secret of our success, I find that I can think only of books by long-dead authors, many of them unread by Americans today. And when they consult American constitutional lawyers on how to go about writing a new constitution, I tremble for their future. It is these same lawyers, for the most part, who are busy rewriting our own constitution so as to rob it of its original merits . . .

Despite all such reservations, however, we are a successful nation—no question about it—and the envy of much of the world. It is perfectly understandable, therefore, that Americans believe we are still "a standing monument and example" to the world (to quote that brilliant rhetorician and much inflated statesman, Thomas Jefferson). But what, precisely, does a "standing monument" do? Our isolationist tradition would have it just stand there, a role model (as we would now say) for the world to emulate. But the American people are of an activist temperament, which is why, as we became a "standing monument" that is also a world power, it has been so easy for a concern for universal "human rights" to grab hold of our imagination.

This concern was first elaborated, in its present form, in opposition to communist totalitarianism, which deprived human beings of all rights—deprived them, in fact, of their humanity. The apocalyptic vision of Orwell's *1984* provided us with the key text. But, in the course of the 1950s and 1960s, the issue was seized by the Left and used as a club with which to batter the moral legitimacy of anticommunism in general and of American foreign policy specifically. The strategy employed was to revise the conception of "human rights" so as to include, as human rights, the civil rights and civil liberties that are to be found in a modern liberal democracy. Since many of our allies in the Cold War were not particularly respectful of such rights and such liberties, we became vulnerable to the accusation of using a "double standard," one for communist regimes and another for non-communist or (especially) anticommunist regimes. Today, this revision of the original idea of "human rights" is so orthodox that liberals and conservatives alike find themselves imprisoned in it.

But this blithely ignores the fact that there are large areas of the world which do not share our conception of civil rights and civil liberties, and are unlikely to move toward any such commonality in the foreseeable future. Saudi Arabia, for instance, does not permit Christians or Jews to become citizens or even permanent residents. Are we to allow this fact to disrupt our relations with that very important and relatively friendly country? Are we to contemplate the religious reformation of Saudi Arabia? No, we are not.

The truth is that, not only does our foreign policy have a double standard with regard to what is now called "human rights," but we have a triple and quadruple standard as well. Indeed we have as many standards as circumstances require—which is as it should be. We react more cautiously to China's antiliberalization than we would to Russia's because our ally, Japan, whose interest in China is considerably greater than our own, has strongly urged such caution upon us. There is nothing "immoral" about such deference. We are free to engage in the quiet diplomacy of persuasion, the open diplomacy of intimidation, a foreign policy that may or may not involve military intervention—always depending on circumstance. If a Pol Pot regime were to be reestablished in Cambodia and reinstitute its genocidal policies, we would surely break off diplomatic and commercial relations. But we would limit our response to that level. Should such a Pol Pot emerge in Cuba, on the other hand, we would almost surely intervene militarily. The reason for this disparity is that our interest in Cuba is radically different from our interest in Cambodia.

All in all, it is perfectly possible to envisage a post-Cold War foreign policy for the United States which, constantly defining (even redefining) our "national interest" as the world changes (and as we change, too), would be sensible and realistic. It would disburden itself of the incubus of liberal internationalism, with its utopian expectations and legalistic cast of mind. It would not be, could not be isolationist—unless, that is, one identifies the abandonment of liberal internationalism as *ipso facto* "isolationist." It would be realistic without being a species of brutal *realpolitik*—itself a special theory of international relations, originating in a special period of European history, that has no relevance to the American position in the world today or to the predispositions of our democracy. Obviously, such a foreign policy will have plenty of room for failures as well as successes. But both failure and success would flow from errors of judgment, not from illusions about the world and the people (including Americans) who inhabit it.

Will we move toward such a foreign policy? It is hard to see what other direction there is for us to move in. But it would be much better for us and for the world if this movement were clear-sighted, rather than if (as is all too likely) we marched backward into our future, constantly troubled by nostalgic intellectual loyalties and inappropriate paroxysms of self-doubt.

7.   What Is the National Interest?

Alan Tonelson

Since the end of the Second World War, Americans have by and large defined their foreign-policy objectives in what may be called globalist or internationalist terms. Internationalism has been protean enough—liberal and conservative, hawkish and dovish, unilateralist and multilateralist—to have commanded the loyalty of figures as different as Ronald Reagan and Jimmy Carter. But its essence springs from three crucial lessons learned by most Americans and their leaders from the Great Depression and the rise of fascism during the 1930s, from the global conflagration that those events helped produce, and from the emergence of a new totalitarian threat almost immediately after that war.

The first lesson was that the United States would never know genuine security, lasting peace, and sustained prosperity unless the rest of the world also became secure, peaceful, and prosperous. The second lesson was that international security was indivisible—that the discontent that produced political extremism and, inevitably, aggression was highly contagious and bound to spread around the world no matter where it broke out. The third lesson was that the only way to achieve these fundamental goals and prevent these deadly dangers was to eliminate the conditions that breed extremism wherever they exist, and somehow to impose norms of peaceful behavior on all states.

The result of all this was a global definition of vital U.S. foreign-policy interests, with globalist

SOURCE: Alan Tonelson. "What Is the National Interest?", *The Atlantic Monthly*, vol. 268, no. 1, July 1991, pp. 35–44; 49–52, excerpts. Reprinted with permission. Alan Tonelson is Research Director of the Economic Strategy Institute, a Washington, D.C., based think tank studying the relationship between trade policy, technology policy, and national security. His essays and reviews on American politics and foreign policy have appeared in many leading national publications, and he is co-editor of *Powernomics: Economics and Security after the Cold War* (Madison Books, 1991).

international-security and economic structures to back it up. . . .

Yet even before the Gorbachev Revolution in Soviet foreign policy—during the Cold War years, when the case could be made for a total response to the ostensibly total Soviet threat—the problems created by the internationalist approach to foreign policy were beginning to loom as large as those that it was meant to solve. Militarily and strategically, internationalism identified America's foreign-policy challenges in such a way as to turn any instance of aggression into an intolerable threat to America's own security, whether or not tangible U.S. interests were at stake, and no matter how greatly the costs of intervention may have outweighed any specific benefits that the United States could plausibly have realized. Vietnam is the classic example. Internationalism also drew America into nuclear alliances—notably, in Europe—deliberately structured to entrap the country in nuclear conflict even in cases when our own national security had not been directly affected.

Economically, as early as the late 1960s internationalism showed signs of turning into a formula for exhaustion. Richard Nixon brought the post-Second World War international monetary system to an end, in 1971, precisely because America could no longer meet its foreign-policy obligations and its domestic obligations simultaneously. Politically, the internationalist strategies and rhetoric employed by U.S. leaders throughout the post-war era generated tremendous pressures on these same leaders to follow through. Remembering the political fire storms that followed the "losses" of China and Cuba, they repeatedly resolved to prove the nation's mettle when the next outbreak of trouble occurred, reducing to almost nil the possibility that non-involvement would even be considered as an option, much less chosen.

Now, in the post-Cold War era, internationalism has become even more problematic. As our chronic budget gap shows, our foreign policy is politically unaffordable in today's America—as opposed to the America of the 1950s, when popular satisfaction with the barest skeleton of a welfare state and the country's economic predominance permitted levels of military spending two and three times as high as those of today (as a proportion of total federal spending). Internationalism continues to deny us a strategic basis for selectivity, a way of thinking about our international goals that would enable our leaders to resist the temptation to plunge into every crisis and right every wrong that life brings along, and to stand aside without being perceived by the American people as impotent or callous.

In fact, internationalism dismisses as morally reprehensible questions that other nations ask routinely in order to inject some discipline into their decision-making: What is it that we need to do in the world to secure a certain level of material and psychological well-being? What is it that we simply would like to do in the world? What are we able to do? How can we pursue our objectives without wrecking our economy, overloading our political system, or convulsing our society?

At best, post-Cold War internationalism is a recipe for intense, genuinely worrisome domestic political frustrations. Repeated failure to achieve declared foreign-policy goals and especially to avert foreign-policy outcomes officially characterized as intolerable or disastrous could poison and destabilize American politics and democracy. A string of such failures could bring calamitous international consequences by undermining America's ability to conduct a minimally responsible, rational foreign policy. At worst, internationalism raises the threat of drawing the nation into dangerous conflicts for the slightest of stakes. And even if such political and military disasters are somehow avoided, internationalism will continue to drain the nation to its core, especially if U.S. allies do not lend enough help.

Internationalism has not only locked the foreign policy of this nation of self-avowed pragmatists into a utopian mold; it has led directly to the primacy of foreign policy in American life and to the consequent neglect of domestic problems which

has characterized the past fifty years. Internationalism encourages us to think more about the possible world of tomorrow than about the real world of today. Thus the strange irrelevance of our recent foreign policy, and even its victories, to the concerns of most Americans.

A NEW FOREIGN-POLICY BLUEPRINT

If internationalism is no longer an acceptable guide for U.S. foreign policy, what should take its place? What *can* take its place? Assuming that the means available to U.S. foreign-policy makers will not change significantly anytime soon—that American scientists will not devise a new ultimate weapon and preserve monopoly control of it; that U.S. allies will remain reluctant to increase their military and foreign-aid spending dramatically or to compensate the United States for its leadership role in other ways; that the American public will remain unwilling to make the sacrifices needed to carry out an internationalist foreign policy effectively (through some combination of higher taxes, reduced consumption, and reduced demand for public services); and that the unprecedented increases in national economic productivity needed to finance such a foreign policy soundly will remain nowhere in sight—the United States will have to make some profound adjustments.

If the United States cannot hope to achieve the desired level of security and prosperity by underwriting the security and prosperity of countries all over the world, and by enforcing whatever global norms of economic and political behavior this ambition requires, then it must anchor its security and prosperity in a less-than-utopian set of objectives. It must therefore distinguish between what it must do that is absolutely essential for achieving this more modest set of objectives and those things it might do that are not essential. It must, in other words, begin to think in terms not of the whole world's well-being but rather of purely national interests.

The adjustments that are required would produce a foreign policy largely unrecognizable to Americans today. The U.S. government would still be a major force in world affairs, and the American people would still trade with, invest in, work in, and travel to other lands. But the preferred instruments of the new foreign policy would differ radically from those of internationalism. And the policy itself would spring from a completely different vision of America, of its strengths and weaknesses and, most important, its basic purposes. The new orientation, moreover, would reflect the manifest (if seldom articulated) wishes of the great majority of Americans, rather than those of the small, privileged caste of government officials, former government officials, professors, think-tank denizens, and journalists whose dreamy agenda has long dominated foreign-policy decision-making in America. For surely American foreign policy has been conducted with utter disregard for the home front largely because it has been made by people whose lives and needs have almost nothing in common with those of the mass of their countrymen.

Unlike internationalism, interest-based thinking rests on a series of assumptions drawn both from common sense and from classical strategic maxims; and it can help prevent counterproductive outcomes by forcing decision-makers continually to examine the impact of their policies on national security and well-being within a finite time frame. In the first place, a foreign policy derived from interest-based thinking would accept today's anarchic system of competing nation-states as a given. It would neither seek to change the nature of this system nor assume the system's imminent transformation. Instead, the new policy would confine itself to securing certain specific objectives that are intrinsically important to America's security and welfare—for example, the protection of regions that are important sources of raw materials or critical manufactured goods, those that are major loci of investment or prime markets, and those that by virtue of their location are strategically vital.

Interest-based thinking holds that in such a world U.S. national interests can and must be distinguished from the interests of the international system itself and from those of other individual states. This is just common sense. Because states differ in location, size, strength, natural wealth, historical experience, values, economic systems, degree and type of social organization, and many other particulars, their foreign-policy needs and wants—their interests—cannot always be identical or harmonious, and will in fact sometimes clash with those of certain other countries and those of whatever larger international community those states are supposed to belong to. Internationalism's assumption of an ultimate harmony of interests among states and between states and the larger system often obscures these critical truths.

In addition, interest-based thinking assumes that since the world lacks a commonly accepted referee or means of resolving clashes of interests, states cannot count on other states or entities to define their interests or to protect them. States therefore need the means to accomplish these tasks on their own. Interest-based thinking assumes that because countries can in the end rely only on their own devices, national self-reliance and freedom of action are intrinsic goods. With an internationalist foreign policy, these imperatives tend to get lost in the shuffle.

Further, interest-based thinking maintains that because resources are always relatively scarce (if they were not, the discipline of economics would not exist), once foreign policy moves beyond the quest for what strategists call core security—the nation's physical, biological survival, and the preservation of its territorial integrity and political independence—the specific, concrete benefits sought must be brought into some sustainable alignment with the policy's economic, social, and political costs. And the payoff of policies cannot be put off into the long-term future. A country with finite available resources simply does not have the luxury of infinite patience.

Thus an interest-based foreign policy would tend to rule out economic initiatives deemed necessary for the international system's health if those initiatives wound up siphoning more wealth out of this country (in the form of net investment, interest on debt, military expenditures, foreign aid, trade credits, jobs destroyed by imports versus those created by exports, and so forth) than they brought in. Similarly, it would oppose economic policies that actually destroyed wealth—for example, by stimulating inflation, by committing excessive resources to economically unproductive military spending and research and development, by necessitating excessive currency devaluations, by requiring exorbitant interest rates that discourage productive investment, or by blithely accepting the loss of industries that have been technology and productivity leaders for the sake of free-trade ideology or alliance unity.

Unlike internationalism, an interest-based foreign policy would not emphasize alliances and multilateral institutions, or promote worldwide economic efficiency to the point at which U.S. dependence on other countries is seen as a good in and of itself. Rather, the new policy would recognize the importance of maintaining the maximum degree of freedom of action and self-reliance in a still dangerous world. Indeed, an interest-based policy would also recognize that the related realms of economics and technology are as nakedly strategic as the military-political realm. While the Cold War was raging, internationalists viewed economic initiatives and technology as little more than assets to deny the Communist world or as a collection of baubles, to be doled out periodically as political favors to allies and neutrals. The end of the Cold War has produced many acknowledgments by internationalists of the rising importance of economic power. But even this outlook still tends to be nonstrategic. Internationalists still assume that, economically speaking, winning and losing have no meaning whatever—unless one cares about national pride—so long as the competition takes place among nonhostile states. And they continue to believe that economic competition can always be kept reasonable and constructive, as if it were an athletic contest. . . .

Perhaps most important, an interest-based U.S. foreign policy would firmly subordinate international activism and the drive for world leadership to domestic concerns. Indeed, it would spring from new and more realistic ideas about what can be expected of a country's official foreign policy in the first place. The new approach would acknowledge that the modest policy tools actually at a government's command—weapons, money, and suasion-

—cannot build a fundamentally new and more benign or congenial world political order, or change the millennia-old patterns of poverty, tradition, and misrule in which so much of humanity is trapped. Such changes can occur only on the organic level of international relations, as the result of informal social, cultural, and economic interactions over long stretches of time. And even if modern science and technology have greatly accelerated the pace of change, there is little reason to think that change can be controlled or manipulated at the operational level of international relations—by a state's day-to-day foreign policy.

The interest-based approach would also eschew any notion of foreign policy as first and foremost a vehicle for spreading American values, for building national character, for expressing any individual's or group's emotional, philosophical, or political preferences, or for carrying out any of a series of additional overseas missions that, however appealing, bear only marginally on protecting and enriching the nation: promoting peace, stability, democracy, and development around the world; protecting human rights; establishing international law; building collective security; exercising something called leadership; creating a new world order; competing globally with the Soviets (or whomever) for power and influence. None of these sweeping, inspiring, quintessentially internationalist goals can serve as guides for U.S. foreign policy. They are simply free-floating ideals. From time to time they may represent ways of advancing particular and advanceable American interests. But first we have to know what interests we want to advance. An interest-based approach would also reject the idea that meeting a set of global responsibilities can be the lodestar of U.S. foreign policy. Whose definition of this unavoidably subjective notion would be chosen? And on what basis?

Nevertheless, the interest-based approach would recognize that in a democracy such views—that is, simple national preferences—frequently influence foreign policy. That is to say, Americans from time to time favor a course of action (invading Grenada, for example, or aiding the Kurds) not because it serves vital national interests but simply because they like it. An interest-based foreign policy would acknowledge that the citizens of a democracy have every right to choose whatever foreign policy they please; certainly they are answerable to no one but themselves. And it would hold that there is nothing intrinsically wrong with sometimes basing a foreign policy on the whim or preference of the majority. The new approach would insist, however, that the American public be willing to finance its whims soundly—something the United States government has not done for decades. If the public favors aid to insurgents around the world, or fighting poverty in developing countries, or helping new democracies in Eastern Europe or Latin America, or defending certain parts of the world because of a shared cultural heritage, then it should be willing to raise the revenues needed to pay for these policies. If the revenues are not forthcoming, the whims are probably not very strong to begin with and are probably best ignored.

The new foreign policy certainly would not preclude acting on principle. But it would greatly deemphasize conforming to abstract standards of behavior. In fact, the new foreign policy would shy away from any overarching strategy of or conceptual approach to international relations. Unlike isolationism, for instance, it would not elevate nonintervention to the status of a commandment. And it would view other popular doctrines of American foreign policy—containment, détente, multilateralism, unilateralism, idealism, realism, the achievement of a global balance of power—with skepticism. It would be free to use whatever approach or combination of approaches seemed likeliest to achieve the best ends for the United States in a given situation. Its only rule of thumb would be "whatever works" to preserve or enhance America's security and prosperity and—provided that Americans are willing to pay the bills—what the country collectively wishes to define as its psychological well-being.

Internationalists worrying about this policy's potential lack of moral content might think harder about channeling more of their compassion into good works at home—where there is no shortage of

grievous wrongs to be righted and where, as is not the case in many other countries, the social and institutional wherewithal for successful reform actually exists.

As for the issue of defining the ends of U.S. foreign policy beyond core security, there are no magic formulas to rely on. Once national survival and independence are assured, all the major objectives of U.S. foreign policy must be subjected to a rigorous cost-risk analysis. If objectives are truly vital—if physical survival or the continuance of America's democratic values and institutions are at stake—costs and risks can never exceed benefits. But if objectives are less than vital, costs and risks can exceed benefits. For a country with America's built-in geopolitical and economic advantages— with its capacity for achieving security, prosperity, and independence—the top priority is not to settle on a fixed definition of vital interests. It is much more important to learn to think rigorously and strategically about foreign policy, in order to ensure that whatever set of interests is chosen is not so ambitious that it exposes the country to more risks than it repulses, drains it of more strength than it adds, and makes Americans feel bad about themselves and their nation more than it makes them feel good.

The new policy's aversion to grand doctrines and frameworks would be in keeping with the conviction that the fundamental purpose of U.S. foreign policy should be nothing more glamorous than attempting to cope with whatever discrete developments arise abroad that could endanger American security and prosperity. The stress would not be on comprehensive initiatives to get at the root causes of the world's ills and conflicts, on promoting greater international cooperation or integration, or on getting on the right side of history—for these favorite internationalist aims entail enormous costs and offer scant promise of success. In a perilous strategic world, it is usually a mistake to consider foreign policy to be an activist instrument at all. Rather, Americans should start thinking of foreign policy in terms of avoiding problems, reducing vulnerabilities and costs, maximizing options, buying time, and muddling through—objectives that may be uninspiring but that are well suited to a strong, wealthy, geographically isolated country. . . .

THE THIRD WORLD: TIME TO DISENGAGE

Internationalism's genius for focusing U.S. attention on sideshows has nowhere been more evident than in America's relations with the generally weak, poor, politically fragile nations of the Third World. During the Cold War, internationalism's characteristically exaggerated fears—of Soviet power and prestige, and of losing valuable military bases, raw-material deposits, and export markets to hostile forces—turned the Third World into the only theater in which U.S. and Soviet ambitions clashed violently, and the theater in which these conflicts most often threatened to ignite wider war, from Korea to Indochina, from Cuba to the Middle East, from Afghanistan to Central America. Meanwhile, internationalism's equally excessive hopes led U.S. policy-makers to try to combat the Soviet threat not only by helping protect these countries militarily and organizing them into facsimiles of alliances but also by spending hundreds of billions of dollars trying to turn them into modern, subversion-resistant societies.

The Cold War is over, but similar fears continue to drive U.S. policy in the Third World. The specter of local tyrants armed with weapons of mass destruction and long-range delivery systems has replaced the specter of the Soviets, while access to the same markets and raw materials and even most of the same bases is considered as vital as ever. Archetypal internationalist policies—regional security arrangements, multilateral arms and technology export curbs, and aid programs to promote economic development and democracy—are still being proposed to deal with potential Third World problems.

With or without the Soviet threat, internationalists have portrayed America's extensive involvement in Third World countries as a security and economic imperative, resulting from tight, indissoluble links between the Third World's fate and our own. To the extent that these links exist, however, they are largely artificial—the products of

internationalist policy. Since well before the Cold War ended, the importance of the Third World to the United States has been shrinking steadily. America's internationalist foreign policy perversely has sought to reverse this process, and to bind America's future ever more closely to these generally woebegone lands and their desperate problems. Worse, where troubles in the Third World do cause America difficulties, internationalism has prevented the United States from pursuing superior non-internationalist solutions.

With respect to security, the value to America of most Third World military bases on the Soviet periphery has been eliminated by the deployment of intercontinental nuclear weapons, which enable U.S. nuclear warheads to strike any spot on earth. And although the military arsenals of many Third World countries will continue to expand, America's military edge over the developing world will probably widen for the foreseeable future, as the latest advances in microelectronics and other technologies are built into American weapons systems. The Gulf War should have made that clear. In this vein, the Vietnam debacle should have taught us only that the United States will have problems using its military to serve its interests in the Third World when those interests are absurdly peripheral, and also when its objectives (in this case, nation-building) are utopian.

As for America's economic stakes in the Third World, they have always been small and they continue to shrink. Take the idea of the Third World and its teeming billions as the world's last great untapped market and the potential salvation of U.S. industry. Meaningless aggregate figures make this broader version of the myth of the China market seem credible. In fact America's Third World trade is dominated by a handful of countries—the so-called newly industrialized countries (the South Koreas and Taiwans of the world), Mexico, and the OPEC oil producers. U.S. trade with the rest of the Third World rose impressively during the 1970s, but only because the West lent those countries so much money that some increase in their purchasing power was inevitable. Unfortunately, when the loans came due, it became clear that the money had been used not to encourage sound, self-sustaining growth—and thus the creation of reliable markets for U.S. products—but to line rulers' pockets and to finance politically popular national shopping sprees. The resulting debt crisis represents simply the return of those nations to their historical state of economic stagnation following an artificially induced spending boom. Consequently, private U.S. and other Western banks are falling all over themselves to cut their losses and get out of the business of making new loans to most Third World countries (except for loans made involuntarily, as part of government-mandated rescue packages). Indeed, on the whole, all forms of private foreign investment in the Third World are in relative decline. In 1956–1960 direct Western private investments in the Third World amounted to 27.4 percent of the $126.5 billion (in constant dollars) in net Western financial flows to those countries. In 1981–1985 such investments represented only 11.1 percent of the total Western financial flow of $442.4 billion— and this period included some of the peak foreign-lending years.

The United States is heavily reliant on Third World countries for many strategically and economically critical raw materials. But resource availability is hardly a cut-and-dried concept. Appearances to the contrary, statistics on the availability of such resources as petroleum and metals do not tell us definitively how much of these substances remains in the ground. Geologists simply do not know enough to provide credible numbers. And the domination of world production of certain resources by certain countries does not mean that those countries possess the planet's sole deposits. It simply means that their easily accessible supplies can be extracted and refined at costs that the market considers profitable at a given time. Import dependence, moreover, is not the same thing as vulnerability to supply cutoffs. Specifically, the more countries that supply a given material, the less likely it is that a price increase or a supply interruption from any single source will be damaging to the United States.

In addition, materials science today is an exceptionally promising research field, and many new forms of plastics, ceramics, and composites are superior to naturally occurring metals and the alloys made from them. As a result, the smokestack indus-

tries now use decreasing amounts of Third World raw materials in their products. (The new information-intensive industries, of course, have never relied heavily on Third World raw materials.) And the development of synthetics will only accelerate, further lessening our reliance on Third World raw materials.

American interests in the Third World in fact boil down to a handful of concrete issues. On the security side the United States needs to worry about only one region: the Caribbean Basin. And in this region it has only two important concerns: that no hostile outside force establish any significant military or intelligence presence, and that Mexico not fall apart economically and socially.

The United States cannot live with social and economic chaos on its southern border, or insulate itself from the consequences. Yet turning such an enormous, corruption-ridden country as Mexico into a success story seems impossible using standard internationalist tools like economic- and political-development programs. The United States might do better to abandon the dream of remaking Mexico and aim instead at keeping the lid on— helping Mexico muddle through as long as possible. Desperation has forced the Mexican government to make some promising economic-liberalization moves. It should be pressured to make more. The proposed U.S.-Mexico free-trade agreement might help as well, provided that Mexico is not permitted to become either an export platform that gives European and Asian companies easy access to the U.S. market, or more of a sweatshop for American firms seeking to evade strict U.S. environmental, child-labor, and occupational-safety laws.

America's policy toward the Caribbean Basin in general has been wasteful and roundabout. Thus, for a decade after the Sandinista revolution, in 1979, liberal and conservative internationalists alike convinced themselves that securing U.S. interests in Central America required turning that region's countries into something they had never been—stable, democratic, and prosperous societies that would never think of hosting unfriendly foreign presences. The Carter and Reagan Administrations both pumped hundreds of millions in aid into the region and oversaw reform programs down to the village level.

Central America isn't in great demand today as a base for operations against the United States, but if this threat returns, Washington should remember that the lack of democracy, development, and social justice in Central America—however unfortunate for people who have to live there—has never appreciably affected U.S. fortunes. We are strong enough to rely on simpler responses than those chosen by Jimmy Carter and Ronald Reagan. The United States should keep unfriendly foreign powers out of the hemisphere by using and threatening to use force unilaterally. Washington could implicitly propose a new regional compact: local populations would be allowed to mismanage themselves to their hearts' content, provided that no foreign-policy decisions were made that America deemed troublesome. Washington alone would be judge, jury, and court of appeals. Countries that disobeyed would be punished—perhaps in the form of air or naval bombardment, or full economic embargoes. Countries that obeyed would be left alone, no matter which political faction happened to be in power in a given week.

The United States also needs to think about the proliferation of advanced weapons and long-range delivery systems throughout the Third World. Even after the Gulf War, however, the most commonly proposed internationalist solution to the threat of missile attack from Third World countries is one that has already failed: multilateral controls on the military and commercial technologies needed to make missile weapons. This solution has failed for entirely predictable reasons. The worldwide economic integration to which internationalists love to point means that technology—knowledge—is excruciatingly difficult to contain. It is all the more so when the line between military and civilian technology in the crucial high-tech sectors is blurry, when, consequently, many of the key technologies are in private hands (or heads), and when demand is high. In other words, the problem cannot be legislated out of existence. It is hard to see that diplomacy can do much either. How could the

West possibly convince Third World countries that nuclear and other high-tech weapons are not valuable assets, especially in the dangerous regions in which many of the countries are located? And regional security agreements aimed at obviating the need for such weapons are little more than pieces of paper. If states felt secure enough to rely on such arrangements, they wouldn't want the weapons so desperately.

Therefore, it's time for approaches recognizing that the genies are out of the bottle. One approach would replace denial with destruction. Israel understood this first: its bombing of Iraq's nuclear facilities in 1981 bought the world ten years of valuable time. Operation Desert Storm has bought much more. Better yet, such operations—especially if they are restricted to bombing runs over weapons factories—can easily be repeated against militarily and technologically inferior nations whenever necessary. The United States could also replace denial with protection. Ronald Reagan's dream of shielding Americans from the kind of mammoth nuclear strike that the Soviets could launch was never attainable. But a thin-shield defense against the kinds of much smaller strikes that developing countries can launch would be fairly easy, and if we lack the capability now, we should hurry up and get it. Financing would require only a small fraction of the money currently spent on protecting Western Europe and Japan.

On the economic side, America needs to make sure that its banking system is not damaged by further Third World stagnation, and it needs more-reliable supplies of key raw materials found in the Third World. In each case, the internationalist solution has been more complicated, more expensive, less direct, and less reliable over the long term than non-internationalist alternatives. Creating flourishing Third World markets for American goods where none currently exist would be marvelous, but it does not seem possible at any cost that the United States could afford. It is true, as foreign-aid advocates note, that America spends a pittance, in relative terms, on development assistance. But aid has been the same kind of bargain as one on a used car with a bum engine. The prospect of any return at all on the money is so remote that the waste is likely to be total.

Moreover, the chief obstacle to modernization and self-sustaining growth in most of the Third World is not lack of money but, rather, the social, economic, and political disorganization and the official corruption from which Third World countries suffer. Indeed, many of these places are not real countries—at least not in the sense that states in the industrialized free world and parts of the Far East are. Third World countries may belong to the UN, they may have their own flags and airlines and armies and postage stamps, but many of them lack the critical attributes of statehood—the institutional structures and the bedrock cohesion needed both to generate resources and to use them productively.

Rather than persist in trying to solve problems that may be unsolvable, the United States should make the best of a less-than-ideal but eminently tolerable situation, and focus on insulating itself as completely as possible from the consequences of prolonged economic stagnation in the Third World. However significant, the costs could be a bargain compared with the costs and the uncertainties of continued bailout attempts and conventional aid programs. The United States should assume that any real economic promise shown by any of these countries will eventually be recognized by the private sector, however gun-shy it is now.

Since the end of the Second World War the United States has generally accepted its dependence on Third World supplies of strategic materials and has sought to secure them through a combination of military and political means—fielding the forces needed to protect the supplies from hostile powers, using foreign aid and diplomacy to court the regimes that controlled the resources, and, when necessary, helping the regimes fend off internal challenges. These national-security programs represent costs that must be added to the price tag of Third World raw materials. In fact, when one considers all the costs and uncertainties of securing access to these materials, the entire policy equation changes. It becomes clear that many "cheap" Third World raw materials are not

cheap at all. In some cases the true cost of these materials may approach or even exceed the true costs of supposedly uneconomical alternatives. Oil provides the most striking example. The cost of the U.S. military forces maintained even in peacetime primarily to protect the flow of oil from the Middle East, together with the cost of U.S. regional-aid programs—not to mention the cost of the Gulf War—increase the real price of Middle Eastern oil to U.S. taxpayers by a staggering sum. Estimates of the actual amount vary, and preoccupy a small cottage industry; the estimates *start* at tens of billions of dollars a year.

These hidden costs of "cheap" foreign raw materials mean that in many cases the United States has the option of greater self-sufficiency. And because in a strategic world self-sufficiency and freedom of action are intrinsic goods that are worth much, Washington should be aggressively exploring alternatives to Third World supplies. The United States should be looking into developing artificial substitutes for both fuel and nonfuel minerals, stimulating alternative international sources of supply, encouraging exploration for new domestic supplies, and more fully exploiting low-grade domestic deposits.

In the Third World as elsewhere, internationalism has its hopes and fears backward. The modernization of most Third World societies may be out of the question for the time being. As a result, integrating those societies into the tightly interconnected, efficiency-oriented global economy envisioned by internationalism may be indefinitely delayed. Those countries cannot be counted on as strategic assets or substantial markets anytime soon. The United States must not concentrate on turning the situation around, and risk its own exhaustion in the process. Strategic and economic disengagement from the Third World, which has already begun, should be allowed to continue unimpeded.

The greatest obstacles to adopting this new Third World policy are plainly psychological. It is difficult in this era of Spaceship Earth, amid rampant talk of interdependence and globalization, to envision a future in which the developed and developing halves of the world are largely decoupled—in which one half continues to make great economic, social and scientific progress while the other languishes in decrepitude and anarchy. Tragically, it is even more difficult to envision the kind of effort that would be needed to prevent this scenario from unfolding.

DOING FOR OURSELVES

A tighter focus on America's national interests could remove many of the political and institutional influences responsible for the seeming other-worldliness of our internationalist foreign policy. If internationalism has not been serving the interests of the nation as a whole especially well lately, it may be, as noted, because few influential internationalists have to live with the domestic consequences of their positions. Many—probably most—are affluent enough to bear a heavy tax load and to secure the best financial advice money can buy. Their children have not, for the most part, been the ones who have fought in the military conflicts of the past. Their jobs rarely are eliminated when predatory foreign trade practices close American factories. They can also shield themselves from the impact of internationalism's indifference to domestic decay. Their neighborhoods are not haunted by violent crime and drugs. Their sons and daughters are not educated at ineffective public schools. They are not struggling to pay medical bills and send their children to college.

Surely one explanation for internationalists' success at making their priorities those of U.S. foreign policy at large involves their belief that, given our perilous world and America's particular vulnerabilities, a democratically made foreign policy could be a dangerous luxury. The notions of globalization and interdependence and the indivisibility of peace and security all reinforce the belief that foreign-policy makers cannot waste time playing by the rules and seeking the consensus that democratic governance rests on. National security in particular, the internationalists seem to believe, is too important to entrust to the ignorant, fickle masses and their only slightly less ignorant, fickle representatives in Congress.

A foreign policy cognizant of America's considerable strengths and dedicated to enhancing them would automatically allow domestic quality-of-life issues priority on the national agenda. And it would also no longer implicitly accept the need for control by an elite. In this more relaxed environment internationalists would find it harder to portray their prejudices and obsessions as urgent national needs. Their priorities would no longer command automatic assent. Their world-order ideas would enjoy no automatic claims on the country's resources, its attention, or the lives of its young men and women.

After half a century of predominance, internationalism would be superseded by a foreign policy for the rest of us.

Questions for Discussion

1. What is meant by the "national interest"? Who decides? On what grounds?

2. How would you differentiate the national interest from group interests?

3. How has the concept of the national interest evolved? What accounts for the changes in the way that different U.S. leaders have interpreted the term?

4. What competing conceptions of the national interest can you identify?

5. When is sentiment detrimental to self-interest?

6. In 1938, Carl J. Friedrich wrote: "The national interest is a useful term when you are engaged in pressing upon public attention your own view about foreign affairs." Comment.

7. Identify an issue in foreign affairs on which you feel strongly and set forth the hierarchy of considerations that lead you to select one from among the several options available.

Selected Bibliography

BRODIE, BERNARD. *War and Politics*. New York: Macmillan, 1973.

CARR, E.H. *The Twenty Years' Crisis: 1919–1939*, 2nd ed. London: Macmillan, 1946.

DIVINE, ROBERT A. *Roosevelt and World War II*. Baltimore: Johns Hopkins Press, 1969.

GLENNON, MICHAEL J. *Constitutional Diplomacy*. Princeton: Princeton University Press, 1990.

HALBERSTAM, DAVID. *The Best and the Brightest*. New York: Random House, 1972.

KENNAN, GEORGE F., JR. *American Diplomacy, 1900–1950*. Chicago: University of Chicago Press, 1951.

LIPPMANN, WALTER. *Essays in Public Philosophy*. Boston: Little, Brown, 1955.

MORGENTHAU, HANS J. *Dilemmas of Politics*. Chicago: University of Chicago Press, 1958.

NUECHTERLEIN, DONALD E. *National Interests and Presidential Leadership: The Setting of Priorities*. Boulder: Westview, 1978.

———. *America Overcommitted: United States National Interests in the 1980s*. Lexington: University of Kentucky Press, 1985.

RAVENAL, EARL C. *Never Again: Learning from America's Foreign Policy Failures*. Philadelphia: Temple University Press, 1978.

SPYKMAN, NICHOLAS JOHN. *America's Strategy in World Politics*. New York: Harcourt, Brace, 1941.

CHAPTER 4

The Moral Dimension and Foreign Policy

The role of morality in the determination of U.S. foreign policy is no longer the exclusive domain of philosophers and preachers. It has become an integral part of the democratization of American politics and the adoption of an agenda for foreign policy. Every political issue is invested with a moral dimension; and every moral issue has a political dimension. Often, the two may be, if not incompatible, then in conflict with each other. An aide to President Jimmy Carter once observed that with Carter "the surest way to lose an argument on policy was to use a political rationale. He believed that politics sullied or cheapened the domestic policy process."[1] It was this aversion to politics and the bargaining, compromise, and trade-offs that are inherent in the process that alienated Congress and beleaguered his presidency.

The morality of the nation-state is different from that of an individual. Whereas individuals bear a responsibility only for themselves and so can follow whatever moral course they choose, the leaders of the state are responsible for the security and well-being of an entire political community. They cannot create their own environment and impose their own values, but rather must operate in the imperfect world of competing interests, cultures, mores, and nation-states. There is no universally accepted morality. None has ever existed. Within the nation, a police force is necessary to maintain order and prevent anarchy, because not all members of the community abide by the law or even accept its premises. Still more in foreign affairs there exists no shared attachment to a universalist morality. As one scholar put it, "The lack of application of moral considerations to the actions of states has numerous parallels in the domestic life of states; it is not so remarkable as is often made out."[2]

Nations must look to their own defense and protect their own interests. Toward that end it would be well to recall the words of Otto von Bismarck, Germany's Chancellor in the late nineteenth century: "A statesman who attempts to conduct his foreign policies on firm principles is like a man who attempts to walk through a dense forest with a long pole clamped horizontally between his teeth."

Ever since the end of the Second World War, the moral factor, especially the concern for human rights, has assumed greater importance in U.S. policymaking and in the international community generally. A revulsion against the horrors perpetrated by Nazi Germany and Japan on captive peoples and a reaffirmation of the core values of Western civilization, the Universal Declaration of Human Rights was adopted by the

[1] *The New York Times*, August 29, 1986.

[2] J.D.B. Miller. "Morality, Interests and Rationalisation" in Ralph Pettman (ed.), *Moral Claims in World Affairs*. New York: St. Martin's Press, 1979, p. 36.

United Nations General Assembly on December 10, 1948 (Reading 8). The only abstentions were the members of the Soviet bloc, Saudi Arabia, and South Africa. The Declaration had no enforcement mechanism, but from the mid-1960s on treaties or conventions have incorporated its provisions, making them binding on all signatories, in law if not in practice. The U.N. Declaration contrasts with the League of Nations Covenant, which mentioned neither individual rights nor economic and social rights.

During the heyday of the Cold War, human rights violations and social and economic inequities perpetrated by one country were grist for the propaganda mills of the other. Thus, Washington condemned Moscow's denial of freedom of religion and disregard of civil liberties, while Moscow criticized the ills of unemployment, lack of economic security, and costly health care in the United States. Ideological hostility polarized the international system, including the United Nations, and military-strategic considerations predominated in the thinking of each side's foreign policy. What was debated in U.N. forums well into the 1980s hardly reflected a consensus on what was important, either from a moral or political perspective: criticisms of Israel for its treatment of Palestinians on the West Bank and Gaza or of South Africa for its policy of apartheid far exceeded the attention to the mass destruction the Soviet Union was engaged in throughout Afghanistan and the Khmer Rouge and Vietnam were perpetrating in Cambodia; Syrian President Hafez Assad's massacre of 20,000 Syrians in Hama for opposing his rule never elicited even mild censure from the United Nations, any more than did Saddam Hussein's use of poison gas against the Kurds in his country

or Uganda's Idi Amin's massive murders; attempts by the Arab Organization for Human Rights, an exile group, to obtain consultative status as a nongovernmental organization were repeatedly rejected by the Arab governments; and U.S. resolutions deploring human rights abuses in Cuba were regularly voted down by Third World groupings unwilling to direct moral opprobrium against one of their own.

All the more remarkable then, in retrospect, the achievement of President Carter. He gave human rights advocacy a new saliency, certainly in U.S. foreign policy, and he made it an international issue that is difficult to ignore. His inaugural address, on January 20, 1977, sounded the theme:

> Our commitment to human rights must be absolute. . . . Because we are free we can never be indifferent to the fate of freedom elsewhere. Our moral sense dictates a clear-cut preference for those societies which share with us an abiding respect for individual human rights. . . .

On assuming office he forwarded a letter to Andrei Sakharov, the Soviet Union's most prominent dissident, and invited an exiled Soviet human rights activist—Vladimir Bukovsky—to the White House, a symbolic gesture his predecessor had decided not to make. In fairness to Gerald Ford, he believed that to do so would jeopardize ongoing diplomatic negotiations for concluding a strategic arms limitation agreement. And indeed, Carter's gestures did chill U.S.-Soviet relations for quite some time. They brought to the fore the inherent tension between the desire to do the morally right thing and the desire to reach agreements to reduce the likelihood of war or possible confrontation with a major adversary. Carter's attempts ran headlong into the insoluble predicaments that face any political leadership.

However, Carter negotiated a treaty with Panama, returning to it full sovereignty over the Panama Canal by the end of the century. This issue exemplified his determination to enhance the role of morality in American foreign policy. Although the groundwork for such a treaty had been laid by previous administrations, Carter made it a priority. He saw it as showing the rest of the world how the United States could deal in a just manner with a small country. In the process, he also sought "to insure the continued safe operation of the canal itself," since the Joint Chiefs of Staff "estimated that it might take up to 100,000 troops to defend the waterway against a full-scale Panamanian attack."[3] Joshua Muravchik comments on Carter's upgrading of human rights and what this means for U.S. policymakers (Reading 9). He notes the dilemmas and raises the imponderables of foreign policy decisionmaking associated with promoting human rights.

Carter's human rights policy was often inconsistent, vacillating between a focus on human rights and the pursuit of other interests. It had a decided Cold War orientation and tended to focus on the violations of some countries but not others, for example, Pinochet's Chile but not the Shah's Iran, the Soviet Union but not China, Brazil, and Argentina and not South Korea or the Philippines. What is the minimum consistency that can be expected of a country aspiring to be guided by moral considerations? Can a policy that is inconsistent avoid hypocrisy?

[3] Robert W. McElroy. *Morality and American Foreign Policy.* Princeton: Princeton University Press, 1992, p. 137.

Or, in an imperfect world, is inconsistency but another of the inevitable adaptations that must be made in an environment that is beyond one's complete control? Does the espousal of self-determination mean support for any and all manifestations of political fragmentation and secession? What criteria can guide the policymaker who must make choices? It is generally deemed moral to use force to resist aggression. Is it also moral to do so against political dictatorship? Or economic exploitation?

The search for ethical standards by which to judge the foreign policies of states was derided by former Secretary of State Dean Acheson in a speech in 1964: "What passes for ethical standards for governmental policies in foreign affairs is a collection of moralisms, maxims, and slogans, which neither help nor guide, but only confuse, decision" on key issues. He called "the so-called principle of self-determination" delusive. According to Acheson, this principle "has a doubtful moral history," since its originator, Woodrow Wilson, used it to dismember our enemies in the First World War "with results which hardly inspire enthusiasm today" (an allusion to the instability created by the Balkanization of Central Europe). Acheson also argued that the use and threat of force, by one state against another, though condemned by the U.N. Charter, is not without weakness as an absolute moral standard: "Is it moral to deny ourselves the use of force in all circumstances, when our adversaries employ it, under handy excuses whenever it seems useful to tip the scales of power against every value we think of as moral and as making life worth living?"[4]

[4] *The New York Times*, December 10, 1964, p. 16.

Hans J. Morgenthau agreed with Dean Acheson that "the intoxication with moral abstractions" was a continuing source of weakness in U.S. foreign policy. But in accord with the belief that even a foreign policy based on realism could not ignore the moral dimension, he enunciated a number of guidelines for determining policy and navigating between the Scylla of idealism and the Charybdis of ineffectiveness (Reading 10).

More recently, with the end of the Cold War, the U.N. General Assembly has supported a greater degree of activism in emergency or catastrophic situations affecting the lives of innocent civilians, even if this entails intervention over the wishes of the interested government: this path-breaking arrogation of authority by the United Nations was affirmed in January 1992, at the Security Council's "first-ever summit-level meeting" where it acknowledged "for the first time the existence of 'nonmilitary' threats to peace and security 'in the economic, social, humanitarian, and ecological fields.' The debate illustrated how views of national sovereignty are evolving. While the leaders of China and India stressed noninterference in their internal affairs, most other Council members argued that governments can no longer abuse the basic human rights of their people."[5] Jarat Chopra and Thomas G. Weiss trace the origins and explore the implications of this assault on the traditional concept of sovereignty (Reading 11).

Though in the international arena a great power cannot always act as it would like, generally speaking it can demonstrate

[5] Paul Lewis. "The Right to Intervene for a Humanitarian Cause," *The New York Times*, July 12, 1992, Sec. 4, p. 18.

what it would like to do if it could. Resisting aggression, assisting friendly governments, encouraging free and open communication, and affirming our commitment to human rights and democratic values by what we do and not by insisting that others emulate our experience or abide by our prescriptions for progress—these are the elements of a policy that could make crystal clear a U.S. commitment to due regard for moral considerations in foreign policy. Perhaps American policymakers need to devote more attention to the questions of what we would like to do if we could and whether our image abroad, the respect and friendship of others, might not be an essential part of the pursuit of our own national interests.

Keeping in mind George Bernard Shaw's dictum that the world is not a "moral gymnasium" may help avoid the paralysis that occurs when every political move in the foreign policy arena elicits a moral outcry. The ethical factor is a potent one, but it needs to be handled with care, lest lack of discrimination breed trivialization of its controlling value, and overassertion yield numbing indifference to its virtue. Perhaps the aim should be to do better morally instead of striving to be morally right. A sound sense of political perspective and priorities is essential to prevent the transmutation of morality into its caricature—self-righteousness. In Shakespeare's words, the danger then is from those who, under that "hot ardent zeal would set whole realms on fire." But at its discriminating, judicious best, attention to the moral dimension can unite and galvanize a democratic society, reaffirming and refocusing the commitments to basic values and beliefs that bind each new generation to the finest in the ideals, institutions, and traditions of its predecessors.

8.   Universal Declaration of Human Rights

The declaration was the work of the UN Commission on Human Rights which met in January 1947 under the chairmanship of Mrs. Franklin D. Roosevelt. The Universal Declaration of Human Rights was adopted and proclaimed by the General Assembly on December 10, 1948. It was the first effort to set common standards of achievement in human rights for all peoples of all nations.

Preamble

Whereas recognition of the inherent dignity and of the equal and inalienable rights of all members of the human family is the foundation of freedom, justice and peace in the world,

Whereas disregard and contempt for human rights have resulted in barbarous acts which have outraged the conscience of mankind, and the advent of a world in which human beings shall enjoy freedom of speech and belief and freedom from fear and want has been proclaimed as the highest aspiration of the common people,

Whereas it is essential, if man is not to be compelled to have recourse, as a last resort, to rebellion against tyranny and oppression, that human rights should be protected by the rule of law,

Whereas it is essential to promote the development of friendly relations between nations,

Whereas the peoples of the United Nations have in the Charter reaffirmed their faith in fundamental human rights, in the dignity and worth of the human person and in the equal rights of men and women and have determined to promote social progress and better standards of life in larger freedom,

Whereas Member States have pledged themselves to achieve, in co-operation with the United Nations, the promotion of universal respect for and observance of human rights and fundamental freedoms,

Whereas common understanding of these rights and freedoms is of the greatest importance for the full realization of this pledge,

Now, therefore,

The General Assembly

Proclaims this Universal Declaration of Human Rights as a common standard of achievement for all peoples and all nations, to the end that every individual and every organ of society, keeping this Declaration constantly in mind, shall strive by teaching and education to promote respect for these rights and freedoms and by progressive measures, national and international to secure their universal and effective recognition and observance, both among the peoples of Member States themselves and among the peoples of territories under their jurisdiction.

Article 1

All human beings are born free and equal in dignity and rights. They are endowed with reason and conscience and should act towards one another in a spirit of brotherhood.

Article 2

Everyone is entitled to all the rights and freedoms set forth in this Declaration, without distinction of any kind, such as race, colour, sex, language, religion, political or other opinion, national or social origin, property, birth or other status.

Furthermore, no distinction shall be made on the basis of the political, jurisdictional or international status of the country or territory to which a person belongs, whether it be independent, trust, non-self-governing or under any other limitation of sovereignty.

Article 3

Everyone has the right to life, liberty and the security of person.

Article 4

No one shall be held in slavery or servitude; slavery and the slave trade shall be prohibited in all their forms.

Article 5

No one shall be subjected to torture or to cruel, inhuman or degrading treatment or punishment.

Article 6

Everyone has the right to recognition everywhere as a person before the law.

Article 7

All are equal before the law and are entitled without any discrimination to equal protection of the law. All are entitled to equal protection against any discrimination in violation of this Declaration and against any incitement to such discrimination.

Article 8

Everyone has the right to an effective remedy by the competent national tribunals for acts violating the fundamental rights granted him by the constitution or by law.

Article 9

No one shall be subjected to arbitrary arrest, detention or exile.

Article 10

Everyone is entitled in full equality to a fair and public hearing by an independent and impartial tribunal, in the determination of his rights and obligations and of any criminal charge against him.

Article 11

1. Everyone charged with a penal offence has the right to be presumed innocent until proved guilty according to law in a public trial at which he has had all the guarantees necessary for his defence.

2. No one shall be held guilty of any penal offence on account of any act or omission which did not constitute a penal offence, under national or international law, at the time when it was committed. Nor shall a heavier penalty be imposed than the one that was applicable at the time the penal offence was committed.

Article 12

No one shall be subjected to arbitrary interference with his privacy, family, home or correspondence, nor to attacks upon his honour and reputation. Everyone has the right to the protection of the law against such interference or attacks.

Article 13

1. Everyone has the right to freedom of movement and residence within the borders of each State.

2. Everyone has the right to leave any country, including his own, and to return to his country.

Article 14

1. Everyone has the right to seek and to enjoy in other countries asylum from persecution.

2. This right may not be invoked in the case of prosecutions genuinely arising from non-political crimes or from acts contrary to the purposes and principles of the United Nations.

Article 15

1. Everyone has the right to a nationality.

2. No one shall be arbitrarily deprived of his nationality nor denied the right to change his nationality.

Article 16

1. Men and women of full age, without any limitation due to race, nationality or religion, have the right to marry and to found a family. They are entitled to equal rights as to marriage, during marriage and at its dissolution.

2. Marriage shall be entered into only with the free and full consent of the intending spouses.

3. The family is the natural and fundamental group unit of society and is entitled to protection by society and the State.

Article 17

1. Everyone has the right to own property alone as well as in association with others.

2. No one shall be arbitrarily deprived of his property.

Article 18

Everyone has the right to freedom of thought, conscience and religion; this right includes freedom to change his religion or belief, and freedom, either alone or in community with others and in public or private, to manifest his religion or belief in teaching, practice, worship and observance.

Article 19

Everyone has the right to freedom of opinion and expression; this right includes freedom to hold opinions without interference and to seek, receive and impart information and ideas through any media and regardless of frontiers.

Article 20

1. Everyone has the right to freedom of peaceful assembly and association.

2. No one may be compelled to belong to an association.

Article 21

1. Everyone has the right to take part in the government of his country, directly or through freely chosen representatives.

2. Everyone has the right of equal access to public service in his country.

3. The will of the people shall be the basis of the authority of government; this will shall be expressed in periodic and genuine elections which shall be by universal and equal suffrage and shall be held by secret vote or by equivalent free voting procedures.

Article 22

Everyone, as a member of society, has the right to social security and is entitled to realization, through national effort and international co-operation and in accordance with the organization and resources of each State, of the economic, social and cultural rights indispensable for his dignity and the free development of his personality.

Article 23

1. Everyone has the right to work, to free choice of employment, to just and favourable conditions of work and to protection against unemployment.

2. Everyone, without any discrimination, has the right to equal pay for equal work.

3. Everyone who works has the right to just and favourable remuneration ensuring for himself and his family an existence worthy of human dignity, and supplemented, if necessary, by other means of social protection.

4. Everyone has the right to form and to join trade unions for the protection of his interests.

Article 24

Everyone has the right to rest and leisure, including reasonable limitation of working hours and periodic holidays with pay.

Article 25

1. Everyone has the right to a standard of living adequate for the health and well-being of himself and of his family, including food, clothing, housing and medical care and necessary social services, and the right to security in the event of unemployment, sickness, disability, widowhood, old age or other lack of livelihood in circumstances beyond his control.

2. Motherhood and childhood are entitled to special care and assistance. All children, whether born in or out of wedlock, shall enjoy the same social protection.

Article 26

1. Everyone has the right to education. Education shall be free, at least in the elementary and fundamental stages. Elementary education shall be compulsory. Technical and professional education shall be made generally available and higher education shall be equally accessible to all on the basis of merit.

2. Education shall be directed to the full development of the human personality and to the strengthening of respect for human rights and fundamental freedoms. It shall promote understanding, tolerance and friendship among all nations, racial or religious groups, and shall further the activities of the United Nations for the maintenance of peace.

3. Parents have a prior right to choose the kind of education that shall be given to their children.

Article 27

1. Everyone has the right freely to participate in the cultural life of the community, to enjoy the arts and to share in scientific advancement and its benefits.

2. Everyone has the right to the protection of the moral and material interests resulting from any scientific, literary or artistic production of which he is the author.

Article 28

Everyone is entitled to a social and international order in which the rights and freedoms set forth in this Declaration can be fully realized.

Article 29

1. Everyone has duties to the community in which alone the free and full development of his personality is possible.

2. In the exercise of his rights and freedoms, everyone shall be subject only to such limitations as are determined by law solely for the purpose of securing due recognition and respect for the rights and freedoms of others and of meeting the just requirements of morality, public order and the general welfare in a democratic society.

3. These rights and freedoms may in no case be exercised contrary to the purposes and principles of the United Nations.

Article 30

Nothing in this Declaration may be interpreted as implying for any State, group or person any right to engage in any activity or to perform any act aimed at the destruction of any of the rights and freedoms set forth herein.

9.   What Jimmy Carter Wrought

Joshua Muravchik

What lessons can be learned from the Carter experience about how the United States should conduct its human rights policy? For all its mistakes and failures, the Carter policy showed the latent importance of the human rights issue. Jeane Kirkpatrick, Carter's most trenchant critic, commented: "not

SOURCE: Joshua Muravchik. *The Uncertain Crusade: Jimmy Carter and the Dilemmas of Human Rights Policy.* Lanham, MD: Hamilton Press, 1986, pp. 221–230, excerpts. Footnotes deleted. Reprinted by permission.

only should human rights play a central role in U.S. foreign policy, no U.S. foreign policy can possibly succeed that does not accord them a central role." This is so because, as Jimmy Carter rightly said, the belief in human rights is the common blood that flows in American veins. Our sense of nationhood flows from the set of principles expressed in the Constitution and the Declaration of Independence. In order for the United States to act in the world with a degree of national unity and with a sense of conviction, our policy must be felt to be grounded in those principles. It is also so because the politics of the modern age are fought not only over territory and resources, and with missiles and factories, but over and with ideas—and human rights is the essence of the American idea.

There are those who doubt that human rights should be a focus of U.S. foreign policy. Some say that it is "wrong" to intervene in the domestic affairs of other countries. But this is not true in a legal sense. The relevant international law, essentially UN law, is a muddle. The UN Charter upholds the sanctity of "domestic jurisdiction" (Article 2[7]), but it also obligates members to respect "human rights and fundamental freedoms" (Articles 55 and 56). The confusion that this contradiction engenders is exemplified by General Assembly Resolution 2131 (XX) which proclaims: "Every State has an inalienable right to choose its political, economic, social and cultural systems, without interference in any form by another State." This seems clear enough, although General Assembly resolutions are not legally binding. But the very next clause of the same resolution flatly contradicts the principle of nonintervention. It enjoins every state to "contribute to the complete elimination of racial discrimination . . . in all its forms and manifestations." In sum, the most reasonable interpretation of existing law is that *armed* intervention is proscribed, except conceivably in very extreme situations, but that moral intervention on behalf of human rights is permissible.

If it is not legally wrong, is it morally wrong to intervene in the affairs of other nations in order to encourage respect for human rights? Only if the nation, rather than the human individual, is regarded as the ultimate moral unit. But by what logic does the nation have moral standing apart from that of the human beings who make it up? The practical fact is that in the twentieth century especially, but throughout all history as well, nations have intervened politically, morally, and intellectually in the affairs of other nations. If we Americans cherish our human rights, and if we share with America's Founders the belief that these rights are "unalienable" or that they are goods with which people have been "endowed by their Cre-

ator," then it is certainly morally permissible, probably even morally obligatory, that we do what we can within reason to help other people to secure theirs. . . .

[One] argument against a human rights policy holds that U.S. foreign policy must be guided by the "national interest" and that such altruistic goals as human rights can play no more than a peripheral part because, as Ernst Haas says: "A consistent and energetic policy in the human rights field makes impossible the attainment of other, often more important, objectives." The critical flaw in this argument is that it is hard to think of any situation where the advancement of human rights conflicts with other U.S. interests. On the contrary, the advancement of human rights almost always serves concrete American interests, both because it is a victory for our system of values and because every country in the world where human rights flourish is friendly, some of course more than others, to the United States.

Destabilizing friendly dictatorial governments may not serve U.S. interests, but it may not serve the cause of human rights either. If a friendly dictatorship gives way to a more democratic government, the cause of human rights will benefit, and the interests of the United States will not ordinarily be harmed. On the other hand, if it gives way to a new dictatorship, ideologically hostile to the United States, that, as we have seen over and again, ordinarily turns out to be a setback not only for American interests, but for human rights as well. In short, the fall of a dictator may or may not be a good thing for the United States or for human rights—that depends on what comes after. The triumph of democracy, however, will almost always be a good thing both for human rights and for the United States. The goal of our human rights policy should not be to destabilize existing governments, but to encourage democratic currents.

Confusion on this score has arisen from the strong association of human rights policy with the use of punitive measures. It is widely taken for granted that cutting foreign aid to dictators is the essence of any human rights policy. But punitive measures, as we have seen, are not very effective in advancing human rights. And, as it turns out, the main impetus behind the growth of punitive measures was the desire not to advance human rights but to diminish American influence. It is not inherently wrong to give aid to dictatorial governments. No ruler in the history of the human race had on his hands more blood of his own citizens than Stalin. Yet who, today, apart perhaps from Solzhenitsyn, argues that it was wrong for the United States to have given aid to his government in the last world war? If punitive measures prove on the whole to be effective in advancing human rights, then it is doubtful that American interests will suffer much from their use. If they prove on the whole ineffective, then their use should be avoided or reserved for special situations.

If we avoid both heavy reliance on punitive measures and avoid destabilizing governments in the face of uncertain futures, then most of the presumed conflict between human rights goals and the national interest disappears. . . .

A well thought-out human rights policy may not be entirely free from conflicts with other U.S. policy goals (what policy is?), but the harm that may accrue to other U.S. interests will be small compared to the benefits that such a policy can bring, benefits that will serve both our ideals and our interests.

What would be the elements of a well thought-out human rights policy? It would, first of all, appreciate that other cultures are different from ours and that every culture is worthy of respect, but it would not be deterred by charges of "ethnocentrism" from recognizing the special relevance of the American experience to the universal quest for human rights. The yearning for human rights, for individual dignity, for liberty, is widespread and age-old. But the achievement of human rights as a system, a way of life, is America's unique and wondrous contribution to mankind.

Of course, the American system was not cut from whole cloth. It built on many traditions. Nor is the American system the last word in human rights. Other systems of freedom have flowered since ours; some may have improved on ours in some respects. Our system is not and was not perfect, especially in the area of race where our flaws were glaring. But all this said, the largest fact remains that it was the

American approach to human rights that made human rights a reality in the world. . . .

The American approach to human rights rests on certain premises about the nature of man and the primacy of the individual over the state; and it emphasizes certain principles—freedom of expression and association, due process of law, government by the consent of the governed. These are the ideas that our human rights policy must try to impart to the rest of the world.

We should work to strengthen and clarify the concept of "human rights." This means resisting the temptation to stretch the term to embrace such seemingly well-meaning ideas as that of "economic and social rights." We should of course be concerned with the economic well-being of people, and probably the amount of foreign aid we give should be greatly increased. This is a matter of basic compassion; to call it a matter of "rights" gains nothing—it will not feed a single extra person—but it endangers something else of great value. We should also cease treating the category of violations of the integrity of the person as if it were a category of rights separable from other rights. Of course we will want to speak more loudly, act more urgently, in response to the rampages of the Khmer Rouge, the homicidal mania of Idi Amin, or the insidious work of the Salvadoran death squads, than, say, to the fact that Jordan continues to be ruled as a hereditary monarchy. But proclaiming special categories of rights doesn't help us to do this; we do it out of common sense and natural revulsion. The only effect of proclaiming special categories of rights is to denigrate other rights.

The UN and its treaties should not be a focus of major attention in U.S. human rights policy. It has often been remarked that a problem with the UN is that it represents governments rather than people. But the problem, insofar as human rights are concerned, is worse than that. The UN isn't made up merely of governments, it is made up primarily of dictatorships. Virtually every violator of human rights in the world has a vote in the UN, but none of their victims has. There are sound diplomatic reasons for the United States to participate in the UN but as an arena for advancing the cause of human rights it holds little promise. The same may be said for the human rights treaties adopted under UN auspices. We should ratify them if we can find a way, through reservations and the like, without jeopardizing our own constitutional processes, but we should not anticipate that they are likely any time in the foreseeable future to constitute anything more than elaborate monuments to hypocrisy. . . .

A sound human rights policy will strive for consistency of application to all countries. Of course this does not mean treating all abusive governments identically. Some governments are worse enemies of human rights than others. And there are some other legitimate reasons for not treating all situations identically. It is legitimate to take into account a country's progress. Thus, for example, Czechoslovakia during the "Prague Spring" and Poland during the heyday of Solidarnosc were both still one-party states, but obviously the much more impressive fact at that moment was how much they had evolved toward respect for human rights. Common sense directed our attention to how far they had come, not to how far they had yet to go. Common sense also commands us to be mindful of a country's background in determining what we can expect from it. The Pinochet government is the more abhorrent for Chile's democratic history; whereas if Tanzania or Mozambique became tomorrow as free as Chile is today we could not help but be very gratified at the progress.

What is *not* legitimate in a human rights policy is inconsistency based on our own self-interest, raising our voice in moral righteousness wherever it seems inexpensive to do so. It is hard to believe that a policy such as this will inspire many people for very long. On the other hand nothing could better impress the world with our moral seriousness than our willingness to stand by our human rights principles uniformly, even where it costs us something. This does mean, as the Reagan administration discovered after a few months, that "if we act as if offenses against freedom don't matter in countries friendly to us, no one will take seriously our words about Communist violations." But the Carter administration showed that it is easy enough to put the squeeze on weak friendly countries. The more important test is whether we are willing to apply our human rights policy to powerful countries resistant to human rights, whether or not they are friendly. The best litmus tests are the People's Republic of China and Saudi Arabia. . . .

Do we have the courage to voice our support for China's democratic dissidents? Or to express our revulsion at the severing of hands of Saudi thieves? What will these countries do to us if we insist on the principle of speaking the truth about human rights as best we can discover it? There is good reason to believe that they will just learn to live with it, probably after first probing to see if they can intimidate us into backing off.

10.   Realism Can Be Consonant with Morality: Criteria for Judging Any Policy

Hans J. Morgenthau

Universal moral principles, such as justice or equality, are capable of guiding political action only to the extent that they have been given concrete content and have been related to political situations by society. I have always maintained that

SOURCE: Hans J. Morgenthau. "Another 'Great Debate': The National Interest of the United States," *American Political Science Review*, vol. XLVI, no. 4, December 1952, pp. 983–987. Footnotes deleted. Reprinted with permission.

the actions of states are subject to universal moral principles, and I have been careful to differentiate my position in this respect from that of Hobbes. Five points basic to my position may need to be emphasized again.

The first point is what one might call the requirement of cosmic humility with regard to the moral evaluation of the actions of states. To know that states are subject to the moral law is one thing; to pretend to know what is morally required of states in a particular situation is quite another. The human mind tends naturally to identify the particular interests of states, as of individuals, with the moral purposes of the universe. The statesman in the defense of the nation's interests may, and at times even must, yield to that tendency; the scholar must resist it at every turn. For the lighthearted assumption that what one's own nation aims at and does is morally good and that those who oppose that nation's policies are evil is morally indefensible and intellectually untenable and leads in practice to that distortion of judgment, born of the blindness of crusading frenzy, which has been the curse of nations from the beginning of time.

The second point which obviously needs to be made again concerns the effectiveness of the restraints which morality imposes upon the actions of states.

A discussion of international morality must guard against the two extremes either of overrating the influence of ethics upon international politics or else of denying that statesmen and diplomats are moved by anything else but considerations of material power.

On the one hand, there is the dual error of confounding the moral rules which people actually observe with those they pretend to observe as well as with those which writers declare they ought to observe. . . .

On the other hand, there is the misconception, usually associated with the general depreciation and moral condemnation of power politics, discussed above, that international politics is so thoroughly evil that it is no use looking for ethical limitations of the aspirations for power on the international scene. Yet, if we ask ourselves what statesmen and diplomats are capable of doing to further the power objectives of their respective nations and what they actually do, we realize that they do less than they probably could and less than they actually did in other periods of history. They refuse to consider certain ends and to use certain means, either altogether or under certain conditions, not because in the light of expediency they appear impractical or unwise,

but because certain moral rules interpose an absolute barrier. Moral rules do not permit certain policies to be considered at all from the point of view of expediency. Such ethical inhibitions operate in our time on different levels with different effectiveness. Their restraining function is most obvious and most effective in affirming the sacredness of human life in times of peace.

In connection with this passage we gave a number of historic examples showing the influence of moral principles upon·the conduct of foreign policy. An example taken from contemporary history will illustrate the same point. There can be little doubt that the Soviet Union could have achieved the objectives of its foreign policy at the end of the Second World War without antagonizing the nations of the West into that encircling coalition which has been the nightmare of Bolshevist foreign policy since 1917. It could have mitigated cunning for its own sake and the use of force with persuasion, conciliation, and a trust derived from the awareness of a partial community of interests and would thereby have minimized the dangers to itself and the rest of the world which are inherent in the objectives of its policies. Yet the Soviet Union was precluded from relying upon these traditional methods of diplomacy by its general conception of human nature, politics, and morality. In the general philosophy of Bolshevism there is no room for honest dissent, the recognition of the intrinsic worth of divergent interests, and genuine conciliation between such interests. On all levels of social interaction opposition must be destroyed by cunning and violence, since it has no right to exist, rather than be met halfway in view of its intrinsic legitimacy. This being the general conception of the political morality of Bolshevism, the foreign policy of the Soviet Union is limited to a much more narrow choice of means than the foreign policies of other nations.

The United States, for instance, has been able, in its relations with the nations of Latin America, to replace military intervention and dollar diplomacy with the policy of the Good Neighbor. That drastic change was made possible by the general conception of political morality which has been prevalent in the United States from its very inception. The United States is a pluralist society which presupposes the continuing existence and legitimacy of divergent interests. These interests are locked in a continuing struggle for supremacy to be decided by force only as a last resort but, normally, through a multitude of institutions which are so devised as to allow one or the other interest a temporary advantage but none a permanent supremacy at the price of the destruction of the others. This morality of pluralism allows the United States, once it is secure in that minimum of vital interests to which we have referred above, to transfer those principles of political morality to the international scene and to deal with divergent interests there with the same methods of genuine compromise and conciliation which are a permanent element of its domestic political life.

The third point concerns the relations between universal moral principles and political action. I have always maintained that these universal moral principles cannot be applied to the actions of states in their abstract universal formulation but that they must be, as it were, filtered through the concrete circumstances of time and place. The individual may say for himself: *Fiat justitia, pereat mundus*; the state has no right to say so in the name of those who are in its care. Both individual and state must judge political action by universal moral principles, such as that of liberty. Yet while the individual has a moral right to sacrifice himself in defense of such a moral principle, the state has no moral right to let its moral disapprobation of the infringement of liberty get in the way of successful political action, itself inspired by the moral principle of national survival. There can be no political morality without prudence, that is, without consideration of the political consequences of seemingly moral action. Classical and medieval philosophy knew this and so did Lincoln when he said: "I do the very best I know how, the very best I can, and I mean to keep doing so until the end. If the end brings me out all right, what is said against me won't amount to anything. If the end brings me out wrong, ten angels swearing I was right would make no difference." The issue between utopianism and realism, as it bears on this point, has been put most

succinctly by Edmund Burke, and what he has to say in the following passage about revolution, that is, civil war, may well be applied *mutatis mutandis* to all war.

Nothing universal can be rationally affirmed on any moral or any political subject. Pure metaphysical abstraction does not belong to these matters. The lines of morality are not like the ideal lines of mathematics. They are broad and deep as well as long. They admit of exceptions; they demand modifications. These exceptions and modifications are not made by the process of logic, but by the rules of prudence. Prudence is not only the first in rank of the virtues political and moral, but she is the director, the regulator, the standard of them all. Metaphysics cannot live without definition; but Prudence is cautious how she defines. Our courts cannot be more fearful in suffering fictitious cases to be brought before them for eliciting their determination on a point of law than prudent moralists are in putting extreme and hazardous cases of conscience upon emergencies not existing. Without attempting, therefore, to define, what never can be defined, the case of a revolution in government, this, I think, may be safely affirmed—that a sore and pressing evil is to be removed, and that a good, great in its amount and unequivocal in its nature, must be probable almost to a certainty, before the inestimable price of our own morals and the well-being of a number of our fellow-citizens is paid for a revolution. If ever we ought to be economists even to parsimony, it is in the voluntary production of evil. Every revolution contains in it something of evil.

Fourth, the realist recognizes that a moral decision, especially in the political sphere, does not imply a simple choice between a moral principle and a standard of action which is morally irrelevant or even outright immoral. A moral decision implies always a choice among different moral principles, one of which is given precedence over others. To say that a political action has no moral purpose is absurd; for political action can be defined as an attempt to realize moral values through the medium of politics, that is, power. The relevant moral question concerns the choice among different moral values, and it is at this point that the realist and the utopian part company again. If an American statesman must choose between the promotion of universal liberty, which is a moral good, at the risk of American security and, hence, of liberty in the United States, on the one hand, and the promotion of American security and of liberty in the United States, which is another moral good, to the detriment of the promotion of universal liberty, on the other, which choice ought he to make? The utopian will not face the issue squarely and

will deceive himself into believing that he can achieve both goods at the same time. The realist will choose the national interest on both moral and pragmatic grounds; for if he does not take care of the national interest nobody else will, and if he puts American security and liberty in jeopardy the cause of liberty everywhere will be impaired.

Finally, the political realist distinguishes between his moral sympathies and the political interests which he must defend. He will distinguish with Lincoln between his *"official* duty" which is to protect the national interest and his *"personal* wish" which is to see universal moral values realized throughout the world.

11. Sovereignty Is No Longer Sacrosanct: Codifying Humanitarian Intervention

Jarat Chopra and Thomas G. Weiss

Eliminating human rights abuses has been a central theme in this journal since its founding. One word explains why the international community has difficulty countering violations: "sovereignty." The distinguishing feature of a new order established by the Treaty of Westphalia, it obscured humanitarian intentions of earlier founders of international law. However, developing guidelines for the forcible delivery of assistance, beyond historical and recent experience, can break the human rights –sovereignty deadlock in a system where states remain the principal actors.

In the bloody aftermath of the Persian Gulf War, the United Nations Security Council passed Resolution 688 on April 5, 1991, which insisted "that Iraq allow immediate access by international humanitarian organizations to all those in need of assistance in all parts of Iraq to make available all necessary facilities for their operations." This ef-

SOURCE: Jarat Chopra and Thomas G. Weiss. "Sovereignty Is No Longer Sacrosanct: Codifying Humanitarian Intervention," *Ethics & International Affairs,* vol. 6, 1992, pp. 95–117, excerpts. Footnotes deleted. Reprinted with permission.

fectively authorized two major relief operations, "Safe Haven" and "Provide Comfort." In spite of host government hostility and widespread reluctance in the region and in UN circles, some 13,000 U.S. troops and 10,000 soldiers from twelve other nations delivered 25 million pounds of food, water, medical supplies, clothing, and shelter to protected areas carved out of northern Iraq.

Several observers labeled these efforts "humanitarian intervention," resuscitating a conceptual debate on the subject. The intervention in Kurdistan reflected growing public outrage with African countries—particularly in the Horn—where both governments and rebels had deprived civilians of international succor as part of their war arsenals. But intergovernmental discussion was divided during the 1991 General Assembly. Representatives of developing countries were particularly sensitive about reform of the UN humanitarian assistance machinery as a possible "Trojan horse" for big-power intervention after the Cold War.

Traditionally, sovereignty has been interpreted to exclude interference in local affairs, thereby preventing international responses to atrocities such as genocide by the Khmer Rouge or gassing of Kurds by the Iraqi government. Hence, the creation of havens in Kurdistan was a watershed and precedent. But deep suspicion of the event highlighted practical inadequacies of humanitarian intervention. The Iraq case was unique and another bad example on which to base general principles; and more significantly, it illustrated motivations that there is no mechanism in place to distinguish truly humanitarian from biased national interests. In his last annual "report on the work of the organization," former UN Secretary-General Pérez de Cuéllar called for reinterpretation of the Charter principles of sovereignty and noninterference in domestic affairs to allow for intervention on humanitarian grounds, as well as identification of the objective conditions under which it should be carried out. . . .

Sovereignty is pivotal in determining whether or not to intervene on humanitarian grounds. Intervention implies violation or intrusion upon authority; and while authority, like sovereignty, is an abstraction, its concrete form consists of territorial boundaries. Controversy over crossing borders occurs not only because they represent the extent of local political control, but because the right to this control is a sacred underpinning of international order as currently understood. Hence, significant legal instruments have been concluded that prohibit action which is considered threatening to the overall system.

However, sovereignty is a legal fiction that continues to evolve. Perceiving it as immutable and beyond question requires resort to selective memory, a tendency in international fora. The family, the tribe, and the city all did quite well without it. Yet the widespread view persists that it is the best mechanism for organizing human society at the global level. The inability of sovereignty to reflect adequately the effective self-development of international society has relegated it to increasing conceptual and practical irrelevance in such fields as trade, famine, and environment. For the protection of human rights too, there has been a perceptible

movement away from the anachronism of exclusive domestic jurisdiction.

Nation-states have been the principal building blocks of the international system, and their measure of legitimacy as states has been the attribution of sovereignty. As the only abstraction, sovereignty is special in the list of criteria of statehood. The 1933 Montevideo Convention on the Rights and Duties of States lists three others: a permanent population, defined territory, and a government. While a state, as any collective construct, is something more than the sum of its parts, sovereignty transforms it into an absolute. Hinsley points out that sovereignty is not a fact, like energy or power; it is a quality of a fact. Sovereignty is a characteristic of power that relegates its holder to a place above the law. A sovereign is immune from law and only subject to self-imposed restrictions. . . .

Whether the power structure of nation-states ever accurately reflected textbook characteristics, sovereignty is no longer sovereign, the world has outgrown it. The exclusivity and inviolability of state sovereignty are increasingly mocked by global interdependence. Electronic communications and media have fostered conscious and unconscious identification among all of humanity. Convenient and accessible transportation has facilitated mass movements of people and, consequently, the increasing de-linkage (psychologically and physically) of populations from territory. The atomic age extinguished boundaries between destruction and the destroyer. Satellites that penetrate "space above any territory of the globe, regardless of 'sovereign' rights over air spaces and duties of 'nonintervention,' serve to emphasize the new openness and penetrability of everything to everybody." "The common heritage of mankind," enshrined in the 1979 Convention on the Moon and Other Celestial Bodies and the 1982 Convention on the Law of the Sea, "marks the passage from the traditional postulate of sovereignty to that of cooperation." It is also the harbinger of an internationalization of "state-territory as a species of property." Interconnectedness has entered the consciousness of public opinion and has been expressed through popular concern for the environment, human rights, and health—including the AIDS epidemic. In fact, the

United Nations Conference on Environment and Development (UNCED), planned for 1992 in Brazil, will debate an "Earth Charter." That the most powerful economies in the world, the G-7, must act in concert on major policies reflects increasing awareness of global financial integration.

At the same time, the fiction of sovereignty has remained greatly intact. The exclusivity of sovereignty has meant that nation-states have been the only members of the international community and the sole "reference points" of international law. In the eyes of the law, individuals do not exist independently of states. There has been no adequate mechanism for redressing state abuse in a system meant ultimately for human welfare. . . .

The supremacy of sovereignty over law is untenable. Sovereignty as a transcendent source of law is supposed to operate hierarchically between ruler and ruled; it is not supposed to function horizontally, or relatively with other sovereigns. Sovereign equality supposedly prevented developing or legitimating *primus inter pares*. The flaw in the theory of sovereignty is that it was a unitary concept operating in a community: mutual respect implied not being sovereign at all. As such, it is universally recognized that in conflicts between laws of a national sovereign and international law, the latter prevails.

The principle of unanimous voting in the League of Nations became decision making by majority in the UN. This means that sovereign states can be bound against their will by the votes of other states. The veto power of the permanent members of the Security Council vitiates the sovereignty of all other members because by definition one cannot be more sovereign than another. Paradoxically, decolonization eroded the concept because newly emerging small states were forced to rely on community laws for security. In any case, the natural law tradition within international legal thought always perceived the ultimate source of law as *supranational*, for only the law is sovereign: "the public interest (state necessity, reason of state, or whatever) cannot be invoked against the law, except to the extent that the law itself so allows. . . .

Political scientists and theorists of international relations have formulated a corruption of sovereignty, which they perceive in terms of degrees. By redrawing strict parameters to include challenges, sovereignty is not seen as incompatible with individual rights, non-state actors, or permeable boundaries. It is possible to be more or less sovereign. Sovereignty becomes an elastic term that refers to a category of social and political organization that is linked geographically to delimited territory. As such, it has no special meaning other than a contextual one. In contrast to international law's objective, largely standardized threshold, political scientists view limits as determined subjectively. Hence, humanitarian interventions, non-state actors, international organizations, and human rights could all be included as exceptions to the anomaly of partially absolute sovereignty.

During the 1991 General Assembly debate on emergency assistance in wars, redefinitions of sovereignty were apparent. The ICRC argued: "In terms of the existing right to assistance, humanitarian assistance cannot be regarded as interference. Far from infringing upon the sovereignty of states, humanitarian assistance in armed conflicts, as provided for by international law, is, rather, an expression of that sovereignty." At the same session, the Soviet Union noted that reservations about "humanitarian intervention" can be addressed by reformulating the issue as "humanitarian solidarity."

Proponents of humanitarian intervention can, and usually do, rely on one of two arguments, both of which lead to the same conclusion. To maintain the traditional concept of sovereignty is to accept its obsolescence and recognize that the emperor has no clothes. If sovereignty is dead, humanitarian intervention does not violate a sacred principle. On the other hand, if humanitarian intervention is permitted as part of an expanded definition of sovereignty and solidarity, then it does not conflict with the remainder of sacrosanct sovereignty.

Eliminating sovereignty from the lexicon of international relations in the foreseeable future is unlikely, however, for state-centered power structures will not agree easily to part with the basis for their status quo. Moreover, sleights of hand and redefinitions that include humanitarian intervention would perpetuate the fiction of sovereignty and continue to slow the acceptance of such rapidly developing concepts as cross-boundary environmental protection. One way to circumvent sovereignty altogether is to explore why human rights constitute a legitimate justification for intervention and how codification could prevent abuse in this area.

Future acceptance of "humanitarian intervention" is linked to a conceptual and practical capacity to reconcile its two conflicting halves. Running through the United Nations Charter are two contradictions: (i) sovereignty and human rights and (ii) peace and justice.

Explicit Charter provisions illustrate the first contradiction. Article 2, paragraph one, bases the organization on the principle of sovereign equality of all member states; paragraph four prohibits the threat or use of force against any state; and paragraph seven protects from UN intervention "matters which are essentially within the domestic jurisdiction of any state." At the same time, preceding these provisions are the first words of the Charter preamble: "We the Peoples of the United Nations determined. . . to reaffirm faith in fundamental human rights, in the dignity and worth of the human person, in the equal rights of men and women. . . ." Article 1(3) then states that "the Purposes of the United Nations are . . . to achieve international cooperation in solving international problems of an economic, social, cultural, or humanitarian character, and in promoting and encouraging respect for human rights and for fundamental freedoms for all without distinction as to race, sex, language, or religion." Under Articles 55 and 56 members are committed "to take joint and separate action in cooperation with the Organization" for the promotion of "equal rights and self-determination of peoples," including "universal respect for, and observance of, human rights." In Article 68, the Economic and Social Council "shall set up commissions . . . for the protection of human rights." Article 76(c) states that a basic objective of the trusteeship system is "to en-

courage respect for human rights and for fundamental freedoms for all. . . ."

The second contradiction is apparent in the following questions: Are human rights exclusively within the domestic jurisdiction of states or are they an international concern with community jurisdiction? What is the separation of powers? Should the prohibition on the threat or use of force against states be applicable to violence against human beings? Or, for that matter, is the threat or use of force against states permissible for the protection of human rights? Which authority is superior, state jurisdiction over individuals within its boundaries, or international jurisdiction over inalienable human rights?. . .

Whether values are universal or culturally or even individually specific is a question that emerged from the earliest human social relations. It is linked to the basic duality that divides all philosophy, religion, and ideology: diversity and unity, the individual and the collective. Despite these persisting dilemmas, there is not disagreement about whether in principle humanitarian intervention is acceptable. The crux of the issue is fear of abuse and how the danger can be mitigated to make the pill of intervention easier to swallow.

Swallowing is particularly difficult for Third World states. Their representatives draw obvious parallels to the unpalatable power of imperialists who intervened on the basis of "principles" such as "civilization," "white man's burden," and "manifest destiny." The fact that in the present international system those with the resources to intervene are former colonial powers or large and traditionally obtrusive neighbors does not facilitate discussion. Nonetheless, there are two starting points for dialogue—codification and decision making. The codification of objective criteria of the circumstances in which humanitarian intervention should be carried out and the type of operation it should be is the first premise. The second is that decisions about humanitarian intervention must be made exclusively on a genuinely collective basis.

Some authors have attempted to identify lists of objective criteria. Lillich enumerates five conditions that would validate humanitarian intervention: immediacy of violation of human rights; extent of violation of human rights; invitation to use forcible self-help; degree of coercive measures employed (i.e., proportionality); and relative disinterestedness of acting state. Moore adds five qualifications: an immediate and extensive threat to fundamental human rights, particularly a threat of widespread loss of human life; a proportional use of force which does not threaten greater destruction of values than the human rights at stake; a minimal effect on authority structures; a prompt disengagement, consistent with the purpose of the action; and immediate full reporting to the Security Council and appropriate regional organizations.

In the context of relief for man-made disasters, Minear has set down nine operational principles governing humanitarian assistance: recognition of the importance of safeguarding human life, including redefining its relationship with sovereignty; motives for assistance missions must be transparent to affirm legitimacy; response to assistance needs must be consistent in each case, and therefore automatic and not selective; assistance must be provided comprehensively to all categories of persons in need, and not according to artificial distinctions such as between "refugees" and "displaced persons"; success of assistance operations depends on local popular participation, or mutuality; civilian management is preferable for civilian humanitarian initiatives; increasing fidelity to international law; disaster prevention measures and methods of peaceful conflict resolution should be fostered to avoid the need for intervention after the fact; and there must be accountability by the assistance donor, as well as by host governments to their own populations.

An essential problem with codification that has re-emerged in the current debate, however, is the desirable degree of specificity: the enumeration of appropriate circumstances might exclude unforeseen situations requiring assistance which do not fall strictly within any agreed categories. As mentioned earlier, definitions cannot be exhaustive, nor can they be extensive without becoming too restrictive. At the same time, flexibility requires

general provisions, which are then open to abuse. The best way to overcome this dilemma and reduce the danger of abuse is to restrict humanitarian intervention exclusively to the category of collective action as understood in Chapter VII of the UN Charter. Prohibiting it as a form of self-help would circumvent the unreliability of unilateral interventions.

To circumscribe illegitimate justifications, the United Nations should have sole responsibility for determining the existence of humanitarian crises, in the manner that it has monopoly to "determine the existence of any threat to the peace, breach of the peace, or act of aggression" under Article 39. Furthermore, direction or conduct of humanitarian operations should be only a United Nations activity, ideally through Chapter VII of the Charter. In the absence of Article 43–47 agreements for a standing UN force and adequate military capacity, much greater thought needs to be given to clarifying the meanings of "collective action" and "subsidiary organ."

"Collective" must mean the subordination of command and control of sovereign armed forces to a centralized instrument, authorized to act by the larger community in the event of a crisis. Action through international organization, or multilateralism, is distinct from multinational action, which amounts to individual states independently cooperating in a particular venture, effectively as a form of self-help. Particularly, collective action is conducted according to standard operating procedures devised and agreed to prior to a crisis, and which are consistently applied whatever the configuration of subjective interests of community members. The importance of "collective" is not necessarily in the operation, which may be executed by one or two or many states, but in the decision to act as well as the continued direction of operation. Given the U.S.–led coalition's prosecution of the Gulf War and the lack of reporting once the decision to authorize "all necessary means" was taken, the nature of centralized command and control has assumed a greater importance. . . .

The erosion of sovereignty and the emergence of a human rights regime converge in the present decade, when it is finally possible to enforce growing recognition of individuals' rights of access to humanitarian aid, irrespective of their governments' permission.

Missing still, however, is what Third World representatives refer to as a lack of moral authority for humanitarian intervention. Recent thinkers have looked beyond sacrosanct sovereignty and the state toward social organization based on culture or society, defined in their widest senses. As these subvert sovereignty, we must better understand the human desire for absolutes, inherent in both individuals and communities. For us to transcend the dictates of sovereignty, we must articulate an ethical vision and so reshape human relations with authority.

While human needs do not as yet override sovereignty in all instances, the latest resolution of the General Assembly nonetheless takes a significant step along the path of establishing more rights for the afflicted. This process is a continuation of the

efforts by the ICRC to protect prisoners, the wounded, and innocent civilians from states during wartime. In the past few decades, humanitarian NGOs have taken matters into their own hands and resorted to cross-border operations, and intergovernmental organs have sought inroads in defining the rights of innocent civilians in war zones. But binding international legal instruments have not kept pace.

With the humanitarian intervention in Iraq and the recent debate at the United Nations, the international community appears perched on the brink of a new era. The international community is moving toward codification of principles and identification of the appropriate conditions under which humanitarian imperatives will override domestic jurisdiction. One million displaced persons in Yugoslavia and 20,000 civilians dead in Somalia are adequate testimony to the need for action.

Questions for Discussion

1. What role should morality play in foreign policy?
2. What criteria can be used to establish the moral dimension in foreign policy?
3. What accounts for the tension between the promotion of human rights and the promotion of the national interest?
4. Should the United States be selective, or principled, in its promotion of human rights abroad? What are the implications of each approach?
5. How can the U.S. commitment to morality in international relations be translated into direct action abroad? Indeed, should it?
6. Why is there often an inherent tension between the promotion of security and the advocacy of human rights?
7. How should the United States respond when elections threaten to replace un-

elected pro-Western leaders with elected anti-Western leaders whose commitment to liberal values—including democracy itself—is suspect at best and overtly hostile at worst?
8. As we enter the post-Cold War era, what moral considerations should influence the national security policy of the United States?

Selected Bibliography

CINGRANELLI, DAVID LOUIS. *Ethics, American Foreign Policy, and the Third World.* New York: St. Martin's Press, 1992.

DONNELLY, JACK. *Universal Human Rights in Theory and Practice.* Ithaca: Cornell University Press, 1989.

FORSYTHE, DAVID P. *Human Rights and U.S. Foreign Policy: Congress Reconsidered.* Gainesville, FL: University of Florida Press, 1988.

GONG, GERRIT W. *The Standard of 'Civilization' in International Society.* New York: Oxford University Press, 1984.

HOFFMANN, STANLEY. *Duties Beyond Borders.* Syracuse: Syracuse University Press, 1981.

JOHNSON, JAMES TURNER, AND GEORGE WEIGEL. *Just War and the Gulf War.* New York: Ethics and Public Policy Center, 1992.

JONES, DOROTHY V. *Code of Peace: Ethics and Security in the World of Warlord States.* Chicago: University of Chicago Press, 1991.

KOREY, WILLIAM. *The Promises We Keep: Human Rights, the Helsinki Process, and American Foreign Policy.* New York: St. Martin's Press.

LeFEVER, ERNEST. *Ethics and United States Foreign Policy.* Cleveland: Meridien Books, 1967.

McELROY, ROBERT W. *Morality and American Foreign Policy: The Role of Ethics in International Affairs.* Princeton: Princeton University Press, 1992.

NARDIN, TERRY. *Law, Morality, and the Relations of States.* Princeton: Princeton University Press, 1983.

NIEBUHR, REINHOLD. *Moral Man and Immoral Society.* New York: Scribner's, 1943.

OPPENHEIM, FELIX E. *The Place of Morality in Foreign Policy.* New York: Lexington Books, 1992.

PETTMANN, RALPH (ED.). *Moral Claims in World Affairs.* New York: St. Martin's Press, 1979.

PIPES DANIEL, AND ADAM GARFINKLE (EDS.). *Friendly Tyrants: An American Dilemma.* New York: St. Martin's Press, 1991.

SMITH, GADDIS. *Morality, Reason, and Power: American Diplomacy in the Carter Years.* New York: Hill & Wang, 1986.

CHAPTER 5

To Intervene or Not to Intervene

Intervention may be interpreted as interference in the internal or external affairs of a state; as coercive or noncoercive intrusion; or as a threat to elicit compliance. In truth, almost any international behavior, depending on the context and the analyst's criteria, can be regarded as intervention. In international relations the line where it begins is difficult to establish. As Talleyrand, a French foreign minister who served both Napoleon and the short-lived monarchy that followed his deposal, once artfully observed, "Nonintervention is a political and metaphysical term and means about the same thing as intervention." Each has consequences. By way of illustration, in April 1967, the U.S. government did nothing when a cabal of colonels seized power in Athens, a seeming acquiescence that alienated a substantial segment of the Greek population. According to a former CIA station chief in Athens, if the United States had privately but forcefully informed the junta that neither it "nor other NATO members would tolerate naked military dictatorship in a NATO country" and given them 30 days or so to hold new elections, it would have produced results: "Perhaps one moral of this story, for Americans at least, is that nonintervention in the internal affairs of others may sometimes have worse consequences than intervention. Neither, of course, is certain to bring desirable results. But the chances were good, I think, that we might have forestalled the 1967 coup if we had used a bit of our substantial leverage. . . ."[1] There was a similar occurrence with respect to the Philippines. In 1972, President Richard Nixon was supposedly alerted by Filipino President Ferdinand Marcos of his intention to declare martial law, yet Nixon did nothing to try to preserve democracy, the consequence being a 14-year dictatorship that bankrupted the country and ultimately weakened the special military-political relationship between the United States and the Philippines.[2]

Such affecting the outcome of events by doing nothing is the norm when the governments in question are, and are likely to remain, pro-American in their foreign policy orientation. U.S. Presidents have been reluctant to interfere in the domestic upheavals and power struggles of friendly states. Faced with a choice between speaking out against assaults on democracy, and in the process possibly alienating the new, dictatorial leaderships, or acquiescing to the imposition of dictatorship, they have, in the interest of continuing a stable relationship, opted for accommodation. Thus, Nixon and Carter catered to Marcos, Carter and Reagan courted Manuel Noriega, and so on. African dictatorships—in Liberia, Kenya, Sudan, Nigeria, among others—rarely occa-

1. John M. Maury. "The Greek Coup," *Washington Post*, May 1, 1977, p. C3.
2. See Raymond Bonner. *Waltzing with a Dictator: The Marcoses and the Making of American Policy.* New York: Times Books, 1987, passim.

sion criticism from the U.S. government or members of Congress, for this reason and because African-American leaders have generally been reluctant to criticize African leadership.

On the other hand, during the Cold War, U.S. Presidents deliberately intervened in the domestic affairs of unfriendly, pro-Soviet regimes whenever it was possible, by funneling assistance and arms to anti-communist insurgencies, for example, in Afghanistan, Angola, and Nicaragua. The aim was the weakening, eventual overthrow, and replacement of the regime by another one prepared to improve relations with the United States. Arming insurgencies was a form of low-level warfare that was engaged in by the United States (and the Soviet Union) with willing proxies. The intervention was indirect, covert, and limited; it was deemed a cost-effective way of draining the resources and diverting the attention of a prime adversary from strategically more important areas.

Overall, old-style, direct intervention involving a resort to force is less favored and less frequent. In the post-1945 era of decolonization, democratization, and interdependency, a number of systemic developments have made direct intervention more difficult: first, the growth of nationalism has given new and vulnerable states the impetus for stiff resistance to invasion; second, during the 1955–1990 period, the Soviet Union armed anti-Western regimes, thereby strengthening their capacity to counter Western threats; third, the diffusion of advanced weaponry has reduced the number of completely weak states and expanded the costs of intrusiveness to great powers, as the United States discovered in Vietnam and the Soviet Union in Afghanistan; fourth, "there has been a weakening in the Western

world of the will to intervene, by comparison with earlier periods"; finally, "the emergence of a new climate of international legitimacy" has profoundly changed "the moral and legal notions of the justification of intervention."[3]

There is another reason, in the case of the United States, for a much-increased reluctance to intervene directly in the domestic affairs of other countries, namely, the Vietnam syndrome, the impact of America's tragic and costly involvement in South Vietnam in the decade between 1962 and 1972. Unhappily, from the beginning of the commitment of U.S. combat forces "there was no agreement on what was at stake and which U.S. vital interests, if any, were involved. Limited military means were gradually introduced because victory in the classical sense was not sought and the war's relevance to the national interest was clouded at best. The U.S. domestic political environment was to a large extent ignored, and the failure of existing U.S. strategic doctrine led to a commitment the American people were not prepared to fully support."[4] It took the American people more than a decade to overcome the aversion to using force abroad in regional situations that did not unmistakably affect the vital security of the United States itself.

The Vietnam experience was to go a long way toward focusing public attention on the circumstances under which the military forces of the United States should be used in conflicts abroad. In the ongoing debate since the last American combat unit left Vietnam in 1972, the concept of intervention

3. Hedley Bull (Ed.). *Intervention in World Politics.* Oxford: Clarendon Press, 1984, pp. 138–140, 146.
4. David T. Twining. "The Weinberger Doctrine and the Use of Force in the Contemporary Era," *Small Wars & Insurgencies*, vol. 1, no. 2, August 1990, p. 101.

is assumed to entail the direct and overt deployment of U.S. troops on behalf of a friend or ally for a clear political purpose. The risk of escalating conflict or of confrontation with a third party is implicit. Intervention is issue-specific or time-specific, the assumption being that the deployment of troops is for a relatively short time only. Its significance generally inheres in the intensive concern that it manifests for a client's security, possibly for his very survival, as in the case of Kuwait. But clashes of personality or a pattern of minor provocations may also trigger an intervention, as was the case in Bush's invasion of Panama in December 1989 to overthrow Manuel Noriega.

The difficult and multifaceted phenomenon of intervention is viewed in historical perspective by Max Beloff (Reading 12). He notes (writing in 1968) that the United States has lurched from one military crisis or intervention to another, without a theory of intervention to guide it.

During the Reagan administration the debate grew heated, in part because of the mutual antipathy between the two leading members of the Cabinet, and spilled over into the public arena. Secretary of Defense Caspar Weinberger insisted that six tests be met before U.S. troops were committed to combat (Reading 13). Secretary of State George Shultz, however, defended the necessity of using force in situations other than those meeting the tests (Reading 14). The differences in nuance reflected substantive disagreements. Both scrupulously avoided involving President Reagan in their highly public dispute. Weinberger wanted to protect the military, to make sure it was not again sent, as it had been in Vietnam, into combat without a clear sense of mission and full political backing by the government and the country. The invasion of Grenada in October 1983, the U.S. Navy's successful interception of the terrorists who hijacked the Italian cruise ship, *Achille Lauro*, in October 1985, and the U.S. raid on Libya in April 1986 as punishment for terrorist acts in Rome and Berlin, these were missions that met Weinberger's stringent tests. He deplored Shultz's commitment of U.S. marines to a peacekeeping operation in Lebanon in 1982–1983, where the objectives were vague and often changed and where, tragically, 241 marines were killed in a terrorist attack on their barracks in Beirut. For his part, Shultz argued for a more flexible approach to the use of force in a wider range of situations (though he, somewhat surprisingly, opposed the raid on Libya). He believed that "a great nation with global responsibilities cannot afford to be hamstrung by confusion and indecisiveness" and that democracies must show that they believed in themselves, by which he meant the United States should be prepared to use its power to advance the cause of freedom.

Since history does not repeat itself, no two instances of intervention or nonintervention are ever exactly alike. Details are often crucial in explaining why force was used on one occasion but not on another. Let us look briefly at U.S. policy toward Panama and Haiti. Tensions between Washington and Noriega were high all through 1989. In October, Bush refused to come to the assistance of a group of officers who tried to topple Noriega, but two months later he ordered a full-scale invasion of Panama, giving three reasons for his action: to safeguard American lives, to defend democracy in Panama, and to defend the integrity of the Panama Canal treaty. Objectively, U.S.-Panamanian tensions were no greater in December than they had been in October; but subjectively, Bush may have decided to act after an American soldier was killed by Noriega's police. In October 1991, Jean-Bertrand Aristide, the democratically elected president of Haiti, was ousted by a military coup. He has received sympathy and favorable declarations from Washington, the Organization of American States, and the U.N. Security Council—but not the military force to restore him to office. Why the use of U.S. forces against Noriega, but not on behalf of Aristide, whose regime was itself guilty of human rights violations? Is the reason to be found in the absence of a direct American involvement, in the absence of a palpable U.S. interest? Should the United States intervene to restore democracy? What of interventions for humanitarian purposes (see Reading 11), as occurred in the waning weeks of the Bush administration, when the United States sent troops to Somalia to help feed starving people? Many in the media strongly urge such interventions and ask, if Somalia, then why not Bosnia as well (Reading 15). In September 1992, when Les Aspin was in Congress, he argued that if force was to be used it should be directed against Saddam Hussein because the United States has vital interests in what happens in Iraq, but not in Bosnia (Reading 16). It will be interesting to see what position he takes as Clinton's Secretary of Defense.

The position that the United States bears some kind of responsibility to intervene in order to right the injustices of this world is deplored by Doug Bandow, a Senior Fellow at the Cato Institute (Reading 17). The maintenance of a large military establishment and the taxation required to sustain it are, in his view, detrimental to U.S. liberties and the growth of America's economy. Intervention is a costly affair and, to paraphrase Bismarck, is not worth the bones of one American soldier. Accord-

ingly, Bandow advocates a "hands off policy," "a policy of benign detachment."

What, then to do?
To intervene, or not to intervene,—that is the question;
Whether 'tis better for one's national interest and the cause of international peace and stability to suffer
The upheavals and coups that remove from power leaders friendly to us
Or to intervene, and prevent those hostile to us from entering office,
and by so doing to make sure that those hostile to us do not succeed.

Not to intervene,—to watch,—
No more; and by not intervening to accept
The heartache and the thousand inevitable shocks
That hostile regimes must inevitably inflict on us.
To watch! To wait! To accept that forces may be set in motion that will cause us grief and trouble and uncertainty for years to come—
All this must give us pause: Do we submit with equanimity to the process that may bring us calamity;
Or do we intervene, though by so doing we incur the wrath of critics and the disillusionment of our idealistic citizenry;
But there is a dread of intervention—
And this dread makes us rather bear those ills we know will surely come from nonintervention
Thus does constraint make noninterventionists of us;

And thus the native hue of resolution and purposefulness and defense of interests
Is sicklied over with the pale brew of idealism, irresolution, and doubting conscience;

And broader goals of great scope and
   promise fade from view
and dissipate
and lose the impetus to action

To intervene, or not to intervene:
We mean well, but do ill, and justify our
   ill-doing by our well-meaning
Which, then?

12.   Reflections on Intervention

Max Beloff

The indignation which the *modern* practice of intervention arouses in the United States is not due to the novelty of the event, but is the result of a still powerful Wilsonian political philosophy. Woodrow Wilson and his successors saw the world as ideally composed of equally sovereign and impermeable political communities, and they based the League of Nations and the United Nations on the assumption that the real coincided with the ideal. This idealistic misconception, moreover, was the result of a confusion of the subject matter of modern international law—self-contained sovereign states—and the subject matter of international relations, which is a far more complex thing. The contemporary resentment toward interventionist politics, then, is not so much due to the novelty of intervention, for intervention is a recurrent feature of the system, but is a result of the aberrations implicit in Wilsonianism.

It is plain that intervention, loaded with normative overtones and plagued by misconceptions, is a difficult concept to analyze. . . . Several observations about intervention may be drawn from Western historical experience. First, it is obvious from Western history that intervention is one of the instruments employed in *any* competitive international system. Thucydides begins his history of the Peloponnesian War with an account of Corcyra's attempt to reinstall the exiled oligarchs of Epidamnus and the counterintervention of the Corinthians.

SOURCE: Max Beloff. "Reflections on Intervention," *Journal of International Affairs*, vol. XXII, no 2, 1968, pp. 198–207, excerpts. Published by permission of the *Journal of International Affairs* and the Trustees of Columbia University in the City of New York.

It is indeed clear that the Greek city-states exploited civil strife to further their own policies, and that political parties existed within the Greek states which depended, or came to depend, upon "foreign" support.

Secondly, intervention clearly becomes more frequent, as well as more dangerous, when party divisions or religious-ideological passions give states automatic access to the sympathies of partisan groups in other states. The struggle between Guelph and Ghibelline in Florence is the most celebrated example of a political party division that led to intervention. Both the invasion of the Spanish Armada, which followed thirty years of almost unceasing intervention by Catholic Spain in the internal affairs of England, Scotland, and France, and the Thirty Years War, when both Catholic and Protestant forces engaged in intervention in Germany on a scale unequalled until the wars of the French Revolution, are notable examples of intervention caused by religious passions.

Thirdly, the wars of the Revolutionary period, the subsequent interventions of the anti-revolutionary Holy Alliance, and Russian intervention during the Revolutions of 1848 make it plain that basic *social* and *political* differences among members of a multi-state system result in conflicts of ideologies and interests. This will, in turn, give rise to the politics of intervention. Thus, Russian policy between 1815 and 1914 was influenced by the desire to defend the monarchical principle as much as by any other aspect of the "national interest." British policy under Palmerston, and more circumspectly later on, was similarly influenced by ideology and national interest. The British desire that constitutional government should prevail, for example, influenced British policy toward the Iberian peninsula and Italy, and affected both of their subsequent political histories. Differing ideological ambitions, as much as any other aspect of their national interest, influenced both Russian and British policies toward intervention throughout the nineteenth century, and gave rise to the politics of competitive interference that characterized Anglo-Russian relations.

This may seem to be laboring a fairly obvious point, but it is necessary to do so to make it clear that when Lenin, Trotsky, and their successors appealed to the working classes of the capitalist countries or the subjects of colonial empires to rise and overthrow their rulers, and then provided them with money and armed force, they were doing nothing that governments before them had not done. Indeed, the Kaiser's government had intervened in Russia's affairs with the financial assistance it had given the Bolsheviks. And while it is true that the motives of the British, French and Americans in the "intervention" in Russia, 1918–1920, were more confused than Soviet historiography allows, it cannot be denied that the Allied forces were trying to bring about a regime in Russia that they preferred to that of the Bolsheviks. And yet at the same time the Bolsheviks were trying to overthrow the Allied governments. . . .

Modern nations tend to judge the practice of intervention by an examination of the means and ends, apparently disregarding ideological sympathies. The West has, for example, ruled out assassination as a method of intervention, although assassination was used during the Counter Reformation in Europe and is now used in some Asian countries. More rigorous criteria of suitable means may be established. For example, one may rule out all armed force and recognize the legitimacy only of peaceful intervention through propaganda or financial assistance, or anything other than overt propaganda may be regarded as over the permissible threshold.

More importantly, however, modern nations have distinguished between genuine national interest and ideological ambitions in formulating and judging interventionist policies. The criterion used to determine national interest in an interventionist situation is *comparative risk*: it is unwise to intervene where the risk involved entails an even greater evil than the one the intervention is intended to prevent. For example, the West's fear that a general war would escalate into a nuclear war caused it not to intervene to assist the Hungarian uprising of 1956 (although it would be hard to think of a case where the other arguments for intervening were more compelling).

Comparative risk or its synonym, *limited liability*, also suggests that there is a little reason to intervene in a situation where the likelihood of success is marginal and the penalties for failure fall on one's allies. The Bay of Pigs fiasco is the best example of this. The limited liability criterion avoids all the apparatus of deception involved in the Bay of Pigs affair and judges the debacle for the failure it was. Intervention, like most other political actions, takes on a very different appearance according to whether it succeeds or fails, for victors write history. This line of argument is bound to be regarded in some quarters as an example of old-world cynicism, but it should not be abandoned on that account—much of the harm in the world has been done by the high-minded.

According to this criterion (comparative risk or limited liability), rapid and easy success *alone* justifies intervention. If this is an acceptable statement, then we may have established a standard which will help us to judge the legitimacy of future cases of intervention. . . .

The United States' task in positive intervention is more difficult than the Marxists' because the Americans would like to see a highly complex social order universally established. But the United States has not yet successfully discovered, either in theoretical or empirical studies, the preconditions of this desired social order (at least not to our intellectual satisfaction). A self-sustaining democratic form of government, able to meet popular demands for rising levels of consumption without the use of more than a minimum of social coercion, is not a norm of human organization, as Wilsonian theory seems to have assumed, but a highly artificial and fragile growth, easy to destroy and very hard to foster. . . .

Latter-day Wilsonians, including Franklin Delano Roosevelt, his advisers, and many recent American policy-makers, have had a worldview which proclaimed the democratic system as the norm. Since all departures from the norm required particular explanations, these latter-day Wilsonians saw most of the world outside Europe as a vast area under alien colonial rule, which they assumed prevented the emergence of full-fledged democratic societies. They believed that if the European overseas empires were swept away, the new nations would emerge in full glory and happily cooperate in the *Pax Americana*. Let the American Prince kiss the Sleeping Beauty, the spell would be removed, and the enchanted palace come to life again.

It was not like that at all. American action, some of which could certainly be called intervention, encouraged the empires to disappear, but the Sleeping Beauty has not shown much appreciation of the lavish gifts with which the American Prince endowed her. For the truth is that it was not the empires that caused the weakness of the ex-colonial peoples as much as their weakness that had given rise to the empires.

America most needs a coherent theory of intervention in dealing with the underdeveloped world. Some of the newly emergent peoples, if given support against other nations' intervention and if *not* propelled along unfamiliar paths in the name of development, democracy, or the latest fad from outside, may be able to build viable institutions. Some may even be able to build systems not too remote from the democratic model. For many, however, the post-imperial phase will merely be a transition to a new colonial era.

It is endlessly surprising, as one studies American experience over the last two decades in Asia and Africa, to see how little the United States has learned from the object lesson provided by Latin America. After nearly a century and one-half of independence, Latin America still shows little if any sign of following the North American model, and United States' intervention in Latin America since the Platt Amendment has almost always proved counterproductive. If it has proved impossible to manipulate a civilization with many of the same roots in European pioneering as the United States itself, how can one expect that Asian and African societies, belonging to quite different cultures, will respond to American guidance? . . . The West may put a high value on racial equality and democratic liberties and be prepared to make supreme sacrifices for them, but there must be some restraint on what may be imposed upon other peoples for ideal ends. The Soviets long ago ceased intervening to pursue purely ideological goals. As for the West, anyone who says "better dead than Red" has all one's admiration, but this is not a choice one can make for others.

If we are to consider intervention seriously we must first clear our minds of cant, and above all, of the rhetoric of Wilsonian idealism. Too many people act from a strictly moral position before they have either ascertained the relevant facts or acquired the intellectual apparatus to deal with them.

The United States may be doomed to continue intervening abroad by virtue of its size, interests, and vulnerability, but if it is to avoid humiliations it badly needs a theory of intervention.

13. On the Need for Restraint in Using Military Power

Caspar Weinberger

Under what circumstances, and by what means, does a great democracy such as the United States reach the painful decision that the use of military force is necessary to protect our interests or to carry out our national policy? . . .

Alexander Hamilton, writing in the Federalist Papers, said that 'it is impossible to foresee or define the extent and variety of national exigencies, or the correspondent extent and variety of the means which may be necessary to satisfy them.' If it was true then, how much more true it is today, when we must remain ready to consider the means to meet such serious indirect challenges to the peace as proxy wars and individual terrorist action. And how much more important is it now, considering the consequences of failing to deter conflict at the lowest level possible. While the use of military force to defend territory has never been questioned when a democracy has been attacked and its very survival threatened, most democracies have rejected the unilateral aggressive use of force to invade, conquer or subjugate other nations. The extent to which the use of force is acceptable remains unresolved for the host of other situations which fall between these extremes of defensive and aggressive use of force.

We find ourselves, then, face to face with a modern paradox: The most likely challenge to the peace—the gray area conflicts—are precisely the most difficult challenges to which a democracy must respond. Yet, while the source and nature of today's challenges are uncertain, our response must be clear and understandable. Unless we are certain that force is essential, we run the risk of inadequate national will to apply the resources needed.

Because we face a spectrum of threats—from covert aggression, terrorism, and subversion, to

SOURCE: Caspar Weinberger is former Secretary of Defense. November 28, 1984.

overt intimidation, to use of brute force—choosing the appropriate level of our response is difficult. Flexible response does not mean just any response is appropriate. But once a decision to employ some degree of force has been made, and the purpose clarified, our government must have the clear mandate to carry out, and continue to carry out, that decision until the purpose has been achieved. That, too, has been difficult to accomplish.

The issue of which branch of government has authority to define that mandate and make decisions on using force is now being strongly contended. Beginning in the 1970s Congress demanded, and assumed, a far more active role in the making of foreign policy and in the decision-making process for the employment of military forces abroad than had been thought appropriate and practical before. As a result, the centrality of decision-making authority in the executive branch has been compromised by the legislative branch to an extent that actively interferes with that process. At the same time, there has not been a corresponding acceptance of responsibility by Congress for the outcome of decisions concerning the employment of military forces.

Yet the outcome of decisions on whether—and when—and to what degree—to use combat forces abroad has never been more important than it is today. While we do not seek to deter or settle all the world's conflicts, we must recognize that, as a major power, our responsibilities and interests are now of such scope that there are few troubled areas we can afford to ignore. So we must be prepared to deal with a range of possibilities, a spectrum of crises, from local insurgency to global conflict. We prefer, of course, to limit any conflict in its early stages, to contain and control it—but to do that our military forces must be deployed in a timely manner, and be fully supported and prepared before they are engaged, because many of those difficult decisions must be made extremely quickly.

Some on the national scene think they can always avoid making tough decisions. Some reject entirely the question of whether any force can ever be used abroad. They want to avoid grappling with a complex issue because, despite clever rhetoric disguising their purpose, these people are in fact advocating a return to post-World War I isolationism. While they may maintain in principle that military force has a role in foreign policy, they are never willing to name the circumstance or the place where it would apply.

On the other side, some theorists argue that military force can be brought to bear in any crisis. Some of these proponents of force are eager to advocate its use even in limited amounts simply because they believe that if there are American forces of any size present they will somehow solve the problem.

Neither of these two extremes offers us any lasting or satisfactory solutions. The first—undue reserve—would lead us ultimately to withdraw from international events that require free nations to defend their interests from the aggressive use of force. We would be abdicating our responsibilities as the leader of the Free World—responsibilities more or less thrust upon us in the aftermath of World War II—a war incidentally that isolationism did nothing to deter. These are responsibilities we must fulfill unless we desire the Soviet Union to keep expanding its influence unchecked throughout the world. In an international system based on mutual interdependence among nations, and alliances between friends, stark isolationism quickly would lead to a far more dangerous situation for the United States: we would be without allies and faced by many hostile or indifferent nations.

The second alternative—employing our forces almost indiscriminately and as a regular and customary part of our diplomatic efforts—would surely plunge us headlong into the sort of domestic turmoil we experienced during the Vietnam War, without accomplishing the goal for which we committed our forces. Such policies might very well tear at the fabric of our society, endangering the single most critical element of a successful democracy: a strong consensus of support and agreement for our basic purposes.

Policies formed without a clear understanding of what we hope to achieve would also earn us the scorn of our troops, who would have an understandable opposition to being used—in every sense of the word—casually and without intent to support them fully. Ultimately this course would reduce their morale and their effectiveness for engagements we must win. . . .

In maintaining our progress in strengthening America's military deterrent, we face difficult challenges. For we have entered an era where the dividing lines between peace and war are less clearly drawn, the identity of the foe is much less clear. . . .

In today's world where minutes count, . . . decisive leadership is more important than ever before. Regardless of whether conflicts are limited, or threats are ill-defined, we must be capable of quickly determining that the threats and conflicts either do or do not affect the vital interests of the United States and our allies . . . and then responding appropriately.

Those threats may not entail an immediate, direct attack on our territory, and our response may not necessarily require the immediate or direct defense of our homeland. But when our vital national interests and those of our allies are at stake, we cannot ignore our safety, or forsake our allies.

At the same time, recent history has proven that we cannot assume unilaterally the role of the world's defender. We have learned that there are limits to how much of our spirit and blood and treasure we can afford to forfeit in meeting our responsibility to keep peace and freedom. So while we may and should offer substantial amounts of economic and military assistance to our allies in their time of need and help them maintain forces to deter attacks against them—usually we cannot substitute our troops or our will for theirs.

We should only engage our troops if we must do so as a matter of our own vital national interest. We cannot assume for other sovereign nations the responsibility to defend their territory—without their strong invitation—when our own freedom is not threatened.

On the other hand, there have been recent cases where the United States has seen the need to join forces with other nations to try to preserve the peace by helping with negotiations, and by separating warring parties, and thus enabling those warring nations to withdraw from hostilities safely. In the Middle East, which has been torn by conflict for millennia, we have sent our troops in recent years both to the Sinai and to Lebanon, for just such a peacekeeping mission. But we did not configure or equip those forces for combat—they were armed only for their self-defense. Their mission required them to be—and to be recognized as—peacekeepers. We knew that if conditions deteriorated so they were in danger, or if because of the actions of the warring nations, their peacekeeping mission could not be realized, then it would be necessary either to add sufficiently to the number and arms of our troops—in short to equip them for combat . . . or to withdraw them. And so in Lebanon, when we faced just such a choice, because the warring nations did not enter into withdrawal or peace agreements, the President properly withdrew forces equipped only for peacekeeping.

In those cases where our national interests require us to commit combat forces, we must never let there be doubt of our resolution. When it is necessary for our troops to be committed to combat, we must commit them in sufficient numbers and we must support them, as effectively and resolutely as our strength permits. When we commit our troops to combat we must do so with the sole objective of winning.

Once it is clear our troops are required, because our vital interests are at stake, then we must have the firm national resolve to commit every ounce of strength necessary to win the fight to achieve our objectives. In Grenada we did just that.

Just as clearly, there are other situations where United States combat forces should not be used. I believe the postwar period has taught us several lessons, and from them I have developed six major tests to be applied when we are weighing the use of US combat forces abroad. Let me now share them with you:

First, the United States should not commit forces to combat overseas unless the particular engagement or occasion is deemed vital to our national interest or that of our allies. That emphatically does not mean that we should declare beforehand, as we did with Korea in 1950, that a particular area is outside our strategic perimeter.

Second, if we decide it is necessary to put combat troops into a given situation, we should do so wholeheartedly, and with the clear intention of winning. If we are unwilling to commit the forces or resources necessary to achieve our objectives, we should not commit them at all. Of course if the particular situation requires only limited force to win our objectives, then we should not hesitate to commit forces sized accordingly. When Hitler broke treaties and remilitarized the Rhineland, small combat forces then could perhaps have prevented the Holocaust of World War II.

Third, if we do decide to commit forces to combat overseas, we should have clearly defined political and military objectives. And we should know precisely how our forces can accomplish those clearly defined objectives. And we should have and send the forces needed to do just that. As Clausewitz wrote, 'No one starts a war—or rather, no one in his senses ought to do so—without first being clear in his mind what he intends to achieve by that war, and how he intends to conduct it.'

War may be different today than in Clausewitz's time, but the need for well-defined objectives and a consistent strategy is still essential. If we determine that a combat mission has become necessary for our vital national interests, then we must send forces capable to do the job—and not assign a combat mission to a force configured for peacekeeping.

Fourth, the relationship between our objectives and the forces we have committed—their size, composition and disposition—must be continually reassessed and adjusted if necessary. Conditions and objectives invariably change during the course of a conflict. When they do change, then so must our combat requirements. We must continuously keep as a beacon light before us the basic questions: 'Is this conflict in our national interests?' 'Does our national interest require us to fight, to use force of arms?' If the answers are 'yes', then we must win. If the answers are 'no', then we should not be in combat.

Fifth, before the US commits combat forces abroad,

there must be some reasonable assurance we will have the support of the American people and their elected representatives in Congress. This support cannot be achieved unless we are candid in making clear the threats we face; the support cannot be sustained without continuing and close consultation. We cannot fight a battle with the Congress at home while asking our troops to win a war overseas or, as in the case of Vietnam, in effect asking our troops not to win, but just to be there.

Finally, the commitment of US forces to combat should be a last resort.

I believe that these tests can be helpful in deciding whether or not we should commit our troops to combat in the months and years ahead. The point we must all keep uppermost in our minds is that if we ever decide to commit forces to combat, we must support those forces to the fullest extent of our national will for as long as it takes to win. So we must have in mind objectives that are clearly defined and understood and supported by the widest possible number of our citizens. And those objectives must be vital to our survival as a free nation and to the fulfillment of our responsibilities as a world power. We must also be farsighted enough to sense when immediate and strong reactions to apparently small events can prevent lion-like responses that may be required later. We must never forget those isolationists in Europe who shrugged that 'Danzig is not worth a war,' and 'why should we fight to keep the Rhineland demilitarized?'

These tests I have just mentioned have been phrased negatively for a purpose—they are intended to sound a note of caution—caution that we must observe prior to committing forces to combat overseas. When we ask our military forces to risk their very lives in such situations, a note of caution is not only prudent, it is morally required.

In many situations we may apply these tests and conclude that a combatant role is not appropriate. Yet no one should interpret what I am saying here today as an abdication of America's responsibilities—either to its own citizens or to its allies. Nor should these remarks be misread as a signal that this country, or this Administration, is unwilling to commit forces to combat overseas.

We have demonstrated in the past that, when our vital interests or those of our allies are threatened, we are ready to use force, and use it decisively, to protect those interests. Let no one entertain any illusions—if our vital interests are involved, we are prepared to fight. And we are resolved that if we must fight, we must win.

So, while these tests are drawn from lessons we have learned from the past, they also can—and should—be applied to the future. For example, the problems confronting us in Central America today are difficult. The possibility of more extensive Soviet and Soviet-proxy penetration into this hemisphere in months ahead is something we should recognize. If this happens we will clearly need more economic and military assistance and training to help those who want democracy.

The President will not allow our military to creep—or be drawn gradually—into a combat role in Central America or any other place in the world. And indeed our policy is designed to prevent the need for direct American involvement. This means we will need sustained congressional support to back and give confidence to our friends in the region.

I believe that the tests I have enunciated here today can, if applied carefully, avoid the danger of this gradualist incremental approach which almost always means the use of insufficient force. These tests can help us to avoid being drawn inexorably into an endless morass, where it is not vital to our national interest to fight.

But polities and principles such as these require decisive leadership in both the executive and legislative branches of government—and they also require strong and sustained public support. Most of all, these policies require national unity of purpose. . . .

14.   On the Importance of Using Military Power

George Shultz

The Talmud addresses a fundamental issue that this nation has wrestled with ever since we became a great power with international responsibilities: How to judge when the use of our power is right and when it is wrong. The Talmud upholds the universal law of self-defense, saying, "If one comes to kill you, make haste and kill him first." Clearly, as long as threats exist, law-abiding nations have the right and indeed the duty to protect themselves.

The use of force must always be a last resort, when other means of influence have proven inadequate. But a great power cannot free itself so easily from the burden of choice. It must bear responsibility for the consequences of its inaction as well as for the consequences of its action.

The lesson [of Lebanon] is that power and diplomacy are not alternatives. They must go together, or we will accomplish very little in this world. The relationship between them is a complex one, and it presents us with both practical and moral issues.

Of course, any use of force involves moral issues. American military power should be resorted to only if the stakes justify it, if other means are not available, and then only in a manner appropriate to the objective. But we cannot opt out of every contest. If we do, the world's future will be determined by others—most likely by those who are the most brutal, the most unscrupulous and the most hostile to our deeply held principles.

Terrorism is a contagious disease that will inevitably spread if it goes untreated. We need a strategy to cope with terrorism in all of its varied manifestations. We need to summon the necessary resources and determination to fight it and, with international cooperation, eventually stamp it out.

SOURCE: From speeches to Yeshiva University in New York on December 9, Park Avenue Synagogue in New York on October 25, and the Trilateral Commission in Washington on April 3, 1984. George Shultz is former Secretary of State.

And we have to recognize that the burden falls on us, the democracies. No one else will cure the disease for us.

We have to be stronger, steadier, determined and united in the face of the terrorist threat. We must not reward the terrorists by changing our policies or questioning our own principles or wallowing in self-flagellation or self-doubt. Instead, we should understand that terrorism is aggression and, like all aggression, must be forcefully resisted.

We must reach a consensus in this country that our responses should go beyond passive defense to consider means of active prevention, preemption and retaliation. Our goal must be to prevent and deter future terrorist acts; and experience has taught us over the years that one of the best deterrents to terrorism is the certainty that swift and sure measures will be taken against those who engage in it. We should take steps toward carrying out such measures. There should be no moral confusion on this issue.

What will be required, however, is public understanding *before the fact* of the risks involved in combating terrorism with overt power.

The public must understand *before the fact* that there is potential for loss of life of some of our fighting men and the loss of life of some innocent people.

The public must understand *before the fact* that some will seek to cast any pre-emptive or retaliatory action by us in the worst light and will attempt to make our military and our policymakers—rather than the terrorists—appear to be the culprits.

The public must understand *before the fact* that occasions will come when their government must act before each and every fact is known—and the decisions cannot be tied to the opinion poll.

The prerequisite for such a policy must be a broad public consensus on the moral and strategic necessity of action. We will need the capability to act on a moment's notice. There will not be time for a renewed national debate after every terrorist attack. We may never have the kind of evidence that can stand up in an American court of law. But we cannot allow ourselves to become the Hamlet of nations, worrying endlessly over whether and how to respond.

A great nation with global responsibilities cannot afford to be hamstrung by confusion and indecisiveness. Fighting terrorism will not be a clean or pleasant contest, but we have no choice but to play it.

15.   The Case for U.S. Intervention: If Somalia, Then Why Not Bosnia?

Trudy Rubin

There is something cockeyed about official U.S. explanations of why intervention is right in Somalia but wrong in Bosnia. Secretary of Defense Dick Cheney says Bosnia is "dramatically different" from Somalia and it would be "inappropriate" to send U.S. ground troops into Bosnia. Secretary of State Lawrence Eagleburger, who equates Bosnia with quagmire, says about Somalia: "This is one that we could do something about."

The implication is that we can do nothing about Bosnia, that our only option there is to send in the Marines, which would be a mission doomed to failure. But no one is suggesting such an option; No critics of U.S. policy toward Yugoslavia are asking the U.S. to send ground forces into that maelstrom.

On the other hand, the United States *can* "do something about" stopping the slaughter in Bosnia.

For starters, the Bush administration could explain to the American public why resolving the Bosnian issue is so important, much more so than the Somalian disaster. In Somalia, the issue is purely humanitarian, saving millions who are starving due to anarchy in their country.

In Bosnia, issue goes beyond the purely human-

itarian. It has become a security issue for Europe. Moreover, in Bosnia the killing of civilians is a deliberate policy of ethnic purification, not the result of anarchy. Taking a stand against such slaughter becomes a key question of principle for all who espouse a peaceful post-Cold War era.

Today in Bosnia, Serbs are massively shelling civilians in Sarajevo and are poised to capture the whole city. Muslim civilians are being raped, tortured, murdered and driven out en masse purely because they are Muslims, whom Bosnian Serbs want to "cleanse" from their territory to make a pure Serbian Christian state.

If unopposed by the world community, this practice could spread to other countries in Europe where virulent nationalism is resurgent. If unchallenged, Serb aggression could ignite fighting in much of the Balkans. That means political and economic instability and more refugees in Europe which is bad for America, too.

The Pentagon response is that America can do nothing. Joint Chiefs of Staff chairman Gen. Colin Powell only wants to send troops where America can "win," like in Kuwait, or achieve "decisive results," as he hopes to do in Somalia.

But what's needed in Bosnia is not a military "defeat" of the Serbs. Rather, the West must take a stand against the practice of "ethnic cleansing,"—by Serbs or anyone else. And it must compel Serbs

SOURCE: Trudy Rubin. "The Case for U.S. Intervention: If Somalia, Then Why Not Bosnia?" *Philadelphia Inquirer* (December 11, 1992). Reprinted with permission by *The Philadelphia Inquirer*.

to sit down in good faith to negotiate a peaceful solution with Muslims and Croats in the former Yugoslavia.

European nations should have taken the lead in this process. They have failed miserably. So have U.N. peacekeepers in Bosnia, who haven't the arms or the mandate to stop Serbs from dirty work. Even the U.N. general in charge of peacekeeping forces in Sarejevo is now calling for international military help.

The situation cries out for the United States to play the role of catalyst (just what President Bush prescribed for America in Somalia), prodding the Europeans to do what they should have done long ago and pressing NATO to take military action under a U.N. umbrella. The list of possible actions is long. The most urgent are as follows:

- Before considering military intervention, Western nations should pay attention to Serbian elections scheduled for Dec. 20.

  Milan Panic, the Serbian-American prime minister of Yugoslavia who wants to stop the fighting, is challenging the chief Yugoslav villain, Serb president Slobodan Milosevic, for his office. Polls show them running neck and neck, reflecting Serb popular weariness with the fighting and the U.N. economic embargo.

  Bush should address the Serbs, emphasizing that America has no quarrel with them, only with their misguided nationalist leaders. He should pledge U.S. support for the international protection of all minorities in the republics of ex-Yugoslavia, including Serbs living in Bosnia and Croatia. Western nations should send monitors to Serbia to help ensure fair election results.

- If Panic loses, NATO should threaten air strikes against Bosnian Serb artillery sites and bases unless Serbs cease their assault on Sarajevo and their "ethnic cleansing" operations. NATO planes should prevent Bosnian Serb planes from violating the U.N. ban on overflights. If U.N. peacekeeping troops on the ground fear retaliation from Serb gunners, they should leave.

- The U.N. embargo should be lifted on arms sales to the Bosnian government. Serbs have huge stocks of guns from the ex-Yugoslav army. But the Bosnian Muslims—the chief victims—have few heavy weapons to defend themselves, one key reason why Sarajevo may fall.

- The United Nations should warn Serbs of military retaliation if fighting spreads to Kosovo, where 1.8 million ethnic Albanians fear "ethnic cleansing."

  War in Kosovo could spill over to Macedonia, Albania, Greece, Bulgaria and Turkey. To help prevent that, U.N. peacekeepers should be dispatched quickly to Macedonia. Serbian leaders should be pressured to let U.N. troops into Kosovo, too.

None of these steps involves sending U.S. ground troops into Bosnia. Nor do they meet Gen. Powell's criteria that they be guaranteed to produce decisive results.

But if America can't take a firm stand against the practice of "ethnic cleansing," it should abandon any pretense of global leadership. Bosnia is more typical of foreign crises America will have to deal with in the future than Somalia. Ignoring it will only encourage similar mayhem elsewhere in Europe. The Pentagon should start rethinking the criteria for U.S. intervention. Now.

16.   We Have More at Stake in Iraq Than Bosnia

Les Aspin

The suffering and human tragedy in Bosnia-Her-zegovina has led many Americans, including many who opposed the use of force against Iraq, to call for military intervention in Bosnia-Herzegovina.

Initially, the Bush Administration acted as if it believed the unfolding crisis in Yugoslavia did not directly affect U.S. vital interests and suggested that Yugoslavia was a "European" problem. Eventually, however, pictures of Bosnian Muslims starving in camps and stories of "ethnic cleansing" forced the crisis on to the international and the American agenda.

Therefore, at the same time the United States, the United Kingdom, and France were building support within the United Nations for a "no-fly" zone over southern Iraq, the Security Council was passing a resolution authorizing the use of force to ensure the delivery of humanitarian relief to Bosnia-Herzegovina.

This coincidence of timing, however, does not mean that the two crises share equal priority. All Americans are repulsed by the tragedy in Bosnia. When considering the use of U.S. military power, however, Americans must understand that we have much more at stake in the Persian Gulf than in the former Yugoslavia.

Indeed, the crises in Iraq and the former Yugoslavia have many similarities. Ethnic conflict and civil war have plagued both countries. The international community can now document the depopulation of villages, mass executions, and other brutal violations of human rights in both countries. Bosnian Muslims and Iraqi Kurds and Shia all fear annihilation at the hands of government forces. In both countries, only international intervention may prevent another genocide.

Our concerns in Iraq, however, extend well beyond these kinds of humanitarian issues. We went to war in the Persian Gulf, because Iraq's invasion

SOURCE: Les Aspin. Floor statement in the House of Representatives, September 16, 1992.

of Kuwait directly challenged vital U.S. interests, namely, access to oil, stopping nuclear proliferation and thwarting aggression. Unfortunately, the job isn't finished and our vital interests are still at risk. We may have won the war, but we have not yet won the peace.

Moreover, how we deal with Iraq has implications far beyond that country. We are establishing the foundation of the post-Cold War era. How we deal with Iraq says a lot about how we will deal with the new nuclear dangers as well as authority of the U.N. in the coming decades.

From the invasion of Kuwait until the cessation of hostilities, the role played by the United Nations heralded a new era of international cooperation and multilateralism. The United Nations seemed poised to seize the opportunities afforded by the end of the Cold War, and lead the world rather than follow it.

But it is now an open question whether the United Nations has the staying power to deal with the challenges of the new era. The answer to that question will be of immense interest to would-be Saddam's of whatever stripe around the world, not to mention a few Serbs who might be watching. . . .

The steady erosion of U.N. authority in Iraq concerns me. The United Nations, and the coalition partners in general, cannot just declare victory in Iraq and move on.

The problems with Iraq are not solved and the job isn't done. We have been waging this battle with the Iraqis for more than 18 months. The credibility of the United Nations is on the line. The resolutions against the Serbians are still in their earliest stages. What lessons will the Serbians take from the Iraqi experience? Do they simply need to outwait the United Nations, or will they learn that waiting is futile because the United Nations means business?

How we deal with both Iraq and Bosnia is not simply a test of the United Nations. It is a test of U.S. leadership, which is necessary to make the

United Nations effective. George Bush doesn't talk much about the "New World Order" anymore, but the future of collective security in the post-Cold War era is what's at stake.

The fact that we have more at stake in Iraq does not mean, of course, that we should not consider using military power in Bosnia-Herzegovina. I believe we should be willing to use air power to ensure delivery of humanitarian aid to Bosnia-Herzegovina. I also believe that we should be willing to use our air power to blunt an Iraqi ground attack against the Shia in Iraq. I believe that is a consistent position.

Some experts and colleagues reject the additional use of U.S. military power in both places. That also is a consistent position.

What is not consistent, however, is to argue that the use of U.S. military power is appropriate in Bosnia-Herzegovina, but not in Iraq. Saddam Hussein's invasion of Kuwait threatened the vital national security interests of the United States. We may decide to use force in response to the tragic conflict in Bosnia-Herzegovina, but we should not delude ourselves. We have more at stake in Iraq than we do in the former Yugoslavia.

17. Keep the Troops and the Money at Home

Doug Bandow

Advocates of an interventionist foreign policy have, of course, advanced many lofty justifications for their policy: To promote democracy. To ensure stability. To protect human rights. To stop aggression. To enforce international law and order. To create a new world order. And on and on. Such appeals to higher principles and values are very seductive. Suggesting that foreign policy should be based on the promotion of the national interest sounds decidedly cold and selfish in comparison.

The moral goals articulated by many interventionists are important, but we should have no illusions about the ability of the U.S. government to promote, let alone impose, them. Furthermore, recourse to such principles is often simply a rationalization for pursuing strategic or political ends. A cursory survey of activist foreign policy decisions ostensibly taken in the name of higher moral principles reveals ample evidence of both naïvete and sophistry.

SOURCE: Doug Bandow. "Keep the Troops and the Money at Home," Orbis, vol. 35, no. 4, Fall 1991, pp. 552–561, excerpts. Footnotes deleted. Reprinted with permission of Orbis: A Journal of World Affairs, published by the Foreign Policy Research Institute. Copyright Foreign Policy Research Institute.

For instance, policy makers in Washington regularly proclaim their love of democracy and the free market, but as of this writing, there is little sign of reform in Kuwait City; American troops have fought to make the Middle East safe for a monarchy that has so far sought to evade its promises of greater domestic freedom. Going further back in history, Washington created the Export-Import Bank in 1934 to underwrite private exports to the USSR, then ruled by the bloodiest dictator to arise in history. More recently, this institution funded Nicolae Ceauşescu of Romania, and continues to subsidize virtually every authoritarian regime to come along. The United Nations Development Program has undertaken projects in North Korea; the World Bank is again lending to China. Mengistu's murderous Ethiopia was a client of the IMF as well as the Bank. The list goes on and on.

Despite its professed ideals, the United States has used its troops to prop up authoritarian regimes in Korea and Vietnam. In two world wars, it cultivated grand alliances with, respectively, an authoritarian Russia (although admittedly, by the time the United States declared war, the tsar had been overthrown) and a totalitarian USSR. It has viewed its bases in and defense treaty with the Philippines as equally important during the presidencies of Marcos and Aquino.

Not only has America's intervention often been motivated by factors other than disinterested selflessness, but Washington has equally often bungled the job. Financial assistance to a host of Third World autocracies has strengthened the enemies of freedom and democracy. Aid and support tied the United States to failing dictatorships in Iran and Nicaragua; their falls resulted in neither democracy nor allies. America's entry into World War I to promote a utopian world order had perhaps the most disastrous consequences of any international meddling by any state ever; by allowing the allies to dictate an unequal and unstable peace, it sowed the seeds of this planet's worst conflagration, which bloomed just two decades later.

Even more important than the question of Washington's sincerity and realism in promoting higher principles in its foreign policy is the question of cost. How much money—and how many lives—are we prepared to sacrifice to bring American principles to other countries? The price of restoring Kuwait's sovereignty proved surprisingly cheap, but nothing guaranteed the paucity of U.S. and allied casualties. Although they refused to discuss specific casualty estimates in advance, U.S. commanders engaged in hostilities fully expecting a casualty figure many times greater. How many American lives did policy makers think Kuwait's liberation would have been worth? Five thousand lives? Fifty thousand lives? And, even if Iraq was the aggressor, the deaths of tens or even hundreds of thousands of Iraqis, many of them either civilians or military conscripts, must also be recognized as a very real cost of U.S. intervention.

How many body bags per foreign life saved would make intervention elsewhere worthwhile? Why did Iraq's earlier brutal assaults on its Kurdish minority not warrant war? How about Syria's depredations in Lebanon? China's swallowing of Tibet? The war between India and Pakistan? Or Pol Pot's mass murder in Cambodia?

If young American males—and now females—are born to give their lives overseas to forestall aggression, protect human rights, and uphold a new world order, should not the United States have gone to war to unseat the two dictators who (unlike Saddam Husayn) truly were the moral equivalent of Hitler—Stalin and Mao? Why was protecting human rights in these instances not worth war? If the answer is that the cost would have been too great, then those who attempt to make moral distinctions between sacrificing 58,000 Americans for Vietnam but refusing to offer up some unspecified larger number to free more than one billion Chinese need to explain their methodology—unless, of course, they believe that the United States really should have ignited World War III in the name of a new world order.

In fact, the United States did not intervene to liberate the two largest communist states because doing so was not perceived to be in America's interest, owing to the catastrophic costs that such actions surely would have entailed. For all the idealism embodied in the moral explanations for U.S. behavior, American intervention is usually animated by a general sense of realpolitik.

In the case of the Gulf war, humanitarian concerns may have eventually come to dominate President Bush's thinking. But had the initial fighting been between, say, Ethiopia and Somalia, the United States is unlikely to have intervened, just as Washington did not act when those two countries fought more than a decade ago. Concerns about the regional balance of power and Iraq's growing arsenal of weapons of mass destruction were also real, but secondary; after all, the United States was prepared to leave Saddam's military strength intact had he chosen to withdraw from Kuwait by January 15. Despite President Bush's rhetoric, Washington's real vital interest in the Gulf was to ensure allied access to oil. Likewise, past aid to President Mobutu of Zaire can be explained only as an attempt to buy influence with a dictator who controls important natural resources. The presence of troops in South Korea is often justified by U.S. officials as giving America an advanced outpost to be used against the Soviets in the event of war.

As unsatisfactory as an emphasis on America's national interests may be to some, it is the only proper basis for U.S. policy. Such an approach reflects the purpose of the United States government—to protect the security, liberty, and property of the American people—in a sense that the international pursuit of utopian ideals does not. Reasons of national interest and security are the only legitimate justification for U.S. intervention abroad.

WEIGHING COSTS

However, it is not enough to decide that the United States has one or more interests at stake in some foreign matter, because interests are not of unlimited value. The benefits of such objectives have to be balanced against the costs of intervention.

Perhaps the most obvious expense is financial. NATO accounts for roughly half of the entire military budget; the defense of the Pacific runs to about $40 billion. Operation Desert Shield cost $60 billion or more (although that bill was largely covered by allied states). Foreign aid adds another $15 billion annually to the deficit. All told, roughly 70 percent of America's military outlays goes to prepare for conventional wars abroad. Observes General Wallace Nutting, former commander-in-chief of the U.S. Readiness Command, "We today do not have a single soldier, airman, or sailor solely dedicated to the security mission within the United States."

Our domestic freedoms also suffer as a result. World Wars I and II resulted in massive assaults on civil liberties, including the suppression of dissent and free speech, and culminated in the incarceration of more than 100,000 Japanese-Americans. Much more modest, but still unsettling, was the anti-Arab sentiment unleashed during the short war against Iraq. Moreover, a panoply of security restrictions that grew out of the cold war continues to limit our freedom. . . .

Similarly, America's interventionist foreign policy has malformed the domestic constitutional system. We have seen both a centralization of power in the federal government and the aggrandizement of the presidency. How far we have come is reflected by the fact that serious thinkers who purport to believe in jurisprudential interpretation based on the original intent of the framers argued that the president had the unilateral authority to move more than 500,000 men and women far from home

and launch a war against another sovereign state without congressional approval. While reasonable people may disagree over the exact demarcation line between presidential and congressional warmaking powers, the Constitution means nothing if it does not require congressional action in this instance. And, although U.S. participation in formal United Nations forces is rather limited, it represents an even greater abrogation of congressional authority, since the U.N. Act dispenses with the need for a declaration of war when such troops are involved. . . .

Finally, intervention could one day threaten the very national survival even of the United States. We live in a world where biological, chemical, and nuclear weapons are spreading, along with the availability of ballistic missiles. Terrorism has become a fixture of international life. With the growing ability of even small political movements and countries to kill U.S. citizens and to threaten mass destruction, the risks of foreign entanglements increase. No longer are the high costs limited to soldiers in the field. In coming years, the United States could conceivably lose one or more large cities to demented or irrational retaliation for American intervention. A modest SDI program would reduce these risks, but it would never be able to provide full protection.

CONSIDERING ALTERNATIVES

How, then, should we formulate a foreign policy? Every action taken abroad should reflect the purpose for creating the U.S. government; namely, to serve the interests of U.S. society and the people who live there. The role of the U.S. state is not to conduct glorious utopian crusades around the globe. It is not to provide a pot of cash for the secretary of state to pass out to friendly regimes to increase U.S. influence abroad. It is not to sacrifice the lives of young Americans to minimize other peoples' sufferings. In short, the money and lives of the American people do not belong to policy makers, even the president, to expend for purposes other than defending the American community.

Of course, some analysts argue that promoting moral values, particularly democracy and human

rights, advances American national interests by
making conflict—or, at least, war—less likely. The
link is tenuous, however. Indeed, in the Middle
East, North Africa, and some other states, true democracy is likely to unleash destabilizing forces,
particularly Islamic fundamentalism. The end of
the totalitarian rule that kept simmering ethnic tensions in Eastern Europe under control has already
resulted in violent conflict in the Balkans. The best
we can say is that democracies generally do not
attack their neighbors.

Further, America's ability to advance democratic
values is inconsistent at best. There is little that the
United States can do to make Serbia a free country,
for example. And Washington's policies often
throw the United States's commitment to democracy into question. Foreign aid, in particular, has
more often assisted authoritarian rulers than liberal
forces throughout the Third World. In the absence
of any direct link between important U.S. objectives and the imperative to advance democracy in a
particular country, Americans' resources should
not be used in this way. This would in no way
preclude private groups from undertaking such efforts, just as many conservative and libertarian organizations are now active in Eastern Europe and
the Soviet Union.

Furthermore, to decide that as specific intervention is consistent with the purpose of the U.S. government is not enough to justify it. We also need to
assess whether there are alternative means of
achieving the goal. A free Europe is certainly important to the United States, but the maintenance of
195,000 soldiers there is not necessary. The Soviet
threat has waned, while Europe's ability to defend
itself has grown. A sharply reduced Soviet threat
may remain in coming years as the USSR struggles
with daunting economic, ethnic, and political
problems, but we are far more likely to see a Soviet
civil war than aggression against the West. Even
General John Galvin, the supreme allied commander in Europe, says that he does not believe the
Soviets are planning an offensive any longer, and
that once they withdraw from Eastern Europe, it
would take them six weeks to mobilize. Thus, there
is no reason why the Europeans, with thrice the
economic strength of a decaying Soviet Union and

a new buffer in the former Warsaw Pact states,
cannot create their own security system that would
deter any potential threat.

Similarly, South Korea is vastly stronger than
North Korea in every way except current military
strength. Seoul's growing edge has become increasingly obvious as South Korea has stripped away the
North's allies, particularly the Soviet Union and
the East European states. The South is fully capable
of eliminating the military imbalance in the peninsula. South Korean officials do not deny their country's ability to sharply increase its defense efforts;
instead, they tend to complain about having to bear
the added expense. This is hardly a justification for
an American presence. Seoul could gradually increase its military spending—which could be unnecessary if the North enters into meaningful arms
control negotiations—as U.S. forces were phased
out. . . .

It might be difficult to fashion alternative solutions that do not involve direct U.S. intervention,
and Washington might not always be fully satisfied
with the outcome. But it is unrealistic to expect the
United States to assume the responsibility for
maintaining global order. Instead, Washington
should seek to promote cost-effective policies that
yield results most consistent with the U.S. government's duty to protect Americans' security and
constitutional freedoms.

Indeed, even if there appear to be no alternatives
to a U.S. commitment, the United States must
weigh benefits against costs before it intervenes,
and avoid or extricate itself from tragic but ultimately irrelevant conflicts.

For example, what if U.S. policy makers concluded that South Korea would not defend itself if
Washington pulled out its troops? In fact, Seoul
would probably be the last American ally to give
up, but what if it decided to do so? A Northern
takeover of the South would be a tragedy for the
latter, but it would have little impact on the United
States, whose security would remain largely un-
changed and whose economy would suffer only
marginally from the loss of a mid-sized trading
partner. Obviously, other deleterious effects are
also possible; it has been argued that China, for
instance, might be more likely to invade Taiwan

absent an American defense guarantee for Seoul. However, like politics, aggression is primarily local, and there are many good reasons for Beijing to exercise restraint irrespective of the likelihood of an American military response. The threat to go to war should be reserved for cases involving vital American interests. Korea is a peripheral, rather than a vital, interest of the United States, and does not warrant spending billions of dollars and risking tens of thousands of lives every year.

A similar analysis could have been performed on the Gulf. Even if the other regional powers had not taken steps to contain Iraq, the likelihood of Saddam Husayn striking Saudi Arabia was overplayed, since it would have left him dangerously overstretched. Similarly, the consequences even of a highly unlikely conquest of the entire Gulf were overstated. Iraq and Kuwait together accounted for about 7.3 percent of international oil production before the embargo; control of Saudi Arabia would have given Saddam 15.6 percent, and if the other small sheikdoms were also included, the total would have increased to 21.5 percent. Thus, in the fantastic worst-case scenario, Saddam would have controlled about one-fifth of international production; enough to nudge prices up, to be sure, but not enough to control prices or wreck the international economy. If proponents of Operation Desert Storm believed that energy prices and the consequent repercussions on the international economy warranted war, they should have been more forthcoming about how many body bags per unit increase in oil prices they believed to be acceptable. Nor did Saddam's invasion of Kuwait threaten America's ally Israel. To the contrary, Iraq only attacked Israel in a desperate attempt to split the coalition; absent the U.S. presence, Baghdad would surely not have attacked Israel, because that country was fully capable and willing to retaliate.

CONCLUSION

The United States enjoys many advantages that provide it with the luxury of remaining aloof from geopolitical conflicts that engulf other countries. The United States benefits from relative geographic isolation, for example. (This does not insulate it

from nuclear attack, of course, which is why sufficient resources should be allocated to develop some form of missile defense.) The United States also has the world's largest single economic market, which reduces the impact of the loss of one or more trading partners. (Germany and Japan, for example, would suffer far more if the U.S. market was denied to them.) Moreover, America has a constitutional system and political philosophy that have endured for more than two hundred years and have proven to be popular around the world.

This unique status allows the United States to balance the costs and benefits of intervention differently from most other states. Alliances make a lot more sense among European states threatened by the Soviet Union, for instance, or between Saudi Arabia and its neighbors when they are threatened by Iraq. Observes Patrick Buchanan, "Blessed by Providence with pacific neighbors, north and south, and vast oceans, east and west , to protect us, why seek permanent entanglements in other people's quarrels?"

For this reason, the United States is rarely open to charges of appeasement, such as are sometimes rightly leveled at other countries, for its vital interests are rarely threatened directly. For example, had France and Britain accurately perceived the potential threat posed by Nazi Germany, they should have blocked the remilitarization of the Rhineland, and they certainly should not have helped dismember Czechoslovakia (through active intervention, it should be noted). Washington's failure to raise a new expeditionary force in 1933, however, did not constitute appeasement. (In fact, there is nothing wrong in principle with appeasement, if that means only diplomatic accommodation among great powers. In the late nineteenth and early twentieth centuries, Austria-Hungary, Britain, France, Germany, and Russia all resolved potentially violent conflicts without war by making concessions to one another that could be called "appeasement." The case of Nazi Germany was different because Hitler wanted far more than could be given to him, and because the allies materially weakened themselves—for example, by eviscerating Czechoslovakia—in attempting to satisfy him.) For a more recent example, it would not be appeasement for the United States to decline to defend a populous and prosperous South Korea; for Seoul to choose not to augment its forces once U.S. troops were gone, however, would be.

The end of the cold war has resulted in a new world order, whether or not the United States defines or polices it. . . .

What should a new, noninterventionist policy look like? It should rest on the following bedrock principles:

- The security of the United States and its constitutional system should remain the U.S. government's highest goal. Individuals may decide to selflessly risk their lives to help others abroad. Policy makers, however, have no authority to risk their citizens' lives, freedom, and wealth in similar pursuits.
- Foreign intervention is usually expensive and risky, and often counterproductive. Many smaller nations may still need to forge preemptive alliances to respond to potentially aggressive regional powers. Because of America's relative geographic isolation and other advantages, however, intervention is rarely necessary to protect its security and free institutions. This is especially true today, with the disappearance of a threatening hegemonic power.
- America's most powerful assets for influencing the rest of the world are its philosophy and free

institutions, the ideas of limited government and free enterprise that are now sweeping the globe, and its economic prowess. These factors ensure the United States's influence irrespective of the size of its military and where that military is stationed. The United States can best affect others through private means—commerce, culture, literature, travel, and the like.
- The world will continue to suffer from injustice, terror, murder, and aggression. But it is simply not America's role to try to right every wrong—a hopeless task in any event. The American people are entitled to enjoy their freedom and prosperity, rather than having their future held hostage to unpredictable events abroad, however laudable the goals of intervention seem to be. Their lives and treasure should not be sacrificed in quixotic crusades unrelated to their basic interests.

The world is changing faster today than it has at any time since the end of World War II. As a result, the United States has no choice but to refashion its foreign policy. While Washington should remain engaged throughout the world culturally, economically, and politically, it should bring its military home and curtail expensive foreign aid programs. After bearing the primary burden of fighting the cold war, the American people deserve to enjoy the benefits of peace through a policy of benign detachment.

Questions for Discussion

1. What is meant by intervention? How does it differ from nonintervention?
2. What right does the United States have to intervene in regional conflicts? In the domestic affairs of other countries?
3. What criteria should guide U.S. policy when intervention is being considered?
4. Leslie H. Gelb of *The New York Times*, for one, opposed the use of U.S. troops to

overthrow Saddam Hussein at the end of the Gulf War or ensure autonomy for the Kurds of Iraq. However, he strongly favored the use of force in Bosnia-Herzegovina. In one instance, he said it was "contrary to America's interests to sponsor Iraq's disintegration"; in the other case, he saw intervention as in the U.S. interest. Discuss.
5. Discuss U.S. options toward a number of crises in which U.S. troops intervened,

or in which intervention was considered, but rejected. What accounted for the differentiated treatment?

6. Should the United States intervene "to stop the killing" in ethnic conflicts, such as in Bosnia-Herzegovina, as Senator Claiborne Pell and others have advocated? Is stopping ethnic strife a legitimate aim of U.S. policy?

7. Where does humanitarian intervention end?

Selected Bibliography

BLECHMAN, BARRY M., AND STEPHEN S. KAPLAN. *Force Without War: U.S. Armed Forces as a Political Instrument.* Washington, DC: Brookings, 1978.

BONNER, RAYMOND. *Waltzing with a Dictator: The Marcoses and the Making of American Policy.* New York: Times Books, 1987.

BULL, HEDLEY (ED.). *Intervention in World Politics.* Oxford: Clarendon Press, 1984.

CAROTHERS, THOMAS. *In the Name of Democracy: U.S. Policy Towards Latin America in the Reagan Years.* Berkeley: University of California Press, 1991.

FALK, RICHARD A. (ED.). *The Vietnam War and International Law,* vol. 2. Princeton: Princeton University Press, 1969.

GEORGE, ALEXANDER L. *Forceful Persuasion: Coercive Diplomacy as an Alternative to War.* Washington, DC: U.S. Institute of Peace, 1992.

GLEIJESES, PIERO. *The Dominican Crisis: The 1965 Constitutionalist Revolt and American Intervention.* Baltimore: Johns Hopkins University Press, 1978.

HALPERN, MANFRED. *The Morality and Politics of Intervention.* New York: Council on Religion and International Affairs, 1963.

KWITNY, JONATHAN. *Endless Enemies: The Making of an Unfriendly World.* New York: Congdon & Weed, 1984.

LEHMAN, JOHN. *Making War: The 200-Year Old Battle between President and Congress over the Way America Goes to War.* New York: Scribner's, 1992.

PALMER, BRUCE, JR. *Intervention in the Caribbean: The Dominican Crisis of 1965.* Lexington: The University Press of Kentucky, 1989.

ROBINSON, LINDA. *Intervention or Neglect: The United States and Central America Beyond the 1980s.* New York: Council on Foreign Relations, 1991.

VINCENT, R. J. *Nonintervention and International Order.* Princeton: Princeton University Press, 1974.

WALZER, MICHAEL. *Just and Unjust Wars.* New York: Basic Books, 1977.

PART THREE

DOMESTIC DILEMMAS, FOREIGN POLICY IMPLICATIONS

CHAPTER 6

The Struggle against Drugs

The oft-proclaimed "war on drugs" is going poorly. President Ronald Reagan's Attorney General identified drugs as "the number one problem in the country," especially in their links with crime. There are upward of seven million drug users in the United States, about one-third of whom are cocaine addicts. The statistics are estimates and could well be on the low side. Of the drugs consumed, 90 percent come from abroad. Cocaine comes primarily from Colombia, Peru, and Bolivia; and heroin smuggling from West Africa is on the rise. Drug production and trafficking are a big business, whose criminal tentacles are increasingly discernible in corrupted institutions, narcoterrorism, swollen prison populations, urban violence, and new markets in the schools and suburbia.

Despite highly publicized drug seizures, the amount entering the country is on the rise: the borders are porous and the traffickers continually develop new ways to smuggle in drugs in bulk. Until the 1970s, the main problem was heroin, a derivative of opium, which is produced principally in Afghanistan, Pakistan, Burma, Laos, and Thailand. While in Vietnam, thousands of GIs became drug users. On returning home, they turned to pushers to sustain the habit. Since the early 1980s, cocaine has dominated the American market. Its base is the coca paste extracted from the coca leaves raised in the Andean highlands. Cannabis, such as marijuana and hashish, is raised throughout the world, but is deemed a lesser problem, because it is bulky, more difficult to smuggle, less addictive, and, because of its ready availability, cheaper and, therefore, not as attractive to crime syndicates. Then there are synthetic drugs, such as LSD and amphetamines. Finally, as a result of the worldwide oversupply of opium, coca, and cannabis products, drug traffickers were motivated to develop a new product, "crack," a mixture of cocaine and sodium bicarbonate "so addictive that it created a new group of habitual abusers—and a new market for coca products."[1]

The internationalization of drug trafficking has had a baleful impact on countries all over the world, but nowhere more than in the United States. If allowed to continue unchecked, the long-term consequences could be catastrophic. Historically, other societies failed to cope and ultimately were subverted. Only after they had undergone an extensive period of foreign domination, revolution, and massive upheaval did they succeed in uprooting or marginalizing a pervasive drug subculture. Reform failed, or was never seriously attempted, in Persia, in the Mughal Empire on the Indian subcontinent in the seventeenth and eighteenth centuries, in China in the nineteenth and first half of the twentieth centuries, and in

[1] Deborah Willoughby. *Cocaine, Opium, Marijuana: Global Problems, Global Response.* Washington, DC: U.S. Information Agency, May 1988, p. 14.

111

the Ottoman Empire of the nineteenth and early twentieth centuries. The ruling and creative elites of these societies were reduced to impotence through drug-induced ennui and enervation.

American officials recognize that an effective policy must reduce both demand and supply. As William J. Bennett, who served as the nation's first drug czar under President Bush, noted: "The reality of the drug problem cannot be met through an exclusive 'law enforcement' strategy on the one hand, or a 'prevention and treatment' strategy on the other."[2]

Ethan A. Nadelmann, who teaches economics at Princeton University, analyzes the background of attempts to control the flow of drugs into the United States (Reading 18). He examines the cost-effectiveness of a two-pronged policy that is trying both to reduce and destroy crops under cultivation and interdict their movement to the market, and to apprehend and prosecute traffickers. The complexity of the overall process of controlling international drug production and trafficking is given comprehensive treatment. In the process of assessing the costs and benefits—and inherent limitations—of any drug policy, Professor Nadelmann tackles head-on the emotional and value-laden option of legalization.

During the 1970s, interdiction did little to stem the tide of drugs. Increasingly, the Drug Enforcement Administration (DEA) turned, with more palpable results, to developing better financial intelligence. Cooperation with other governments in following the money led to the conviction of some big-time drug barons. However, when Ronald Reagan came to office, his obsession with the communist threat in Central America led to a significant shift in DEA resources from drug enforcement to hunting for connections between Marxist-Leninist insurgents and drug dealers. Ideology distorted his priorities, as the search for communists overrode any concern over drugs. For example, in June 1984, the DEA's attempt to use a valuable informant, one of Colombia's Medellín drug barons' trusted pilots, was upset, probably by a White House aide eager to publicize recently acquired intelligence showing a tenuous connection between the drug traffickers and the pro-Soviet Sandinista regime. On another occasion, according to an incarcerated Medellín bigwig, Carlos Lehder Rivas, U.S. officials offered to let him ship cocaine into Florida "if he would only help them ship weapons to the [anti-Sandinista] Nicaraguan contras."[3] Ironically, both Washington and the Medellín drug traffickers backed Noriega in the mid-1980s, at the time he was successfully ingratiating himself with each of them.

One of President Bush's aims in invading Panama in December 1989 was to introduce a democratic government that would work with the United States to curb drug trafficking. According to a report of the U.S. government's General Accounting Office, this effort has been a failure (Reading 19). Washington's reliance on the Endara government is misplaced. Not only is the drug trade flourishing, but the level of U.S. aid to help Panama's law enforcement agencies has been paltry. No significant incentives to cooperate have been offered Panama's corrupt oligarchy.

There are calls in Congress and occa-

---

[2] National Drug Control Strategy. Washington, DC: The White House, January 1990, p. 2.

[3] Larry Rohter. The New York Times, November 24, 1991.

sionally in the media to enlist the military in fighting drug trafficking (Reading 20). This seems to some like a plausible way to prosecute the war against drugs. However, most military men have serious reservations: they do not see drug-busting as a function of the armed forces. Also, there are those who believe the mission is too vague, too politically charged; and still others doubt Congress's commitment to an all-out war, given its unwillingness to sanction hunt-and-destroy missions against aircraft or ships suspected of trying to smuggle drugs into the United States. In time, such Draconian measures may be adopted, especially if the limited success in detection and interception continues to be not nearly enough to stem the flood of drugs into the country. Nadelmann's assessment of the limited ability of the Department of Defense (DOD) to interdict the flow of drugs has regrettably been confirmed by recent government reports.

Under the best of circumstances, the choices available to the U.S. government are limited. The most powerful country in the world finds itself hamstrung in its aspiration to rid itself of the impoverishing assault by the drug barons. Like a Gulliver at bay, the United States is caught in a maze of restraints that emanate from the democratic system the government seeks to protect. The dilemmas and the policy choices facing the United States are set forth by Rensselaer W. Lee III, President of Global Advisory Services and author of *The White Labyrinth: Cocaine and Political Power* (Reading 21).

At a summit meeting in Cartagena, Colombia, in February 1990, President Bush convinced the presidents of Colombia, Peru, and Bolivia that the Andean nations and the United States had to pursue a two-front strategy: to undertake a strong antidrug offensive using police and security forces, and to encourage farmers to grow products other than coca leaves. Two years later, at a follow-up summit, the disillusionment of the Latin American states with the United States was obvious: most of the U.S. funding had gone to the military, which was using the weapons against insurgents rather than drug traffickers; and the economic assistance from the United States had not really added up to much at all.

Can a rational strategy be devised to cope with the drug problem? Writing in *The New York Review of Books* (July 16, 1992), Luc Sante, a student of the American drug scene, suggests that the drug problem is symptomatic of a profound societal malaise; that drugs are taken for more than merely to "numb pain or enhance pleasure or induce entertaining perceptual distortions. They are a weapon against the void."

> The potent illusion that drugs provide is called upon when the more commonplace illusions fail, and especially when life appears as nothing more than the conduit between birth and death. Drugs populate the empty landscape, supply the missing heaven, extend the movie into the third dimension. Drugs impose their own structure—customs and language, goals and priorities, rewards and punishments—on lives in which all belief has collapsed, and with it conventional structures.
> The alternate world that drugs create is only made more concrete and urgent by the fact of their illegality. Users, suppliers, and agents of the law become locked into an unbreakable circular mechanism. Although individual users can, with great effort, free themselves from the cycle, the social causes are too profound for there to be any widespread solution short of social upheaval; the results, meanwhile, are all too apparent. The popular media and the popular mind—

including that of the government—can do nothing more with this unbearable truth than to demonize it or turn it into an abstraction.[4]

Sante's conclusion that a total societal transformation is the only answer needs to be kept in mind in efforts to reduce the flow of drugs and the country's insatiable appetite for them. The main suggestions for public policy have been the following:

- education to better inform our citizenry, particularly the youth, of the harm from drug use;
- decriminalization to take the profits out of the selling of drugs and, in the process, to avoid making criminals out of those who are unable to resist the attraction (just as prohibition was repealed, so, too, goes the argument, should the laws against marijuana);
- drug treatment to help users stop using drugs and to make available maintenance doses to confirmed addicts;
- better law enforcement, which would entail emphasis on intelligence-gathering, auditing to check for money-laundering through banks, and tracking prime offenders with special task forces;
- seizure and confiscation of the assets of convicted drug dealers;
- death penalty for traffickers smuggling drugs into the United States;
- U.S. government subsidies to farmers abroad who agree to crop substitution;
- expanded use of the military, including

[4] Luc Sante. "The Possessed," *The New York Review of Books*, July 16, 1992, p. 23.

search-and-destroy missions, if necessary, to curb the inflow of drugs;
- extensive spraying of poppy fields and coca plants, despite the damage this may cause the environment.

It is true that the drug problem would be of little consequence if most users decided to desist. But the social, economic, and psychological causes of the crisis will not soon disappear. Accordingly, policymakers responsible for the community and the nation must creatively adapt the available instruments and ideas as best they can.

For the first time in its history the United States is engaged in a war it can neither wage nor win without help from others. It has to work closely with friendly foreign governments, particularly in Central and South America. Multilateral diplomacy, however, requires a due respect for the views and interests of others that has not exactly been a hallmark of Washington's approach in the past. A sense of partnership will not be developed quickly or easily, yet it is essential for long-term cooperation.

In order to persuade Latin American leaders to adopt tough measures against their drug traffickers, the United States must first demonstrate that it has a consistent, no-nonsense, unwavering commitment to the war on drugs and to the punishment of drug dealers: plea bargaining, minimum sentences, early parole, erratic decisions—these characteristics of the American judicial process are viewed disdainfully in Latin America and encourage the attitude that the United States is prepared to be tough on drug dealers *elsewhere* but not at home. If our domestic policy is marked by indecisiveness, rhetoric not reform, hypocrisy rather than honesty in debating the alternatives, and the search for the quick fix instead of lasting solutions, it will undermine efforts to enlist cooperation abroad.

Finally, the drug war mandates that the United States give far greater attention to the economic plight and political problems of our Latin American neighbors. Their well-being is integral to our own. At this moment, however, the criminals are winning the war.

18.   U.S. Drug Policy: A Bad Export

Ethan A. Nadelmann

Almost everyone seems to agree that the "drug problem" is now a major international issue. U.S. relations with several Latin American countries are seriously strained because of these countries' inability to control the drug trade. Political leaders across the spectrum are advocating U.S. military involvement in suppression efforts; U.S. troops have even been deployed abroad in an effort to disrupt the production and export of cocaine from Bolivia.

At home political figures endorse increasingly repressive measures to try to stamp out drug use. There are calls for more widespread drug testing, increasingly powerful investigative tools for drug enforcement agencies, and greater expenditures on all aspects of drug enforcement.

The political tide is now so strong that drug policy, perhaps more than any other domain of public policy, has been captured by its own rhetoric and effectively immunized from critical examination. Clearly the time has come for a more rational discussion of the drug problem—one that attempts to distinguish the problems of drug abuse, on the one hand, from the problems that result from drug prohibition policies, on the other.

Obsessed with the need to control drug trafficking, governments have enacted and enforced in-

SOURCE: Ethan A. Nadelmann. "U.S. Drug Policy: A Bad Export," *Foreign Policy*, no. 70, Spring 1988, pp. 83–108, excerpts. Reprinted with permission from *Foreign Policy* 70 (Spring 1988). Copyright 1988 by the Carnegie Endowment for International Peace.

creasingly harsh criminal penalties regulating virtually every aspect of drug use with little regard for the costs imposed by these laws. These costs can be measured not just in tax dollars, but also in individual lives, personal liberties, political stability, social welfare, and moral well-being. Federal and state governments spend several billion dollars each year to enforce the increasingly repressive laws inside the United States. And U.S. diplomats press governments around the world to follow the American lead and enact their own harsh measures against drug use and trafficking. Meanwhile, there is no indication that the magnitude of the worldwide drug abuse problem is declining. Indeed, there is good reason to believe that the current American approach actually may be exacerbating most aspects of what is commonly identified as the drug problem.

Sixty years ago, most Americans demonstrated a clear ability to distinguish between the problems of alcoholism and alcohol abuse and the costs imposed by the prohibition laws. The debate between proponents and opponents of Prohibition ultimately revolved around conflicting interpretations of what both sides regarded as a cost-benefit analysis. Unfortunately, today few Americans demonstrate any aptitude for distinguishing between the problems of drug abuse and those occasioned by the drug prohibition laws. Yet so much of what Americans typically identify as part and parcel of the drug problem falls within the latter, not the former, category.

No doubt most people resist thinking about the drug problem in terms of the Prohibition analogy because the notion of repealing the current drug laws is not regarded as a viable policy option. Indeed, the very suggestion of such a possibility quickly conjures up images of an American transformed into a modern-day Sodom and Gomorrah. Yet there are powerful reasons to at least attempt a reasoned analysis of the costs and benefits of current drug policies. First, an optimal drug policy must aim to minimize not just drug abuse but also the costs to society imposed by drug control measures. Second, there are numerous alternatives to current policies, among which the libertarian vision of unrestricted access to all drugs is only one and certainly the most radical. Third, there is good reason to believe that repealing many of the current drug laws would not lead to a dramatic rise in drug abuse, especially if intelligent alternative measures were implemented.

All public policies create beneficiaries and victims, both intended and unintended. When a policy results in a disproportionate magnitude of unintended victims, there is good reason to re-evaluate its assumptions. In the case of drug prohibition policies, the intended beneficiaries are those individuals who would become drug abusers but for the existence and enforcement of the drug laws. The intended victims are those who traffic in illicit drugs and suffer the legal consequences. The unintended beneficiaries, conversely, are the drug producers and traffickers who profit handsomely from the illegality of the market while avoiding arrest by the authorities and violence by other criminals. Each of these three categories is readily recognizable. The unintended victims of drug prohibition policies, however, are rarely recognized as such. Indeed, they are most typically portrayed as the victims of the unintended beneficiaries—that is, the drug traffickers—when in fact the drug prohibition policies are the principal cause of their victimization.

In certain respects, the Latin American countries are among the principal unintended beneficiaries of U.S. drug policies. The international demand for illegal drugs such as marijuana and cocaine has proved to be an economic boon for Latin America. This has been especially true for the main source countries—Bolivia, Colombia, and Peru. Much, but by no means all, of the economic benefit has derived from the market's illegality. Government repression of the market has had the same effect as a huge tax except that the revenue is collected not by governments but by illicit sellers. Hundreds of thousands of farm families, primarily in Bolivia, Colombia, and Peru, have earned far more from growing coca, the agricultural raw material for cocaine, than they would have from growing any other crop. The same is true of tens of thousands of marijuana growers in Belize, Colombia, Jamaica, and Mexico. Others involved in refining, transporting, or protecting the illegal product have supplemented or replaced meager incomes earned in the legitimate economy. Countless corrupt officials likewise have pocketed money from the illicit trade. In addition to these groups that benefit directly, significant sectors of the population in several Latin American countries have benefited indirectly from the trickle-down effects of the trade. . . .

Today many drug specialists, including Drug Enforcement Administration chief John Lawn, concede that stopping the flow of drugs is impossible. They know that whenever drug control efforts succeed in cracking down on one source country or disrupting one major trafficking route, another soon emerges in its place. International drug enforcement efforts are thus justified on the grounds that they are essential in limiting consumption by keeping the retail street price of the substances as high as possible. . . .

Limitations on the ultimate success of the international regime to control drug trafficking are best comprehended by comparing the drug regime with other international law enforcement regimes. In certain important respects the drug regime resembles other international law enforcement regimes, such as those that nearly eradicated piracy and slavery during the previous century or those established more recently that deal with counterfeit currency and airplane hijacking. In each case, the vast majority of governments ultimately recognized a mutual interest in not participating, directly or indirectly, in such illegal acts and in cooperating in their suppression. Moreover, each act has come to be regarded in international law as in some sense an international crime.

However, the drug regime differs from other international law enforcement regimes in at least two significant respects. First, despite rhetoric to the contrary, it lacks a deeply rooted moral consensus that the activity in question is wrong. Second, crimes that require limited resources and no particular expertise to commit, that are easily concealable, and that create no victims with an interest in notifying authorities are most likely to resist enforcement efforts. Each of these characteristics describes drug trafficking. For instance, unlike counterfeiting, no particular expertise is required to become a drug smuggler. Even in the United States, marijuana is grown profitably by tens of thousands of people with no more training than can be acquired in a local library. In the less developed countries where opium poppies, coca, and cannabis for foreign markets are grown and refined, hundreds of thousands of poorly educated farmers participate in the market. Nor does it require any special expertise to be a drug courier. The potential number of successful counterfeiters is an extremely small number; the potential number of successful drug traffickers is virtually infinite.

Most aspects of drug trafficking are easily concealable. The crops are often grown in inaccessible hinterlands and camouflaged with legitimate crops. Their transport to the United States is also exceedingly difficult to detect. . . .

Although the international slave trade, like the drug traffic, was driven by the prospect of higher profits than could be attained in legitimate commerce, it was a far more visible trade. Ships carrying slaves from Africa usually could be identified far more readily than the vessels that transport marijuana and cocaine today. Even more important, the purchasers of slaves had much more difficulty concealing their illegal "property" than do the ultimate customers of illicit drugs.

Finally, the victims of slavery, piracy, counterfeiting, and hijacking are eager to have others know of their plight. But the willing "victims" of the drug trade have no intention of notifying the authorities. Drug trafficking, which involves willing buyers

and sellers, unlike the other targets of international law enforcement regimes, is an entirely consensual activity.

In the case of each successful international law enforcement regime, the activity could not be effectively suppressed until a broad consensus had developed across diverse societies that viewed the activity as morally noxious. Such a consensus in regard to the immorality of piracy developed throughout much of the world during the 18th century. A similar consensus evolved with respect to slavery during the 19th century. The reason these and subsequent consensuses underlying other international law enforcement regimes evolved was essentially the same: the activity itself directly victimized innocents. The basic problem of the antidrug regime, and for that matter of the efforts in the early part of this century to create antialcohol and antiprostitution regimes, has been the absence of just such a consensus. For all the undeniable victims of these vices, many others involved in the activities were not, and did not perceive themselves as, victims. Thus despite the efforts of the United States and some other governments to create the veneer of an international moral consensus on the drug issue, a true consensus does not exist—and will not be attained—either within the United States or around the world.

Comparing Risks

The case for legalization is particularly convincing when the risks inherent in alcohol and tobacco use are compared with those associated with illicit drug use. Both in Latin America and in the United States, the health costs exacted by illicit drug use pale in comparison with those associated with tobacco and alcohol use. In September 1986, the Department of Health and Human Services reported that in the United States, alcohol was a contributing factor in 10 per cent of work-related injuries, 40 per cent of suicide attempts, and also 40 per cent of the approximately 46,000 traffic deaths in 1983. That same year the total cost of alcohol abuse to American society was estimated at more than $100 billion. An estimated 18 million Americans are currently reported to be either alcoholics or alcohol abusers. Alcohol has been identified as the direct cause of 80,000 to 100,000 deaths annually and as a contributing factor in an additional 100,000 deaths. The health costs of tobacco use in the United States and elsewhere are different but of similar magnitude. In the United States alone in 1984, more than 320,000 deaths were attributed to tobacco consumption. All of the health costs of marijuana, cocaine, and heroin combined amount to only a fraction of those of either of the two licit substances. . . .

Drug-Policy Alternatives

There are those who acknowledge the greater harms caused by alcohol and tobacco but who justify the criminalization of other substances on the ground that two wrongs do not make a third wrong right. The logic of their argument, however, ultimately crumbles when the costs of the drug laws are considered. There is little question that if the production, sale, and possession of alcohol and tobacco were criminalized, the health costs associated with their use and abuse could be reduced. But most Americans do not believe that criminalizing the alcohol and tobacco markets would be a good idea. Their opposition stems largely from two beliefs: that adult Americans have the right to choose what substances they will consume and what risks they will take, and that the economic costs of trying to coerce so many Americans into abstaining from those substances would be enormous and the social costs disastrous.

An assessment of the costs and benefits of current drug control policies in the United States requires some sense of what the alternatives would be. When Prohibition's proponents and opponents debated the merits of the 18th Amendment, they were able to draw on their recent memories. The difficulty in contemplating the alternatives to drug prohibition is that few people can remember when heroin, cocaine, and even marijuana were legally available. The first federal legislation severely restricting the sale of cocaine and the opiates was the 1914 Harrison Act. Marijuana did not become the subject of federal legislation until 1937, when Congress passed the Marijuana Tax Act. In both cases,

however, state legislatures around the country already had imposed their own restrictions on the availability of these drugs, motivated in good part by the popular association of these substances with feared minorities—the opiates with the Chinese immigrants; cocaine with blacks; and marijuana with blacks and Hispanics. Even so, the late 19th century and the first years of the 20th century could be described as a period in which most of today's illicit drugs were more or less legally available to those who wanted them. The United States at that time had a drug abuse problem of roughly similar magnitude to today's problem, but it was perceived almost entirely as a public and private health issue. Crime and law enforcement played little role in the nature, perception, and handling of the problem.

In 1987 direct expenditures on drug interdiction incurred by the military, which markedly underestimate actual costs, increased significantly from almost nothing in 1981 to about $165 million. Expenditures in this area by the three principal intelligence agencies—the CIA, the Defense Intelligence Agency, and the National Security Agency—also have increased dramatically. The Drug Enforcement Administration's budget has risen from about $200 million in 1980 to a projected $500 million in 1988, and almost all of the other federal law enforcement agencies—in particular, the FBI and the U.S. Customs Service—have increased dramatically the proportion of their resources devoted to drug enforcement activities. In an August 1987 study prepared for the U.S. Customs Service by Wharton Econometrics, state and local police were estimated to have devoted about one-fifth of their total budgets, or close to $5 billion, to drug-law enforcement in 1986. This represented a 19 per cent increase over the previous year's expenditures. All told, 1987 expenditures on all aspects of drug enforcement, from drug eradication in foreign countries to imprisonment of drug users and dealers in the United States, probably totaled at least $8 billion. . . .

Other costs are equally great but somewhat harder to evaluate: the governmental corruption that inevitably attends enforcement of the drug laws; the effects of labeling the tens of millions who use drugs illicitly as criminals, subjecting them to the risks of criminal sanction and obligating many of those same people to enter into relationships with drug dealers—who may be criminals in many more senses of the words—to purchase their drugs; the cynicism that such laws generate toward other laws and the law in general; and the sense of hostility and suspicion that, many otherwise law-abiding individuals feel toward law enforcement officials. . . .

Voices for Legalization

Despite the soaring costs—economic, political, and social—associated with drug prohibition policies, little popular support can be found for repealing the drug laws. The percentage of Americans supporting legalization even of marijuana has dropped markedly since the late 1970s. Liberal politicians tend to choose the drug issue as the most profitable one on which to abandon their liberal principles and prove their tough-on-crime credentials. Even the civil liberties unions shy away from this issue, limiting their input primarily to the drug-testing debate. The minority communities in the ghetto, for whom repeal of the drug laws promises the greatest benefits, fail to recognize the costs of the drug prohibition policies for what they are. And typical, middle-class Americans, who hope only that their children will not succumb to drug abuse, tend to favor any measures that they believe will make illegal drugs less accessible to them.

The few scholars who have spoken out in favor of repeal are primarily from the conservative end of the political spectrum: the economists Milton Friedman and Gary Becker, the criminologist Ernest van den Haag, and the magazine editor William F. Buckley, Jr. However, there is also a significant silent constituency in favor of repeal found among the criminal justice officials and scholars, intelligence analysts, and military interdicters who have spent the most time thinking about the problem. More often than not, job-security considerations combined with an awareness that they can do little to change official policies ensure that their views remain discreet and off the record. . . .

There can be no guarantee, of course, that legalization would lead to better and healthier societies in either the short or the long run. Indeed, the possibility cannot be excluded that drug abuse would become more widespread than it is now. But that prospect is by no means a certainty. At the same time, it is certain that most of the costs of current drug policies would be reduced dramatically in both North and South America. If the objective of American and international drug control policy is to consider the costs not just of drug abuse but also of drug control measures, then it is essential to consider the legalization option.

Of course, there is no single legalization option. Legalization can mean a free market, or one closely regulated by the government, or even a government monopoly. Just consider the range of regulatory regimes for the control of alcohol that state and even municipal governments have devised. Nor does legalization imply an end to law enforcement, as the Bureau of Alcohol, Tobacco and Firearms can attest. Legalization under almost any regime, however, does promise many advantages over the current approach. Government expenditures on drug-law enforcement would drop dramatically. So would organized crime revenues. Between reduced expenditures on drug-law enforcement and increased revenues raised by taxing drug consumers and producers, the net benefit to government treasuries in the United States would easily be many billions of dollars per year. In Latin America, the net benefits would be smaller in terms of dollars, perhaps only a few billion, but far greater in terms of social gains—less corruption, more law and order, and a strengthening of the role of government in society.

It is troubling to note the opposite trends in the purity of legal and illegal substances. The average tar content of cigarettes is declining as smokers seek relatively safer products. Similarly, alcohol drinkers are shifting away from hard liquor and toward wine and beer, motivated in good part by health concerns. During the same period, conversely, the average amount of THC, the primary psychoactive ingredient of marijuana, has increased significantly; the average purity of cocaine has risen from 12 per cent to 60 per cent; and smoking crack has become far more widespread. In addition, the spread of high-potency "black tar" heroin from Mexico has contributed to an increase in the drug's average purity. Government law enforcement efforts help explain these trends in that they place a premium on minimizing the bulk of the illicit product to avoid detection. But the increasing purity is also an indication of the failure of law enforcement efforts. Under a legal drug regime, government regulators could establish relatively low purity levels, thus reducing the potential for drug abuse and addiction. They also could ensure quality and provide warnings as to the potential dangers of the licit substances. A black market still would exist for higher purity and even more dangerous substances, but it would be a fraction of its current size. Given the option of obtaining reliable supplies from government-regulated vendors, few drug users would have much to gain by resorting to the black market. And the government could set drug prices at a level high enough to discourage consumption but low enough to minimize black market opportunities.

Of all the drugs that are currently illicit, marijuana perhaps presents the easiest case for repeal of the prohibition laws, in good part because it presents relatively few serious risks to users and is less dangerous in most respects than both alcohol and tobacco. Moreover, the available evidence indicates no apparent increase in marijuana use following the decriminalization of marijuana possession in about a dozen states during the late 1970s. In the Netherlands, which went even further during the 1970s in relaxing enforcement of marijuana laws, some studies indicate use of the drug has actually declined. Marijuana arrests may not account for most of the drug offenders in U.S. federal and state prisons, but they do account for most of the drug arrests as well as for a large portion of the money spent on local drug enforcement by municipal criminal justice systems and on interdiction by the Coast Guard and the military.

Cocaine, heroin, and the various amphetamines, barbiturates, and tranquilizers that people consume illegally present much tougher policy problems. If they were legally available at reasonable prices, would millions more Americans use and

abuse them? Drawing comparisons with other countries and historical periods provides clues but no definitive answers for the simple reason that culture and personality often prove to be the most important determinants of how drugs are used in a society. Availability and price play important roles, but not as important as cultural variables. There is good reason to assume that even if all the illegal drugs were made legally available, the same cultural restraints that now keep most Americans from becoming drug abusers would persist and perhaps even strengthen. . . .

A similar commission, composed of North and South Americans, could evaluate the costs and benefits, as well as the potential and limits, of the international drug control regime. Unlike the recently created White House Conference for a Drug Free America, this commission could examine the entire range of options for reducing not just drug abuse but also the costs of drug prohibition policies. It would not begin its investigation, as the White House Conference has, with the unquestioned assumption that any use of illicit drugs is by definition drug abuse. Nor would it automatically assume that increased law enforcement and increasingly harsh criminal sanctions can produce a more effective drug control strategy. Rather, its mandate would include intensive scrutiny of the very assumptions that underlie current drug policies. For instance, the commission could make recommendations on how to deal more effectively with the violence, crime, and corruption that stem in good part from current drug prohibition strategies. In short, it would be an inter-American commission mandated to evaluate the value and effectiveness of current drug control strategies and to consider any and all alternatives.

In the final analysis, the drug problem remains an international problem that needs international solutions. Latin American governments realize the consequences for their countries of the U.S.-inspired policies, but they are unable to offer alternatives. They are hampered not only by their historical incapacity for concerted action but also by their recognition that the drug issue is one on which the U.S. government is liable to act impulsively, and even irrationally, to the detriment of everyone's interests. So rather than seek more effective and less costly drug policies, the Latin American governments find themselves torn between trying to appease their powerful neighbor to the north and trying to minimize the harmful consequences of a problem that lies beyond their control. Publicly they proclaim their adherence to the chimerical objectives of eliminating illicit drug production and use. But in practice they pursue "drug control" policies that really are nothing more than damage-limitation strategies designed to keep the drug traffickers from taking over their countries and the U.S. government from striking out at or abandoning them.

One of the most important steps the U.S. government could take, therefore, would be to let the

Latin Americans evaluate their own best interests independent of U.S. demands. If they determine that their overall interests are best served by policies designed not to suppress but to control and regulate the production of marijuana and cocaine, then the U.S. government should be willing to consider policy alternatives that acknowledge those interests. Indeed, it is far from certain that the interests of the United States in this regard necessarily conflict with those of Latin America. For U.S. interests lie not only in reducing the costs of drug prohibition policies abroad but also in developing alternatives to a drug control policy that has proved both largely unsuccessful and increasingly costly at home.

19. The Case of Panama: The More Things Change, the More They Remain the Same

Although U.S. officials lack comprehensive statistics on narcotic-related activities in Panama, they believe that drug trafficking may be increasing and that Panama continues to be a haven for money laundering. U.S. and Panamanian efforts to reduce the flow of illegal drugs into the United States have been hindered because Panama's law enforcement agencies lack the training and resources necessary to conduct effective anti-narcotics operations. In addition, Panama's environment is conducive for money laundering because of the large volume of transactions processed through the banking and commercial sectors.

Panama has taken measures to help identify potential money laundering activities, and the governments of Panama and the United States have signed agreements to promote cooperation in reducing drug trafficking and money laundering. The United States is also providing Panama with a total of about $1 million in aid for fiscal years 1990 and

SOURCE: U.S. General Accounting Office. *The War on Drugs: Narcotics Control Efforts in Panama*. Washington, D.C., July 1991, pp. 1–4, GAO/NSIAD-91-233.

1991 to assist Panama's law enforcement agencies in reducing narcotics-related activities, but these assistance programs have experienced delays.

General Manuel Noriega was removed from power in late 1989 during Operation Just Cause, a U.S. military operation. One of the operation's objectives was to combat drug trafficking by apprehending Noriega and bringing him to the United States to be tried for drug trafficking. The operation was the culmination of 2½ years of U.S. pressure against the rule of General Noriega. After the operation, the civilian government that was elected democratically on May 7, 1989, and led by President Guillermo Endara, was installed.

Under the Noriega regime, all military and law enforcement agencies were part of the Panama Defense Forces. General Noriega was the commander of these forces. After the operation, President Endara abolished the Panama Defense Forces and in early 1990 established law enforcement agencies with minimal military functions. The agencies involved in anti-narcotics activities are the Special Anti-Narcotics Unit of the Judicial Technical Police, the National Maritime Service (a Coast Guard), and the Customs Service. With these changes, Panama has had to create its drug enforcement capability from scratch.

Although reliable statistics are not available, U.S. officials believe that drug trafficking in Panama may be increasing. According to a Drug Enforcement Administration official, the actual volume of drugs passing through Panama is not known. However, the amount of cocaine seized in Panama has increased. According to Drug Enforcement Administration data, Panamanian authorities seized 3,959 kilograms of cocaine in 1990 compared to 1,728 kilograms in 1989. According to State Department records, seizures in 1990 included the largest single seizure in Panamanian history—2,118 kilograms—during an operation in Colon that was directed by the Drug Enforcement Administration. In addition, data on monthly seizures of cocaine from September 1990 to March 1991 showed an increase. Over 1,300 kilograms were seized from January to March 1991 compared to the 418 kilograms seized during the prior 3-month period. Although seizure amounts may not reflect actual amounts of drugs passing through Panama, on the basis of these data, most U.S. officials we interviewed believe that trafficking may be increasing, and a Drug Enforcement Administration agent believes that trafficking may have doubled since Operation Just Cause.

According to U.S. Embassy officials, drug trafficking continues because Panama's law enforcement agencies are unable to patrol all of the known transshipment points and areas around Panama's border. In addition, according to a Drug Enforcement Administration agent, traffickers no longer have to make large payments to Panama Defense Forces officials for drug shipments to pass through Panama.

U.S. officials believe that money laundering is Panama's most serious narcotics-related problem, although the extent of this problem is unknown. According to the economics advisor at the U.S. Embassy, comprehensive statistics on the volume of money being laundered through Panama are not available, but an Embassy official estimated that billions of dollars were laundered during the Noriega regime. According to the State Department and the Drug Enforcement Administration, Panama continues to be a haven for money laundering due to its commercial and financial infrastructure. Panama has numerous banks and trading companies. In addition, Panama's dollar-based economy, weak economic conditions, reputation for not enforcing laws that prohibit narcotics-related activities, and geographical proximity to cocaine-producing areas in South America make Panama's environment conducive to money laundering.

Until recently, Panama did not require banks to report large cash transactions, which facilitated money laundering. However, to curb money laundering, the Panamanian government issued regulations that require banks to record certain information concerning currency transactions for amounts of $10,000 and greater. These regulations are intended to prevent and penalize banking operations with funds originating from narcotics-related activities. The regulations went into effect in May 1990, and Panamanian government officials reported that banks have been complying with the regulations. The Drug Enforcement Administration indicated that banks' compliance with the regulations was sporadic. In January 1991, the regulations were strengthened to include all easily negotiable items such as travelers and cashiers checks. Fines for violating these regulations range between $100,000 and $1 million. In addition, the Panamanian Supreme Court has reinterpreted certain banking laws to allow greater access to bank records during criminal investigations for drug-related crimes.

A political adviser at the U.S. Embassy believes that Panama is experiencing an increase in money laundering. The advisor stated that narcotics-related activities temporarily slowed after Operation Just Cause until traffickers could assess the new government's ability to deal with drug trafficking and money laundering. Once the traffickers became aware of the government's inability to detect and deter drug activity, money laundering flourished.

According to U.S. Embassy officials, traffickers are able to disguise illegal transactions among the high volume of legitimate transactions at the Colon Free Zone. When funds from money laundering activities are commingled with legitimate business revenues before they are deposited into banks, efforts to identify and prosecute drug traffickers become complicated. In addition, according to a Drug Enforcement Administration official, drug cartels continue to establish corporate entities in Panama as a front for their laundering activities.

Panama lacks the enforcement capability to address the current drug trafficking and money laundering problems. Each of the law enforcement agencies involved in anti-narcotics activities—the

Special Anti-Narcotics Unit of the Judicial Technical Police, the National Maritime Service, and the Customs Service—is staffed with new recruits that are not adequately trained to combat narcotics-related activities. These agencies also lack the necessary equipment for conducting effective anti-narcotics operations. The government of Panama has provided limited funding for law enforcement efforts against narcotics activities.

20. Call Out Troops in the Drug War

Claude Lewis

The war against narcotics in Colombia—the country that is said to be the source of 80 percent of the cocaine flowing into the United States—may signal a new beginning for America.

Attorney General Dick Thornburgh is absolutely correct when he suggests that America should consider sending troops into Colombia even though Colombian President Virgilio Barco has said that they aren't necessary. The battle against drug trafficking is as much our fight as it is the fight of our Latin neighbors.

Recently, Colombian officials, responding to the assassinations last week of presidential candidate Sen. Luis Carlos Galan, a judge and a police chief, launched an offensive that resulted in the arrest of nearly 11,000 individuals, including a reputed top official of the Medellin cartel.

All this activity heartens me because—with the exceptions of racism, sexism and abortion—no problem has been as important to me as a columnist and as an American as the problem of addiction. The use and abuse of narcotics in our country is now more widespread and devastating than governmental corruption, the incompetence of government bureaucrats, the escalation of violence and the intransigence of poverty and hunger.

SOURCE: Claude Lewis. "Call Out Troops in the Drug War," *Philadelphia Inquirer*, August 23, 1989. Reprinted with permission of *The Philadelphia Inquirer*.

I think this is true because illicit drugs have had a persistent and direct impact on all of these difficulties. Indeed drug addiction has been so immobilizing that it has even limited freedom in America, forcing law-abiding citizens to abandon their streets and, in some cases, to turn over their homes to dealers and traffickers.

Almost no discipline, ranging from the arts, to government, to blue collar workers, has been immune from drugs. Despite efforts to curb the problem, despite appeals from the White House, America is the leading market for drug dealers.

Through the years I have interviewed teenaged addicts, visited the ugly dungeons of squalor and death where many wind up. Repeatedly, I've heard the complaints of addicts who in the beginning boasted that "heroin is my hero," and in the end discovered that "narcotics are hell."

I have known addicts, boys and girls, who have committed suicide. I've sat with mothers with no lights left in their eyes because of the sad events surrounding their children's addiction. I know a family that has five addicted daughters.

The problem is too widespread, too much a part of the American culture to be eradicated through slogans and appeals. It is too late for that, though steps to eliminate the *demand* for narcotics must be found.

I have never been impressed by government efforts to clean up the drug mess. Indeed, the extent of the problem we face today is the result of a series of impotent or ignorant leaders who failed to recognize the potential for disaster stemming from drugs during the last 30 years.

After years of denying the enormity of our problem, government has approached it in fits and starts. At first it promised to wage an "all-out war" against drugs, then argued that it is impossible to commit the needed funds for such a battle. The truth, however, is that America cannot afford to allow this ravenous affliction to continue to spread. It has infected almost every community and is sapping the national will, having a devastating impact upon the military, the work force, professional sports and educational institutions.

Once the perception was that most addicts lived across town, largely in America's ghettos. Today's reality is that as many of them sit across from us at our dining room tables. Just last week, a physician at the Medical College of Pennsylvania told me that fully "50 percent of the births at the hospital involve mothers abusing drugs." At many other hos-

pitals in American cities, the figure for babies born into addiction ranges from 10 percent to 30 percent.

The battle in Colombia has the strongest of implications for Americans. I am against sending U.S. troops into foreign countries to wage or direct wars. However, in the case of Colombia, I side with Thornburgh.

Thornburgh and Bill Bennett, Bush's drug czar, know that further chaos lies down the road unless America takes its gloves off in the battle against drugs. Sending American troops to Colombia, Bolivia and Peru or anywhere else to stop or slow narcotics trafficking is as much a responsibility of America as of our Latin neighbors.

We have long since passed the point where we may simply advise children to "just say no." A war to end the illicit industry that yields billions of dollars can be won. As things now stand, when it comes to drugs, when Latin America sneezes, America gets pneumonia. Decisive action must be taken.

21   The Limits of Choice

Rensselaer W. Lee III

U.S. and Latin American efforts to curb the supply of cocaine have failed abjectly. Some 200–300 tons of cocaine may flow into U.S. markets yearly; as University of Michigan researcher Lloyd Johnston notes, "the supply of cocaine has never been greater in the streets, the price has never been lower, and [the] drug has never been purer." The U.S. government supports a number of programs meant to reduce supply in the Andean countries, but

SOURCE: Rensselaer W. Lee III. "Why the U.S. Cannot Stop South American Cocaine," Orbis, vol. 32, no. 4, Fall 1988, pp. 513–519, excerpts. Footnotes deleted. Reprinted with permission of Orbis: A Journal of World Affairs, published by the Foreign Policy Research Institute. Copyright Foreign Policy Research Institute.

these programs amount to perhaps $40–$50 million a year, a pittance when compared to the South American cocaine industry's earnings of $3–$5 billion a year. Yet more resources may not be the answer. Structural barriers block effective drug enforcement in poor countries, and such barriers could well be insurmountable.

First, Andean governments worry about the impact of successful drug-control programs. The consequences would be exacerbated rural poverty and new legions of the unemployed, both of which would strengthen anti-democratic or communist movements. Imagine 200,000 coca-growing peasants marching on Bolivia's capital, La Paz. In Peru and Colombia, the war against drugs has proved difficult to reconcile with the struggle against communist insurgency. The threat of eradication alienates coca growers from the government and enhances the appeal of insurgent groups. In the Upper Huallaga Valley, for example, the U.S.-backed eradication effort has doubtless driven many peasants into the ranks of Sendero Luminoso.

Second, many Latin Americans see the economic benefits of drug trafficking. . . .

Third, Latin Americans tend to see U.S.-imposed drug enforcement measures as infringements on their national sovereignty. According to a recent poll, two-thirds of Colombians oppose the extradition of drug traffickers to the United States. . . .

Fourth, governments often exercise little or no control over territories where drug production flourishes, for these are remote from metropolitan centers, relatively inaccessible mountainous or jungle terrains which are patrolled by guerrillas or other hostile groups. In this way, drug traffic encourages territorial disintegration. . . .

Finally, corruption severely undermines criminal justice systems in cocaine-producing countries. Law enforcement in Latin American countries often represents simply a way to share in the proceeds of the drug trade: the police take bribes not to make arrests and seizures. When the police do make successful busts, the drugs are often resold on the illicit market.

These barriers mean that anti-drug activities in Latin American countries are largely cosmetic. Governments draw up elaborate plans to eradicate coca—the police make a few highly publicized arrests and cocaine seizures, fly around the countryside in helicopters, terrorize villages, and knock out an occasional cocaine laboratory—but with little effect. The core structure of the cocaine industry remains, and the industry's agricultural base continues to expand. Farmers in the Upper Huallaga Valley plant four or five acres for every hectare of coca eradicated, according to a professor at the Agrarian University of Tingo María, the capital of an important cocaine-growing province in the Valley. . . .

Unfortunately, there may no useful way to upgrade the war against cocaine that is not counterproductive. Virtually every prescription under discussion carries major disadvantages.

Enhancement of Drug-Fighting Capabilities in Producer Countries. Under this proposal, Andean governments would be provided with firepower, transport, communications, and intelligence support to establish their authority in drug-trafficking zones and destroy the cocaine industry's infrastructure. But the prevailing pattern of corruption in Andean countries makes many U.S. observers skeptical of the utility of such buildups. RAND economist Peter Reuter has suggested that better-equipped governments might mean no more than greater payoffs from the drug traffickers.

"Americanization" of the War on Drugs. In this approach, the U.S. receives permission to take over drug enforcement that producer countries cannot perform. . . .

Income Replacement. "If we are to make a difference in cocaine control," declares a Department of State report, "a massive infusion of economic assistance will be required." Such assistance compensates countries for the economic and social costs of shutting down cocaine production. Possible measures include hard currency loans to compensate for the reduced flow of dollars and lowering import barriers for legitimate products, such as textiles and sugar.

But what about the hundreds of thousands of small farmers who cultivate coca? A coca farmer in the Bolivian Chapare can net up to $2,600 per hectare per year, over four times what he can earn from cultivating oranges and avocados, the next most profitable traditional crops. Thus crop substitution offers few attractions. The U.S. government is now indirectly paying $2,000 for each hectare of coca eradicated in Bolivia, but the Bolivian government estimates that the social costs of eradication—the cost of redirecting farmers into the licit agricultural economy—would be at least $7,000 per hectare. For Bolivia, where coca grows on 50,000–70,000 hectares, the cost of total eradication would be a mind-boggling $350–$490 million. Even if the money were available, it might be misspent; there are persistent rumors that some coca farmers in the Upper Huallaga Valley and the Chapare have used the cash payments for eradication to underwrite the costs of planting new coca fields in other locations.

Sanctions. Perennially popular with Congress, this course of action includes withholding aid, prohibiting trade, cutting off international lending, and restricting the flow of travelers. Yet the record shows few cases where sanctions have achieved the desired objective. To cut off aid to the Andean countries would probably provoke intense anti-Yankee feeling, poison the diplomatic atmosphere, and reduce the resources available for anti-drug campaigns. . . .

Negotiating Cutbacks in Drug Production. This approach requires a dialogue with the Escobars, the Ochoas, the Rodríguez Gachas, and the other chief executives of the cocaine industry. The idea of a dialogue has enormous public support in Colombia. Supporters include a number of distinguished figures: a former head of Colombia's State Council (the country's top administrative court), a former acting attorney general, two Catholic bishops (of Popayan and Pereira), and several congressmen and academics. The traffickers themselves made a formal offer to the government in 1984—to withdraw from the cocaine industry, dismantle their laboratories and airstrips, and repatriate their capital. In return, they wanted guarantees against extradition, which would have amounted to a safe haven in Colombia. The Colombian government has said officially that it will not negotiate with traffickers.

Certainly, selective amnesty arrangements for criminals can and have been tried as tools of law enforcement. (The United States has its own witness protection program, for example.) Cocaine chiefs could reveal much about the structure and operations of the international cocaine industry— its supply channels, distribution networks, personnel policies, financing, and the names of corrupt U.S. officials who abet the trade. They could also provide information about guerrilla operations, for the two often use the same territory, the same clandestine methods, the same smuggling channels, even the same overseas banks.

Yet it is hard to see how the proposal would work in practice. One problem is timing: when the traffickers made their original offer to the government, they were under great pressure. Colombia had a functioning extradition treaty with the United States, and traffickers were being tried in military courts, which have a higher conviction rate than civilian courts. Thanks to Colombian Supreme Court decisions, neither of these conditions is operative today, and the Barco government does not have a great deal of bargaining leverage vis-à-vis the country's cocaine syndicates.

Further, monitoring an amnesty arrangement— the repatriation of capital and the shutting down of a multi-billion-dollar industry—would present fundamental problems. How many Colombian and American law enforcement officials would it take to oversee such a program, and who would monitor the monitors? Too, the traffickers might be unable to deliver on their promises. Is the cocaine industry so tightly structured that a few kingpins can command a larger number of lieutenants to order an even larger number of subordinates to stop producing a product that earns so much? Possibly, but an amnesty might constitute little more than a retirement program for the chief executives of the cocaine industry. They would have to make a practical demonstration of their market power— say, by shutting down 80 percent of Colombian cocaine production for a six-month period. Amnesty is at best a futuristic option—the idea has some theoretical merit, but it would be extremely difficult to implement.

These difficulties suggest that curbing the supply of cocaine from producer countries may not be effective, no matter how much money the United States government devotes to overseas programs.

Are there better ways to spend the U.S. drug-enforcement dollar? The options seem to be increased interdiction, stepped-up enforcement against drug dealers and pushers, and such demand-reduction steps as stiffer penalties for users, "Just Say No" programs, and drug testing. Many U.S. experts expect these measures also may not work very well. Moreover, as the national controversy over drug testing indicates, there are political and legal limits to controlling drug consumption, just as there are limits to controlling production in the Andean countries. Short of legalizing cocaine use (which carries the danger of stimulating even more addiction) or changing the habits and preferences of U.S. consumers, there seems to be no way out of the cocaine morass.

The solution, if there is one, lies not in the An-

dean jungles but in the United States. The six million people who now consume cocaine must be persuaded to change their habits and preferences. Perhaps they will grow tired of cocaine and switch to designer drugs; or perhaps they will find more productive and healthy forms of recreation.

Questions for Discussion

1. Does the drug problem have a solution? Is it to be found at home or abroad?
2. Drug abuse is sustained by external sources of supply. What can the United States do to eliminate or reduce foreign sources of supply?
3. Friendly governments such as Turkey, Thailand, and Pakistan are not doing all that they could to ban and destroy opium-poppy cultivation, which provides income for their farmers. What should U.S. policy toward these and similarly caught regimes be?
4. Do other U.S. national interests in maintaining close ties to drug-producing countries take precedence over the concern for the smuggling of drugs into the United States?
5. Should the United States be prepared to appropriate much more money to subsidize crop substitution programs in Latin America? What if such crops then compete with those that American farmers are seeking to sell abroad? Should the U.S. undertake nonetheless to finance such programs? What assurances are there that this will end the drug problem?
6. Should the United States push a massive spraying program to destroy opium and coca fields? Should it use pesticides to destroy marijuana?
7. Why has international cooperation been of limited use in curbing the flow of drugs into the United States?

Selected Bibliography

COCKBURN, LESLIE. *Out of Control.* New York: Atlantic Monthly Press, 1987.

EHRENFELD, RACHEL. *Narco-Terrorism.* New York: Basic Books, 1990.

GROB, GERALD N. *Narcotic Addiction and American Foreign Policy: Seven Studies, 1924–1938.* New York: Arno Press, reprinted edition, 1981.

GUGLIOTTA, GUY, and JEFF LEEN. *Kings of Cocaine: Inside the Medellín Cartel.* New York: Simon & Schuster, 1989.

KLEIMAN, MARK A. R. *Against Excess: Drug Policy for Results.* New York: Basic Books, 1992.

LEE, RENSSELAER W. III. *The White Labyrinth: Cocaine and Political Power.* New Brunswick: Transaction Publishers, 1989.

MILLS, JAMES. *The Underground Empire: Where Crime and Governments Embrace.* Garden City: Doubleday, 1986.

REUTER, PETER, GORDON CRAWFORD, and JONATHAN CAVE. *Sealing the Borders: The*

Effects of Increased Military Participation in Drug Interdiction. Santa Monica: The RAND Corporation, 1988.

SHANNON, ELAINE. *Desperados: Latin Drug Lords, U.S. Lawmen, and War America Can't Win.* New York: Viking, 1988.

TAYLOR, ARNOLD H. *American Diplomacy and the Narcotic Traffic, 1900–1939: A Study in International Humanitarian Reform.* Durham, NC: Duke University Press, 1969.

ZIMRING, FRANKLIN E., and GORDON HAWKINS. *The Search for Rational Drug Control.* New York: Cambridge University Press, 1992.

CHAPTER 7

Illegal Immigration: Manageable Problem or Growing Threat?

Illegal immigration, a burgeoning global problem, is the direct consequence of the population explosion and the poverty explosion. It is in its early stage and could harbinger an extended period of mass migrations, whose impact could be as momentous as that of the Huns on Europe in the fourth, fifth, and sixth centuries, or the Turkic-speaking tribes of Central Asia on the Middle East in the tenth to the thirteenth centuries. The rich, stable, democratic societies of the West are in danger of having their institutions overwhelmed and their resources drained by the unwanted influx of desperate, restless people. For Europe, the demographic pressure comes from the south (Africa and the Middle East) and the east (Eastern Europe and Russia); for the United States, primarily from Latin America. Because of the complex political issues that cause and underlie them, long-term or durable solutions have thus far proved elusive.

The problem of illegal immigration is far more serious today than in the early 1980s, when President Reagan said "We have lost control of our borders" and ordered the Coast Guard to intercept and turn back boatloads of Haitians trying to enter the country. The challenge for policymakers and the complexities they have to handle were apparent then (Reading 22). In the intervening years, the situation has merely gotten worse.

Regardless of the perspective one brings to this problem, two things need to be kept in mind. First, U.S. immigration policy is the most fair-minded and generous in the world: the 600,000 to 800,000 immigrants admitted annually exceeds "the total annual immigration allowed into all other countries of the world combined."[1] Second, a country that cannot, or will not, control its borders is courting disaster. Every government must, if it is to preserve its social system, draw a line somewhere. To how many illegals should the United States, out of humanitarian concern, permit entry? Will well-intentioned exceptions merely encourage new waves of illegals? In *The Camp of the Saints*, a novel written in 1970 by a Frenchman, Jean Raspail, one million Indians head for the West, for France. Poor, angry, without hope, they have no plan, only an implacable drive to gain access to the wealth in the West. In the course of the novel, the author explores every moral, political, economic, social, and military argument for and against permitting the intruders to land. In the end, the elites, unwilling to use force, flee to Switzerland, leaving the less fortunate citizenry to their fates. A bleak but powerful story, with troubling insights into the human condition.

[1] Russell W. Peterson. " . . . Spills Over U.S. Borders," *The New York Times*, May 8, 1984, p. A31.

In microcosm, the position of the United States vis-à-vis the Haitians epitomizes the dilemmas raised by Raspail. The particularities of their situation in late 1991–early 1992 are discussed and put in broader historical perspective by Charlotte Allen (Reading 23). Congress has groped for a sustainable national policy, starting with the 1882 law that excluded the Chinese, then the national origins quota system, instituted in 1924, favoring immigrants from Europe and excluding those from Japan, up to the 1986 Immigration Reform and Control Act that penalizes employers who knowingly hire illegals. Interestingly, there were no quotas on immigrants from within the Western Hemisphere until 1965, after which time illegal aliens in substantial numbers appeared for the first time inside the borders of the United States.

The Haitians are only one part of a continuing flow from the Caribbean and Central America comprising Nicaraguans, El Salvadoreans, Jamaicans, Dominicans, and Mexicans (the most numerous of all). Seeking illegal entry are those who do not or cannot obtain a regular visa for immigration under their country's official quota. For them, the wait is too long.

Most illegals hope for admission as "refugees." In 1980, Congress adopted the United Nations' definition: refugees are persons who fear personal persecution by their government because of their race, religion, or political beliefs. About 125,000 applicants are admitted annually under this category. Others seek asylum. However, to be considered for asylum, a foreigner must be on American soil, hence the interception of the Haitians at sea, before they enter U.S. territorial waters. As many as 10,000 people a year may qualify and be granted permanent residence. This is in addition to the regular admissions under official immigration quotas for every country.

Human rights activists—civil libertarians, the Roman Catholic Church, the American Baptist Churches, and many other lobbying organizations urging leniency and easy admission to the United States—contend that in the past those fleeing from communism were unquestioningly admitted as "refugees"; whereas those from noncommunist dictatorships were invariably turned back, allegedly because they were fleeing poverty not political persecution. There the battle remains, waged in the courts, the media, and the Congress.

Emma Lazarus's inscription on the Statue of Liberty is the cry of those who favor open and unrestricted mass immigration:

> Give me your tired, your poor
> Your huddled masses yearning to
>   breathe free,
> The wretched refuse of your teeming
>   shore,
> Send these, the homeless, tempest-
>   tossed to me:
> I lift my lamp beside the Golden Door

The opposing view says this sentiment does not come to grips with reality. To illustrate the concerns of those fearing the consequences of unlimited migration, there is the apocryphal story of President Carter's visit to China in 1978, and his attempt to persuade Premier Deng Xiao-ping to be less repressive and permit dissidents wanting to emigrate to do so. Deng, so goes the tale, archly asked: "How many do you want? Ten million? Fifteen million?"

Unfortunately true, however, is the still politically vivid incident in the spring of 1980, when Fidel Castro suddenly emptied his prisons and mental institutions and permitted 125,000 Cubans to sail from Mariel

Harbor for Florida. All were poor and deemed undesirable for some reason or other, including an inability to contribute to the economy or a history of criminal activities. In the confusion, 15,000 Haitians crossed over with the Cubans. Floridians were irate over the ensuing economic and social problems, and the federal government was helpless. At first, Castro refused to agree to any repatriation. An agreement was worked out in 1984 to repatriate about 2,700 of the detainees, but Castro equivocated and eventually took back only about 25 percent of the group. Though several thousand continue to be kept in detention, eventually most of the Cubans and all the Haitians were allowed to remain in the United States. In the 1990s, another Mariel-type exodus is a perennial political nightmare in Florida and other states of the region.

Clearly, there must be an orderly way to manage the immigration crisis. Thus far, there has been no consistency in where U.S. presidents have drawn the line: When do human rights take precedence over national sovereignty? What standards and who are to differentiate among the illegals? Who is to take in how many of whom?

In 1991 President Bush opposed the agreement between Britain and Vietnam arranging for the mandatory repatriation from Hong Kong of those Vietnamese whom the British determined to be economic migrants, not "refugees" (that is, those who fled out of fear of political, racial, or religious persecution). The matter was aggravated in February 1992, when Vice-President Dan Quayle described the Vietnamese as "political refugees." However, Bush refused to admit additional Vietnamese from the camps in Hong Kong, Malaysia, and Thailand, on the grounds that the United States had already admitted over 600,000. And in late May

1992, he issued an executive order to the Navy and Coast Guard ordering them to repatriate all Haitians being housed temporarily at the U.S. Navy base at Guantánamo Bay, Cuba, and to intercept the Haitians in international waters and send them back to Haiti. So much for the confidence expressed earlier by one administration official that "Bush has been pretty consistent in maintaining opposition to any involuntary repatriation."[2] Bush's explanation was the standard one: the United States could not open its doors to all those seeking to come to the United States for economic reasons. True, but then he might have shown more understanding of the British dilemma in Hong Kong. By July 1992, the nine-month imbroglio, which had started when Bertrande Aristide was deposed on September 30, 1991, was over: of the approximately 37,000 Haitians involved, about 11,000 were granted permission to enter the United States and the rest were returned.

The consequences of illegal or, as it is sometimes euphemistically described, undocumented immigration—the economic and social costs and the implications for U.S. policy—are analyzed by Jeffrey S. Passel, a specialist at the U.S. Census Bureau (Reading 24). Since he wrote, the facts have become grimmer. In the 1980s, twenty million immigrants were admitted to the United States, of whom about six million were already illegally residing in the United States and were accorded legal status by the Immigration Reform and Control Act of 1986. The act sought to curb illegal immigration by imposing penalties on employers who hire illegal aliens. To gain enough support for its passage, it granted amnesty to

[2] Nick Lewis. *The New York Times*, October 3, 1991.

those who had entered the country illegally prior to 1982.

The failure of the act to halt the flood of undocumented immigrants is already evident in the early 1990s. Reinforcing the gloomy assessments of other specialists, Nathan Glazer, a sociologist at Harvard University, stresses that no U.S. policy can be effective unless it takes into account, and enlists the cooperation of, the national interests of other countries, especially Mexico (Reading 25).

The pressure from migrants in search of a better life will increase markedly in the coming decades. According to the U.N. Population Fund, the flight of "environmental refugees" from areas unable to feed their populations or sustain growth is inevitable. The numbers will rise dramatically, if global warming, droughts, shortages of water, and population growth continue unchecked. The United States cannot remain an island, separate unto itself. Its support of human rights stimulates the politically and economically downtrodden to flee to the West, where anxiety over the sheer numbers is occasioning demands for barriers against "the strangers at the gate." Does legalizing illegals not encourage others to follow? Does it thereby intensify political opposition to admitting more immigrants? What can the United States do that it has not so far done?

The specialists are divided. In reading their accounts, one is reminded of the proverbial story of the blind men who were asked to describe an elephant. Each reached out and touched a different area of the large animal—one, the trunk, another, the foot, and so forth, so all had limited and varying answers on the nature of the beast. The literature on illegals reveals similar confusion as each discipline rides its own hobbyhorse:

> Economists differ over the point of balance between restrictive domestic policies and the relative benefits of overseas development assistance, including trade, aid, and investment. Social scientists have taken several tacks to describe the issue, alternately targeting the locus for policy intervention in poverty, in racist and xenophobic public reaction, or in controlled population growth. Demographers, perhaps, have been most cognizant of the constraints to policy recommendations based on population projections.[3]

The explosiveness of the issue demands attention from political leaders—national and international. Time is not on the side of those who counsel delay and further study.

[3] Kimberly A. Hamilton and Kate Holder. "International Migration and Foreign Policy: A Survey of the Literature," *The Washington Quarterly*, vol. 14, no. 2, Spring 1991, p. 209.

22.   Illegal Immigration: Background to the Problem

Immigration is one of the most important and complex problems that the United States faces today. It

SOURCE: "Illegal Immigration: Challenge to the U.S.," Report of the Policy Panel of the Economic Policy Council of the United Nations Association of the United States of America (December 1981), as reprinted in *Current*, March/April 1982, pp. 39–41, excerpts.

is, however, a problem with a mixture of opportunities as well as dangers. If the U.S. develops appropriate immigration policies, it can continue to benefit from the rich quality of life that comes from cultural diversity, material progress, and amicable relations with other countries. On the other hand, improper immigration policies can threaten this country's national sovereignty, widen income disparities and damage the quality of life, generate racial and social tensions, and exacerbate relationships with foreign countries.

If immigration is an important and complex problem, it is also an increasingly urgent national issue. First, there is the pressing problem of gaining control of illegal immigration. The United States is currently experiencing a large illegal or undocumented influx. As is the case with all clandestine processes, it is almost impossible to obtain accurate data on such migration, but most observers would agree that the annual inflow of illegals is between 500,000 and one million a year and that this inflow has greatly accelerated over the last 10 years. This constitutes a flagrant violation of national sovereignty, as control over entry by noncitizens is one of the two or three universal attributes of nation states. Apart from the fact that the U.S. seems to have less control over its borders than any other major industrial country, this illegal inflow is creating a large pool of persons (estimates are in the four to six million range) who live and work in its society with less than the full protection of its laws. This obviously makes these people a target of exploitation and intimidation.

Second, there is growing concern over the rate of growth and the sheer size of the inflow. Net immigration (legal and illegal, immigrants and refugees) is now well in excess of one million per year, which means that the U.S. accepts twice as many immigrants and refugees as the rest of the world put together. This rate of inflow is at the highest level in the nation's history. It is usually not recognized that the country's largest number of immigrants came not in 1833 or 1911, but in 1980. Legal and illegal immigration accounts for half of the United States' population growth rate and a rising percentage of its crime and welfare statistics, and is bound to have an impact on the society and on the economy. Can the United States successfully integrate the newcomers, or will it find, particularly in times of rising unemployment, that xenophobic impulses and racial and ethnic tensions become more pronounced as citizen workers feel increasingly threatened by immigrants? Perhaps the most sobering factor in these calculations is that unless a restrictive policy is put into place, the rate of in-

flow in the future is likely to accelerate rather than to stabilize or diminish, generating even greater domestic problems.

The pressures that will make for an accelerating inflow (in the absence of tighter controls) are fairly obvious and stem from the inability of third world countries to absorb their rapidly expanding populations into productive, decently paid occupations. The world's population was about four billion in 1975 and will reach 6.4 billion by the year 2000. Most of this population growth is in developing countries, which already have serious unemployment and underemployment problems. These nations will need 600 to 700 million new jobs between 1980 and the year 2000 just to keep unemployment from rising. To put this in perspective, 600 or 700 million is more jobs than existed in 1980 in all the industrialized countries combined. These pressures will not be lessened by declining birth rates, which tend to accompany the industrialization of third world nations, since most of the people who will enter the work force during the next decades have already been born. Of course, the U.S. may be more affected by the specifics of the Mexican situation than by the general characteristics of the third world. But Mexico, despite its high growth rates and oil wealth, reproduces the picture described above. The Mexican population of over 70 million will double by the year 2000, and the total number of jobs that would have to be created in Mexico during the next 20 years in order to (a) accommodate all new entrants to the labor force, (b) absorb the present arrears of unemployed and underemployed into productive full-time employment, and (c) reintegrate those who would otherwise be employed in the U.S. is 31 to 33 million. Even if Mexico is to sustain a growth rate of 6.6 percent a year (a record of sustained economic growth that is virtually unprecedented among developing countries), only 20 million new jobs would be created before the end of the century, which leaves a sizable deficit. It must also be recognized that no matter how many new jobs are created in Mexico during the next 20 years, the real wage differential and changing currency values between Mexico and the U.S. will draw workers across the border.

In summary, the United States has a massive

illegality problem and a massive numbers problem, and external pressures are such that, left to themselves, both problems will get much worse over the course of the next two decades. Despite the urgency of these problems, there are a variety of difficulties that hinder the formation of a more effective and coherent national immigration policy.

The pressures to migrate from the underdeveloped countries are so strong that some third world leaders are beginning to assert an international right to immigrate and others believe that migration forces are so strong that they cannot be stopped. The President of Algeria, for example, has declared: "No quantity of atomic bombs could stem the tide of billions . . . who will some day leave the southern part of the world to erupt into the relatively accessible spaces of the northern hemisphere looking for survival." Additionally, Mexican Foreign Minister Jorge Castaneda told a Washington audience in 1978: "No matter what restrictive measures you may adopt, the United States will continue to absorb for some time to come part of our excess population." These views raise important sovereignty issues, especially the right and the ability of the United States to control its borders.

The second deterrent to the development of an effective immigration policy for the United States is the diversity of interests, and the lack of political consensus, on this complicated issue. Unlike other political problems, there is no clear ideological division on these matters. Allies on economic policy, for example, often disagree on immigration policy. There is no sharp "conservative" or "liberal" division. Moreover, immigration is a highly emotional issue involving ethnic and racial agendas, attitudes, and fears that are not always clear or expressed. Immigration, in addition, involves emotions and principles that are not easily compro-

mised. It is no wonder, then, that most experienced politicians see the immigration question as dangerous territory with serious short-run costs and no clear advantages, despite the fact that public opinion polls repeatedly show that the overwhelming majority of Americans are greatly dissatisfied with the U.S. immigration policy and want the Government to take action to solve the problem.

Another important deterrent to effective immigration policy is the absence of acceptable data to resolve disputes about the number and impact of illegal immigrants. The data problem is, of course, inherent in any illegal activity and is therefore not likely to be satisfactorily resolved until immigration is legalized. Because of the absence of reliable statistics, interpretation tends to be colored by the biases of the interpreter. Those who favor relatively unlimited immigration minimize the numbers and tend to exaggerate the positive effects of legal and illegal immigration. Those who want to restrict immigration tend to exaggerate both the numbers and the negative impacts.

Another complication is the dynamic long-run nature of the immigration problem and the difficulty that many public and private systems have in dealing with events that will impact 10 or 20 years in the future, even when these events are demographically determined and are therefore highly predictable. In too many cases, the United States has developed policies after crises have occurred rather than in order to avoid crises. Furthermore, the dynamic nature of this process causes conclusions that are made about the impact of immigration at one stage to be invalid at another, even though these stages have demonstrated a high degree of regularity and predictability through time and in different countries. . . .

23.   American Restricted Territory: The Haitian Influx

Charlotte Allen

The Haitian boat people—the 16,000 whom Coast Guard cutters have intercepted in international waters since October and the more than 4,000 of those shipped back to Haiti since the beginning of February—are victims of pandemic violence and poverty in their eroded Caribbean island nation. It has always been that way. The country of 6 million is the poorest in the Western Hemisphere. Ever since revolutionaries overthrew and widely slaughtered their French slave masters in 1804, there has hardly been a moment's peace (the most stable and prosperous interlude was the glitzy but tyrannical reign of the Duvalier dynasty from 1957 to 1986). The latest upheaval, a military coup Sept. 30, ejected the Rev. Jean-Bertrand Aristide, a firebrand left-wing Roman Catholic priest who had been elected Haiti's president with 67 percent of the vote nine months earlier.

The boat people are also victims of conflicted U.S. policy on how to treat refugees. It has always been that way. Even as the Statue of Liberty was going up in New York Harbor more than 100 years ago, with its language about welcoming "the wretched refuse of your teeming shore," Congress was banning immigrants from one teeming shore, China's, from setting foot on U.S. soil.

Sentiment about the Chinese has changed. Now, in the wake of the Tiananmen Square massacre of 1989, they enjoy a kind of favored-refugee status with Congress and the White House. Not so with the Haitians. Except for one federal law—passed in 1986, it legitimized the status of 15,000 Haitians who had arrived without visas along with 125,000 Cubans in the Mariel boatlift of 1980—Haitians have received no special immigration breaks from this country.

Quite the contrary: Since 1981, Haitians, and Haitians alone, have been the subject of a Coast Guard interdiction program designed to ensure that there would be no more Mariel flotillas. During the program's first 10 years, cutters plying the high seas near Haiti stopped nearly 22,000 Haitians.

Almost all were taken back to Haiti after brief interviews with Immigration and Naturalization Service officers to determine whether they had conceivably valid asylum claims. Over the entire decade, the officers found only six likely candidates for asylum who were allowed to proceed to the United States to make their claims formally. The current interdiction program continues the policy, except that the Coast Guard now detains the Haitians in a camp the U.S. government set up hastily in November at its naval base at Guantanamo Bay, Cuba.

"They're black, they're seen as poor, they're seen as users of services with very little to offer," says Robert Juceam, a New York big-firm lawyer who is donating his services to the Miami-based Haitian Refugee Center and is weary from staying up all night to file papers with the Supreme Court, in an effort, ultimately unsuccessful, to stop the forced repatriations on grounds that the returned Haitians faced reprisals by an out-of-control military. "They have a low standard of living, and they are users in the early stages," he says. "They're very visible where they're held, and South Florida has seen more than its share of refugees. They just got hit with [100,000] Nicaraguans. They're suffering from compassion fatigue."

Juceam does not even mention AIDS. About 10 percent of Haiti's residents are believed to carry the human immunodeficiency virus, and in Belle Glade, Fla., where many Haitian immigrants work the sugarcane fields, full-fledged acquired immunodeficiency syndrome has reached epidemic proportions.

"A refugee is supposed to be someone who applies to come here because of a well-founded fear of persecution," says David Ray, spokesman for the Federation for American Immigration Reform, the nation's largest group working to limit immigration. "Haiti shares an island with another nation," the Dominican Republic, says Ray, and it's "a little closer than Fort Lauderdale, which is across 600 miles of shark-infested ocean. But [Rep. Charles] Rangel," a New York Democrat and a member of the Congressional Black Caucus, "says the Dominican Republic doesn't have a Statue of Liberty. These people want to come here, not go there. They're fleeing economic bullets. If you create this animal called an economic refugee, you've qualified the entire country of Bangladesh."

That about sums up America's abiding split personality when it comes to immigration, leading to a policy informed by alternating bursts of hospitality and hostility, Metternich-style considerations of foreign policy and just plain politics.

The official stance of the U.S. government toward Aristide's ouster is disapproval. Years ago, when the Soviet Union still existed, subsidized Fidel Castro's Marxist dictatorship in Cuba and underwrote leftist guerrilla movements all over Latin America, the United States backed Haiti's Duvaliers, who, whatever their grave faults, were staunchly anticommunist. Now, with the "new world order," the United States supports democracy everywhere, no matter how unsavory the elected product (Aristide egged on his supporters to violent reprisals against his political enemies). The State Department has refused to recognize Haiti's post-coup military government, has engineered an Organization of American States trade embargo and has worked within the OAS to broker an agreement that would restore Aristide to power.

Nonetheless, the State Department, whose Bureau of Human Rights and Humanitarian Affairs sets the refugee policy implemented by the Immigration and Naturalization Service (a branch of the Justice Department), takes the position that Haitians are fleeing their country not because they have the "well-founded fear of persecution" on the basis of political beliefs, as federal law requires to qualify as a refugee, but simply because they cannot make a living in Haiti.

Pro-Haitian organizations such as the Haitian Refugee Center take issue with this characteriza-

tion, citing what they say are concrete examples of harassment of forcibly returned Haitians (Amnesty International has accused the military junta of murdering 1,500 people). But the State Department is probably right, says Michael Wilson, a Central America expert with the Heritage Foundation, a conservative think tank.

"Haiti is a country with no tradition of the democratic process, no tradition of law and order, no modern judicial system or police force," says Wilson. "Everyone uses violence to accomplish their goals, and that tends to breed an atmosphere of violence. There have been five or six coups since Baby Doc's ouster" in February 1986, when the younger Duvalier left Haiti. "There is an issue of, if they're refugees, why not the Dominican Republic? If you're politically persecuted, you'll go anywhere. Jews in Poland during World War II would gladly go anywhere." Adding weight to Wilson's assessment is the fact that a stream of Haitians, far smaller than the latest outflow but still significant, spilled out of the island in boats last summer, when Aristide was still in power.

The State Department's view of the Haitians has generally prevailed in the federal courts. The Haitian Refugee Center during November and December secured three temporary orders from U.S. District Judge Clyde Atkins in Miami halting the forced repatriations on a variety of grounds: that INS screening procedures were inadequate, that Haitians had a right to have a lawyer present, and that the agency was not following its own guidelines for assuring that the Haitians did not face reprisals on their return, a violation of U.N. refugee protocols.

But the Atlanta-based 11th U.S. Circuit Court of Appeals issued a 2-1 ruling Feb. 1 that foreigners intercepted on the high seas have no legal or constitutional rights. The Supreme Court has turned down two requests to halt repatriations, most recently on Feb. 24, when it also declined to review the 11th Circuit ruling. Throughout, the Coast Guard has been ferrying as many Haitians as it can back to Port-au-Prince from Guantanamo.

This has been a bad year so far for asylum seekers at the Supreme Court. On Jan. 22, the high court, in an opinion written by Justice Antonin Scalia, ruled that a Guatemalan's claim that his refusal to join antigovernment guerrillas when he was living back home in 1987 was not enough to support his claim that he had a "well-founded fear" of persecution on account of his political beliefs. Scalia's opinion, joined by five other justices, was a signal that lower federal courts should read the language of federal refugee laws narrowly.

The ruling in *Immigration and Naturalization Service vs. Elias-Zacarias* dashed the hopes of open immigration advocates that courts would recognize the concept of an economic refugee as indistinguishable from a political refugee (both flee oppressive systems). Based on the Supreme Court decision, Congress would have to rewrite the immigration laws for those hopes to prevail.

For most of this country's history, since the Jamestown settlement of 1607, there were virtually no restrictions on immigration. Anyone could come: political refugees, religious exiles, the desperately poor.

In 1873 there was a depression, and with it began a debate that has raged in America ever since: whether high levels of immigration remain good for the country. The debate centers on the question of whether, as the country's population grows, its economy is able to absorb proportionately more people.

Also by the middle to latter part of the 19th century, such organizations as the Know-Nothing party began to worry about immigration by groups other than Northern Europeans, who had until then formed the bulk of settlers. This was the beginning of a strong strain of anti-immigration sentiment among the American public that persists to this day. For example, a 1990 Roper poll indicated that 77 percent of respondents believed that there should be no increases in immigration.

In 1882, Congress passed the Chinese Exclusion Act, barring the admission of Chinese workers for 10 years and denying citizenship to all foreign-born Chinese. That same year, Congress denied entry to idiots, lunatics and anyone likely to become a public charge. Subsequent laws barred other Asians, paupers, anarchists, radicals, illiterates and those too disabled to work. In 1921, Congress set up a visa system for the first time, instituting numerical caps on immigration and a quota system favoring Northern Europeans and disfavoring Mediterra-

neans (later laws modified the system to a more equitable worldwide one, with preferences for skilled workers and relatives of U.S. residents). The quotas did not apply to the Western Hemisphere, whose inhabitants could freely enter the United States as long as they were healthy and had jobs awaiting them. Congress did not set up Western Hemisphere quotas until 1965, thereby creating the first illegal aliens in substantial numbers inside U.S. borders.

All of these measures were perfectly constitutional despite their obvious discrimination against some races some of the time. Immigration is one of the few areas in which the courts have declined to interfere, with regard to substantive policy, giving Congress almost unbridled authority to decide who gets to enter the country and to control them once they are here (Congress has delegated much of its enforcement authority to the INS).

For example, federal law bars resident aliens from collecting welfare and related benefits for the first five years, although their U.S.-born children may do so. Plenary congressional power has meant enormous scope for public passions and sentiments to play against one another. However, once aliens are inside the country, legally or illegally, they acquire basic constitutional and procedural rights, the courts have ruled.

More recent laws have involved tensions and trade-offs between gradually increasing the number of legal immigrants (unpopular with the public but popular with some members of Congress as the years have passed) and cracking down on illegal immigrants. The 1986 Immigration Reform and Control Act instituted sanctions for the first time for employers who hire illegals (the sanctions have had no effect on such immigration) at the price of an amnesty program that legalized the status of 1.6 million people. In 1990, Congress raised the number of available legal immigrant visas to a record 714,000 a year, while again trying to appease anti-immigration sentiment by beefing up enforcement.

As for refugees and asylum seekers, the United States practically ignored them from 1921 until after World War II, even turning away Jews fleeing Hitler's Germany if they did not have proper visas. The first refugee law was the Displaced Persons Act of 1948, welcoming Europeans who had no other place to go at the end of the war. The American public was not particularly enthusiastic about displaced persons, sociologist Rita J. Simon reported in her 1985 book, *Public Opinion and the Immigrant*.

What changed the public's mind about refugees was the spread of communism throughout Eastern Europe and elsewhere during the next two decades. Presidential orders and laws welcomed Hungarians, Cubans and Indochinese exiles. Congress granted the INS authority to "parole" into the country whole ethnic groups on a temporary basis, then later granted them permanent residency. Of 1.5 million refugees admitted from 1954 to 1978, Cubans alone accounted for more than 40 percent. Refugees, unlike ordinary immigrants, can qualify for about $5,000 in welfare benefits when they arrive in this country.

In 1980 Congress passed the Refugee Act, adopting U.N. standards for treatment of refugees and asylum seekers (technically, refugees are people outside the United States; asylum seekers are people who otherwise qualify as refugees but have entered the country illegally or overstayed a visa). The definition of a refugee as someone having a well-founded fear of persecution on account of race, religion, nationality, membership in a particular social group or political opinion derives from the U.N. definition. The act restricted the immigration service's parole power, giving the president and Congress the authority to designate how many refugee visas it would allot among strife-torn areas. The number of refugee visas is currently about 125,000 a year, and 10,000 asylum seekers may obtain permanent residence. More than 900,000 refugees have gained legal status in the United States since 1980.

A 1990 change in the law created a new humanitarian-relief category called "temporary protected status," which allows the attorney general to let illegal entrants who do not qualify for asylum stay in the United States for a set period if the national interest permits and conditions are chaotic at home (a natural disaster as well as a civil war can trigger the required chaos). As its name indicates, the relief is supposed to be temporary, but in fact, hardly anyone who gets permission to stay on humanitarian grounds ever has to go home.

These changes in the law were supposed to introduce evenhandedness into treatment of claimed refugees, but in some ways they have had the opposite effect. Typically, refugee allotments have favored exiles from communist countries. The INS has generally maintained a border-patrol attitude toward asylum claims, treating them with suspicion. And in decisions whether to grant asylum or issue refugee visas, the State Department's Bureau of Human Rights and Humanitarian Affairs plays a key role that derives not from any particular statute but from the president's constitutional authority to make foreign policy. The department issues an advisory opinion in every case in which someone fights deportation by claiming asylum, and foreign policy considerations play a bigger role in that decision than the individual asylum seeker's problems abroad. The INS almost always follows State's advice (a 1987 legal change gives the asylum seeker a chance to rebut the opinion, but that seldom affects the outcome).

"What you have is foreign policy versus immigration control," says Arthur Helton, head of the refugee project for the Lawyers Committee for Human Rights. "Some groups have been favored on foreign policy grounds, others disfavored. We have a refugee policy that operates differently in the way it treats certain groups."

Helton is referring to the different ways in which different branches of government treat claimed refugees from communist-dominated countries and those from noncommunist authoritarian regimes. Take Nicaragua and El Salvador, both locales for civil wars for much of the 1980s. The difference was that Nicaragua had a Marxist Sandinista government, while El Salvador had an array of U.S.-supported centrist to right-wing elected administrations.

Originally the INS treated asylum claims from both countries identically, rejecting almost all of them on the theory that most Western Hemisphere immigrants in the United States illegally were simply looking for better-paying jobs. Then after Ukrainian sailor Miroslav Medvid jumped from his Soviet ship into the Mississippi River in 1985, only to be forcibly returned by INS authorities, Attorney General Edwin Meese set up a special asylum review group for claims from Eastern Europe and

Nicaragua. The Nicaraguan success rate jumped to 26 percent, while the Salvadoran rate stayed at 3 percent. But the Salvadorans got some relief from liberal federal judges who sympathized with their claims, and when a Democrat-dominated Congress instituted temporary protected status in 1990, Salvadoran exiles were the only ones to get the status by law instead of having to wait for the Justice Department to take action.

Disparate treatment for communist and noncommunist refugees might make some sense—after all, there was a Cold War for four decades—but some ethnic groups have won special niches in immigration law by sheer dint of political clout or connections. More people want to emigrate to the U.S. than there are visas available (the waiting period for an ordinary immigrant visa can be as long as 10 years, and by conservative count an estimated 200,000 people move here illegally without detection each year), so jockeying for some sort of government break is crucial.

Mexican illegals, well represented by Mexican-Americans in Congress, were the chief beneficiaries of the 1986 amnesty. A "diversity" lottery in the 1990 law, which handed 55,000 extra visas to people from countries where immigration was once high but now is low, contained qualifications that throw nearly half to the Irish, probably thanks to Democratic Sen. Edward Kennedy of Massachusetts, chairman of the Judiciary subcommittee that oversees immigration. The law also elevated Hong Kong to the status of a separate country for immigration, quintupling the annual visas for its residents, to 25,000. And a three-year, 12,000-visa bonus goes mostly to employees of Citicorp's Hong Kong branches and their immediate family members.

But for Haitians, there is nothing. Cubans just across the Windward Passage from Haiti in the Caribbean's second-poorest country generally get a warm welcome and quick processing from immigration authorities because Castro is still in power and they fall under a 1966 law that grants them permanent U.S. residence if they want to leave Cuba. The contrast represents more than official loathing for Castro and ambivalence about Aristide, however.

"The Haitians are a border-control problem for the INS," says Helton. They are more than that; they symbolize the border that can be controlled (unlike the porous 1,500-mile Mexican border). They are a locus for Americans' frustrations about immigration, welfare and, as the Cold War becomes a memory, likely unwillingness to take in more refugees.

The 1981 interdiction program, entered into by President Reagan and the Duvalier government, is the only one of its kind. Reagan's executive order declared that the Haitian boat people had become "a serious national problem detrimental to the interests of the United States," even though Haitians accounted for less than 2 percent of illegal aliens in the country. The same year, the INS decided to detain Haitian asylum seekers who managed to avoid interdiction in camps before deporting them, something it had done with no other group (the previous policy had been to detain only dangerous aliens). When critics called the move racist, the service began a policy of automatically detaining all aliens deemed excludable, including Afghans and other victims of communism.

What galls the Haitians' advocates is that this immigrant group has resided in the United States practically since the ratification of the Constitution (Pierre Toussaint, the former slave who is a candidate for Catholic sainthood, lived in a Haitian community in New York City during the early 19th century). About 700,000 Haitian immigrants currently live in this country; the 300,000-member working-class Haitian neighborhood in Brooklyn, N.Y., bustles with small shops and restaurants and is touted as an example of how immigrants can bring a dying urban neighborhood back to life.

The Supreme Court, with its Feb. 24 [1992] ruling on repatriation, continues to express a lack of interest in the Haitians. It is also highly unlikely that Congress would amend the refugee laws to include economic victims, as some have suggested; that would be tantamount to opening U.S. borders to all comers. . . .

24.   **Undocumented Immigration**

Jeffrey S. Passel

CONSEQUENCES OF UNDOCUMENTED IMMIGRATION

Evidence regarding the effects and consequences of undocumented immigration—and immigration in general—is often contradictory and subject to individual interpretation. For example, the econometric models used to assess whether undocumented immigrants displace native workers require a number of assumptions and simplifications before they can be evaluated. The nature of these assumptions can sometimes determine the outcome of the modeling exercise. As a consequence, analysts argue on the basis of what should happen logically or what they think will happen rather than on the basis of empirically verifiable research findings. Meanwhile, the debate rages on.

A whole spectrum of positions can be found on undocumented immigration. At one extreme, people argue that undocumented immigration has a beneficial effect on the American economy. Undocumented aliens take jobs that legal residents—citizens and aliens—will not. In doing so, they increase economic growth, create more jobs, and better the overall condition of American workers, it is argued. Furthermore, undocumented aliens do not burden social services and governments because the taxes paid by them exceed the costs of services provided; in fact, undocumented aliens actually generate a surplus in government coffers. In support of this overall position, its adherents point out that undocumented immigration acts as an outlet for surplus workers in Mexico and other sending countries; the remittances by undocumented aliens also help the balance of payments of the home countries.

SOURCE: Jeffrey S. Passel. "Undocumented Immigration," *THE ANNALS* of the American Academy of Political and Social Science, vol. 487, September 1986, pp. 194–200. Footnotes deleted. Reprinted by permission of Sage Publications, Inc.

At the other extreme, opponents of undocumented immigration argue that the undocumented immigrants compete directly with minorities and young workers—groups with the highest levels of unemployment—in secondary labor markets. The undocumented aliens displace native workers and depress wages. They also perpetuate low-wage, low-productivity jobs. If there were no undocumented workers, then employers would have to raise wages, make the jobs more attractive, or otherwise enhance productivity in order to fill the jobs and compete. The costs of undocumented aliens, these proponents argue, include unemployment compensation for displaced workers, lost tax revenues—both from the aliens who do not pay their share of taxes and the displaced workers who are not earning income on which to pay taxes—plus the costs of the extensive social services used by the undocumented aliens. These costs are alleged to outweigh by far any benefits of undocumented immigration.

Economic Effects

The major debate surrounding undocumented immigration is about job displacement: do undocumented immigrants take jobs from citizens? Another way of stating this argument is this: Are enough jobs created by the employment of undocumented aliens to offset the jobs that they themselves fill? The available evidence does not support the idea that there is massive job displacement. Huddle and his colleagues argue otherwise—that for every 100 undocumented aliens working, 65 jobs are taken away from legal residents—but their conclusion is based on a very small-scale study in one locality. On the other hand, in a study of the labor market in Los Angeles, an area with a large proportion of all undocumented aliens in the country, no evidence was found to support the notion that undocumented aliens were taking jobs away from blacks, the group with whom the aliens were most likely to be competing.

Some authors have argued that undocumented aliens do not displace citizens, that the aliens fill jobs that citizens refuse to take. However, the recent studies of the characteristics of undocumented aliens have shown very clearly that not all jobs held by undocumented aliens are universally unattractive. To the extent that such job refusals do occur, it is probably because the jobs are unattractive at the wages being offered. Undocumented aliens are willing to take jobs at low wages in the United States because even the low U.S. wages are substantially higher than wages in the home countries.

If job displacement does occur, low wages are the most likely culprit. Studies on the macro level tend to support this reasoning. DeFreitas and Marshall found that the rate of wage growth between 1970 and 1980 in a group of 35 metropolitan areas was inversely related to the size of the immigrant populations of the areas. In a similar vein, Espenshade and Goodis found some evidence of wage depression in Los Angeles in the 1970s attributable to immigration. The presence of a growing immigrant work force was apparently responsible for the slower rate of wage increase in manufacturing in the Los Angeles area. They also noted two countervailing trends. The slower rate of wage growth was thought to be responsible for some of the large growth in employment in the area. In addition, the slowing in wage growth that did occur had only a very small effect on black family income.

The benefits to employers of the low wages that undocumented aliens will accept are obvious, but studies have found other benefits as well. Many employers feel that the undocumented aliens make better employees because they are easier to control, they work harder, and they complain less. In addition, some employers may be able to exploit the undocumented aliens in other ways, such as not paying withholding taxes, Social Security taxes, and other taxes.

There is another—more legal—reason why employers prefer undocumented aliens. The baby bust of the late 1960s and 1970s has recently led to declines in the number of persons in the age group of 15 to 24 years. This group supplies most of the employees in entry-level and low-skill positions. Already a labor shortage is apparent in some parts of the country. Undocumented aliens may increasingly be sought by employers to fill a demand for entry-level and low-skill workers that is not being met in the marketplace.

Social Costs

Undocumented aliens use services supplied by the public sector. They also pay taxes of various kinds: income tax, Social Security tax, property tax, either on property that they own or on property they rent, sales tax, and so forth. One of the major debates among immigration analysts is whether the money paid in taxes by undocumented aliens offsets the costs of services used by the aliens; in other words, do undocumented aliens cost society money or do they pay their own way?

There are major methodological problems involved in answering this question. First is how to partition the costs of social services between legal residents and undocumented aliens. Then there is the problem of estimating how much undocumented aliens pay in taxes. Finally, there is an even more fundamental problem, that of determining the indirect costs of undocumented immigrants. For example, is the cost of unemployment compensation paid to a worker who was displaced by an undocumented alien to be included in the calculation? Are the taxes paid by a worker in a job created by an undocumented alien to be included? Even if both of these questions are answered in the affirmative, there is the problem of measuring job displacement and creation, which, as we have seen, has not been done satisfactorily. Consequently, in addressing the issue of social costs, these indirect costs are omitted from most discussions—this one included.

Many undocumented aliens have income tax withheld from their paychecks, yet they never file for the refunds due them because of their fear of the federal government. Many also pay into Social Security, either into a bogus account, another individual's account, or a fraudulently obtained account in their own name. Yet, they are either too young to receive benefits or ineligible ever to receive benefits because of their legal status. Thus, at the federal level, undocumented immigrants pay into the system, but are ineligible to receive anything from most of its benefit programs, such as food stamps, Medicare, and Social Security.

Undocumented aliens tend to be young and to have families, and they are ineligible for many welfare-type programs. Consequently, most of the social costs incurred by undocumented aliens are for education or health care. Because the costs of these programs are allocated differently in various states, studies at the state and local level paint a mixed picture. Weintraub found that, in Texas, the state showed a net surplus from undocumented immigrants, but the local governments of six major cities incurred costs in excess of revenues. The state gained its surplus because its revenues from individuals came mainly from a sales tax, which is a regressive tax that would affect all residents regardless of legal status. The local governments, on the other hand, had to pay for the education of undocumented aliens' children. Any group with children tends to cost money under this definition of costs to local governments, and undocumented aliens tend to have children. The state surplus did exceed the local costs, so the net to all governments in the state was a surplus.

If undocumented immigrants were legalized, it is difficult to predict what the net cost to the public might be. Certain costs would be expected to increase. For example, at some point, former undocumented aliens would become eligible for social programs for which they are currently ineligible. Education costs might increase as more children of undocumented aliens took advantage of public education, but because many of these children are already being educated in public schools, the costs might not go up. These costs, however, could and probably should be considered an investment by society in the next generation. Revenues might also increase, though, as the former undocumented aliens and their employers paid the taxes due. On balance, it would not be unreasonable to expect an immediate net contribution to society from legal-

ized undocumented aliens. Even if this were not the case, legalized undocumented aliens and their descendants can be expected, in the long run, to make a net contribution to American society just as the immigrant groups before them have.

IMPLICATIONS FOR POLICY

On all sides of the immigration debate, there is a growing feeling that something must be done to reform our immigration laws and to control undocumented immigration. On neither side of the debate do the parties argue for perpetuating the status quo. Everyone recognizes that the current system is out of control and needs changing. The undocumented aliens and their native-born children, who are U.S. citizens by birth, form an underclass that is ripe for exploitation. In addition, the next generation of Americans will undoubtedly face a political crisis from this underclass and their children.

The opposite poles of the immigration debate differ in how they would respond to the current situation. One side would opt for regularizing much of the current flow of undocumented immigrants by granting more temporary work permits and increasing the number of aliens admitted for permanent residence. In the extreme, this position calls for completely open borders. The opposing position calls for greater enforcement activities to regain control of U.S. borders and extremely stiff penalties for hiring undocumented aliens.

Passing legislation to deal with the immigration problem has proved to be extremely difficult, in part because there is no consensus on what should be done and in part because any specific proposal tends to generate strong and vocal opposition. Furthermore, opposition to various segments of proposed legislation tends not to come from the same groups. Consequently, packages of reform proposals tend to be opposed by groups from all parts of the political spectrum, who have thus far been able to unite, after a fashion, and defeat all legislative attempts to deal with immigration.

To be successful, any immigration policy must, at a minimum, deal with three specific issues: the lure of U.S. jobs to foreign workers, the pressures toward clandestine entry into the United States, and the current population of undocumented aliens. Solutions to these problems raise a number of peripheral issues. In addition, there are other areas related to immigration that can and should be dealt with, but these three are essential for immigration reform to succeed.

The vast majority of undocumented immigrants—and legal immigrants, too—have an economic motivation for coming to the United States. They believe, and usually correctly, that they can have a better life for themselves and their children in the United States than in their home country. They come looking for jobs and willing to work hard to succeed. To remove the motive for entry, it must be made illegal for employers to hire workers who are ineligible to work in the United States. There must be effective enforcement of such a provision, together with penalties severe enough to deter employers from breaking the law.

An effective method of validating an individual's right to employment is a corollary to employer sanctions. Employers must be able to differentiate between eligible and ineligible workers in order to comply with the requirements of such a law. Two objections must be dealt with in developing a worker-identification system. The system must avoid employment discrimination against people who look or sound foreign or who have foreign-sounding names. Second, the civil liberties of all Americans must be protected.

Clandestine entry into the United States must be made more difficult. At a minimum, this would mean additional resources for the INS to regain control of the borders. One recent proposal relating to this area is to increase the cost to the undocumented immigrant of an unsuccessful border crossing. Currently, an undocumented alien who is apprehended crossing the border or in the interior is given a trip out of the country and is free to attempt another clandestine entry immediately. There is no effective deterrent to repeated attempts at entry.

Pressure for illegal entry to the United States comes from the great demand to immigrate and the very long waiting lists to do so in many countries. These pressures will only intensify in the future as

the populations in sending countries continue to increase. For example, between 1980 and 2000, the labor force of Mexico will double. These additional people will have to earn a living—either in Mexico or in the United States. Additional foreign aid to assist economic development in the countries that send undocumented immigrants has been proposed as one method of lessening pressure on the United States. In the long run, economic development is probably the answer, but the appropriate role for the United States is not clear.

Increased quotas for legal immigration are another proposal that would alleviate somewhat the pressures for illegal entry. Under current policy, the United States is willing to accept a certain number of people each year—amounting to roughly 550,000 in recent years. It is the popular belief that the population increases from immigration by this same amount. However, more than 100,000 former immigrants emigrate from the country every year. Thus, net immigration is actually quite a bit less than the number of foreign-born persons admitted for residence every year. If the United States is willing to accept an annual increase from immigration of 550,000, then the actual immigration ceiling could be increased by at least 100,000 and still the net effect would be no more than the prescribed amount.

The current population of undocumented aliens must be dealt with in any successful immigration program. Many of these people have been in the United States for many years, have lived within the laws of the land—with the obvious exception of their own immigration status—and built significant equities in this country. Any attempted mass deportations would be inhumane, would be perceived as racist, and would create significant international problems. Therefore, in the interests of fairness and expediency, undocumented aliens who meet certain minimum criteria should be granted status as permanent resident aliens.

The details and execution of the legalization program are less important than the existence of such a program. Planning for such a program should recognize the differences between undocumented settlers, sojourners, and commuters by having a minimum continuous-residency requirement. Furthermore, policymakers and those who design a legalization program should be aware of the true size of the undocumented population so that reasonable alternatives are not dismissed as too expensive.

There are many other items that have been proposed for immigration programs and many other aspects to be considered. The demand for labor in the United States in the absence of undocumented immigrants must be dealt with. One proposed solution has been a guest-worker program, similar to the *bracero* program in the past. Guest-worker programs have not met with resounding success in places where they have been attempted—Germany provides an example—but such programs remain as an alternative. Other options would include increased mechanization, increased wages to attract more employees, making the jobs more attractive, improved management and productivity, and, finally, moving the jobs outside the country. The foreign-relations aspects of any immigration pro-

posal must also be considered carefully, particularly those relating to Mexico.

Undocumented immigration continues to be one of the most explosive issues in the contemporary United States. No legislative attempt to deal with undocumented immigration has emerged from Congress. Solutions to the problem remain vexing; it is not clear whether any program, even one with the essential features discussed here, could meet with success. Nonetheless, we must continue to address the issue. Even though the number of undocumented aliens in the United States and the annual growth of that number are not as great as the most popularly quoted figures, the best estimate of 2 to 4 million persons increasing at 100,000 to 300,000 persons per year still represents a sizable number of people. Whatever their current numbers and effect on the economy, the potential effect on the next generation will be enormous if the current problems are not resolved.

25. New Rules of the Game

Nathan Glazer

American immigration policy in the course of our two hundred year history has been determined by many factors. These have included our need for workers and population, our ideological fear of the ideas immigrants might be bringing (beginning as early as Federalist fear of French revolutionaries, leading to the Alien and Sedition Acts in 1798), racial prejudice (leading to the restriction of the Chinese in 1882, the Japanese in 1907, and culminating in the banning of all Asian immigration and the sharp reduction in immigration of Jews from Eastern Europe and Italians in 1924), and humanitarian concerns. Foreign policy considerations have dominated our policies on refugees

SOURCE: Nathan Glazer. "New Rules of the Game," *The National Interest*, no. 8, Summer 1987, pp. 64–70, excerpts. Reprinted with permission. ©*The National Interest*, no. 8, Washington, D.C.

since the end of World War II, but have rarely affected the shaping of our overall immigration policy. But just as the American economy becomes increasingly entangled with the world economy, so that we can no longer conduct our economic affairs in isolation from or indifference to other major economies, so too with the flow of people. The domestic influences that have dominated immigration policy in the past will have to be viewed in the light of that policy's impact on other countries. Conversely, we will have to be increasingly concerned with how other countries, because they wish us ill or wish some part of their population ill, may try to overwhelm our own immigration decisions with crises of their making to which we must respond and which we cannot shape. We have seen this in the case of the Cuban Marielitos and the Vietnamese boat people—and we must legitimately fear that we have not seen the end of mass expulsions in which we are targeted as the residual country of refuge. All this is new, and we have hardly considered how to respond to these developments.

Some relations between immigration and foreign policy are not new, and we have lived with them a long time: I have in mind the impact of immigrants and their descendants on foreign policy as it affects their homelands' interests. Charles Mathias has suggested that immigration is possibly "the single most important determinant of American foreign policy." That may be going too far. Senator Mathias was thinking, of course, of the strong influence of various ethnic groups in affecting American foreign policy, an influence that could be discerned a hundred years ago or more, as American politicians tried to appeal to or respond to the strong anti-British feelings of Irish Americans. In World War I and World War II, a host of ethnic groups, formed by our free immigration, entered into the political battle around American neutrality, their leaders staking out positions on the basis of whether neutrality or intervention hurt or aided their homelands or (as in the case of those wishing to achieve national independence for their native group) their hoped-for putative homelands.

We are ever more aware and accepting of these influences. It is a rare American political figure who would lash out against "hyphenated Americanism," as both Theodore Roosevelt and Woodrow Wilson did in the run-up to World War I. We are also rather more sophisticated about such loyalties and identification, understanding that they will exist and will make themselves felt. Perhaps one reason we are more sophisticated is that the entire question of national interest is less clear-cut than it once was. It was Samuel Lubell who pointed out that one possible reason the South was the most interventionist section of the country in the prelude to World War II was because it was primarily English and Scottish in origin (leaving aside the blacks), and had been less affected than the Northeast and Midwest by massive Irish, German, and Italian immigration. But did this mean the South was defending the national interest, and the other sections were disloyal? Misguided, perhaps, and defending an evil and unwise policy, but if both

sections were being influenced by ethnic origins, it was not easy to see where a sharply defined national interest independent of ethnic allegiances came into play.

These ethnic influences on foreign policy have, if anything, grown, as ethnic groups are less and less inhibited by fears of disloyalty and charges of "hyphenated Americanism" from engaging in open lobbying and pressures to advance the claims of homelands or countries (such as Israel) that have become symbolic homelands. Senator Mathias might well have had in mind the involvement of his own Greek community in exerting pressure on American policy toward Greece and Turkey.

The rapid creation in the past twenty years of large new ethnic groups as a consequence of our 1965 immigration act has increased the number of ethnic players in American foreign policy. For thirty-five years, the United States could lean toward Pakistan and against India without worrying about domestic pressures—there were no Pakistanis or Indians to pressure their Congressmen. That situation has changed. A half million Asian Indians are now on the scene in the United States, their numbers growing through immigration and natural increase at a rate of more than 20,000 a year. Their leaders will undoubtedly be heard from as we debate additional military aid to Pakistan; in fifteen years, they may be as influential in shaping American policy on issues affecting the military balance between India and Pakistan as a million Greeks have been in the policy debates affecting the military balance between Greece and Turkey.

All this is well known, but it is not likely that Congress will allow this common knowledge to affect our immigration policy. No one, at the time we expanded the categories of those who could enter in 1965, by eliminating the national-origins quotas which strongly favored Northern Europe, looked ahead to consider what the impact of the creation of many large ethnic groups, not previously present in any numbers on American soil, would be on foreign policy. Indeed, whatever prescience anyone might have possessed, they could not have made such an estimate. The best informed observers of the day expected that our immigration policy shift in 1965 would lead to an increase in

Italian, Greek, and Jewish immigrants, not Asian and Latin American immigrants—for it was the European groups that had fought for the revision of the immigration act. No one expected that the effect of the new law, in combination with other unforeseeable events, would be to shift the weight of immigration from Europeans to Asians and Latin Americans; to create in the United States large new ethnic groups of Koreans, Asian Indians, Vietnamese, Dominicans, Colombians, and others; and to expand greatly the number of Chinese, Filipinos, Mexicans, Jamaicans, and others.

Two other kinds of relations between immigration policy and foreign policy have come to the fore since 1965, and will have to be taken into account. The first, which we have considered in relation to Mexico, is how our openness or restrictiveness to immigration affects other countries. The impact of mass emigration on home countries is not new, and has in the past been a subject of concern to many countries. The loss of skilled manpower, for the economy and the military, the depopulation of agricultural areas, and concern over how one's countrymen would be treated abroad have been factors that played a role at given times in all the countries that were the sources of the growth of the American population. In our need for labor, we sucked in millions, unconcerned as to what that might mean for Sweden or Norway, Bavaria or Sicily, Bohemia or Galicia. Just how the governments of those countries responded to a wave of emigration that at times approached depopulation would be an interesting question to examine; on the whole, it has been neglected. . . .

Even if we insist that American immigration policy is our concern alone, other countries can make that claim a mockery. Cuba can, and has, by forcing us to accept 120,000 Marielitos we had no intention of accepting. Vietnam can, by expelling (or allowing to leave) hundreds of thousands of boat people who in the end will find their major destination of refuge the United States. Mass expulsions, as Michael Teitelbaum has pointed out, are a new twist in the relations between immigration and foreign policy, one we did not have to deal with before World War I. Persons who fled because of political persecution there were, but they were

individuals or small groups of leaders and activists, not masses. Nor did we have to deal with the issue in law at all as long as immigration was essentially uncontrolled, as was the case until the early 1920s, though polygamists, anarchists, and some other categories were banned. Even though anarchism was then something of a mass movement, the impact of this prohibition was on individuals.

It is primarily in our terrible twentieth century that political and religious persecution producing masses of refugees has become a major issue. For a while, we ignored it: the fact that Jews had to leave Germany and Eastern Europe to escape persecution made no dent on our immigration policies at all. If they were German Jews, they had the accidental benefit of the ample German quota of the act of 1924. If they were Polish, hard luck. A considerable degree of anti-Semitism in the State Department (and the country as a whole) made it hard, even while Jews were being sent by the millions to death camps, to effect even the slightest bending of our harsh immigration laws in their favor during World War II.

We were more considerate of refugees from communist countries in the postwar period. Our first refugee act that responded to the reality of mass emigration for political or religious or racial and ethnic reasons was passed only in 1953, and that defined a refugee as a person fleeing "from a Communist dominated country or area, or from any country within the general area of the Middle East." In 1980, a new act adopted the politically neutral language of the 1967 United Nations Protocol on Refugees: a refugee is someone who "owing to a well-founded fear of being persecuted for reasons of race, religion, nationality, membership of a particular social group or political opinion, is outside the country of his nationality and is . . . unable or . . . unwilling to return to it." A new right of asylum was also established in the act. In 1978 the number of refugees granted this was about 2,000; the new act raised the number to 5,000. It is one of the ironies of our age of persecution that laws designed for individuals are soon overwhelmed by masses. So with the refugee act of 1980, where it was assumed that a relatively modest number of refugees, set by the president and

Congress each year, would deal with the problem. The Marielitos and Vietnamese soon showed us how naive that would be, and we have set figures for refugees each year far larger than anticipated in the legislation, and still not enough to respond to mass expulsions.

Similarly with seekers of asylum: A mere 5,000 at the time of the passage of the Refugee Act of 1980, they had ballooned to 164,000 by 1984. In our age, persecution, and the resulting status of refugee and asylum seeker, once the mark of an exceptional individual, become the condition of masses.

It is here that relations between immigration policy and foreign policy become most controversial and most delicate. We find it easy, understandably, to accept refugees from communist countries with whom we are at odds, and whose deprivations of human rights we emphasize—and in some cases may for political reasons exaggerate. We find it hard to accept that countries that are allied with us politically will also have people who flee in fear of persecution for their politics. A simple insistence that *no* political considerations at all may enter into decisions on admitting refugees or granting asylum status, as demanded by human rights advocates, is unrealistic. In addition, they often ignore real differences. In all the countries around which disputes as to whether to admit refugees or grant asylum status now rage, economic problems are so severe that there is a real question how to separate economic reasons for immigration—which are accommodated within the main body of immigration law—from political reasons, which are accommodated within the Refugee Act. War alone and its disorder create fear and real physical threats—but the Refugee Act was not written to aid victims of civil war.

Another difference ignored is that between persecution by government—which is the kind of persecution foreseen and attended to by the Refugee Act—and fear of reprisal by non-governmental agents. The latter is or should be a law-and-order problem within the country itself, and should not be solved by granting the right of asylum. Admittedly, for the individual threatened with death by non-governmental agents, it is hardly satisfactory

to be told that his problem is not foreseen by the Refugee Act, yet in fact there are different causes of fear, and the Refugee Act does not deal with all of them. It would be difficult to take the position that law and order have so broken down in a country that we must grant refuge to its citizens in this country because their own government cannot protect them.

I think the distinctions are real ones, whether or not they should affect our policies. However, the fact is that the demand for refuge is so great and comes from so many sources that regardless of how we decide individual cases from El Salvador or Guatemala, some kind of overall cap must be set on the demand for asylum. In some countries where we are reluctant to grant asylum for political reasons, the numbers of potential seekers of asylum are so great that even if we were to accept the claims that they advance, we would have to find other means for regulating the flow of refugees and asylum-seekers into the country.

Can foreign policy attempt to mitigate this terrible development of great streams of people being forced out of their country or desperate to leave because of persecution and internal war? Ideally, yes. Thus, the overthrow of Duvalier and Marcos, assisted or encouraged by the United States, meant that some refugees from those countries would return home. However, it hardly affected the great number of immigrants from those countries, who have reasons other than political for wishing to live in the United States. Improving the economic circumstances of those countries, which would reduce the flow, raises certain questions, as we indicated in the case of Mexico. First, do we know how to do it—and our aid policies are no sterling demonstration that we do. Further, even if we knew, would we want to spend the money and exert the political pressure that might improve their economic circumstances?

The United States has been spared up to now the most extreme consequences of immigration on foreign policy, consequences a good number of countries in the developing world have had to deal with. In some cases, a delicate ethnic balance has been threatened by immigration. This is what has been happening in Assam, as Bengalis move in, often over the international frontier with Bangladesh, with results leading to massacre and a situation of near open rebellion and threatened civil war. In the Punjab, an opposite situation exists, in which Sikh extremists are trying to drive Hindus from the state through terrorism to ensure Sikh dominance. In Lebanon, a delicate balance between various Muslim and Christian groups was upset by the mass entry of Palestinian refugees, which was undoubtedly one factor in the complicated skein of events that has resulted in endless and bloody civil war. The oil-rich Gulf countries have feared the impact of immigrants from other Arab countries—one reason they have preferred workers from Pakistan and India and Korea who cannot participate in local politics. So immigration, which may be seen as only a means of dealing with labor shortages or fulfilling humanitarian responsibilities, may under certain circumstances threaten the balance of internal politics, and even threaten the subversion of the state.

This is one rarely stated element of American concern with Mexican immigration. About ten years ago, during an early congressional inquiry into immigration issues, one witness asserted that by the end of the century there would be 140 million Mexicans, half of them living north of the Rio Grande. This was wildly exaggerated—a reflection of a time when American officials could assert there might be as many as 12 million illegal immigrants, a figure now thought to be at least three times as large as the real one. Nevertheless, at some point one will have to think about the impact of Mexican immigration on our relations with Mexico, not from the point of view of annoyances created by restricting immigration, but from the point of view of the creation of what may be considered a Mexican lobby dwarfing any other potential immigrant-ethnic lobby. This may seem highly unlikely. The assimilatory power of American society has

been enormous. The fact that the Germans are the largest immigrant ethnic component of the American population, next to the English, Welsh, and Scots, has had hardly any effect on American foreign relations. It did not prevent us from entering into two wars against Germany; if there has been an underground influence of greater sympathy with Germany in American foreign relations as a result of this large component of the American population, it has not been obvious.

And yet, the past may be no guide to the future. One can list many differences between the mass immigration of the nineteenth century and immigration today that would suggest a different course of assimilation, with different consequences. These considerations play no role in shaping our immigration policy. In time one suspects they will.

To say something is affected by, and affects foreign policy, is to suggest that there is an answer in foreign policy. If there is, it is unfortunately no simple answer. It takes no great prescience to look around the globe and see possibilities—perhaps probabilities—that we will be faced by new streams of refugees, created by political developments, knocking at our doors. One hesitates to make a list of these possibilities. But consider, to take only one example, what is likely to happen when blacks rule South Africa. One need not take the gloomiest scenario to project that hundreds of thousands will want to, perhaps have to, move elsewhere—and may have some claim that puts them under the Refugee Act. This is hardly the kind of factor that should play the largest role in determining our South African policy. But it is a consideration that at some point should come into play. Just how it might affect that policy is a delicate matter. But it should be thought about, for our immigration problems are no longer a matter that can be determined solely by domestic considerations.

Questions for Discussion

1. When, and why, did illegal immigration become a U.S. foreign policy problem?

2. What proposals have been offered for its solution?

3. What makes any solution difficult?

4. Does permissiveness toward illegal immigrants encourage even greater influxes?

5. As the magnitude of the problem of illegal immigration is increasing, and as past reforms and concessions have not stemmed the tide, what do you think needs to be done? What does the national interest require?

Selected Bibliography

BRIGGS, V.M., JR., and MARTA TIENDA (Eds.). *Immigration: Issues & Policies.* Washington, DC: National Council on Employment Policy, 1984.

CAFFERTY, PASTORA SAN JUAN, et al. *The Dilemmas of American Immigration: Beyond the Golden Door.* New Brunswick: Transaction Publishers, 1983.

EHRLICH, PAUL R., and ANNE H. EHRLICH. *The Population Explosion.* New York: Simon and Schuster, 1990.

HARRINGTON, MICHAEL. *The Vast Majority: A Journey to the World's Poor.* New York: Simon and Schuster, 1977.

LOESCHER, GIL, and LAILA MONAHAN (Eds.). *Refugees and International Relations.* New York: Oxford University Press, 1989.

MITCHELL, CHRISTOPHER (Ed.). *Western Hemisphere Immigration and United States Foreign Policy.* University Park, PA: Pennsylvania State University, 1992.

ORGANIZATION FOR ECONOMIC COOPERATION AND DEVELOPMENT. *Migration, Growth and Development.* Paris: OECD, 1979.

RASPAIL, JEAN. *The Camp of the Saints.* New York: Simon and Schuster, 1975.

SIMON, JULIAN L. *The Economic Consequences of Immigration.* Cambridge: Basil Blackwell, 1989.

TEITELBAUM, MICHAEL S. *Latin Migration North: The Problem for U.S. Foreign Policy.* New York: Council on Foreign Relations, 1985.

WEINTRAUB, SIDNEY. *A Marriage of Convenience: Relations Between Mexico and the United States.* New York: Oxford University Press, 1990.

CHAPTER 8

The United States and the Global Economy

The plight of its economy may be the most immediately pressing problem of the United States. It is losing its competitiveness abroad, running annual trade deficits of more than $100 billion, becoming dependent on cheap Middle East oil, and relying on foreign borrowing to finance ballooning domestic expenditures. Unemployment remains high, the costs of health and welfare services are out of control, functional illiteracy is the highest in the industrial world, and one in five children lives in poverty.

C. Fred Bergsten, Director of the Institute for International Economics and chairman of the Competitiveness Policy Council created by Congress, explores the growing primacy of economic considerations in U.S. foreign policy, the dilemmas the United States faces, and the essentials of what are needed if the downward spiral is to be reversed (Reading 26). His assessment highlights the historical roots of America's current condition as a declining hegemon and the complex interrelatedness of the main problems.

The sources of America's economic troubles are both political and structural. In the 1960s, politics led successive presidents to deplete the nation's wealth in Vietnam. Kennedy made the first major commitment of U.S. forces; Lyndon Johnson quickly expanded the number of troops to more than 500,000; and Richard Nixon, in trying to leave with some assurances that the status quo would be maintained, held on longer

than he should have. Yet none of them was willing to raise taxes to pay for the enormously increased military budgets. And when President Johnson adopted a myriad of social programs to build "the great society," again no plan was made for financing the inflationary policies, except through increased borrowing. The dollar weakened, inflation eroded American competitiveness, and foreign borrowing became an essential feature of government policy. During the 1980s, the huge defense buildup and continuing outlays for social programs, which increased the national debt from $1 trillion to $4 trillion, was possible only because of Japanese, European, and Middle Eastern purchases of U.S. government securities. In less than two decades, the United States went from being the world's most important creditor to being its biggest debtor. As recently as the late 1970s, U.S. imports and exports each represented about 6 to 7 percent of total GNP (Gross National Product); but a decade later the relationship between them had altered, creating a troubling disequilibrium, with imports soaring to 13 percent of GNP and exports lagging behind at about 9.5 percent.

Structural changes have also contributed to a decline of America's once unchallenged hegemonic position. At the end of the Second World War, the United States was the industrial engine of the international system. But in time new industrial powers emerged, most with American assistance—Germany and Japan, in particular, but also France, Italy, Taiwan, and South Korea. They captured a hefty part of world trade, with a concomitant, and inevitable, decrease in America's disproportionately large share. Throughout the Cold War, the United States assumed the military responsibility for protecting allies and friends in Europe and the Far East from the Soviet threat and diverted its resources from productive to nonproductive (that is, defense) uses. As a result, it found itself economically and commercially lagging at a time when competitors were proving more adept at exploiting new technologies, outpacing it in industrial productivity, and investing heavily in more efficient plants and new infrastructure. By the time of the Reagan years, the situation was critical and many predicted that with its "decreased rate of economic growth and a low rate of national savings, the United States was living and defending commitments far beyond its means. In order to bring its commitments and power into balance once again, the United States would one day have to cut back further on its overseas commitments, reduce the American standard of living, or decrease domestic productive investment even more than it already had."[1]

To compound the American predicament, there was a corrosive financial crisis that threatened the very stability of the international banking system. Awash with petrodollars (surplus funds acquired by oil-rich countries when oil prices soared in the 1970s and were deposited abroad for interest income), U.S. banks lent to Third World countries, which borrowed at high rates of

interest, but found themselves unable to repay from commodity exports because of the global downturn in economic activity. In addition, rising interest rates increased the cost of the indebtedness of Third World countries precisely when they were least able to cope with debt-service payments. Banks that had lent in excess of $500 billion found themselves on the threshold of bankruptcy. Through creative financing, debt relief and rescheduling, and large-scale loans, this crisis was managed without a systemic collapse, but at the expense of economic growth.

At another level, the interdependency and fragility of the international banking system were demonstrated when one rogue bank facilitated the spread of crime and corruption across national borders. The story of the nefarious activities of the privately owned Bank of Credit and Commerce International (BCCI) is not yet finished, but enough is known for us to understand how it was transformed from a legitimate lending institution for Third World enterprises and immigrants into a haven for drug laundering operations and fraudulent investment schemes. Established in Pakistan in 1972, by the time of the crackdown on its activities in July 1991, the BCCI had enmeshed eminent Washington insiders and foreign intelligence services into its orbit of illegality.

Somehow, the international system has survived intact. But its structural vulnerability was laid bare in September 1992, when European financial markets panicked because of fears that Western Europe's political leaders were having second thoughts about the desirability of European economic integration. Currency speculators "forced Italy to devalue the lira by 8 percent while Britain was forced to raise its prime lending

[1] Robert Gilpin. *The Political Economy of International Relations.* Princeton: Princeton University Press, 1987, pp. 347–348.

rate by five percentage points in a three-day period and to sell 25 percent of its dollar reserves to save its currency from free fall."[2] The dangers for the United States are clear. One stems from the combination of technology and the globalization of world financial markets which enables investors to shift overnight from one currency to another; if investors lose confidence in the dollar, they could stampede a run from the dollar, forcing the U.S. government "to raise interest rates to stop huge capital outflows, which would plunge the economy back into recession."[3] Another inheres in huge perennial budget deficits financed by extensive foreign borrowing. With the largest foreign debt in the world, the United States needs to find a way to reduce the deficit and at the same time foster economic growth.

The problems are easier to analyze than solve. Two examples provide a hint of the complexity that faces the Clinton administration. First, what to do about the cutting-edge, high-tech industries that have lost their once-dominant positions. As far back as 1984, the United States started to import more electronic products than it was exporting. The stunning decline was dramatically manifested at the end of 1992 in the plight of IBM. Long one of the pillars of American technological prowess, IBM's fall from favor was due to poor management decisions, a sluggish response to new technologies, and an unwillingness to adapt fast enough to changed market conditions. Some critics have linked this to American management's fixation on showing profits rather than building for the future; this "short-termism" translates into low investment in research

and development and in a failure to work continually to upgrade the quality of the work force.[4]

Second, what to do about trade, which is one of the fundamental types of interactions among nations.[5] According to the theory of comparative advantage, which is the traditional explanation for trade, each nation specializes in producing those goods that it can produce relatively most efficiently, "that is, those goods that consume the least amount of a country's resources in comparison to other countries," and it trades these for the goods of other countries. Specialization is the key to success, but it requires a high degree of cooperation among nations. In the interest of facilitating international trade, the General Agreement on Tariffs and Trade (GATT) was established in 1948 to eliminate protectionist barriers and ensure reciprocity among trading partners.

Japan, in the view of a growing number of U.S. analysts, has been practicing protectionism in order to provide advantages for its own firms. Clyde Prestowitz, for one, author of *Trading Places: How We Allowed Japan to Take the Lead,* contends that Japan (and South Korea and Taiwan, as well) subsidizes key industries to give them an edge in developing overseas markets. Through its Ministry of International Trade and Industry, Japan targets industries of the future and then proceeds to subsidize home enterprises until such time as they have acquired the technology, know-how, and servicing capability to strike out on their own.

---

[2] Madis Senner. "The U.S. Isn't Immune to Global Chaos," *The New York Times,* September 27, 1992, p. F13.

[3] Ibid.

[4] Ray Marshall and Marc Tucker. "Building a Smarter Work Force," *Technology Review,* vol. 95, no. 7, October 1992, p. 54.

[5] Dan Haendel. "Economic Power: A Base for National Security and Foreign Policy," unpublished manuscript.

Moreover, as Robert B. Reich, a Harvard economist and President Clinton's Secretary of Labor, has argued, the United States should not sell its patents and experience merely to obtain some inexpensive and easy financing, as Western Electric did in 1953 when it "licensed its newly invented solid-state transistor to Sony for $25,000" (!); or a few years later as RCA did, when it "sold its color television technology to the Japanese," a sale that triggered "the beginning of the end of video electronics in America."[6] Rather, he believes that the United States should adopt an industrial policy along the lines of what Japan has done, that is, the government should provide capital and subsidies for American industries that are deemed to be of critical importance for our export earnings and our national security. Perhaps nothing illustrates more clearly the extent to which the United States has come to depend on Japanese high-tech products than the U.S. military's realization "that many of the weapons it used to beat Iraq could not have functioned without Japanese components."[7]

There are no easy answers. Merely getting tough with Japan will not make U.S. industry more efficient: emulating its low capital gains tax for businesses investing in new plant and research might. Nor will mirroring Japan's industrial policy necessarily bring the desired cooperation among U.S. enterprises: perhaps less stringent anti-trust regulation might. Moreover, as a government-sponsored report prepared by a panel of influential Japanese businessmen made clear, Japan will fight back, if the United States uses "tax and trade laws to impede

the American operations of Japanese companies," or limits Japanese access to markets because of preferences for Mexico and Canada under the North American trade agreement.[8]

Closer to home is the problem of Mexico, an economic and political partner of major importance. Economically, the United States is Mexico's main trading partner; and Mexico is third only to Canada and Japan among countries trading with the United States. Mexico's enormous reservoirs of oil and natural gas are of strategic as well as economic significance. But the problems straining the U.S.-Mexican relationship are politically explosive: a burgeoning population, which will exceed 120 million by the turn of the century; an already large-scale unemployment and underemployment, which have led to substantial illegal immigration to the United States; and drug trafficking, which worsens from year to year. The two countries have also differed markedly in the past over foreign policy, especially with respect to Castro's Cuba and Central America. Always in the background is Mexico's remembrance of Yanqui imperialism in the nineteenth century. The dictator, Porfirio Diaz, once lamented, "Poor Mexico, so far from God, so near the United States."

However, there is a new mood of optimism in the relationship and a new experiment in partnership underway—the North American Free Trade Agreement (NAFTA). The initiative came from Mexico. In 1990, President Carlos Salinas de Gortari proposed a free trade agreement, perhaps as a response to the U.S.-Canadian agreement that was signed in the fall of 1989; perhaps

[6] Robert B. Reich. "Boeing's Joint Venture: A Faustian Bargain with the Japanese," *The New York Times,* April 6, 1986.

[7] James Fallows. "Is Japan the Enemy?" *The New York Review of Books,* May 30, 1991, p. 31.

[8] David E. Sanger. "Japanese Warn U.S. Not to Act Rashly on Trade," *The New York Times,* December 23, 1992, pp. D1–D2.

as a result of the assistance the United States had provided in the late 1980s, when it took the lead in arranging for debt relief for Mexico (and other Latin American and Third World countries). For Salinas, then embarked on a course of extensive economic reform, it was a bold step to take, an integral part of his ambitious program of development and modernization. His domestic opponents, however, believe he is jeopardizing Mexico's independence and economic prospects.[9] A searching examination of the pros and cons of the NAFTA accord is presented by two Mexican analysts (Reading 27). Their assessment may find a sympathetic audience in the White House, because President Clinton has expressed a number of reservations, similar to theirs, about the agreement negotiated by his predecessor.

Shortly before taking office, President Bill Clinton convened an economic conference to identify and analyze the principal economic problems facing the country. Stressing the long-term nature of the solutions that had to be found, he set out the parameters of what his administration intended to do:

- "First, we must invest in our people, their education, their training and their skills . . . ;

- second, we must increase investment, both public and private, to create jobs—investment in technology, investment in infrastructure, investment in plant and equipment, investment in research and development;
- third, we must stop the cycle of borrow and spend economics;
- fourth, we need a new approach to energy and to the environment . . . ;
- finally, we must make a personal commitment to our government . . . and [show] a willingness to give something back to the country and to challenge the way the government does its business so that we are not wasting so much money and not wasting so much of our future."[10]

These are strong words and provide criteria with which to evaluate the performance of the new administration in reversing America's economic decline, and the ability of the United States to take the lead in restructuring the multipolar world we are entering.

[9] See, for example, Cuanuhtemoc Cárdenas, "Misunderstanding Mexico," *Foreign Policy,* no. 78, Spring 1990, pp. 113–130. Cárdenas opposed Salinas in the 1988 elections.

[10] *The New York Times,* December 15, 1992, p. B10.

26.   The Primacy of Economics

C. Fred Bergsten

American foreign policy is at sea. With the collapse of communism and the disintegration of the Soviet Union, the principles that guided past behavior are gone or are going fast. Replacements have not yet been discerned and agreed upon. Decisions on individual issues are ad hoc and without context.

For the past half century, four basic concepts defined both international relations as a whole and American external interests in particular:

The first was the dominance of security issues. Military capability lay at the center of America's international engagement. Most U.S. global economic initiatives, especially those attempting to create systemic structures in the early postwar years, were primarily motivated by security concerns.

The second core concept was bipolarity. World order (or disorder) was based on the existence of, and relationship between, the two military superpowers. The struggle between the United States and the Soviet Union largely defined the international environment.

Third, the bipolar rivalry contained an important ideological dimension. America espoused democracy and capitalism. The USSR embodied totalitarian politics and command economics under the banner of communism.

Fourth, each superpower erected an alliance system to support its objectives. The United States embraced past enemies to construct NATO and the U.S.-Japan Security Treaty, and built multilateral organizations to pursue its goals. The USSR created the Warsaw Pact. Each superpower sought to align as many countries as possible with its bloc. The universal organizations that embodied both groups, notably the United Nations, foundered as each of the chief antagonists blocked actions that could favor its rival.

SOURCE: C. Fred Bergsten, "The Primacy of Economics," *Foreign Policy*, no. 87, Summer 1992, pp. 3–24. Copyright © 1992 by the Institute for International Economics. Reprinted by permission.

With the end of the Cold War, American policymakers must reappraise the precepts that will define world affairs, and clearly link those precepts to American interests. Today's external challenges will have to be clarified for the American public and met in ways that will garner broad support. There will be great virtue in again articulating a central theme that will be readily perceived and accepted.

Traditional security issues such as nonproliferation and regional conflicts will of course remain important. Rogue countries will have to be deterred and, if necessary, repelled. In addition, the United States will want to project its key values, including democracy and human rights, around the world— as in the current transition in Eastern Europe and the former Soviet Union. Such "new global issues" as the environment, migration and refugee flows, population growth, arms transfers, and the drug trade are increasingly salient. Continued, even accelerated, support for development in the poorer countries must also be on the agenda.

But the central task in shaping a new American foreign policy is to set priorities and select central themes. Those choices must derive from America's national interests, which have shifted sharply in the direction of economics. The share of trade in the U.S. economy has risen by two and a half times since 1960. Exports and imports of goods and services amount to nearly one-quarter of total gross domestic product. The United States now depends as heavily on trade as do the European Community (EC) as a group and Japan. As the world's largest debtor country, and one still running large external deficits, the United States also relies on sizable inflows of foreign capital.

Moreover, the American economy has become deeply dependent on export-led growth: The annual trade balance has improved by more than $120 billion in real terms since 1987, providing half the country's growth in 1990 and cutting the recession in half in 1991. The massive budget deficits inherited from the 1980s preclude any significant use of fiscal policy to stimulate economic activity; the need to reduce the deficit will in fact depress the economy for some time. The fragility of the financial system and the overhang of private debt limit the impact of easier monetary policy, as illustrated by the meager response to repeated and substantial cuts in interest rates by the Federal Reserve. The United States thus enters the decade without the usual policy tools to promote domestic demand and will have to rely on foreign markets well into the 1990s.

American foreign policy will also be shaped by an external environment that has moved sharply in the direction of economics. Even during the Cold War, most countries placed economic concerns at or near the top of their foreign policy agendas. Japan chose to do so; most developing countries were forced to do likewise by their circumstances. America's European allies, and a few countries such as South Korea and Taiwan that faced unique security threats, devoted substantial resources to military preparedness but still emphasized economic concerns much more than did the United States.

With the elimination of the principal threat to world peace, the priority most countries attach to economic issues will rise substantially. That tendency will be reinforced, at least over the next few years, by slower global economic growth as the United States struggles with its deep structural problems, as the West European countries reduce their inflation rates and budget deficits to qualify for economic and monetary union, and as Japan adjusts to labor shortages and the collapse of its financial bubble. The result will be even fiercer competition for markets and investments around the world. The prospect of a global savings shortage, when and if more rapid growth were to resume, would sustain and even intensify the struggle to attract capital. If the Uruguay Round of the General Agreement on Tariffs and Trade (GATT) were to fail, primarily because of European unwillingness to reform its agricultural policies, European-U.S. trade conflict would join existing Japanese-U.S. tensions to threaten a two-front trade war that would elevate the economic priority even more rapidly.

Even the "non-economic" issues cited above embody considerable economic content. Conflicts in the Persian Gulf, the most volatile of all the regions, often center on oil. Third World growth is important as an outlet for American exports as well as for humanitarian impulses. The population explosion will ultimately be checked only by faster economic development. It is becoming clear that environmental degradation can carry large economic costs. Arms transfers are motivated at least as much by economic as by security interests. The foreign policy agenda for the future repeatedly returns to economics.

The primacy of economic over security issues will produce a second basic change: Three roughly equal economic superpowers (tripolarity) will replace two roughly equal military superpowers (bipolarity) at the center of the world stage. The European Community already has a larger economy than the United States and will function as a single actor on global economic issues to an increasing degree. Japan is already the world's largest creditor country and a leader in many technologies, and its economy will become as large in absolute dollar terms as America's early in the next decade (if it grows annually at about 4 per cent to America's 2–2.5 per cent and the yen appreciates to 100-to-1 against the dollar). The United States, Japan, and the EC depend about equally on international trade and financial flows—so none could wage or welcome a trade war believing that others would lose more. The three large economic areas are already equivalent, or shortly will be, in the key criteria that determine global status.

Third, the Cold War ideological confrontation between capitalism and communism is likely to be replaced by competition among alternative versions of market economies. In Japan's "non-capitalist market economy," corporations pursue the interests of employees, suppliers, and communities more than those of shareholders, and hence have very different governance systems than American firms. It is clear that Japan values production, relative to consumption, much more than the United States does. Government of course plays a far more active economic role in the Japanese than in the

Anglo-Saxon model. Western observers are closely studying the Japanese and other Asian models to see what could be learned to improve Western economic performance.

The social welfare systems of continental Europe present another alternative to the U.S. model. Government plays a considerably greater role in guiding, if not supplanting, private activity. Banks play a much larger role in corporate management, especially in Germany.

The fourth potential change lies in alliance arrangements. The Cold War regime of bilateral and multilateral alignments that centered on the United States and the Soviet Union, some extending as far as South Vietnam and Cuba, is giving way to very different, in some cases more natural, regional groupings. The East European members of the former Warsaw Pact are already signing association agreements with the EC and will presumably become full members within a decade. The Baltic states, and several other republics that have risen from the ashes of the Soviet Union, seek similar arrangements. Russia itself may associate with Western Europe in the foreseeable future. NATO is already working out new modes of cooperation with the former adversaries.

In Asia, adoption of the East Asia Economic Caucus proposed by Malaysia would represent the first modern pan-Asian grouping. It could bring former adversaries—notably China but potentially also Vietnam and North Korea—into the fold, just as Russia may be brought into the European compacts. Similar patterns can be seen in Latin America with the recent explosion of subregional pacts like the Southern Cone common market (Mercosur) and a revitalized Andean Pact. Those Latin American efforts are partly motivated by desires to qualify for, and strengthen their positions in, subsequent negotiations with the United States that would expand the North American Free Trade Area (NAFTA) to create a Western Hemisphere free trade area.

All those changes are highly desirable. Even trade wars are far less threatening than nuclear holocaust. Competition among fellow democracies with market economies is far preferable to confron-

tation with an implacable ideological foe bent on world domination. The change in scenery represents a historic triumph for the United States and its allies.

But the world moves on to new challenges, new configurations of power, and even new threats. There is no time to bask in the successes of the recent past. The United States must understand and respond to the new realities if it is to pursue its national interests effectively and refashion a coherent foreign policy.

AMERICAN TASKS, AMERICAN DILEMMAS

American foreign policy must achieve three major objectives in this new era, each of which poses a major dilemma for the United States. The most important aim will be the pursuit of U.S. economic goals. It is impossible to envisage a prosperous America, or an America that retains world leadership, without a foreign policy that effectively supports that country's economic interests.

America's economic goals center on raising the standard of living of the average American and the competitiveness of the country's economy by achieving and maintaining open markets for international trade and investment. Despite its size, the American market cannot be fully competitive and efficient unless its firms and workers are constantly stimulated by the availability of foreign products and services. Nor can American firms and workers realize their full potential without access to major markets abroad, since the global economy is four times the size of their own. Domestic and external liberalizations must of course proceed simultaneously because of their impact on the U.S. trade balance, the competitive position of individual American industries, and the domestic politics of trade policy—since fair treatment of U.S. exports by others is essential to enable the United States to retain an open market at home.

Restoration of America's competitive strength is also central to the country's global status. Japan could be described as "an economic giant but a political pygmy" during the Cold War, but the

United States must avoid the reverse appellation in the years ahead. Chancellor Helmut Kohl of Germany is reported to have remarked that "we know who will win the medals in the economic Olympics of the year 2000 but we do not know which nations will bring home the gold, silver and bronze." Full American participation in the key global decisions, let alone a U.S. ability to continue playing a leadership role, is at stake—as the British learned during their decades of decline earlier this century.

Yet just as America's interest in pursuing its economic goals has risen sharply, the country's ability to do so has dropped precipitously because of the rise of the new economic superpowers and other highly competitive countries (such as the Asian newly industrialized countries).

That is the first dilemma now facing U.S. foreign policy: The United States will increasingly be the *demandeur* in international economic negotiations, but it will be less able to achieve its objectives. That in turn will make it extremely difficult to sustain an activist foreign policy because weakness in the domestic economy will increasingly be blamed on external factors and a failure of the country's negotiators to deliver. Just as organized labor left the liberal trade coalition in the 1960s and 1970s when it concluded that free trade was no longer in its interests, business and other groups that have supported America's world involvement will grow ambivalent—or even defect—if Washington does not pursue their pocketbook concerns diligently. America's new foreign policy will need both a strong economic foundation at home and successful economic initiatives abroad.

A second critical task for American policy will be to maintain smooth relations among the economic superpowers, much as it previously sought to limit tensions with the Soviet Union. There are both positive and negative reasons to do so. On the positive side, all countries benefit (at last in the aggregate) from open flows of international trade and investment. Hence the achievement of maximum prosperity for people throughout the world, including Americans, requires cooperation to those ends among the economic superpowers. They can now place priority on the positive-sum game of global economics instead of the negative-sum security game of the Cold War era.

At the same time, the inevitable disputes over economic and other issues must be prevented from escalating into damaging conflicts among relative equals—conflicts the United States could now lose. Moreover, it is hardly inconceivable that tensions among the economic giants could degenerate into broader conflicts. There are frequent historical examples of such degeneration when international regimes failed to accommodate the status and legitimate aspirations of rising powers.

In addition, as *New York Times* columnist Flora Lewis perceptively noted in her winter 1991–92 essay in FOREIGN POLICY, "it is a unique phenomenon of [this] era that economic and military might tend to be in separate hands"—as opposed to previous historic periods. In the spring 1992 issue of FOREIGN POLICY, *Asahi Shimbun* columnist Yoichi Funabashi noted that disputes between the United States and Japan are already moving beyond economics and into the political sphere. Hasty U.S. military withdrawals from Europe and Asia could even induce the other economic superpowers to devote more of their resources to military forces and further increase the risk of future confrontations.

Economic disputes among Europe, Japan, and the United States are of course nothing new. However, their nature, and perhaps depth, will now be quite different. The onset of power equality among the three means that Washington can no longer dictate outcomes on the basis of superior economic clout. But neither Japan nor Western Europe can replace the United States as a systematic arbiter of economic disputes, and the three have neither acted collectively to do so nor conferred that authority on existing international institutions. So there is no reliable mechanism for amicable dispute settlement among the economic superpowers.

Even more important, as predicted by this author in the summer 1990 issue of *Foreign Affairs*, American, European, and Japanese political leaders are no longer compelled, as in the Cold War, to place overriding importance on preserving their alliances and thus to suppress conflict on economic and other issues. Without the security "glue" to hold them together, the economic superpowers can much more easily fall into severe antagonisms. It would be an enormous irony of history if the Marxist prediction of inevitable conflict among the capitalist nations were to come true as a result of the collapse of the Marxist political systems. Nevertheless, containment of the risk of conflict among the economic superpowers must replace the Cold War's containment of military risk as a primary purpose of U.S. foreign policy.

There is of course inherent tension between defending U.S. economic interests and maintaining smooth relations among the economic superpowers. Aggressive pursuit of its national economic interests will often pit the United States against the EC or Japan, or occasionally both, and thus threaten relations among the three. That is the second dilemma confronting an economics-centered U.S. foreign policy.

A third major goal of America's post–Cold War foreign policy will be promotion of collective security arrangements. The United Nations provided an umbrella for the anti-Iraq alliance in the Persian Gulf war, and the U.N. (as well as some regional organizations) is being extensively tapped to handle difficult and costly regional peacekeeping. Collective security arrangements will probably play a central role in U.S. security goals.

As in the Gulf war, the world will probably want to continue drawing on American military strength when regional instability requires an armed response. But the United States must continue to insist that other countries also provide military forces and that the other economic superpowers, in addition to those countries directly affected that can afford it, pay a large portion of the bills.

"Collective leadership" in the Gulf war meant that the United States led and the United States collected—overfinancing its marginal military costs and thus turning an economic profit on the conflict. As a result, nerves were rubbed raw in several capitals, notably Tokyo and Bonn. Burden sharing and the accompanying responsibility sharing will have to be organized in the future to sustain political support in all participating countries.

But the imperfect overlap between the key countries in the security and economic spheres makes it difficult to do so. An enhanced U.N. role in security matters endows the members of the Security Council—China, France, Russia, the United Kingdom, and the United States—with critical authority. The main financiers, however, will be Japan and the EC as a group (with Germany central), and they can hardly be expected to pay unless their views are fully represented in security decisions The third dilemma for U.S. foreign policy is how to reconcile that mismatched influence on security and economic issues.

In fashioning a new foreign policy, the United States will thus need to advance three related objectives and overcome three dilemmas. It will have to promote its own economic interests despite a sharp decline in its relative economic clout. It must maintain friendly relations among the economic superpowers and work with them to preserve an open, globally oriented economic order while pursuing its narrower domestic economic goals. And it will need new collective security systems that depend on political and economic contributions by different sets of countries.

Those aims have not been at—or usually even near—the top of Washington's previous agenda. Some of them have been pursued in the past but with a rationale that was rooted in the Cold War struggle. Clearly, a new approach is needed.

A NEW FOREIGN POLICY

A policy that promotes U.S. economic interests and forges strong new economic and security systems would have five major components:

- substantially reforming domestic institutions to improve the competitive performance of the American economy, including its international trade and financial position;
- calibrating America's military drawdown to minimize inducements for the new economic superpowers to militarize;
- maintaining close bilateral ties with the key economic actors, notably Western Europe and Japan but including Saudi Arabia and others that are essential to the world economy;

- launching a series of initiatives through which America, a uniting Europe, and Japan (the Group of Three, or G-3) would recreate an open world economic order based on shared rights and responsibilities; and
- institutionalizing a collective security regime, mainly through the U.N., that would encompass political-military and economic-financial arrangements.

The centerpiece of any effective U.S. foreign policy must be a substantial improvement in the performance and international competitiveness of the American economy. Wholly or partly as a result of its reduced economic standing, the United States is perilously close to being unable to play a serious role—let alone a leading one—in a growing number of global issues. Examples include support for economic reform and democracy in Eastern Europe and the former Soviet Union, energy policy and the related problem of global warming, and even the activities of "its own" international financial institutions (the International Monetary Fund and World Bank). Even more important, domestic support for an activist foreign policy will wither if the economy continues to perform poorly with as much international engagement as it now experiences.

Further erosion of America's economic position will invite increasing exasperation and even disdain from other major countries. That distressing trend will encourage them to go their own way without the United States. In the late 1970s, the EC created the European Monetary System largely to escape the instability generated by relying on the dollar. More recently, America's seeming inability to support the IMF and World Bank contributed to European desires to create an alternative organization—the European Bank for Reconstruction and Development—that they could dominate and use to support economic reforms in Eastern Europe and the former Soviet Union. Japan's tacit acceptance of Malaysia's proposed East Asian Economic Caucus that excludes America is hardly unrelated to Japanese doubts about the future strength and policies of the United States.

Achieving the needed economic improvement will require action at three levels, as described

recently in the First Annual Report to the President and Congress of the Competitiveness Policy Council, a bipartisan national commission of 12 business, labor, government, and public leaders appointed by the president, Senate, and House. Significant changes in macroeconomic policies will be needed to boost the country's saving and investment rates, which are crucial to fostering national productivity growth but which are now by far the lowest in the industrial world. That will require converting the budget deficit into a surplus through a carefully crafted combination of cuts in defense spending and entitlement programs, and pro-saving tax increases. It may also require basic changes in the tax system to induce more saving and investment. (The United States is already the world's largest debtor country and further borrowing from abroad to finance domestic spending is both uncertain and unwise.)

Structural reforms are essential to strengthen U.S. education and worker training systems, cut health care costs, and improve corporate governance and commercialization of technology. Thoughtful sector-specific domestic policies can assist the development of crucial industries, as in the past with respect to agriculture and commercial aircraft and numerous other defense-related products. A comprehensive competitiveness strategy incorporating these three elements, including governmental assistance to those who are hurt in the process of required adjustment, can provide an alternative to protectionism or managed trade policies, which would undermine rather than promote American competitiveness. Such a strategy, in addition to restoring American economic strength, can help maintain an open global economy and resolve the dilemma of simultaneously pushing U.S. economic interests while limiting conflict with other economic superpowers. The strategy is required for foreign policy as well as for "purely economic" reasons.

The second element of a new foreign policy is to temper the speed and distribution of American military retrenchment. New military buildups in Europe, and especially Japan, would cause considerable unease, but there are few historic examples of economic powers that eschewed responsibility for their own security. Those who have, such as

Kuwait and Saudi Arabia today, have often found themselves in need of an outside rescue. Germany and Japan have relied on others throughout the postwar period only because of their unique historical circumstances.

The United States will for some time enjoy a "comparative advantage" in providing military protection, both nuclear and conventional, to other countries. It is hardly irrational for the United States, having invested trillions of dollars to create that advantage, to deploy its resources in ways that advance its economic and continuing security goals. The best way to do so now is to retain an adequate military presence overseas and an adequate overall security capability to deter the new superpowers from taking actions that could set the stage for frictions. Fortunately, most Europeans and Asians, including the economic superpowers, want American forces to stay. It is also cheaper to station U.S. troops abroad than at home, especially in Japan where the Japanese government pays most of the costs.

Acting as a military leader while asking allies to share the costs does not make the United States "the Hessians of the twenty-first century" any more than did its insistence that others finance the Gulf war. The United States would be pursuing its own national interests by keeping troops abroad. It would continue making all key decisions concerning their use, either unilaterally or with others collectively, where it undoubtedly would retain veto power.

Difficult tradeoffs are again apparent. Large reductions in defense spending are needed to help convert the budget deficit into a surplus. The freeing of high-quality human and financial resources will contribute to restoring American economic strength. But America's economic and broader security interests would be jeopardized by excessive cuts, and policy therefore must attempt to strike a careful balance.

The third element in U.S. foreign policy strategy should be the maintenance of close bilateral ties with the primary economic actors. Relations with Japan cannot be allowed to deteriorate to a point that could trigger concerted withdrawals from the dollar, that would push up both U.S. inflation and interest rates and deny world-class technologies to the American market. Relations with Saudi Arabia must preserve Washington's ability to call on that country to ensure adequate supplies of oil at moderate prices.

Those relationships should be relatively easy to maintain since neither Japan nor Saudi Arabia has other friends around the world to which it can turn. Domestic Japan-bashers and anti-Arabists resist such ties, but they are crucial to an economics-centered foreign policy. U.S. military protection of these countries against security threats would remain an essential part of the implicit bargain.

The problem is more complicated with Europe, which does have real alternatives to tight relations with the United States. It is already prioritizing its neighbors to the east and launching initiatives to expand ties to Asia, deepening the shallowest part of the tripolar relationship. At a minimum, it is imperative that the United States avoid encouraging Europe and Asia to gang up against it, a response that could be triggered by any number of events: a sharp outbreak of protectionism in Congress, a continued erosion of the American economy and especially a perception that this country is "never going to put its house in order," or a precipitate withdrawal of U.S. troops abroad. Any such development would, of course, further weaken American leverage on crucial future issues.

The biggest challenge to a new U.S. foreign policy is the need to build systems of collective leadership in the economic and security spheres. Doing so is essential to future U.S. interests because of the end of America's dominant position, the unwillingness of the American public to "go it alone," and the resulting need to share both costs and responsibilities. The creation and maintenance of such systems will require years of patient U.S. prodding, along with a willingness in the other key countries to institute the new regimes and accept an equal role in managing them.

The economic effort needs to begin with a political statement, probably by the Group of Seven (G-7) at its summit meeting in Munich in July 1992 or at a special session called for such a purpose, that recognizes the new world milieu and sets a goal of establishing a collective leadership structure. Such a statement would note that the end of the Cold War, among other things, calls for a reexamination of the economic institutions that had been created during the period of military confrontation and American hegemony. It would recognize that the existing economic order has been eroding for some time, as evidenced by international monetary instability since the collapse of fixed exchange rates in 1971–73 and by the erosion of world trade policies for the past decade as 20 of the 24 countries in the Organization for Economic Cooperation and Development were, on balance, moving toward managed trade. It would reject the view that "international cooperation" imperils "the pursuit of domestic objectives" by noting that the former almost always *helps* achieve the latter except in the very short run.

The heads of government could then instruct their officials to go to work on the new rules and institutional arrangements. For example, finance ministers would be charged with creating more stable monetary arrangements to underpin sustained world growth and avoid the huge trade imbalances that, as in the mid-1980s and again now with renewed soaring of the overall Japanese surplus, cause severe economic dislocation and incite protectionism. One possible arrangement would be target zones for the key currencies, building on the reference ranges adopted by the G-7 in 1987; another option would be to globalize fixed but adjustable parties like those implemented by the European Monetary System since the late 1970s.

In the trade area, the U.S. goal should be to resuscitate an open and globally oriented international system. A clear preference for such a regime, as opposed to regional blocs, should be expressed. Regional arrangements, such as the EC and NAFTA, should be endorsed only if they meet standard GATT criteria of non-discrimination and are supplements, rather than alternatives, to a globally oriented system.

The relevant ministers could start the process by bringing the Uruguay Round—if still unfinished—to a rapid, far-reaching, and successful conclusion. Agricultural trade would have to be liberalized, requiring additional concessions from the EC and Japan. So would textile trade, requiring concessions from the United States and Europe. Services trade would have to be liberalized, with no major

sectors exempted, requiring concessions from the United States and Japan. Developing countries would have to recognize intellectual property rights, and market access for both goods and services would have to be enhanced everywhere.

But the Uruguay Round, ambitious as it may seem, will at best leave unresolved many issues that plague world trade policy. The ministers should thus move promptly to address a new agenda, preempting in the process the usual post-round protectionist backsliding. Those topics include the linkages between trade and environmental policies, harmonization or at least some convergence of national competition and tax policies, agreements on foreign direct investment, and perhaps new standards for immigration. Beyond money and trade, the new leadership could also seek to develop collective approaches to the world's continuing energy problem, environmental degradation (especially global warming), and the arms trade.

In all those areas, the G-3 (or, for the moment, the G-7) would operate as an informal steering committee to galvanize positive action. It would neither create new institutions nor dictate decisions in the existing organizations. It would consult with other key countries, factor their views into its own plans to help form a global consensus, and seek to implement the new approaches in the global institutions.

The G-3 would, however, recognize that its members—the United States, Japan, and an expanded EC—account for about two-thirds of world output. It simply must assume primary responsibility for making the system work, to foster both world economic progress and to prevent its members' drifting apart. It could make tradeoffs across issue-areas as the process proceeded, as necessary, as it did so successfully at the Bonn summit in 1978. Because "the mice get trampled when the elephants fight," smaller and developing countries would in fact be the main beneficiaries if effective G-3 leadership could produce a more open and prosperous world economy.

The new systemic arrangements proposed here will give the United States its best chance to reconcile the dilemma between pursuing its narrow economic interests and avoiding constant conflict, and possible sharp deterioration, in relations with the other economic superpowers. There will always be some friction between major trading and financial partners, but such frictions can become endemic if sector-specific disputes are permitted to dominate economic relations and are dealt with only on an ad hoc basis. That pattern is reemerging between Japan and the United States, as epitomized by President George Bush's January 1992 trip to Tokyo and its aftermath, after their previously healthy focus on macroeconomic issues in 1985–87 and on structural impediments in 1989–90. Only new systemic mechanisms that channel disputes into procedures governed by negotiated rules can resolve economic problems and simultaneously prevent scapegoating and bashing. The Japanese-U.S. relationship, in particular, must emphasize cooperative systemic management both to place the countries' sector-specific disputes into proper context and to provide techniques for resolving them with less acrimony. The United States led the world wisely in creating multilateral institutions for the initial postwar era. In today's very different circumstances, it needs to take the lead again—this time to revitalize the institutions by forging collective leadership techniques to replace its own hegemony.

Such reforms will also best enable the United States to resolve the dilemma of achieving its national economic goals despite the decline in its relative economic power. The United States has maintained much closer relations with both Europe and Japan than they have with each other and is thus in the best position to advocate and implement new international arrangements that protect its interests. It is in America's interest to create new regimes as soon as possible, while it retains this unique position. The positive-sum nature of the outcome should bring the other key countries along as well.

The final element of U.S. foreign policy should be an initiative on collective security in which joint action, whether to carry out intervention when needed or deter proliferation and regional conflicts, is the centerpiece. Here too the existing institutions should be the central tool: the U.N. and, to a degree, regional organizations. But an institutional innovation would be needed to include the eco-

nomic superpowers in the informal steering committee that would take the lead. As proposed by political scientist Joseph Nye and his colleagues in their July 1991 report to the Trilateral Commission, the most promising approach is the creation of a political "P-7," including Japan and Germany (until the EC can act together on security issues) along with the five current members of the U.N. Security Council (the "P-5"), that would consult before formal collective security decisions were made. A less formal variant, as already applied in the Cambodia situation through a "P-10," is to create ad hoc consultative groups for each crisis that always include the economic superpowers. Such a regime, whatever the precise technique, would reconcile the mismatches between countries that now dominate security and economic issues.

It is crucial to note that only the United States and Japan would participate at the outset in both the economic and security steering groups. The EC cannot for some time function as a unit on security issues. Japan, though it would be involved in the informal P-7 consultations on security, is not a permanent member of the Security Council. Hence the United States would be the only member of all components of the process and would assume a unique role as "steerer of the steerers." That would befit its status as the only superpower in both military and economic terms. It would also enable the United States to link economic and security issues in its bilateral relations with Japan and the key European countries, maximizing its comparative advantage across the two spheres.

ALTERNATIVE COURSES

Given the primacy of economic issues and the increasing domination of the three economic superpowers, global economic (and security) arrangements are likely to follow one of two paths. The first is collective leadership by the major powers, operating informal steering committees within the existing international framework, as proposed here, to create a collective security regime and revitalize an open world economy. The other path is toward regional blocs that would become increasingly restrictive and exclusionary. Such blocs would initially develop in the economic sphere mainly in response to failings of the global economic system, but history reveals that they can easily spill over into the political and even military domains. Those tendencies could be accelerated by a premature American withdrawal from its global security role—an all too plausible prospect in light of America's internal economic needs and the insensitivity of other countries, as in the Uruguay Round, to the links between economic and military issues in domestic U.S. politics.

A world of blocs would run counter to fundamental American interests. Europe and Japan are by far the world's largest economies outside the United States, and any serious erosion of ties with them would severely cripple America's efforts to expand exports rapidly and attract foreign investment.

In addition, America's "natural" bloc would be the Western Hemisphere; Japan would dominate Asia, and the EC would attain primacy in Eastern Europe, including much of the former USSR, and the Middle East. While Latin America is clearly on the path to recovery, as country after country begins to enjoy the fruits of the painful reform efforts of the 1980s, every state in the region remains at a relatively early stage of modernization and is a net debtor. A Western Hemisphere economic grouping, as proposed by Bush in his Enterprise for the Americas Initiative, could help the entire region improve its competitiveness but would hardly augment the global position of the United States if more dynamic areas were ceded to the other superpowers.

If the world were to move toward hostile blocs, the United States would therefore seek to develop Pacific Basin arrangements as well as pursuing its Western Hemisphere initiatives by building on the Asia-Pacific Economic Cooperation group. But such efforts might be quickly derailed by the same rivalry with Japan that precluded G-3 cooperation in the first place, leaving yet another dilemma: either a foundering of the entire Pacific Basin cooperative effort or a version that would try to exclude Japan and thus intensify dangerous nationalist reactions in that country.

Devolution of the world economy into hostile blocs would be extremely risky for the United

States, and American foreign policy should do its best to prevent it. Cooperative initiatives to organize collective security (through the P-7) and global economic arrangements (through the G-3) are far superior. Regional arrangements would still form, but, with relations among them governed by effective global accords, discriminatory and hostile competition could be avoided. Indeed, new collective leadership at the global level should make the world safe for constructive regionalism.

If the United States restores its competitiveness by implementing the domestic reforms at the core of the proposed strategy, those collective arrangements would facilitate the vigorous pursuit of U.S. economic interests despite its relative economic decline. At the international level, the arrangements would create a new glue to hold the allies together and preempt the risk of new economic conflict that could lead to deeper hostilities. They would also provide an effective security regime that should deter or contain new Saddam Husseins.

Such an ambitious "new world order" will come about only if the United States devotes its foreign policy to that end. Adoption of that strategy will require a difficult psychological adjustment for Americans: They will have to undertake a painful comprehensive effort to restore their own competitiveness while simultaneously accepting a more collegial role in global management. But the country's deep economic interdependence will not permit it to withdraw from the world despite the pleas of a few to "Come Home, America." The only real alternative is a forlorn effort to maintain hegemony. The Pentagon's strategic plan leaked in March 1992 contemplates that course, and current Bush administration policy seems to be pursuing it: seeking to maintain most decision-making power, at least on security issues, while asking others to foot the bill. But objective global and domestic circumstances will simply not permit such a course. New collective arrangements, based on revitalization of America's domestic economy, offer the only constructive possibility.

The shift to tripolarity has already occurred in the economic arena, where the EC and Japan can clearly veto American initiatives. Yet even in economics there has been no shift to positive collective leadership. One clear indicator is the continued foundering of the Uruguay Round; another is the G-7's failure to head off a possible world recession and the recent renewed surge in trade imbalances, especially the Japanese surplus.

Nevertheless, the G-7 (or its predecessors) has been meeting regularly for seven years and irregularly for nearly two decades. It has had spectacular successes, as with the 1978 Bonn summit package and the 1985 Plaza Agreement, as well as periods of sustained progress, as with fixed exchange rates in the 1960s and with Third World debt. The two previous multilateral trade agreements, the Kennedy Round of the 1960s and the Tokyo Round of the 1970s, were largely worked out by the United States and Europe. So there is reason for hope that collective economic leadership can be achieved, if the United States can convince others that it is prepared to share decision making as well as costs.

The spotty records of the G-7, International Monetary Fund (IMF), and GATT, however, reveal the weaknesses of the current institutions. The G-7 has no institutional memory. It was totally ineffective in curbing the huge currency misalignments and trade imbalances of the early 1980s. It has relied inordinately on supportive personalities like James Baker, Kiichi Miyazawa, and Gerhard Stoltenberg, who together implemented the Plaza and Louvre exchange rate strategies in the 1980s. The IMF offers the needed institutional framework but the G-7 has chosen to sharply limit its competence rather than use it to pursue the core issues of the global economy. The GATT has failed to bring central issues of world trade—agriculture, services, and

intellectual property—under its domain. It falls into disuse after each negotiating round, allowing new protectionist activities, as it did throughout the 1980s. Much more systematic arrangements will be necessary to achieve positive and predictable results.

Collective security collaboration is an old idea but one with which the United States and others have very little experience. It has become possible only with the Cold War's end, and the Gulf war is its main test to date. Fortunately, security arrangements by their nature are tested much less frequently than economic arrangements. An effort to construct a global security structure might reach fruition in time to deal with the next major crisis.

The strategy proposed here responds to America's chief interests in a post–Cold War world where economic issues have taken preeminence over security concerns, but where the latter remain important and must be addressed effectively as well. It recognizes that the United States, like all countries, lives in a highly interdependent world of pluralistic power configurations in which it has already lost a great deal of real sovereignty over its own affairs. It concentrates on relations among the three economic superpowers. It assumes that competition in the new world will take place among different market-based economic models rather than antithetical ideologies with a heavy military component. It is a strategy that could both meet America's central international needs in the post–Cold War era and provide the foundation for world peace and prosperity well into the twenty-first century.

27.   Another NAFTA: What a Good Agreement Should Offer

Jorge G. Castañeda and Carlos Heredia

Most Mexicans, and probably many Americans and Canadians, believe that a North American free-trade agreement is inevitable and that the agreement now before the three governments will benefit all. But they are wrong. There is no reason to believe that the almost century-long process of economic integration between Mexico and the United States (leaving aside Canada for now) would halt without some kind of formal trade agreement. Nor is it at all certain that this particular agreement is good for all involved. The agreement is advertised as a commercial accord suitable for two individualistic and deregulated market economies. But the question is: Do we Mexicans really want a market economy like the one the United States has? No one has asked us. Neither President Carlos Salinas de Gortari nor President George Bush even suggested that their agreement surreptitiously chooses between two different market economies and types of economic integration: Anglo-Saxon neo-liberalism and a European Community-style social market economy.

In the same way that Bill Clinton's election opens the possibility for a free-trade agreement that is quite different from the current Bush-Quayle, trickle-down, conservative agreement, the debate in Mexico is shifting toward the formulation of a viable alternative. And indeed, the entire NAFTA process involves considerably more complex and substantive nuances than Republican conservatives—in Mexico and the United States—have acknowledged.

FALSE CHOICES

There is a process of economic integration under way between Mexico and the United States, and if

SOURCE: Jorge G. Castañeda and Carlos Heredia. "Another NAFTA: What a Good Agreement Should Offer," *World Policy Journal*, vol. IX, no. 4, Fall/Winter 1992, pp. 673–687. Footnotes deleted. Reprinted with permission.

anything is inevitable in today's world, that process probably is. But it is a process that did not just begin with President Salinas or former president Miguel de la Madrid, or on the basis of the economic reforms set in motion in 1983. Economic integration began toward the end of the last century, when the United States became Mexico's major trading partner. Since then between 60 percent and 90 percent of Mexico's trade (depending on the period of time and method of reckoning) has been with the country north of us, as have comparable shares of foreign investment, tourism, and credit.

In principle, we could sufficiently diversify trade, investment, financing, and tourism to bring about a real shift in our ties with the United States. If we were to withdraw from the General Agreement on Trade and Tariffs (GATT) and adopt tariffs of 100 percent on U.S. products and 0 percent on Japanese or European products, if we were to maintain that policy for 20 years, and if we could close the border, perhaps we could manage to diversify our external trade. If the cost of an American product were twice that of its Japanese or German equivalent, diversification would surely become feasible.

But the cost to Mexico of making that attempt would be extremely high, both politically and economically. And Mexican society is not prepared to pay that cost. This, and this alone, is why the process of economic integration is inevitable.

While trade is inevitable in this sense, is a formal free-trade agreement? Do we need to regulate, administer, and codify economic integration? Probably not. The informal process has been going on for half a century without being governed by any agreement at all and would doubtless continue.

Finally, is there anything indicating that this agreement is the only possible one? Even if the abstract process of economic integration is inevitable, and even if some kind of agreement is also inevitable, there is no reason to suppose that *this* agreement, as negotiated, must be the one. In fact, the agreement signed by Salinas, Bush, and Canadian Prime Minister Brian Mulroney differs significantly from the one they began with. It now includes many issues and regulations that were not on the original agenda and rules out others. Similarly, the agreement that will ultimately be ratified by the U.S. Congress and the Canadian parliament (the Mexican Congress has no voice in the matter) will undoubtedly be different from the text agreed upon in August 1992.

The government of Mexico, and the Bush administration to a lesser extent, have set up a false choice that many have fallen for: either this agreement or autarchy. It is simply untrue that the only alternative to the Bush-Salinas agreement is autarchy, protectionism, or a return to the status quo ante. There is a wide range of agreements concluded around the world in the last 30 years that provide many options for formalized integration. In reality, the choice is between the agreement already negotiated, a right-wing agreement of a neoliberal Republican cast, and an agreement of some other kind, more like a social-democratic agreement, with a strong dose of regulation and planning, inspired by an emerging progressive social compact for a new North America. The choice is between what is called an exclusively commercial agreement, proper to the Anglo-Saxon world's individualistic and deregulated capitalism, and an accord that would go beyond the strictly commercial, also encompassing social issues and the relation between the state and the market. The contrast between those two agreements, the "bad" one we have and the "good" one we want, reflects the difference between the kinds of market economies that exist in the world today.

WHAT WE GOT FROM NAFTA

What is the bad agreement all about? Its conceptual premise is to leave free trade exclusively to the free market. In Mexico, leaving everything to the market means giving free rein to those who command it: the most powerful, the richest. Second, the agreement supposedly covers only economic issues. In reality, NAFTA is an agreement that encompasses

not only financial matters, investment, intellectual property, and of course commerce, but also dispute-resolution, banking, transport, and services. Clearly, the agreement is not solely commercial.

But it *is* a strictly economic agreement, one that does not include other possible issues: social, political, environmental, cultural. What we have here is an accord that is fundamentally opposed to the idea of planning, to choosing what each country will produce, to defining how established goals will be met, and to clarifying how certain sectors will be protected or exposed in order to reach long-term objectives.

Just as deregulation was a major feature of the economic policy of both the Bush administration and the Salinas government, so, too, NAFTA lacks a strict regulatory framework. To the greatest extent possible, it seeks to eliminate all social, economic, consumer-protection, and environmental regulations. True, that is no easy task, since the United States and Canada have legislative bodies, courts, and citizens' organizations that have struggled for years to pass the present regulatory framework.

Here, the Salinas government stands to the right even of the Bush administration. It was the Mexicans who insisted on dismantling the various regulations in force in the United States, alleging that they constituted disguised forms of protection (in some cases true). Ironically, Mexico, completely lacking in effective regulation of anything, lacking a minimum regulatory framework in any area, now opposes the preservation of the U.S. regulatory framework, arguing that it is contrary to the market and free trade.

Finally, the bad agreement is an agreement without asymmetries, without real recognition of the enormous disparities between Mexico and the United States. From the beginning, the Mexican government sold the United States and the Mexican public on the idea that Mexico did not need longer time-spans for removal of restrictions and deregulation or greater protection for its producers because the country was becoming part of the First World, competitive and modern. However, Mexican negotiators, realizing that the country might need some special treatment, stressed asymmetry. But they were never really able to carry forward this argument to its ultimate conclusion—except perhaps as regards energy—because it was contrary to the spirit of the agreement and the negotiation itself. Salinas, in effect, was saying: The only thing we need is open markets. Just take your foot off the brake, you don't even have to put it on the accelerator.

WHAT WE WANT FROM A FREE-TRADE AGREEMENT

It is easy enough to criticize a bad agreement. But what is the alternative? The alternative is an agreement that includes compensatory financing, encourages industrial planning and a common regulatory framework, confronts the issue of worker mobility, harmonizes upward labor standards and rights, creates an environmental and consumer protection charter, and institutes a broad multipurpose dispute-resolution mechanism.

The premise underlying a good agreement is that there is no single model of formal economic integration, just as there is no single model of a market economy. In the past, the diametrical clash between capitalism and real socialism tended to obscure the contrasts between the various market economies in the industrial world. But today the differences between individualistic, predatory Anglo-Saxon capitalism and the social-democratic market capitalism of Germany (or of the Rhineland, as some European observers have put it) or the public-private capitalism of Japan are striking. The U.S. model, presently under severe strain, is highly dynamic but antisocial, short-term oriented, anti-interventionist, and tends to exacerbate inequalities. The European and Japanese models—looking beyond their differences—are less dynamic but more socially oriented and regulated with a more active and dominant role for the state, and tend to forge more egalitarian homogeneous societies.

There are also various models of formal economic integration, from the U.S.-Canada model of 1988, which leaves almost everything to the will of the market, to the European plan of Jean Monnet and the Treaty of Rome, which emphasizes the state's role in planning, regulation, and social policy-making.

The free-trade agreement proposed and imposed by Salinas and Bush is not the only possible scheme for Mexico. Actually the conservative agreement is probably the worst program.

Paying the Costs of Adjustment

A good agreement would call for compensatory financing or the creation of regional funds. As markets are integrated painful adjustments often occur: as the factors of production are redistributed with greater efficiency, some industries are weakened, others lost altogether. In theory, the costs of such adjustment are equitably shared. In practice, however, Mexico will bear a heavier burden than the United States. Our per capita income is eight to 10 times less than that of the United States, the distribution of income is much more skewed, levels of wages, productivity, efficiency, and technology are clearly inferior.

Although parts of the United States and Canada will also suffer disproportionately great adjustment costs, even larger than those borne by some parts of Mexico, in general Mexico's situation will be worse because we are starting from a weaker economic position. Other trade agreements have redressed such disparities among partners by creating compensatory financing facilities.

The European Community established structural adjustment funds to mitigate economic and social differences and strengthen economic and social cohesion. EC members seek to stimulate productivity and enhance development in depressed areas by strengthening infrastructure, training workers, and introducing appropriate technology. This is a policy specifically designed to redistribute wealth to the poor: the funds are given to the *most impoverished* areas, not necessarily those *most affected* by the integration process.

In Europe, the amount of money involved has been large. Ireland, perhaps the European country that has benefited most from regional funds, receives 8 percent of its annual GDP from community aid. It is as if Mexico were to receive $20 to $25 billion a year from the governments of the United States and Canada. In the Maastricht Treaty, the Spanish and Portuguese persuaded other members that they should continue receiving help, even with a per capita GDP above 75 percent of the European average. The per capita GDP of Mexico is about 15 percent of the U.S.-Canada average. This injection of resources is in no way a disguised form of charity: in fact, out of every 100 ecus the EC invests in Portugal, 46 return to the other member states by way of increased exports to Portugal.

In North America, the transfer of resources would have three aims: to improve infrastructure, harmonize standards, and subsidize excessive adjustment costs. It is clear how additional funds could be used to achieve the first two goals. Some explanation is needed, however, of how regional aid could be used to lessen local burdens. Certainly factories, farms, and firms in Mexico (and in the United States and Canada) will be forced to close as a result of the new North American competition. This will mean layoffs, which will indirectly affect suppliers and cities that depend on one or two companies, and a drop in the tax base for certain entities. Regional funds could be used to establish a temporary unemployment insurance scheme for those laid off by companies forced to close due to the free-trade agreement, or to finance programs of conversion or vocational training, or to alleviate drops in income.

The central problem of compensatory financing is finding the resources. The European approach ranges from adoption of a general value-added tax to direct governmental transfer payments. This has not been accomplished without controversy, particularly by the more conservative governments. And, given the prevailing ideological climate in the United States, the idea of transferring resources from U.S. taxpayers to build Mexican roads seems a bit far fetched.

There are, however, several ways of financing the transfer of resources from rich areas to poorer ones without passing on the bill to every U.S. taxpayer. The first is a tax on cross-border transactions, such as the one proposed by the Democratic leader of the House of Representatives, Richard Gephardt, to finance an environmental clean-up program along the border. Another mechanism is to tax the windfall profits that some companies would make upon moving to Mexico (by reducing their labor costs

and continuing to sell their products at the same price in the United States and Canada).

Still another way to raise funds would be to create a North American Development Bank and an adjustment fund to provide compensatory financing to Mexico. For U.S. taxpayers and Mexican citizens to accept such a program the bank and/or fund would have to finance poor areas or groups of people *in all three countries*. Also, negotiators would have to decide whether only governments can apply for loans or subsidies, or whether private parties would have access to the resources. Finally, the three governments must ensure stable and sustained sources of funding. For NAFTA, there might be a combination of public and private resources, channeled both in the form of loans (development bank) and subsidies (support fund for depressed areas). Ideally the bank would finance projects submitted directly by organized groups of citizens—rural or urban community organizations.

Finally, the Mexican external debt could be renegotiated to free up funds. Resources earmarked for debt servicing could be recycled by using debt-for-investment swaps to finance social development funds in agreement with the creditors.

Compensatory financing facilities, of course, face serious challenges. This is a policy whose results become apparent only over the medium term, and which may lead to the most depressed areas becoming dependent on external transfers. In Europe, however, the gap between rich and poor areas has been narrowing.

Strategic Alliances

A good agreement includes the idea of a trilateral industrial policy—a strategic alliance between the private sector and states to capture markets, develop technologies, achieve dynamic competitive advantages, and reach new levels of competitiveness.

What is needed is active and effective coordination among the three countries. The idea is explicit involvement by government. But success depends on the *meaning* and *purpose* of government intervention. It is not enough to expand physical infrastructure and make things easier for the transnational corporations whose investments are being courted. Each country must invest in social infrastructure to improve wages and standards of living.

A Regulatory Framework

To complement a North American industrial policy, the three countries should create an economic commission to plan which industries should be developed and where, how each stage will be reached, where the money will come from to reach that stage, and what regulations will be established. In Mexico we do not have excessive regulation, on the contrary, we suffer from a notoriously sparse regulatory environment.

Worker Mobility

If NAFTA is to improve access to the United States market for our exports, then two major exports have been left out of the agreement: drugs and people. Call it what you will, but Mexico has been exporting Mexicans for over a century now. Yet those who negotiated NAFTA almost completely ignored this situation.

It is not true that it is impossible to legalize migration from a poor to a rich country. On the contrary, the great discovery of the Europeans was legalizing the previously existing movements of undocumented people. When the Treaty of Rome entered into force there was already a very large number of workers from southern Italy working in Germany, Belgium, Holland, and France. Most were undocumented. The only solution was to give them papers, granting them entitlements, rights, and power. Indeed, in the United States, the process of legalization in recent years has been impressive: nearly three million Mexicans have benefited from it. Many Americans understand that it is not possible to have an enormous undocumented population concentrated in 10 or 15 cities. The result will be more disturbances such as the one in Los Angeles last May. The problems began in the Afro-American community, but Mexicans and Salvadorans did much of the looting. A population flow that cannot be stopped or controlled has to be legalized.

The negotiation of the free-trade agreement was a good opportunity to move in that direction. Obviously, complete legalization of all the undocumented Mexicans in the United States, or free entry for all those still in Mexico, would not have been possible. But including the topic of migration was possible, just as the United States succeeded in including oil on the negotiating agenda. Mexico should have insisted on the gradual and selective liberalization of migration, offering in exchange much of what Mexico's immigration authorities are unfortunately already granting unilaterally.

The free-trade agreement says little about the free movement of unskilled labor. Only some provisions concerning temporary and limited entry for professionals have been included. The Mexican authorities have been unable to explain why the negotiations resulted in free entry for officials, bankers, or consultants, but not for everybody else. Worse, entry for professionals from the United States and Canada into Mexico was significantly liberalized. The governments are opening borders to goods and capital flows, while labor, Mexico's main export, is barred from entry.

A Social Charter

A good agreement will provide for upward harmonization of labor standards and rights—not just labor legislation but also implementation of standards. Harmonizing standards would sometimes mean improvements by the United States, since its legislation occasionally falls short of Mexican legislation (although the enforcement of the Mexican laws is often lax).

Including a social charter is the best way of starting to minimize differences between productivity and wages. It does not guarantee it, but it is a start. The case of the auto industry, especially the Ford-Mazda plant in Hermosillo, Mexico, illustrates a well-known paradox. The plant manufactures vehicles at a productivity rate and quality comparable or higher than the Ford plants in Dearborn or Rouge, and slightly below those of Mazda in Hiroshima. Nevertheless, the wage of the Mexican worker with equal productivity is between 20 and 25 times less than that of the U.S. worker. The

Mexican government argues that the wage differential between the two countries is justified because productivity is not comparable: workers cannot expect equal pay for unequal productivity. But what about when the productivity *is* the same?

One reason why workers at factories belonging to the same company, producing the same cars with the same quality and productivity, earn 20 times less, is that the right to strike in Mexico is more a metaphor than anything else. Because of the union-exclusion clause and the unions' subordination to the state and its party, the workers' ability to use the strike as a weapon is negligible. Although it is difficult to legislate equal pay (though not guidelines for gradual equalization), it is possible to harmonize standards for collective bargaining, labor tribunals, the right to strike, and wider union freedom. With such power the workers themselves can achieve, over time, those levels of wages and benefits, as well as dignity in the workplace.

Beyond harmonization of labor standards, a free-trade agreement should promote workers' rights. One way to do this is to allow workers to organize and negotiate collectively at a continental level. NAFTA allows General Motors to decide what to produce in North America and where, but does not create conditions so that workers in Michigan and Coahuila can act jointly to influence industrial policy and wages in their areas. A good agreement will also require the United States and Mexico to adopt the Canadian system of recognition of unions as a de facto matter, so that collective bargaining begins when the majority of the workers at a company decide to form a union or join an existing one. Finally, a social charter should include the adoption of workers' councils, establishing the right of workers' representatives to participate in decisions regarding contracts or layoffs, assignment of workers to a particular place of work, matters of health and safety in the workplace, and access to training. The idea is that all of these rights go hand in hand with the commitment to increase productivity.

Other elements of the social charter might include: no favorable tariff treatment for goods whose production fails to comply with given conditions; prohibiting child labor (under age 16); and requiring employers to provide a healthy workplace, without exposure to toxic substances.

An Environmental and Consumer Protection Charter

One of the biggest incentives for U.S. companies to move to Mexico is to evade environmental protection laws. In Mexico, the environment is not protected, nor is society itself very comfortable with the idea. Harmonizing consumer protection and environmental standards, which tend to be similar, is intended to prevent Mexico from becoming like the border—a toxic waste-dump for the United States.

The *Coalición para la Justicia en las Maquiladoras* (Coalition for Justice in the Maquiladoras), a bi-national body made up of workers and social groups in the United States and Mexico, has proposed a code of conduct for labor and the environment for those enterprises. Unfortunately, not only Matamoros and Ciudad Juárez are disaster areas, vast areas of Mexico's territory are deteriorating. In order for any environmental program to succeed it must encourage citizen participation. It is possible to include in a good agreement a bill of rights for the defense of the environment and the consumer and to establish a common regulatory framework, on the condition that the costs of these measures are equitably financed. And that means that the polluters pay for what they have polluted.

Dispute-Resolution Mechanisms

If there is no mechanism available to all sectors, not just governments and corporations, then many of the features outlined above will not get beyond the drawingboard. And if the machinery created lacks its own resources and full competence to cover all aspects of the issues, the best free-trade agreement will remain a dead letter.

There is no point in harmonizing standards for environmental, labor, and consumer protection without providing sanctions for those who violate them. It is impossible to determine who is complying and who is not if the matter is left entirely in the hands of governments. In this respect, it is indispensable to have a mechanism for dispute resolution that is supranational, autonomous, with resources, and open to all.

If the dispute-resolution mechanism decides that a standard has indeed been violated, the manufacturers would lose the free–trade privilege, the only sanction that a mechanism of this kind can impose, but one which would prove to be highly effective. It implies a real cost for the violating party. Anyone should be able to use the dispute-resolution mechanism to report violations and demand inspection, monitoring, control, and, if necessary, a ruling and the determination of a sanction. The costs of using the mechanism by all the parties concerned is less than that of indiscriminate violation of harmonized standards. Again, citizen participation is a key element. The mechanisms should be open to organized citizens and to governmental bodies from each country.

A PROGRESSIVE SOCIAL COMPACT

The agreement suggested here implies greater transfers of sovereignty to supranational entities than that of Salinas and Bush; it may even imply a more substantive abdication of sovereignty. Not that the regime's conservative agreement preserves sovereignty as well as it pretends to. But it would be illusory and dishonest to pretend that the accord proposed here does not involve curtailments in several areas.

At the same time, this kind of agreement seeks to enable Mexico to more vigorously and effectively defend what sovereignty remains to it; it proposes achievements and changes so that the defense of the Mexican nation as a whole will be a more plausible undertaking than it is today. A good agreement involves going further toward integration, building more supranational forums, dovetailing our society and institutions more fully with those of the United States and Canada.

The elements of a good agreement do not amount to a list of protectionist measures or suggest that workers should be a privileged group. The idea is simply to put into practice the principle that governments often repeat, but seldom live up to, that a country's most valuable asset is its work force, the majority of the population who are systematically left out of decision making circles but are affected by what the elites decide. The idea is also to go

beyond the myopic vision that seeks to divorce the free-trade agreement from labor, emigration, environmental, or human rights provisions on the ground that it is only a commercial agreement. This narrow view overlooks an incontrovertible truth: flows of trade, capital, and investment bring with them social implications that cannot be divorced from their causes and have to be addressed. The only way of guaranteeing compliance with social, labor, or environmental standards is to link them to the granting or denial of tariff relief. Otherwise, there are a thousand ways of getting around them, as the Mexican experience proves.

This agreement is not a socialist or statist or populist agreement; nor is it a nationalist agreement. It is an accord based on the operation of a particular type of market economy. It is an accord that is typically reformist: hence its virtues and its shortcomings—it is viable but filled with costs. The agreement between Salinas and Reagan-Bush-Quayle is a classically conservative agreement, whose premise is the traditional functioning of the U.S. market economy, while the agreement proposed here is based on a European-style or Japanese-style capitalism. It is neither left-oriented nor right-oriented. Instead, the proposed agreement takes as its premise a different market economy. Some believe that it is preferable, others believe it is worse: these are political-ethical choices. Either way it is outlandish to suggest that the only agreement and the only type of market economy that is possible is the declining and obsolete model of the most uncouth hard-line conservatives in the United States, just booted out of office by more than 60 percent of the electorate.

There remains the problem of the viability of a scheme such as that suggested here. Many may argue that such a plan is desirable but neither viable nor acceptable to Americans under present conditions: we will never get the money out of them, or the worker mobility, or even the type of regulatory and environmental protection machinery described here. But who is it that will never accept these things, the Republicans or the Democrats, in 1992 or in 1994?

A new, progressive North American social compact could become an example for the rest of Latin

America; a bad agreement is merely a Trojan horse for the most reactionary sectors in the United States and the rest of the hemisphere. A conservative covenant can never become a step toward a progressive program; on the contrary, it makes such an agree- ment all the more difficult and remote a prospect. NAFTA should not become a legacy of the Reagan-Bush era, but a precedent for a different North America.

Questions for Discussion

1. What are the international implications of the U.S. budget deficit?
2. What are the sources of U.S. economic problems?
3. Should U.S. economic concerns be accorded as much weight as national security interests in the formulation of foreign policy?
4. Is Japan a tough competitor or a dangerous rival?

5. What is meant by NAFTA? Is it in the U.S. national interest?
6. Should the United States maintain high military spending?
7. What are the dilemmas of a neo-mercantilist policy?
8. Is President Clinton's commitment to protect the environment compatible with his objective of promoting economic growth?

Selected Bibliography

CHACE, JAMES. *The Consequences of the Peace.* New York: Oxford University Press, 1992.

ENCARNATION, DENNIS J. *Rivals Beyond Trade: America Versus Japan in Global Competition.* Ithaca: Cornell University Press, 1992.

GARTEN, JEFFREY E. *A Cold Peace: America, Japan, Germany, and the Struggle for Supremacy.* New York: Times Books, 1992.

GILPIN, ROBERT. *The Political Economy of International Relations.* Princeton: Princeton University Press, 1987.

HOWELL, THOMAS R. (ED.). *Conflict Among Nations: Trade Policies in the 1990s.* Boulder: Westview Press, 1992.

HUFBAUER, GARY CLYDE, and JEFFREY J. SCHOTT. *North American Free Trade.* Washington, DC: Institute for International Economics, 1992.

KENNEDY, PAUL. *The Rise and Fall of the Great Powers.* New York: Random House, 1987.

MARKUSEN, ANN, and JOEL YUDKEN. *Dismantling the Cold War Economy.* New York: Basic Books, 1992.

NAU, HENRY R. *The Myth of America's Decline.* Rev. ed. New York: Oxford University Press, 1992.

VOLCKER, PAUL, and TOYOO GYOHTEN. *Changing Fortunes: The World's Money and the Threat to American Leadership.* New York: Times Books, 1992.

WEIDENBAUM, MURRAY. *Small Wars, Big Defense: Paying for the Military After the Cold War.* New York: Oxford University Press, 1992.

PART FOUR

ALLIANCES AND ALIGNMENTS IN TRANSITION IN A POST-COLD WAR WORLD

CHAPTER 9

On the Utility of Existing Security Systems in Europe and the Far East

When confronted by aggressive powers threatening their security or the stability of the international order, nations join together in alliances. Such cooperation is temporary, its catalyst a common adversary, its focus the creation of a new constellation of forces, a balance of power that will deter or, if necessary, repel and defeat the challenger(s) to the status quo. At such a time security needs overshadow possible ideological, economic, or political differences. By entering into formal alliances members affirm, in the strongest possible manner, their common interest in resisting a potential aggressor, and they obligate themselves to come to the assistance of any member who is attacked. Historically, alliances disbanded or fell into desuetude once the threat that triggered their creation had passed.

At their best, alliances are presumed to deter war, though it is difficult to prove that the absence of war—a nonevent—was directly attributable to them. After all, major wars have occurred even in times of a system of countervailing alliances. This failure to deter can sometimes be explained by an inadequacy of military capability. For example, on the eve of the First World War (1914–1918), the military strength of the Franco-Russian alliance proved insufficient to deter Germany. The situation might have been quite different had Britain unequivo-cally committed itself to side with France and Russia in the event of an attack by Germany. The lesson in this seems to be that deterrence requires overwhelming military power. Being merely as strong as your main adversary is not always good enough. In general, alliances are most effective when the members share a common political philosophy, interests that are broadly convergent rather than divergent, and an unmistakable common danger.

Not until the Second World War did the United States need military alliances. Uninvolved in the quarrels of Europe until World War I, it fought on the side of the British, French, and Russians, but withdrew soon thereafter, largely because of domestic politics. It could afford to be aloof from "the game of nations": power politics. Protected from invasion by the two oceans on its east and west, a weak Mexico on its south, and a friendly and nonthreatening Canada on its north, the United States was, indeed, fortunate; as Otto von Bismarck is supposed to have said, "God protects infants, drunks, and the United States of America."

The Second World War, which began on September 1, 1939, when Hitler invaded Poland, transformed U.S. foreign policy. Britain and France honored their treaty commitments to Poland and declared war on Germany. By May–June 1940, however, German armies had overrun France, Belgium, the Netherlands, Denmark, and Norway, and soon controlled Western Europe. Britain fought on alone. On June 22, 1941, Hitler turned on Stalin, with whom in late August 1939 he had concluded a surprise agreement carving up Poland, the Baltic states, and the Balkans. Though ideologically hostile to one another since the Bolshevik Revolution of November 1917, Britain and the Soviet Union made common cause against a shared enemy, Nazi Germany. Under President Franklin D. Roosevelt, the United States tilted toward Britain, providing Lend-Lease Aid, but remained a nonbelligerent partisan. However, after Japan attacked Pearl Harbor on December 7, 1941, and Hitler gratuitously and unexpectedly declared war on it, the United States joined in alliance with Britain and the Soviet Union to defeat the Axis Powers (Germany, Italy, Japan).

The defeat of Nazi Germany and Japan ushered in a period of Cold War, not peace. The inability of the victors to maintain their wartime cooperation led to the division of the world into two hostile ideological-political-military camps. Stalin's aim in the immediate post-1945 period was security for the Soviet Union along its western border. To him this meant Soviet domination of Eastern Europe and the installation of puppet Communist regimes. Moscow's commanding position was reinforced by extensive territorial acquisitions: from Finland, the ice-free port of Petsamo and territory extending the Soviet frontier to Norway; seventy thousand square miles of eastern Poland; the province of Ruthenia from Czechoslovakia and northern Bukovina and Bessarabia (and control of the Carpathian mountain passes into Central Europe and the Danubian plain) from Romania. Annexing land from the countries of Eastern Europe and subordinating them to

its rule, the USSR advanced its power into the center of Europe. Its continued occupation of East Germany turned a temporary expedient in the closing days of the Second World War into a permanent threat to the countries of Western Europe. In 1948, Stalin's attempt to force the Western Powers out of West Berlin, which was located 110 miles inside the Soviet zone of occupation (East Germany), heightened the West's sense of vulnerability.

On April 4, 1949, the governments of Belgium, Canada, Denmark, France, Iceland, Italy, Luxembourg, the Netherlands, Norway, Portugal, the United Kingdom, and the United States established the North Atlantic Treaty Organization (NATO); they were joined in 1951, by Greece and Turkey, and in 1955, by West Germany. In the long-established tradition of other military alliances, NATO was defensive in character, created to act as a deterrent against any Soviet move to expand into Western Europe.

For the more than forty years that the Cold War was waged between the Soviet Union and the NATO countries, there was no war in Europe. The periodic crises over Berlin, Moscow's suppression of revolts in East Berlin in 1953, Hungary in 1956, and Czechoslovakia in 1968, its forward deployment of nuclear-capable intermediate nuclear missiles in 1977, and massive military buildup in East Germany aggravated tensions, but these were managed without upsetting the stability of a divided Europe. Each bloc avoided an armed attack on the other. The combination of the U.S. nuclear umbrella and the Western alliance's firmness and resolve to counter the USSR's forward deployment of combat-ready divisions served as an effective deterrent.

When Gorbachev came to power in March 1985, he set about improving relations with the West. He and President Reagan met at summit meetings in Geneva, November 1985; Reykjavik, Iceland, October 1986; Washington, D.C., December 1987; and Moscow, June 1988. Each meeting marked a big step toward accommodation and détente: Gorbachev's change of Soviet policy from acrimony to accord was matched by Reagan's shift of U.S. foreign policy from militant anticommunism to far-reaching arms control agreements. By 1990 Gorbachev was committed to a historic accommodation with the United States and a comprehensive reconciliation with Western Europe. He terminated Moscow's empire in Eastern Europe, permitted the peaceful re-unification of Germany, and moved from rivalry to cooperation in the Third World. Inexorably, the U.S.-Soviet Cold War was ending.

A dramatic sequence of events led to a completely unforeseen dénouement. On August 19 to 21, 1991, Gorbachev's closest associates mounted a coup that failed, but that, in the process, set in motion not only Gorbachev's downfall but also the dissolution of the entity known as the Union of Soviet Socialist Republics. Though surviving the coup, Gorbachev found his influence waning and the instruments of power at his disposal increasingly unable to cope with the deteriorating economy and rising ethnic nationalism. The disbanding of the Communist Party of the Soviet Union, the rejection of Marxism-Leninism and the ideological underpinnings of the Soviet state, and separatist pressures from the Baltic states, Ukraine, Armenia, and Georgia, all proved too much for Gorbachev and the infirm political system.

On December 9, 1991, the presidents of Russia, Belarus, and Ukraine met in Minsk, declared "that the USSR has ceased to exist as a subject of international law and as a geopolitical reality," and formed a Commonwealth of Independent States. By this time helpless and without political allies, Gorbachev bowed to the inevitable: on December 25, he resigned as President of the Soviet Union. The Soviet Union no longer existed, as each of the fifteen constituent republics reaffirmed their independence and gained admission into the United Nations. The Cold War was now truly over.

As we move into a post-Cold War world, U.S. leaders need to rethink basic assumptions about security. The Soviet menace, which NATO was created to deter, is no more. Nor is there any discernible military threat to the nations of Western Europe. Accordingly, the time may be appropriate for a searching reexamination of U.S. interests. An alliance, after all, is not to be confused with a love affair. There is no doubt that NATO no longer operates in a hostile or threatening environment. Presumably, if it is to be continued, calculations must demonstrate that it enhances U.S. security and well-being.

After all, other Cold War alliances were disbanded, though for reasons that lack particular pertinence to the situation of NATO. There was the Southeast Asia Treaty Organization (United States, Britain, France, Thailand, the Philippines, Australia, New Zealand, and Pakistan), established in 1954, ostensibly as a deterrent to Chinese expansion into Southeast Asia. In reality it was a U.S.-generated (the driving force was Secretary of State John Foster Dulles) attempt to multilateralize support for South Vietnam, which, along with North Vietnam, had become independent in the wake of France's withdrawal from its former colony. Ironically, South Vietnam was never a member of SEATO. After North Vietnam triumphed in 1975, the alliance was clearly anachronistic and was allowed to expire on June 30, 1977. Another alliance that went out of existence was the Central Treaty Organization (the United States, Britain, Turkey, Iran, and Pakistan). A successor to the Baghdad Pact of 1955, CENTO replaced it in 1959 after Iraq had experienced the coup that overthrew the pro-Western Hashemite monarchy. But with the fall of the pro-U.S. Shah of Iran in January 1979, CENTO, too, went out of existence. In both instances, alliances were abandoned because of changes in the political outlooks or affiliations of key members.

General Alexander M. Haig, Jr., whose record of public service includes having been Secretary of State during the Reagan administration and Supreme Commander of NATO forces in the 1970s, argues that the peace of Europe depends upon America's remaining a European power (Reading 28). His case is premised more on political and economic trends than on any military threat.

Hugh De Santis of the National War College, Washington, D.C., believes that NATO should not exist indefinitely but should be replaced by a new security framework built, without U.S. participation, on the existing Western European Union (WEU) to promote integration and stability in Europe (Reading 29). His hopes for the WEU rest on success of a set of overlapping initiatives: the creation of localized security pacts in the Baltic region and in the Balkans, the incorporation of Eastern Europe into the new security system, and the sustained movement of the West Europeans to contain emerging ethnic conflicts in post-Cold War Europe.

Although not a part of his assessment, the future of NATO cannot be divorced from consideration of the German Question. Throughout the twentieth century, general war in Europe has been a function of Germany's foreign policy. With reunification in 1990 and with the collapse of the former Soviet Union in 1991, Germany finds itself once again the preeminent power on the European continent. Economically and industrially, it already dominates Europe; potentially, it could do so militarily in the future as well. Inevitably, its growing assertiveness, for example, in Eastern Europe and the Balkans, raises the question of how best to contain the explosive force of German nationalism. Should NATO be preserved, if only to keep Germany anchored to an alliance system in which the United States can serve as a countervailing force? Is NATO's continuation the most feasible way to ensure that Germany remains a nonnuclear power? How much of the defense burden should the United States be prepared to assume for retention of the Atlantic alliance? Any discussion of NATO's future needs to explore such issues.

For the United States, Northeast Asia is as important economically and strategically as Europe. However, as the result of a Eurocentric cultural bias, there has been much less public debate on U.S. options in dealing with Japan, China, and the two Koreas. A continued U.S. military presence, combined with U.S.-Russian agreements on force reductions and confidence-building measures, could assure deterrence and an absence of war in the region. But there are certain obstacles. Both Japan and South Korea have shown a readiness to increase their defense spending, but a more difficult determination is how much more they are prepared to pay to enable U.S. forces to remain deployed in strength in the area. The U.S. Congress wants them to bear more of the financial burden. Washington also has serious problems with China—in the fields of trade, human rights, and arms sales.

Colonel Ralph A. Cossa, Jr., a Senior Fellow at the National Defense University's Institute for Strategic Studies, examines the origins of America's key Asian security alliances and assesses their durability (Reading 30). In the absence of strong treaty ties to the United States, Japan and South Korea could embark on major military buildups, which would be politically disruptive, causing regional instability. Hence, Cossa argues, the strategic necessity for sustained American engagement in East Asian affairs.

Jung-en Woo of Northwestern University disagrees, seeing rather the need for an "attenuation of bilateral relations between East Asia and the United States. While in the short run this could lead to tense and unstable relations, in the long term," he believes, it would "give the United States greater flexibility" in its foreign economic policy (Reading 31).

The United States faces major choices, not only in its relations with old friends but also with former adversaries. The ultimate decision will hinge on many variable factors: strategic assessments, the responses of East Asian allies, and domestic pressures rising out of concerns over trade imbalances, unfair trade practices, and burden sharing. How the United States responds to the changing strategic environment in Northeast Asia will have momentous consequences for the region and for the United States.

A. THE FUTURE OF NATO

28. NATO's Continuation Is in the National Interest

Alexander M. Haig, Jr.

On the face of it, the United States has rarely been in a better international position than we are in today. Many believe that we defeated our Soviet adversary in the Cold War, and in the aftermath of that war, we used that same American strength to defeat a regional predator, Saddam Hussein. Our allies in Europe and Asia are prosperous and democratic. The nuclear threat has receded. In short, the great political, military, and economic trends appear to be moving in our favor and, therefore, all will be right with the world.

SOURCE: Alexander M. Haig, Jr. "The Future of American Foreign Policy," Testimony before the House Foreign Affairs Committee, U.S. Congress, May 20, 1992, excerpts.

This is a comforting vision and perhaps the most comforting part of it is that it promises an easing of American effort. The Cold War is won. There is a new World Order and we can all go home. . . .

There is only one problem with this view of our situation. It is wrong, fundamentally wrong. There is no new World Order, only a group of new states —Russia foremost among them—looking for a new order. These states may choose to join the Western camp, based on democracy, free markets, and peaceful settlement of international disputes guided by rule of law. Or they may find their way once more into the other camp: Those governments who prefer to rule by force and to settle disputes by force, the dictators and the tyrants who are still too numerous, although less numerous than before.

An undue focus on the end of the Cold War and an unwarranted belief in a new World Order may blind us to the three great changes transforming our times, and the challenges they present to our future. Two of those changes—multipolarity and interdependence—are evolutionary and we take them for granted, although we shouldn't. The third, the collapse of Soviet-style Marxist-Leninism, is revolutionary. Together, these historic changes are the raw material from which we must fashion the future.

This committee and every student of international relations is familiar with the technical term for the first great change, multipolarity. To me it means that the artificial post-war division of the world between the superpowers is passé. That is good news. Cultural diversity and economic progress have long been the watchwords of American society and we have never feared these characteristics in other nations nor envied their success. Our allies are alive and kicking and we no longer have to carry the burden of the world's troubles on our heads alone nor, in fact, will such an approach succeed. . . .

The point is that we are not moving from a world run by two superpowers to a world run by one superpower in Washington. Instead, we are moving from a world based on strife to a system based on cooperative diversity. At least that is the potential. . . .

Together, multipolarity and interdependence have brought two profound changes that affect the conduct of statecraft. One is that the old distinctions between domestic policy and foreign policy no longer apply. Before a government acts at home, it had better consider the consequences abroad— and vice versa. It would be tragically shortsighted to become preoccupied with domestic economic issues, for example, while expecting international political trends automatically to be benign. And it would be an equally profound mistake to expect a foreign policy to remain robust in the midst of chaos on the home front.

The second is that the old distinctions in statecraft among politics, economics, and security are also being blurred. A new mosaic is taking its place. A country's strategy for making its way in

the world must be based on an integrated view of how each of these assets affects the other. The decline of the Soviet military threat, for example, has turned our attention far more to the economic dimension of foreign policy than ever before.

More than any other nation, the United States has benefited from multipolarity and interdependence. Today, our domestic economy relies ever more heavily on free trade, real-time communications and multilateral arrangements such as the GATT. An increasing portion of our GNP is due to exports, the fastest growing segment of our economy. Our allies have also grown under multipolarity into sources of real strength and not weakness.

Still, I am not so sure that we Americans are ready to bring our thinking into accord with these new realities. Just take a look at our own political scene. A philosophic confusion has produced some of the strangest political bedfellows in American history. Old style liberals and new style conservatives are rallying around an attitude best described as the new isolationism.

American liberals were once the conscience and driving force of America's international commitments. It was the liberals, aided by the Cold War, who moved this country from its traditional isolationism to an enlightened engagement with the rest of the world. But this is not the driving force of many liberals today. After Vietnam and Watergate, they became estranged from America's international role. The ills of American society, such as social and economic injustice, poor schools, the drug culture, a collapsing urban infrastructure, were attributed in part to the diversion of resources on behalf of a failed international vision. And these ills now threaten to become an exclusive preoccupation so that those who used to push America outward now press America inward.

While this is occurring on the left of the political spectrum, many on the right of the political spectrum have joined in rejecting the realities of the international situation. Already in the Reagan era, some believed that a massive military build-up and muscular rhetoric would enable America to reclaim the mantle of superpower from the mythical age of the late 1940s. Today, these conservatives want America to go it alone. They would attribute to our allies most of our economic problems because in their view, our allies shirked their responsibilities.

These unnatural bedfellows from the left and the right have been reinforced by the fall of the Soviet Union, and America's current economic difficulties. Many on the left would back the U.S. out of international commitments in the name of domestic need. Many on the right would back the U.S. out of its alliances the better to go it alone. Nowhere is this more in evidence than in the debates and actions of the Congress of the United States. And make no mistake about where this is leading our country. A fitful unilateralism that bashes our allies, embraces economic protectionism would make of America a wrecking force in a world already shaken by uncertainty.

These symptoms are not confined to the United States. They can be found in Europe, in the concept of the EC [European Community] as an exclusive club. I would add here that because of the EC's size and preference, it is vitally important that the results of greater European economic harmony make the continent more open to world trade. The recently reached agreement between the EC and the European free-trade area countries is a good sign. I hope too that the EC becomes more helpful to the newly free countries of Central and Eastern Europe, and more receptive to the problems of the developing countries. Finally, it would indeed be a good sign if the stories about Germany adopting a more constructive approach to the EC's ruinous Farm Subsidy Policy turn out to be true. That could contribute mightily to the success of the current GATT round and signify a new Europe open to North American and Pacific commerce. The current drift toward exclusive regional trading blocs would be arrested. . . .

The preoccupations of left and right that feed a new American isolationism and economic nationalism are also fed by serious misinterpretation of the great revolution of our times: the collapse of Soviet-style Marxist-Leninism. I have chosen these words carefully because that is the reality upon which we must focus, not simply the end of the Cold War. But here too we are in danger of misread-ing what has brought us to the current happy state of affairs. Today, we are confused by two errors in interpreting the course of events.

The first error is that America's toughness in the 80s brought Moscow down. Some would claim that the Reagan era defense build-up and U.S. actions around the world in Grenada, Afghanistan, and even Nicaragua caused the Soviet collapse. As President Reagan's first Secretary of State and the source of some fairly robust rhetoric, I would like to believe this but it is simply not true. The U.S. policy of containment, pursed by all post-war presidents of both parties—though with varying skill—undoubtedly did make an important contribution to the Soviet disaster. But that disaster was fundamentally made in Moscow. The fact is that until the opening of the Berlin Wall in 1989, the Brezhnev era Soviet empire was still intact in Europe, in Asia, in Africa, and in Central America. The real story of the Soviet collapse is not our storming of the barricades but instead how a militant multinational empire gripped by an archaic ideology gradually choked on its own inherent contradictions, inefficiencies, and corruption.

If we accept the idea that our toughness was the major contribution to the Soviet collapse, then we are in danger of accepting the next logical step: the war's over, so let's go home. We no longer face any dangers to our security and we do not need to worry about what happens "over there." Such a misjudgment focuses exclusively on the end of the Cold War as the supreme event of our times, inevitably missing the most important event, which is the collapse of Soviet-style communism.

A second error is that we are witnessing a triumph of Western values. But it is *not* a triumph of Western values. It *is* instead, a triumph of Western systems: ours works and theirs does not work. This kind of victory, however, does not speak to the far more important moral issues that matter most over the long haul. Are our values worth adopting because our society is one of moral worth and excellence? Are we making adequate headway against the drug problem, inferior education and the gross fiscal irresponsibility exposed over the last several years? I think that most people lately freed from communism are not so sure that Western societies are such paragons of virtue as we would like to believe. . . .

It is not the case of Western values suddenly winning the hearts and minds of our adversaries but of our adversaries dramatically casting aside their own failed ideology in an effort to improve their lot. If, out of a sense of false triumphalism that borders on arrogance we become complacent about ourselves and the world, if we do not offer a society of excellence committed to a better world, then democracy will become just a discarded slogan for those nations newly free of Marxism-Leninism. And they'll be driven by confusion to new extremes to the right or left.

With this in mind, I would make the following observations about the new Russian revolution now taking place. *First, there is a political vacuum because the revolution was unintended.* Moscow has seen a coup and a counter coup but the outcome remains in doubt. . . .

The consequence of this unintended revolution is a dangerous political vacuum with the democrats badly divided while the old communists, still entrenched in the bureaucracy, weigh the new Russia down like an albatross.

Second, power and bad memories, not economic logic or democracy will dominate events. While the Russians try to sort themselves out, the desire of the underdogs to become the overdogs will rule the politics of the other republics—taking power and blaming the economic disaster on the old Soviet Union or some hated ethnic group will be the prime forces and in the absence of legitimate government, power will descend from the republics to the provinces to the cities and eventually to the streets. The various republics will be held together not by their vision of a harmonious commonwealth with Russia but their fear of civil war. And no one can be sure that this fear alone will be enough to prevent a massive tragedy. I am especially concerned about Russia's two large border states—Ukraine and Kazakhstan—where large Russian minorities live.

Third, the true democrats are in a distinct minority. In the coup of last August, only thousands came out to defend Yeltsin, not hundreds of thousands. While Yeltsin himself is the first freely elected leader of Russia in its thousand-year history,

there are no democratic institutions, legal systems, tradition of representative government, or broad understanding of democracy as we know it. The existing legislatures contain many appointed former communists and, in any event, they do not enjoy popular support. I would even say that elections are already somewhat discredited because so many were held so often with so little result over the last several years. In the absence of institutions and traditions, democracy now in the former Soviet Union really depends on the convictions of a very few, and whether democracy can be associated with a successful economic program. . . .

Amid this growing confusion, ethnic animosity and the politics of disintegration, what can we do?

First, our approach must have a humanitarian dimension. Even in the depths of the Cold War, our quarrel was not with the Russian people but their oppressive government. We should help the Russians in their hour of need. . . .

Second, we should target economic assistance to the micro, not only the macro economic policies. No amount of money will prop up a discredited approach for long. If you think otherwise, just ask the Germans who sank billions into the abyss of Gorbachev's indecisive last phase.

I am not an economist but of this I am sure: decontrolled prices and a convertible ruble in the context of an economy still run by state monopolies is certain to ruin any chance for free-market economics. Instead, we can try to encourage the only development that will pull Russia and its neighbors out of the morass—the private sector. Once we isolate what a private sector needs to function, we can push in that direction and give our businessmen and others incentives to invest and to help.

Third, and finally, we should recall that certain geopolitical facts, as old as European history, will not change. Russia will continue to be the largest state. The relations between Russia, Ukraine, and Kazakhstan will determine whether that part of the continent will see a new birth of sovereign peoples, or a rebirth of Russian domination of their immediate neighbors. History, as we know, is not encouraging. Soviet imperialism was preceded by two centuries of tsarist imperialism. And whether Russia repeats another such cycle of aggressive expansion, after the brutal contraction of these last few years, depends on whether democracy triumphs there.

Whatever the outcome, we know already that the consequences of the collapse of Marxist-Leninism in Russia are global and in each region presents us with a challenge and an opportunity.

I'll begin with Europe. Churchill once said that where there is a great deal of free speech there is always a certain amount of foolish speech. The foolish speech we hear nowadays are the dissertations that after the Cold War, the American role in Europe is finished. I believe just the reverse is true. Many nations have re-emerged as a consequence of the Soviet collapse. One is the united Germany, this time democratic and integrated economically and militarily with its neighbors and the United States. Another, of course, is Russia itself. And between these two, over a hundred million people in half-dozen states, including Poland, Hungary, and Czechoslovakia have emerged from tyranny.

We can be frank in this hearing and we ought to be. Only one security organization in history has dealt successfully and simultaneously with Germany and Russia. That is NATO, and NATO has worked because we are in it: politically, legally, and militarily on the ground.

To be for NATO, however, does not mean to be against a European security pillar. We cannot deny the Europeans the right to examine their security problems and come up with their own suggestions. In fact, we have been asking them to do that from the beginning of the alliance. But the result of that

examination will not alter the geopolitical realities. None of the major European states has either the strength or the moral authority to articulate a common European vision or to solve the enduring problem of European imbalance. I do not see that the failure of the Soviet attempt to impose its own vision on Europe changes this fact. Certainly, a Franco-German brigade or even a corps will not change it and can anyone imagine a danger to the security of the European Community that its members would prefer to handle by excluding the United States? This is what I call "foolish speech."

Both Americans and Europeans must therefore confront the hard truth: The peace of Europe depends upon America remaining a European power—a military, economic, political, and especially a moral power. Otherwise, the crisis of the East will become, sooner or later, a crisis for the West.

Still less can the CSCE [Conference on Security and Cooperation in Europe] be counted upon. Like the General Assembly of the United Nations, its strength is its weakness. There may yet be a need for a kind of European Security Council to deal with problems such as Yugoslavia and to give the new Russia a constructive role. But America's role will not change.

In short, American participation is more than ever the key to the whole and free Europe we all desire. And as the Russians sort it out, both the EC and NATO must find a way to extend the benefits of prosperity and security further eastward but without injuring the cohesion of these institutions.

29. The Graying of NATO

Hugh De Santis

From a political viewpoint, it is hard to imagine any West European state, except possibly the United Kingdom, justifying the perpetuation of NATO on the basis of an extra-European threat. In

SOURCE: Hugh De Santis. "The Graying of NATO," *The Washington Quarterly*, vol. 14, no. 4, Autumn 1991, pp. 54–64, excerpts. Reprinted by permission of the MIT Press, Cambridge, Massachusetts.

this case, past is prologue; neither European publics nor governments can be expected to extend NATO's mandate outside the treaty area, including Eastern Europe. The glaring lack of allied unity during Operation Desert Shield/Storm underscores the point.

Indeed, the politics of postwar Europe are likely to trend toward particularism rather than globalism. As reflected in the growing self-absorption of Germany—a condition that is bound to create strains with France—the European allies are investing their energy in the politics of Europeanization. To be sure, they would still like the United States to underwrite their security until some other European entity can supplant it. The United States, too, would like to preserve its dominant security role on the continent to maintain its status as a world power and to inhibit the European Community from formulating policies that will restrict its export of goods and capital. But the U.S. desire to sustain its influence in Europe and the allied preference to limit its role to that of security caretaker do not augur well for the longevity of the Alliance.

ALTERNATIVES TO NATO

If NATO's days are numbered, which institution is likely to replace it? Until recently, many European officials believed that the new security order should be built on the foundations of the Conference on Security and Cooperation in Europe (CSCE), a Soviet-inspired forum that ironically became the catalyst for détente during the Cold War. Buoyed by the collapse of the Soviet empire and the sweeping public repudiation of communism from Berlin to Bucharest, Germany's foreign minister, Hans-Dietrich Genscher, and Václav Havel, president of the Czech and Slovak Federal Republic, trumpeted the CSCE as the harbinger of the millennium of peace in Europe.

In contrast to NATO, the CSCE contains all the European countries except Albania. It also includes the Soviet Union, thereby enhancing the prospect of European integration. Unlike NATO and, to a lesser degree, the WEU or the Council of Europe, the CSCE is not freighted with the cultural baggage of the Cold War. As the child of détente, the CSCE shares with the Harmel Report a vision of a reunited Europe committed to progress on political, security, economic, and human rights activities. Finally, the membership of the United States and Canada in the CSCE gives it a Euratlantic character. More important, it enables it to address European aspirations without sacrificing the stabilizing presence of the United States.

Convinced that the democratic paroxysms of 1989 prefigured the emergence of a peaceful and prosperous Europe, the leaders of the CSCE states convened in Paris in November 1990 to celebrate their new world order. Officials and pundits alike compared the gathering to the Congress of Vienna in 1815. . . .

The peaceful revolutions of 1989 and 1990 seem to have mesmerized too many people into believing that collective security would be the rationally ordained outcome of democratic reform. Unfortunately, the end of the Cold War has not transformed human nature. The CSCE might succeed in damping down regional quarrels between its member states, but it would be no more capable of preventing armed conflicts among revisionist states than was the League of Nations unless it were prepared to use military force to enforce its collective decision-making authority.

To compound the security problem, a CSCE-centered Europe, whether it nurtures peace or not, is not likely to sustain an active U.S. commitment. The U.S. public has never been interested in the CSCE. Given that public's chronic complaint about having to defend rich and ungrateful allies and its new worries about an emerging European economic fortress, the emphasis on a CSCE "architecture" for postwar Europe may accelerate the process of U.S. military retrenchment at the expense of continental stability.

Disillusioned with the CSCE, Euro-optimists seem to be gravitating toward the European Community. Although West Europeans continue to believe that NATO and the U.S. military presence are necessary for their near-term security, a majority of them would prefer to see the Community form a common defense organization to protect their interests in the future, according to a recent EC poll. . . .

It is only natural that Europeans would hope that the considerable progress the EC has made toward economic integration might eventually extend to political and security matters. For the French and others who suspect that the U.S. presence in Europe may soon be coming to an end, the EC represents the only institutionally viable way of providing for European security and ensuring that Germany remains institutionally tethered to the West.

At its present state of development, however, the EC is just as ill-suited as the CSCE to assume the security trusteeship of a reunited Europe. Efforts to establish an adjunct defense role in a body that includes neutral or security-phobic members such as Ireland, Denmark, and (Turkey aside) Greece are bound to founder. The key to the development of a peaceful Europe is economic integration. To divert the EC from its single-minded pursuit of this crucial objective by burdening it with a security function that it is unprepared to accommodate is to retard and possibly undermine European unity. . . .

If neither the EC nor the CSCE is capable of replacing NATO, one could always opt for a new security organization. But one might wait forever for a new security structure to emerge. Membership, the role of nuclear weapons, and burden-sharing arrangements would provoke disagreements far more intense than anything the allies have encountered in the past. While the allies tiresomely debated the future, Europe might enter a dangerous period of drift. In the process, Germany might eventually opt for neutrality or a policy of military unilateralism. And the United States would sooner or later be pressed by Congress and public opinion to remove its forces from the continent.

Besides, there is no need to create a new edifice when there may already exist a better alternative to NATO than either the CSCE or the EC or some hybrid of these and other organizations: the Western European Union. The WEU is the only European institution whose members have pledged to defend one another. Moreover, given its explicit commitment to European integration, it is the security analogue of the EC and the CSCE in their respective economic and political domains.

True, the WEU has not had a distinguished history as a collective defense organization. Established in 1955 as a successor to the Brussels Treaty Organization to monitor German rearmament, its security functions were preempted by NATO after the Federal Republic's entry into the Alliance. Except in Paris, where it still excited *troisième voie* fantasies of a French-led European defense organization, the WEU served thereafter mainly as a souvenir of security cooperation immediately after the war, a sort of monument to good intentions. In the United States, it was all but forgotten until its resuscitation during the intermediate-range nuclear forces (INF) crisis, when the overly sensitive administration of President Ronald Reagan publicly renounced its deliberations and gave it more attention and status than it deserved.

Since then, however, the WEU has taken on new life. At the end of 1987, as the outlines of change in the Soviet Union became more sharply etched, it adopted a "Platform on European Security Interests," which called for more active cooperation among its signatories in support of rather than in opposition to NATO in the areas of arms procurement and arms-control verification. Free of legal constraints on its activity outside Europe, the WEU authorized European participation in the 1987 reflagging of Kuwaiti tankers and in the U.S.-led coalition against Iraq in the Gulf War.

Quietly, interest in the WEU is intensifying in allied capitals. On December 6, 1990, the German chancellor, Helmut Kohl, and President François Mitterrand of France sent a letter to the heads of the European Council expressing the hope that the WEU would become the centerpiece of European security. Rumors are also circulating that the WEU may move its headquarters from Paris to Brussels, which would allow the member states to accredit their ambassadors simultaneously to NATO.

Still, the European allies are treading softly on the issue. The Kohl-Mitterrand letter reportedly triggered a stern demarche from the United States to allied capitals. In response, Genscher and the French foreign minister, Roland Dumas, issued a bland statement on European unity that subordinated the WEU to NATO. Fearful of alienating Washington and thus precipitating a U.S. withdrawal from the continent, the allies, led by the British and Dutch, have resumed referring to the WEU as a "European pillar" within NATO.

But this transatlantic dance cannot continue indefinitely. The tune is already changing, and the partners risk getting uncomfortably out of step. Whether the United States likes it or not, Europe is Europeanizing. Consequently, U.S. influence will inevitably decline. But a reunited Europe must also accept the responsibility for its own defense. It cannot, therefore, expect the United States to maintain an indefinite military presence on the continent.

To be sure, U.S. leadership will be needed in the short term to provide stability and reassurance to an unsettled continent. But the role of the United States as well as NATO in the unfolding postwar Europe can only be transitional. In the long term, the Western European Union, or whatever it may then be called, is the most likely steward of a united Europe's security. . . .

Throughout this process of integration Europe would be simultaneously denuclearizing. The removal of all ground-based, short-range weapons, including nuclear artillery, from the continent is predictable. Furthermore, motivated by the desire to speed the withdrawal of Soviet troops from its territory and to establish closer ties to the new democracies in the East, Germany is likely to reject the deployment of air-delivered nuclear weapons (so-called TASM).

To be sure, the British and French will maintain their nuclear deterrents to bolster the development of the WEU and to hedge against Soviet or, more likely, Russian expansionism. Nonetheless, to alleviate anxieties in Bonn that British and French nuclear forces were aimed at Germany, and to preclude German nuclearization, London and Paris would probably be forced to scale back the size of their nuclear arsenals in proportion to the reduction of conventional and strategic arms in Europe.

The Soviet Union would still possess strategic weapons. But so would the United States. Given the enormous uncertainty that will attend the process of European unification, and the nagging worry about the dispersal of nuclear weapons to the restive Soviet republics, it seems unlikely that either Moscow or Washington will agree quickly to a START II treaty. Although the condition of strategic standoff will be far from ideal, it will give assurance to all participants in the process of Europeanization, the United States and the Soviet Union included, that the transition from bipolarism to multilateralism will not undermine the state of mutual deterrence that sustained European stability during the Cold War. Although the European states would maintain defense forces tethered to the WEU, or ESU, they would have no incentive to build nuclear forces.

Like the regional associations and the Warsaw Pact, NATO will gradually wither away. The skeletized force of two U.S. divisions and three air wings in the mid-1990s, say, will be phased out by the end of the decade. To allay allied anxieties about the return to neo-isolationism in the United States, however, U.S. officials would be well advised to underscore their continuing commitment to European security. At a minimum, this would require the United States to leave prepositioned equipment in Europe for the foreseeable future, maintain adequate airlift and sealift capability to respond to crises, if necessary, and foster a consultative relationship with the WEU Council on a broad range of defense topics, especially nuclear weapons policy.

PLANNING FOR THE FUTURE

The envisioned evolution of European security in the emerging postwar period does not anticipate some millennium of peace. The resumption of the interrupted process of nationalism in Eastern Europe may overcome efforts to establish cooperative structures. Societies that mortgaged their futures to the illusion of a socialist utopia may not be able to defer economic and social gratification. Further, it may be a fantasy to believe that Turkey, which is likely to experience rising Islamic fundamentalism and a growing security threat on its southern borders, can be fitted into the mosaic of a Europeanized Europe. But to repose one's hopes for the future in the strength of institutions like NATO that belong to another time in the history of both Europe and the United States is to induce a dangerous complacency that invites instability.

Conflict cannot be prevented in the emerging postwar Europe. It can be contained, however. In order to do so, the United States and the European allies must first part with their illusions. Efforts to superimpose prefabricated architectures on the new Europe without examining and shoring up, if necessary, its existing foundations are bound to fail. Viewing the future through the lens of 1949 gives an equally distorted picture of reality. Neither approach is rooted in the present.

At the same time, political leaders in the United States and Europe must have some vision of the future that they would like to see emerge from the present. The EC should figure prominently in their thinking—it has the quintessential role to play in the new Europe as the engine of economic unity. So should the CSCE. Just as the CSCE provided a process of interaction that sustained détente in Europe during the superpower chill of the 1980s, it can perform an equally valuable service as a conciliator and mediator in the ethnic, religious, and territorial disputes that lie ahead. But Western leaders also need to develop a new concept of security to replace the alliance structure that has served peace so well for the past four decades. The WEU appears to be the only viable institutional base on which a new structure can be built.

The WEU is no panacea for the problems that await the new Europe; it may struggle to manage the process of integration. Unlike NATO, however, it points the Euratlantic community in the direction of tomorrow rather than yesterday. That alone is a hopeful sign. For its part, the United States should assist rather than resist the development of the WEU. After all, no country has made a greater contribution on behalf of European unity. Besides, the security and stability that a collective defense organization will provide to a continent that is about to resume responsibility for its own affairs can only enhance the long-term geostrategic interests of the United States.

B. THE FAR EAST

30. Toward a New Pacific Strategy

Colonel Ralph A. Cossa, USAF

As with Europe, "containing communism" was the primary motivating factor behind the various Asian security alliances. However, the threat historically emanated not just from the former USSR but from the People's Republic of China, North Korea, and Vietnam, with each of these nations presenting a threat in its own right. The degree to which each threatened its neighbors—and U.S. interests—has varied over time.

There is also a (usually subtle) ethnocentric bias on the part of most Americans toward the region. Although in economic terms America is becoming more and more Pacific-oriented, culturally and emotionally we remain a European nation. We have also been twice-burnt in Asia—the lack of a clear-cut victory in Korea and a defeat in Vietnam—as opposed to our string of victories in Europe and elsewhere. A defense commitment in Asia appears harder to "sell" to the American people

SOURCE: Ralph A. Cossa. "Toward a New Pacific Strategy," *Strategic Review*, vol. XX, no. 2, Spring 1992, pp. 70–74, excerpts. Reprinted with permission.

and Congress, especially at a time when the economic balance of payments equation is tilted so heavily in Asia's favor.

Europe and the Pacific do share one major characteristic, however. Since World War II, both have fallen under an American security umbrella which has provided the sense of security essential to each region's social and economic development. Few nations in either region are eager to see this umbrella close, even as they acknowledge that some change in its size and orientation appears inevitable (and necessary).

A useful parallel can also be drawn between Asian fears of a resurgent, remilitarized Japan and Europe's lingering fears over a resurgent, reunified Germany. Like Germany, Japan already is an economic superpower. And, with the world's second or third largest annual military budget (measured in total expenditures rather than as a percentage of GNP), it is already seen by most Asians as a regional military power—one who previously cast a long shadow across much of Asia. *Although the United States may not fully share the fears of Japan's (and

Germany's) neighbors, we must understand these security concerns and ensure that our policies assuage rather than exacerbate their fears.

The underlying premise of this piece is that the United States has vital economic and security interests in the Asia-Pacific theater. The question is how best to protect these interests. On this basis we can properly assess the utility of existing security relationships, or force deployment patterns.

Currently, five security alliances provide the framework for our military interaction with our Asia-Pacific neighbors. Maintenance of these security relationships underscores the U.S. commitment to remain both a Pacific and a global power. Although these alliances were initially aimed at—and justified in terms of—containing Soviet or communist expansion, the actual threat environment defies simple description. In reality, few outside Japan and China ever saw the former Soviet Union as the primary threat. Many see threats emanating from non-communist sources, with a resurgent Japan being primary among potential alternate threats. Notably, no Asia-Pacific nation outside North Korea sees the United States as the primary threat.

The Asia-Pacific region is in the front yard of two major world powers, Japan and China, and in the back yard of two others, the United States and Russia. Major regional military powers include India, Vietnam, and both Koreas. All told, seven of the world's ten largest military forces reside in or adjacent to the Asia-Pacific region. It was, is, and appears destined to remain a multi-polar region. With some notable exceptions, the U.S. military presence—and U.S. intentions—have been seen as largely benign and more stabilizing than threatening. U.S. security relationships are aimed as much at promoting regional stability and enhancing security cooperation as they are at countering a specific military threat.

These alliances also help promote and protect America's growing economic interests throughout the region. It is an established fact that since the mid-1970s, the United States has conducted more trade with its Asia-Pacific neighbors than with any other region of the world. This trend is expected to continue. One significant change has occurred,

however. Whereas a decade ago, the United States was the number one trading partner with virtually all free world nations in the region, today Japan enjoys that status. At the same time that the region is becoming more important to the U.S. economically, U.S. economic leverage on a country-to-country basis is declining. This, in turn, enhances the relative importance of the U.S. military presence as an instrument of American influence. . . .

JAPAN

The U.S.-Japan security relationship serves a number of mutually supportive objectives. It provides a common security bond between two major powers, based on defense cooperation rather than competition. It provides U.S. military access to Japanese facilities, to assist both in the defense of Japan and in the protection of U.S. security interests throughout Asia. Most importantly, it provides an alternative to a massive Japanese military build-up that neither side (or anyone else in Asia) wants to see. As one strategic analyst observed, "It serves to keep the Japanese in a box that they want to remain in."

The fact of the matter is that the only thing that stands between Japan and true world superpower status is Japan's lack of a nuclear arsenal. Economically, Japan is already there. In terms of conventional military power, it has one of the best equipped, most capable armed forces in the region, if not the world. Its limited ability to project this power far from its shores (no aircraft carriers, long-range bombers or strategic missiles) could easily be overcome—it previously built carriers, has a burgeoning aircraft industry, and already has sufficient rocket technology to place satellites in orbit. It is the presence of the U.S.-Japan security relationship that removes the need for Japan to develop an independent nuclear capability.

To the extent that the U.S. relationship/presence persuades Japan not to expand its military capabilities, regional security is enhanced. If Japan were to remilitarize, and particularly if it were to "go nuclear," the global balance of power equation would be significantly altered. Even the North Koreans—who otherwise would prefer to see the United States as far away from their shores as possible—would most likely prefer a U.S.-Japan security relationship to a remilitarized (particularly a nuclear) Japan.

Most Japanese share this outlook. The sentiments against remilitarization in Japan run deep. There is no need to convince Japan in this regard; there is a need to avoid policies and actions that will convince them to modify or abandon these beliefs. Tokyo realizes that its economic health is totally dependent on overseas sea lanes. To argue, therefore, that a withdrawal of the U.S. security umbrella would not result in Japanese remilitarization is to argue that Japan would not take whatever steps are necessary to ensure that its security interests remain protected. If Japan were denied the U.S. nuclear umbrella, it would have only two reasonable options: develop its own nuclear capability, or align itself with another nuclear power—and it appears difficult to imagine Japan placing its security in Soviet or Chinese hands.

Given Japan's current military capabilities and past history, U.S. calls for Japan to increase its defense spending raise concerns throughout Asia. Such demands reflect a lack of awareness regarding both current Japanese capabilities and the extent of regional concerns. Indeed these demands are not even genuine. What we are really seeking is for Japan to spend more on *our* defense; i.e., to share an even greater portion of the cost of U.S. forces based on their territory. While Japan can certainly afford to spend more to keep us there, we must recognize that Japan already pays more toward the maintenance of U.S. forces on its soil than any of our other allies. More importantly, these forces are present not just to protect Japan but to preserve and protect our own and other regional nations' interests as well.

There is another aspect of the U.S.-Japan security relationship which needs to be addressed. As U.S. economic leverage over Japan continues to diminish, the importance of our security relationship conversely grows. This does not mean we can or should wave the security umbrella over Japan as a sword. It does mean that the security link, the strongest link between our two nations, provides the greatest leverage in dealing with Japan. Indeed, it may be our *only* source of leverage. As long as

Japan's physical security is tied to the United States, we enjoy a special relationship that should, if properly managed (and not abused) pay dividends in the course of economic and other non-security-related discussions—provided the various U.S. agencies involved figure out how to cooperate on Japanese issues, rather than engage in internecine warfare.

CHINA

China's role in the Asia-Pacific balance of power equation must be more clearly defined. It should come as no surprise that China looks out for China first. It distrusts both the Russians and the Japanese but desires normalized, if not cordial, relations with both nations. It seeks closer cooperation with the United States, but on its own terms, and not as a "card" to be played against Moscow or any other power. The United States, for its part, has never needed China as an ally in the traditional sense of the word. During the Cold War, China's role in the event of a global conflict was to tie down a half million Soviet forces by virtue of its presence alone. Even a neutral China could serve this purpose.

Nonetheless, it is clearly in the U.S. interest to maintain a dialogue with the world's largest nation; one which by virtue of size alone is destined to remain a regional power and whose nuclear capabilities and expanding ties with the Third World make it a major global power as well. More importantly, most definitions of a "new world order" place increased emphasis on a multinational approach toward conflict resolution and tension reduction, with the United States as the most likely vehicle. This enhances China's international power and prestige, given its veto powers as a permanent member of the U.N. Security Council. (Ironically, many proponents of increased U.N. involvement are also proponents of hardline policies that would isolate and alienate China; these policies seem uncomplementary.)

It is also essential to put current developments in proper perspective. Tiananmen Square notwithstanding, China has come a long way in the past decade in terms of economic and political reform, and Deng Xiaoping has recently provided strong signals that he remains committed to liberalization. But Deng continues to move cautiously, ever mindful that going too fast could destroy his own power base. More importantly, he has seeded the bureaucracy with like-minded reformers who are poised to lead China even further along the path of reform once the current generation of leaders passes from the scene. But, regardless of their policies, the next generation of Chinese leaders will likely be just as stubbornly committed to enhancing China's role in the region and world.

China's three largest neighbors (Russia, Vietnam and India) all place the PRC high on their list of potential adversaries, and a deep sense of mutual distrust lies not-so-deeply buried beneath the currently cordial Sino-Japanese relationship. In many parts of Southeast Asia, China is seen as part of the problem rather than as part of the solution. In fact, one of the greatest fears among our Southeast Asian friends in the early 1970s was that the *quid pro quo* for China serving as a balance to Soviet power in Northeast Asia would be U.S. acquiescence in a predominant Chinese role in the region. These fears of U.S.-Chinese collusion have been largely overcome, but concerns about long-term Chinese intentions remain, especially in nations with large ethnic Chinese communities.

Sino-Russian relations are expected to improve since both sides need a period of reduced tensions in which to undertake widespread economic reforms. It is important to note, however, that the initial improvement in Sino-Soviet relations engineered by Mr. Gorbachev came about almost exclusively on Chinese terms. To the extent that there was ever any self-doubt among China's leaders as to the wisdom of stubbornly holding one's ground until the other side finally comes around, their success in dealing with Gorbachev removed this doubt. As a result, Chinese diplomatic inflexibility is likely to increase (and not just when dealing with Moscow).

KOREA

Now that East and West Germany have reunited, is the reunification of the two Koreas close at hand? The answer, regrettably, is "not necessarily." True,

both have been divided about the same length of time, but the circumstances are significantly different. Germany was divided because it fought a war and lost; Korea was divided as part of the spoils of war. North and South Korea then fought a bloody civil war in which neither side won and both suffered greatly. While the dream of reunification is as sincere in Korea as it was in Germany, the level of mistrust and animosity between the two Koreas makes progress more difficult.

North Korea remains one of the most closed, repressive, heavily armed and economically backward societies in the world and the prospects of significant reform from within appear slim as long as North Korean President Kim Il-Sung is alive. Most analysts also predict a potentially volatile leadership transition following Kim's death, given his desire to have his son replace him.

The U.S. presence in South Korea has been instrumental in preserving peace on the peninsula. It has provided the security shield behind which the Republic of Korea's military forces have developed and behind which Korea's economy has blossomed, to the point that Korea stands today as a model of economic development, in sharp contrast to the North. U.S. force levels in Korea have never been sufficient to defeat an all-out North Korean attack. U.S. forces are aimed at deterring such an attack, by presenting a symbol to the North of U.S. commitment. Politically, they serve in a "tripwire" capacity; one that "guarantees" the North that the United States will be involved. Militarily, they are there to help delay a North Korean advance until U.S. reinforcements arrive. The amount of forces required to serve as a tripwire is open to debate. But, the need to continue sending a strong signal of U.S. commitment and support during a time when North Korea's future direction is uncertain and potentially volatile appears essential.

Of note, the U.S. commitment to Korea is also seen as a signal of U.S. resolve throughout the region. Of all of America's security agreements, the U.S.-Korea arrangement is the least susceptible to the charge of having been rendered obsolete due to the absence of a credible threat. To appear to renege on this commitment would raise considerable doubts as to the viability of all other U.S. defense commitments.

CONCLUSIONS

U.S. forward deployed forces, in conjunction with our treaty relationships, represent a force for stability in the Asia-Pacific region. The U.S. presence has traditionally served to balance not just the former Soviet threat but the overall mosaic, which includes a nuclear China, a Japan with unrivaled economic power and growing military potential, a volatile North Korea, and many other security concerns and issues. First and foremost, however, they protect and promote U.S. security interests in Asia.

Discussions on appropriate U.S. force levels need to proceed, but they should be based on a realization of how important a U.S. presence is in maintaining the current balance. Also of importance is the realization that, as our relative economic clout declines, our military presence becomes more important. This is not to predict that the United States is destined to become a one-dimensional power in Asia—we remain a major player economically and we continue to provide a political and economic model which, with minor modifications to fit Asian culture, continues to be attractive. But we should recognize that our security commitments, and thus our military presence, represent a powerful instrument of goodwill and potential influence even in peacetime, given regional threat perceptions that do not always coincide with our own.

Defense Secretary Cheney's planned Phase One cuts in U.S. Asia-based forces have been accepted as reasonable and non-threatening by most Asians but are unlikely to appease Congress or escape further challenge as defense cuts continue. The question of how low we can safely go remains to be answered. Forward-deployed forces cannot be addressed in a vacuum however. They underscore the various regional defense commitments that promote our own economic and security interests and hold intra-regional rivalry in check. Force cuts that undermine the regional security mosaic will work to our long-term detriment.

Ultimately, it is the viability of the U.S. defense commitment to Asia that will ensure continued stability and thus protect our political, economic and military interests. The real challenge for the United States, over time, is to break the mindset that equates commitment with presence. Instead, we must seek more creative, less costly ways to continue playing the role that only we are equipped to play. More frequent exercises, exchange visits, port calls, civil engineer and other nation-building projects, more access to our military schools and training programs, and a greater level of security assistance, all provide alternative means of demonstrating commitment and building good will. The challenge will be to find the proper mix between forces on the ground and alternative, more creative means of demonstrating that the United States intends to remain a force for peace and stability in Asia.

31. East Asia's America Problem

Jung-en Woo

Despite their newfound self-assertiveness, the capitalist states of Northeast Asia remain semi-sovereign in their politics and defense, and barely sovereign in their mass culture—the epicenter of

SOURCE: Jung-en Woo. "East Asia's America Problem," *World Policy Journal*, vol. VIII, no. 3, Summer 1991, pp. 458–468, excerpts. Footnotes deleted. Reprinted with permission.

the latter still being firmly in Hollywood and New York. They are regionally bereft of anything akin to the European Economic Community, let alone a sense of "East Asianness," or common adherence to the legitimacy of social democratic ideals. Japanese, Koreans, and Chinese barely talk to each other, if truth be known.

For all the talk about Japan as "number one," Japan remains utterly unable to fashion an alternative hegemonic discourse, one that can leap across civilizational boundaries to create a universal appeal and turn Japan's solipsism into everyone else's universalism. There is little indigenous weight to offset the overwhelming influence of the United States, save the increasingly slim reed of "the East Asian tradition." Money can buy culture and ideology, as demonstrated by Sony's and Matsushita's respective purchases of Columbia and MCA, but it has not—as yet—created one. As one literary critic explained, Japan can produce "the signifiers, but not the signified."

THE POLITICAL ECONOMY OF AMERICA'S EAST ASIA

This poverty of philosophy stems from the reality of postwar U.S. hegemony in East Asia, which has been much more overwhelming and unilateral than in Western Europe. Starting with Gen. Douglas MacArthur's suzerainty during the occupation of Japan, the United States has had, until recently, nearly unilateral sway in the region. Thus over the years it has treated East Asia in a cavalier manner, one best symbolized by its frequent apologetics for forgetting to "consult" with its East Asian allies about monumental shifts in U.S. policy like opening relations with China, withdrawing troops from Korea, or forgiving debts to the Poles (which caused a recent brouhaha in Japan). And however penetrated the U.S. market may be by Asian imports, that market, despite concerted efforts recently to diversify, remains the lifeline of East Asia's economic success, providing the United States with a reverse influence over the region that is rarely acknowledged. . . .

Through the San Francisco framework of postwar peacemaking, Japan essentially gave up its military power and its autonomy in foreign policy-making. South Korea did the same at the time of the Korean War. For that reason, the state's role in mediating the relationship between the domestic and the international spheres remains decidedly weak in East Asia, at least where the United States is concerned.

National defense, which would ordinarily be a primary task of any state, Japan included, was handed over to Washington, and to the U.S. bases in Japan and Korea. Even after the Korean War, the Korean peninsula continued to be an armed-to-the-teeth tinderbox as Washington created under its nuclear umbrella a modified version of Japan's pre-war military empire, using South Korea's massive military as a regional gendarme to protect not just the Republic of Korea, but also to fight communist insurgents in Vietnam in the 1960s. Vietnam's 17th parallel was to have been another *cordon sanitaire.* Thus former colonies and dependencies, not to mention GI's stationed at bases in the Pacific, were to do their bit protecting the big enchilada, the Japanese archipelago. This was not a bad deal for Japan, of course, and the compact was justified by a weird formula that reverberates today: the Japanese really had to be protected from themselves. . . .

From 1948 to 1978 Taiwan had a similar compact with the United States, with the Kuomintang mainlanders dealt the best hand. Native Taiwanese were excluded from power and another huge military organization deleterious to democracy was created, while all the islanders were left free to make money. In 1978, of course, the United States demonstrated once again that it holds the ultimate trump hand, switching this China for the other one, and leaving Taiwan to make the best of its very bad deal—the saving grace being that the islanders were still free to make money, which they have done with a vengeance.

A virtual monopoly on the means of violence and the whip hand in important foreign policy decisions is one aspect of U.S. hegemony in East Asia. The other compact shaping the region is economic—the maintenance of a U.S. market open to East Asia's capitalist upstarts. The history and the workings of this compact are complicated, but the upshot was to deny the states of the region national agency in the conduct of domestic politics and economics. We can call this the compact of single-market dependence, and seek to understand its political logic.

The three Northeast Asian capitalist economies are remarkably dependent on the U.S. market. Canada and Mexico are the only other countries more singularly dependent on the U.S. market; no other West European, African, or Middle Eastern nation shows any comparable level of single-market dependence for its exports. . . .

By 1971, all that changed. Throughout the 1960s, the United States had supported a regime of fixed exchange rates and convertible currencies. But with inflation on the rise and the dollar heading for a fall, Nixon resorted to his "new economic policy," a mercantilist revolution that suspended indefinitely the dollar's official convertibility into either gold or foreign currencies, leaving the Japanese and the Europeans holding the bag. Nixon also slapped a discriminatory 10 percent duty on Japanese imports. The hell with you, said Nixon and Secretary of the Treasury John Connally; and Europe and Japan took it because they had nowhere else to go.

The Japanese did not respond at the time with tit-for-tat mercantilist policies, however. Despite the erection of new barriers to entry in the U.S. market and what we might call "hegemonic irresponsibility" on the part of the United States, Tokyo's commitment to GATT, though slow in coming, continued to grow steadily over time. The problem was that the U.S. commitment to the same GATT system became more capricious as protectionists made inroads into U.S. trade policy despite the professed support for GATT by free-traders and presidents alike.

This "hegemonic irresponsibility" continued throughout the 1980s as the U.S. Treasury bill market came to be financed by Japan. The United States now combines selective closing of the U.S. market ("voluntary restrictions") with mysterious codes— MOSS (market-oriented, sector-specific), SII (structural impediment initiative) and Super 301—to restructure the way domestic politics and markets are organized in Japan. It has had more success than many observers realize. For example, a recent survey of U.S. businesspeople in Japan found few complaints about closed markets and other obstacles to foreign commerce.

The smaller East Asian countries have been subjected to similar pressures and have had even less leverage on the United States than does Japan. Besides, their politics are much too brittle and their societies much too fragile to accommodate U.S. demands for liberalization, open markets, and democratized states without setting off tidal waves of change. South Korea is one such country. Despite all its visceral animosity toward Japan, it nonetheless fashioned its political economy after Japan's, in large part because neomercantilist alchemy had industrialized Japan rapidly, and was there to be emulated. But the essential difference between South Korea and its much envied "mirror of the future" (that is, Japan) was that South Korea was a bulwark of containment; thus, instead of the "soft authoritarianism" of Japan, Korea ended up with hard-core military authoritarianism.

Another difference was that South Korea industrialized even later than the relatively late developing Japan. The United States allowed South Korea to have a more insular political economy, so long as it occupied an innocuous place in the pores of the international market. The result was neomercantilism with vengeance, a developmental economy that was more tightly sealed and orchestrated from above than even Japan's.

In the 1980s, when the United States began a frontal assault on South Korea to liberalize its commodity and financial markets, the authoritarian state went into a tailspin. The power of the South Korean state had been predicated on its ubiquitous ability to control developmental resources, to mold the investment pattern by selectively allocating credit, to supplant and supplement the market, and thereby to create and control a huge constellation of entrepreneurial forces. U.S. demands for economic liberalization helped to shift power from the state to the society, and from the domestic to the international sphere as U.S. firms sought to enter the Korean market and exploit their comparative advantage in the agribusiness, high-technology, and service industries. The military regime collapsed like a house of cards in 1987, as Korea's *haute bourgeoisie* sat on the sidelines, silent spectators to a massive revolt begun by students and workers but swelled by members of the middle class. This was an unexpected outcome for a regime that had been so tightly embraced by the Reagan administration: it became a victim of the antinomies in U.S. foreign policy.

The point here is not to argue the merits of this outcome, nor to say that the Koreans were mere puppets of the United States, but merely to point out its structural logic. The regime's demise came about mainly because of widespread popular dissatisfaction, but U.S. pressure was a factor that helped shape the outcome. Hounding out a military dictator like Chun Doo Hwan may be a good thing in itself, but a situation whereby a hegemonic power undermines and compromises the political economy underpinning another society is profoundly problematic. This is a dilemma for the semi-sovereign states of East Asia as they grapple with U.S. hegemony, which still structures much of the political discourse by which we understand Asian politics.

THE STATE IN WEST AND EAST

The U.S. policy of restructuring East Asian economies is generally viewed as valid and enlightened, while Asian—especially Japanese—resistance to U.S. pressures to remake their societies and their economies is seen as devious and self-interested. From the East Asian perspective, however, it looks very different. Why this is so requires some discussion of how Asians think about the question of national agency and purpose, and the role of the state in society. At bottom are divergent views about the purpose of politics and government.

Liberal political theory has always seen state power as problematic, if not dangerous. In the view of many Americans, the state is a vacuity in which interest groups contend and conflict. According to pluralist theory, the state is merely a referee that maintains rules and the political order, and thus lubricates the market and the society. To the extent that the state is perceived to be autonomous of society, it has a negative image: a brooding presence that, as it grows, threatens to expropriate the market and civil society. These assumptions are so strong that it is often difficult even to discuss alternatives to the U.S. political pattern; state intervention or state autonomy conjures up in the liberal mind the Fascist regimes of Europe in the 1930s, and there discussion ceases and the shouting begins.

Alternative views of the state exist, however, apart from the extremes of Fascism and Stalinism. The state, for instance, can be benevolent, protective, and exemplary; it can be bountiful and generous, and it can be harsh and disciplinarian. Catholic cultures believe that, and so do Confucian cultures. In their view, state and society do not compete in an adversarial relationship or expropriate each other. Instead, the state is seen as an exemplary and meritocratic order that guides and educates the society. The Anglo-Saxon tradition of the minimal state is the exception, not the rule (rather than the other way around, as the Orientalist discourse would have you believe).

It would be fair to say that the peoples of China, North Korea, South Korea, Japan, and other Confucian cultures deeply believe that the state ought to provide not only material wherewithal for its peoples but moral guidance. And in that sense, the distinction between state and society is not one that is sharply drawn. By and large, Westerners have no way to understand this point except to assert that the Asian countries suffer from a series of absences: no individual rights, no civil society, no Enlightenment, and thus a weak or absent liberalism. In so doing they are saying little more than that northern Europe and North America had a different historical pattern than did other parts of the world. But too often this particular pattern presents itself as universal.

The state as conceived by East Asians is, furthermore, a practical necessity of development. Karl Polanyi, who was a Catholic socialist of sort, thought of the modern state (however tragically flawed it was at times) in similar terms—as a prophylactic to protect the society against the ravages of the world market. The resulting protected economy may have its inefficiencies—antique rice farmers and family store owners in East Asia, as well as higher prices for consumers to cover the costs of this "moral economy"—but who is to say, except the hegemonic power that believes in mammon and Adam Smith, that efficiency ought to reign as the only acceptable doctrine of political economy? And is it not true that the American state might have done *more* in recent years to protect its peoples—especially blue-collar workers—against the vicissitudes of international competition? . . .

Simply to make this argument opens one up to attack given the current climate in the United States. U.S. pressure on the Japanese domestic market is a counterpart to the interior desires of American Orientalists, who find the Japanese soul insular and unempathetic to the rest of the world, and want to turn it inside out, into a gleaming reflection of the American liberal self. U.S. policymakers see the potential for another triumph for "the end of history," for the vanquishing of one more perceived illiberal polity after the demise of the Stalinist systems in Eastern Europe.

EAST ASIAN SOLUTIONS FOR THE 1990S

While the more deeply rooted and contrary ways that Americans and East Asians think about the state and politics are likely to persist, it does appear that the East Asian states are moving slowly to attenuate the economic Gordian knot that ties the region to the U.S. market. The single-market dependency that characterized previous economic relationships now seems to be approaching the point of unsustainability. This is because of U.S. protectionism, but also because, as I have argued, this dependency has led to unwanted reciprocal pressure by Washington on Japan and Korea to "open markets" and cease to protect the moral economy of small producers—that is, to give up national autonomy. Single-market dependency is something that policymakers in East Asia can change, however, and they have recently begun to do so.

The single-market dependency that has for decades characterized East Asia's economic relationship with the United States is rapidly being reduced, as Japan, South Korea, and Taiwan diversify with an eye toward Europe and their neighbors. Recent figures suggest that a dramatic shift is under way. For instance, Japan's dependence on the U.S. market has dropped from 33 percent of its total worldwide trade in 1986 to 27 percent in 1990, while the estimate for 1991 is 25 percent.

To the extent that this pattern to diversify markets continues, it means a move away from the previous structure whereby the United States interacted bilaterally with Western Europe and Japan while Japan and Europe had little interaction. In the future we are likely to see an increasingly triangular pattern as investment and trade between Europe and East Asia continue to grow. Japan is also likely to continue strengthening its economic and political ties with its East Asian neighbors and to be more reluctant to let Washington mediate its relations with Taiwan, South Korea, and other Asian nations. Over time, we can expect that the more prosperous nations of Northeast Asia will become more integrated and begin to look like something akin to the European Community, while links will deepen between Northeast Asia and Southeast Asia, a region that is likely to give birth to the next generation of NICs.

These trends bespeak an East Asia that wants to set itself free from its asymmetric and often smothering relationship with the United States and wrest greater autonomy from the world system. The United States should welcome this development, for as Washington attempts to forge a "new world order," East Asia affords Washington an opportunity to disengage from some of its costly hegemonic burdens. . . .

As the security situation in the region continues to relax, U.S. leverage over the East Asian states will lessen further. Tensions in East Asia have eased significantly since 1985 with the Soviet Union's withdrawal of 200,000 troops from the Sino-Soviet border, and China's massive troop demobilizations. The preponderance of U.S. and Japanese conventional air and naval power in the North Pacific looks increasingly like an anachronism now that the Warsaw Pact does not even exist.

A relaxation of tensions, then, is clearly going on in East Asia. But in contrast to what is occurring in the economic realm, these changes have not begun to touch the basic security structure. As a result, it is much harder to project what will happen to the international Brumairean compact; what will be the future role of the United States in Asian regional security? The United States has been slow to let go in East Asia, and vice versa. Japan has thus far been content to keep the postwar security arrangement, and Japan's neighbors prefer U.S. troops to, say, Japanese ones.

As one Chinese strategist noted, Japan has 300,000 troops, 70 percent of whom are officers and noncommissioned officers. Thus it is quite capable of quickly increasing its troop strength. In addition, Japan has the economic and technological capabilities needed to leap over several generations of weapons technology and develop intelligent or "smart" weapons. This is not a proposition that Japan's neighbors want to test. Regional security, then, is likely to remain in Washington's hands for some time to come. It is likely that the United States will seek to hold onto the levers of security so as to stem the erosion of its influence in the region.

The change that will be the slowest in coming (if at all) will be with regard to what one might call the hegemonic psychology in East Asia. The United States is still the world's greatest and most vibrant center of cultural and ideological production. Japan may slowly replace the U.S. lead in finance, manufacturing, and technology, but it has yet to begin to articulate a post-hegemonic ideology, nor does its culture have a regional, let alone a universal, appeal. At best, Japan's cultural "contributions" are Nintendo hardware (the signifier without the signified), maudlin songs, karaoke bars (where drunken males mimic pop hits), and sex tours.

Tensions are likely to persist, at least for some time, because of this vast cultural and rhetorical divide between East Asia and the United States, and because East Asians may prove less adept at reducing their political and cultural dependency on the United States. The key obstacle is that East Asia remains an area without an identity, a region incapable of imaging itself as a community, to borrow academic Benedict Anderson's conception. Former victims of Japanese aggression, like Korea and China, also partake of the either/or absolutes of the new Orientalism, projecting for the future either a dreaded neo-Co-Prosperity Sphere, or the capitalist utopia of the Pacific Rim. That Alvin Toffler is listened to as a prophet throughout the region, including China, is merely a token of the utter absence of any regional self-definition.

East Asia lacks the language and psychology for self-assertion, which is an artifact of its long domination by the West. This palpable absence is also testimony to the terrible difficulty of hegemonic transfer across a civilizational divide, something that has never before occurred. When England passed the hegemonic baton to the United States in the 1940s, it passed it to an ally sharing much of its culture and tradition. With Japan's meteoric rise, another such transition perhaps beckons on the horizon. But all too many pundits can only greet this change with talk of conflict, eternal differences, the dire absence of (our) "transcendental truths," and even "the coming war with Japan." Surely our imaginations ought to do more than merely project into the future a past that everyone—the Japanese included—would rather forget.

Japan's neighbors can hardly bear to watch Japan again assert itself as a superior, homogeneous nation uniquely fit among Asians to the tasks of the modern world. But then they have also felt uncomfortable as they have watched Americans "going nationalist" over the past decade, with huge displays of flag waving that perhaps began at the Los Angeles Olympics in 1984, and certainly continued through the national celebration of the humiliation of Iraq.

The new Orientalism coupled with East Asian aphasia does not make for happy prognostication about the future of U.S.-East Asian relations. In the absence of a full airing of the issues that separate Americans and East Asians, public utterance becomes euphemistic, private thoughts run rampant, and slips of the tongue swelling up from the viscera taint the relationship and poison the atmosphere.

It would be far better if we would extrude antique conceptions of race and of Orient and Occident entirely from the ongoing debate. Instead we should focus on what really divides East and West, which is almost always some predictable and intelligible conflict of interest, and recognize what unites East and West in a common endeavor of development.

A U.S. policy of "constructive disengagement" from the asymmetrical relations of the past would not only leave more room for Asian autonomy, but also aid the United States by reducing its security burdens. In addition, such a policy could lead to a productive period of "looking inward" that could help domestic U.S. industries revive and flourish—

which after all is the best way to meet the "Asian challenge."

We need to think about a positive disengagement that prepares for truly equal and mutually beneficial relations in the future. We need to talk openly about what ties us together and what pushes us apart, what we really think about each other, how to build bridges of mutual understanding, and what America's East Asia has truly been about.

Questions for Discussion

1. Does the United States need allies in a post-Cold War world?
2. Should NATO be disbanded, the way SEATO and CENTO were?
3. What is the case for retaining NATO?
4. Should NATO assume new functions, for example, be used to support U.N.-sponsored humanitarian relief activities?
5. What role should the United States aspire to play in Europe?
6. Should the United States continue the security relationship with Japan? What changes, if any, should be made in it?
7. How will trade wars between the United States and allies in Europe and the Far East affect security relationships?

Selected Bibliography

ABSHIRE, DAVID M., RICHARD R. BURT, and R. JAMES WOOLSEY. *The Atlantic Alliance Transformed.* Washington, DC: Center for Strategic and International Studies, 1992.

BRADY, LINDA P. *The Politics of Negotiation: America's Dealings with Allies, Adversaries, and Friends.* Chapel Hill, NC: University of North Carolina Press, 1991.

BURSTEIN, DANIEL. *Turning the Tables: A Machiavellian Strategy for Dealing with Japan.* New York: Simon and Schuster, 1993.

CALLEO, DAVID P. *Beyond American Hegemony: The Future of the Western Alliance.* New York: Basic Books, 1987.

CARPENTER, TED GALEN. *A Search for Enemies: America's Alliances after the Cold War.* Washington, DC: Cato Institute, 1992.

FRIEDMAN, JULIAN R., CHRISTOPHER BLADEN, and STEVEN ROSEN (Eds.). *Alliance in International Politics.* Boston: Allyn and Bacon, 1970.

HARDING, HARRY. *A Fragile Relationship: The United States and China Since 1972.* Washington, DC: Brookings, 1992.

HARKAVY, ROBERT E. *Great Power Competition for Overseas Bases: The Geopolitics of Access Diplomacy.* New York: Pergamon Press, 1982.

of *Access Diplomacy.* New York: Pergamon Press, 1982.

MULLER, STEVEN, and GEBHARD SCHWEIGLER (Eds.). *From Occupation to Cooperation: The United States and United Germany in a Changing World Order.* New York: W.W. Norton, 1992.

OSGOOD, ROBERT E. *NATO: The Entangling Alliance.* Chicago: University of Chicago Press, 1962.

_____. *Alliances and American Foreign Policy.* Baltimore: The Johns Hopkins Press, 1968.

TREVERTON, GREGORY F. *America, Germany, and the Future of Europe.* Princeton: Princeton University Press, 1992.

ULLMAN, RICHARD. *Securing Europe.* Princeton: Princeton University Press, 1991.

WALT, STEPHEN M. *The Origins of Alliances.* Ithaca: Cornell University Press, 1987.

CHAPTER 10

Dealing with Russia

The collapse of the Soviet Union in December 1991 and the consequent end of the Cold War ushered in a new era in relations between Washington and Moscow. Although no longer the hub of a vast imperial system, Moscow is the capital of the Russian Federation, the largest of the fifteen republics to emerge to independence as a result of the USSR's demise. It is the most powerful republic, by virtue of its possession of a preponderance of the former Soviet Union's nuclear and conventional forces, and it is the richest in resources. Of the approximately 290 million people in the former Soviet Union, Russia has a population of about 150 million and "maintains 90 per cent of Soviet oil, nearly 80 per cent of the natural gas, 62 per cent of electricity, 70 per cent of gold production, and 70 per cent of the trained workers."[1] Though fallen on hard times, Moscow is very much in the league of great powers.

In terms of the U.S.'s geopolitical and military interests, the Russian Federation is the most important successor state of the former Soviet Union, the one with whom it has the greatest interest in establishing a friendly, cooperative relationship. Historically, the United States and Russia/Soviet Union have shared certain characteristics that kept their rivalry within acceptable limits, even in the worst periods of the Cold War, and that hold the promise of sound, stable relations for the future.

First, despite tense crises and regional conflicts in the Third World in which each backed opposing clients, Russia/Soviet Union and the United States have never fought a war against one another, not over Berlin in 1948–1949, Korea in 1950–1953, Hungary in 1956, Cuba in 1962, Czechoslovakia in 1968, Vietnam in the late 1960s to early 1970s, the Middle East in 1970 or 1973, or Nicaragua or Afghanistan in the 1980s. Both powers refrained from taking steps that might have pitted their own troops directly against each other and precipitated a direct confrontation between them.

Second, neither covets the territory of the other. There are no outstanding irredentist claims. Real estate is not and never has been at the heart of their difficulties. Their rivalry was imperial rather than nationalist in character, making it far easier for the elites in power to manage domestically. Each side could accept limited gains by the other in marginal areas, that is, areas that did not threaten the core security interests of the other.

Third, as peoples, the Russians and Americans have many positive images of one another. They appreciate each other's literature, music, theater, and sports, as is evident in the widespread popularity of the visiting artists and cultural troupes of both countries.

---

[1] Dimitri Simes. "Russia Reborn," *Foreign Policy*, no. 85, Winter 1991–92, p. 42.

Fourth, Russians and Americans share the belief of the eighteenth-century Enlightenment that through science, education, and man's reason, society can be perfected. This fundamental outlook continues to prevail in both countries despite mushrooming economic, ecological, and social problems, and despite disillusionment with the unanticipated consequences of social engineering. For both, gleaming technology still stands at the center of the societies that they strive to build.

Fifth, as urban, industrialized societies, the two countries face common problems, such as alienation, resource depletion, environmental deterioration, drug addiction, impoverished segments of the population, ethnic tensions, and so on. Their racial and nationality problems cause political unrest and absorb an increasing amount of the attention of the leaderships.

Finally, both face the supreme paradox of the nuclear age: Despite awesome military power, their influence in the world is difficult to manage and maintain. Small nations have found a new lease on autonomy and independence of action in this nuclear age.[2]

The new post-Soviet Russian leadership under Boris Yeltsin is committed to the return of Russia to Europe, to ending the isolation toward the West that was the dominant characteristic of the period of Soviet rule. This process started under Gorbachev, whose acquiescence to decommunization in Eastern Europe, reduction of Soviet forces from the area, and agreement to the reunification of Germany were intended to foster the Europeanization of Moscow's policy. In the interest of pursuing a "common European home," Gorbachev had implicitly accepted the dismantling of the common socialist alliance. However, there has always been a certain ambivalence toward Europe among Russia's ruling elites. In the mid-nineteenth century, two competing conceptions crystallized: Slavophiles versus Westernizers. The Slavophiles believed in the superiority and historical mission of Russia's Byzantine, Eastern Orthodox, autocratic tradition; they exalted messianic nationalism, unity of the Slavs, and expansion on the Eurasian landmass. The Westernizers argued that Russia was part of Europe, albeit at a less advanced economic and political stage of development; they espoused liberalization of society and a constitutional system modeled on the British experience. Both of these currents of thought are very much alive in the Russian Federation today and the outcome of their competition will affect the kind of foreign policy that Moscow follows and that the United States can support.

A number of Western commentators have correctly noted that the return of Russia to Europe is by no means a foregone conclusion: "It is more than a question of appropriate institutional mechanisms of integration, more than a matter of Marshall Plans, more than a matter of constitution making—essential as all of these things are. Ultimately, the return of Russia to Europe is a cultural process—the implantation in hearts and minds of a democratic, non-tribal temper."[3] Russian nationalism is one potentially destabilizing uncertainty: critics of Yeltsin's are using the precarious situation of the more than twenty-five million

[2] Alvin Z. Rubinstein. *Soviet Foreign Policy Since World War II*, 4th ed. New York: HarperCollins, 1992, p. 308.

[3] Michael Ignatieff. "Falling Apart and Coming Together: Russia and Europe in the 1990s," *Queen's Quarterly*, vol. 98, no. 4, Winter 1991, p. 810.

Russians living outside of the Russian Federation in newly independent republics as a rallying cry for intervening there "to defend our people." Another source of discord is Yeltsin's economic policy. Aleksandr Rutskoi, Vice-President of the Russian Federation, has bitterly and persistently attacked President Yeltsin's economic program, alleging that it has created "a dangerous situation of anarchy." He said that speculation has grown to impermissible levels, privatization is proceeding without regard for the real worth of the government enterprises that are being sold, and budgetary considerations are ignoring the plight of workers and pensioners. Ethnic nationalism and economic deterioration were instrumental in weakening Gorbachev's reform efforts; they could do the same to Yeltsin's.

The immediate problem for the United States is how extensive a commitment to make to the transformation of Russia. In early 1992, concerned that too little was being done by the Bush administration, Richard Nixon used the media to make his point: Help Yeltsin now. His speech on March 11, 1992, emphasized the importance of helping Russia move toward a "free market economy" and making the most of Yeltsin's leadership. Rating both Gorbachev and Yeltsin "as political heavyweights," he observed that Yeltsin, unlike Gorbachev, "has repudiated not just communism but socialism, as well," and has moved far beyond his predecessors in the field of arms control: "Yeltsin is the most pro-Western leader in Russian history. Under those circumstances then, he deserves our help":

Charity, it is said, begins at home and I agree. But aid to Russia, just speaking of Russia specifically, is not charity. We have to realize that if Yeltsin fails the alternative is not going to be somebody better, it's going to be somebody infinitely worse. We have to realize that if Yeltsin fails, if freedom fails, the new despotism which will take its place will mean that the peace dividend is finished, we will have to rearm, and that's going to cost infinitely more than would the aid that we provide at the present time. . . .

It also means, if Yeltsin succeeds, if democracy survives, that our children and grandchildren will have removed a fear of a possible world nuclear war that now haunts them, because democracies do not begin wars.[4]

As if in response to Nixon's prodding, on April 1, 1992, President Bush announced that the United States would contribute about $4.5 billion and join with Germany, Japan, France, Britain, Italy, and Canada to provide Russia with a $24 billion one-year aid package, to be used for stabilizing the ruble ($6 billion), debt rescheduling ($2.5 billion), credits and essential purchases ($11 billion), and funding for the International Monetary Fund (IMF) ($4.5 billion). Two weeks later, the IMF's Managing Director noted that in addition to the $24 billion for Russia, the international community and international institutions would have to help the fourteen other republics of the former Soviet Union with about $20 billion in 1992, and that over the next few years the need would be for more than $100 billion in outside assistance. At a time of sluggish international economic growth and mounting demands from Third World countries for investments and credits, the prospects for massive transfers of assistance to former Soviet bloc countries are not bright.

4 Richard M. Nixon. Speech delivered at a Nixon Library Conference in Washington, D.C., March 11, 1992.

On June 1, 1992, Russia's admittance as a member of the IMF marked a significant step toward its full integration into the world economic system. Implementation of the extensive aid package, however, will not be accomplished quickly, because Russia and the other republics of the old USSR must comply with the IMF's stringent financial conditions. In fact, in 1992, Russia received less than $18 billion of the $24 billion promised; the $6 billion stabilization fund was not provided, according to the IMF's managing director, Michel Camdessus, because Russia had failed to make structural and fiscal reforms necessary to curb the danger of hyperinflation.

Politics may have dictated Bush's aid package to Russia, since no administration wants to be blamed for "losing Russia," for failing to do what it could to help Russia make the transition to democracy and a market economy. Nonetheless, critics contend that the package is too open to waste and diversion, too loosely structured, too removed from stringent supervision and expressed linkage between reforms implemented and aid rendered. Leon Aron and William D. Eggers, analysts at The Heritage Foundation, a conservative think-tank in Washington, D.C., identified five problems that may lessen the economic impact of U.S. aid: 1) the "general aid" is helpful to Yeltsin politically, but does not necessarily translate into effective programs; 2) the effect of massive loans may be to add to Russia's huge foreign debt and to hamper economic growth; 3) aid that does not result in a convertible ruble will perpetuate budget deficits and discourage Western investment; 4) loan guarantees to purchase American grain may hurt the nascent emergence of a private agricultural sector in Russia; and 5) aid given without criteria established for as-

sessing progress in reforming Russia's economy may be a waste of scarce resources.[5]

These reservations were underscored by information presented to a Congressional committee by the Central Intelligence Agency's Director of Slavic and Eurasian Analysis, John McLaughlin. He substantiated Russia's attempts to reduce its budget deficit (which remains large), set exchange rates at more realistic levels, and accelerate cuts in defense spending, probably by about 15 percent. However, Russia still has a long way to go to create a market economy. Only 2 percent of its farmland has been privatized. Russia's "failure to permit the private resale of land or even pass a law on bankruptcy illustrates how much work lies ahead. Little progress has been made in privatizing state assets. And the government's fiscal and monetary restraint is showing signs of weakening in the face of pressures from the old establishment—especially defense industry—for increased spending and easier credit."[6]

Prior to the Yeltsin–Bush summit meeting in Washington, D.C., in June 1992, Douglas Seay, Deputy Director of Foreign Policy and Defense Studies at The Heritage Foundation, prepared a checklist of Dos and Don'ts that was intended to make people think about what should be discussed between the two leaders in the interest of strengthening U.S.-Russian relations (Reading 32). Taken as a whole, the points pro-

[5] Leon Aron and William D. Eggers. "Five Problems with the Bush Aid Package to Russia," *Backgrounder Update*, no. 178, April 8, 1992. Published by The Heritage Foundation.

[6] Statement for the Record, John McLaughlin, Director of Slavic and Eurasian Analysis, Central Intelligence Agency, to the Technology and National Security Subcommittee of the Joint Economic Committee of Congress, June 8, 1992, p. 11.

vide a usable baseline against which to evaluate progress in the countries' relations.

Although experiencing "a time of troubles" whose end is nowhere in sight, Russia remains a formidable military power. The shift from the subsidized, secretive, still-influential military-industrial complex to civilian production will be difficult; military conversion is proving extraordinarily complicated and encountering the tenacious resistance of powerful bureaucratic elites. Nonetheless, there are two reasons for guarded optimism about the long-term character of Russia's military policy. One is Yeltsin's foreign policy orientation and strong attachment to détente. The other is the erosion of the military establishment under the pressure of ethnic nationalism, societal alienation, economic privation, a diminished pool of new manpower, and budgetary constraints. Both Yeltsin and his Acting Defense Minister, General Pavel Grachev, are committed to a professional and much smaller army.

The atmosphere in Washington and Moscow is conductive to efforts to shed vestiges of the Cold War and further reduce the threat of war. For example, on December 12, 1991, President Bush signed into law the Nunn-Lugar Amendment, formally known as the Soviet Nuclear Threat Reduction Act, which provides for the United States to assist the countries of the former Soviet Union to dismantle their tactical nuclear missiles as expeditiously as possible. To this end, Congress appropriated $800 million. On January 3, 1993, Bush signed a SALT-2 treaty in Moscow with Yeltsin. If ratified, this landmark treaty would reduce each side's nuclear arsenal by about two-thirds by the early twenty-first century.

Perhaps the boldest proposal comes from Fred Charles Ikle', Under-Secretary of Defense for Policy in the Reagan administration and currently a Distinguished Scholar at the Center for Strategic and International Studies, Washington, D.C. He suggests the creation of a "defense community" linking Russia and the United States which "should not be confined to bilateral nuclear issues and to issues raised by the global proliferation of weapons of mass destruction," but must also promote a constructive relationship at the level of conventional forces as well. It should aim at reducing military secrecy between Russia and the United States and at promoting "democratic practices and traditions for civilian control of the military" in Russia.[7] The difficulties inherent in his proposal are formidable, but the strategic benefits could be incalculable.

President Bill Clinton's policy toward Russia was foreshadowed in a speech that he delivered on the subject during the 1992 campaign (Reading 33). His views are remarkably similar to those set forth by former President Richard Nixon, thus suggesting the possibility of an essentially bipartisan approach to the challenge of dealing with Russia, at least as long as Yeltsin is President.

When Yeltsin's political future was in jeopardy in March 1993 as a result of a move by opponents in the parliament to impeach him, Clinton strongly affirmed U.S. support for him:

> He is, after all, the first elected President in a thousand years. He has the mandate of having been voted on in a free and open election where people were free to vote and free to stay home—something that was not true previously. . . . He has shown a great

[7] Fred Charles Ikle'. "The Case for a Russian-American Defense Community," *The National Interest*, Winter 1991–1992, pp. 30–31.

deal of courage in sticking up for democracy and civil liberties and market reforms. And I'm going to support that.[8]

[8] Transcript of Clinton's First News Conference at White House, *The New York Times*, March 24, 1993, A9.

Prior to a summit meeting with Yeltsin in Vancouver, Canada, Clinton offered a comprehensive package of assistance designed to foster Russia's reforming efforts and emphasize the U.S. commitment to its attempt to democratize the political system and introduce a market economy.

32. Forging a Political Partnership between America and Russia: A Checklist of Do's and Don't's

Douglas Seay

Declare strong support for Russia's new government, for its reforms, and for Yeltsin personally.

Because it is identified with democracy, America commands tremendous moral authority throughout Eastern Europe and the former Soviet Union, including Russia. An embrace of Yeltsin by Bush and strong statements backing his government and the reform process would be a considerable political boost for the Russian president at a time when he is under great pressure to reverse course on reforms.

Those who argue that the U.S. should keep Yeltsin at arm's length because he may prove to be a transitional figure are profoundly mistaken. With little support from Western governments, and even outright opposition in the past from the Bush Administration, Yeltsin and the democratic forces in Russia and throughout the former Soviet Union succeeded in overthrowing the Soviet regime. In so doing, they advanced U.S. and Western interests far more than any Western government could have accomplished on its own.

SOURCE: Douglas Seay. "The Bush-Yeltsin Summit, June 15–17, 1992: Forging a U.S.-Russian Partnership," *Heritage Talking Points*, June 12, 1992. Published by The Heritage Foundation, excerpts. Reprinted with permission.

In this effort, Yeltsin acted with great political courage. As important, he repeatedly has demonstrated superior understanding and judgment regarding the political situation in Russia—far more acute than those of his many detractors in Russia and the West. He also has demonstrated a commitment to far-reaching political and economic reform, even if his efforts are only in their beginning stages. As such, Yeltsin remains the best hope for Russia's democratic reforms. It would be difficult to identify a replacement for him who would do better.

Refuse to take sides in the dispute between Russia and Ukraine.

Since the demise of the Soviet Union last fall, many disputes have arisen between Russia and the other former Soviet republics, especially Ukraine. Russian-Ukrainian tensions are among the most serious, given the size of the two countries and the growing vituperation between them. The list of disputes is long and growing and includes the treatment of national minorities, the status of Crimea, the division of the Black Sea Fleet, and many others. . . .

Already, various participants in these disputes have called upon the U.S. for support. The U.S., however, has no interest in choosing sides. Its interests lie in keeping the peace and preventing the outbreak and spread of conflict. Therefore, Bush should emphasize in his public and private statements that the U.S. will not choose sides in these and other disputes; instead, it will insist that all such disputes be settled peacefully. He must remember the lessons of the Yugoslav conflict where Western warnings were correctly interpreted in the region as empty rhetoric and were brushed aside by those government leaders, such as Serbian President Slobodan Milosevic, who are intent on achieving their goals by force. Bush must make very clear that the U.S. will seek to isolate and punish governments which resort to force against their neighbors.

Pledge U.S. support for the protection of Russian minorities in other countries.

The dissolution of the Soviet Union into several countries has meant that the poorly drawn boundaries of the former republics have become international borders. Included within these borders are millions of ethnic minorities, including Ukrainians, Armenians, Uzbeks, and many others. Russians constitute the largest of these minorities, around 25 million, and number over 10 million in Ukraine alone. Each of these ethnic groups faces the possibility of discrimination and persecution. Political forces in Russia and the other countries of the former Soviet Union have seized upon the alleged mistreatment of their ethnic kin to demand action in their support. For example, Russian Defense Minister Pavel Grachev declared on June 5 that the mistreatment of ethnic Russians would bring "the most iron-handed measures, including the use of armed force." As in Yugoslavia, real grievances have been used as cover to advance cynical political agendas; in Russia, anti-democratic forces are attempting to use the issue of the treatment of Russians in other countries to embarrass and thereby undermine Yeltsin's government and to provoke Moscow's intervention in these countries.

Bush must make clear that the U.S. opposes any such intervention by any of these new countries, regardless of the pretext. The problem of the protection of ethnic minorities is a difficult one—Russia itself harbors a large number—but the U.S. must insist that only peaceful solutions are acceptable. Moreover, a requirement of these countries' entry into the world community and continued cooperation with the West is protection of their minorities. If U.S. support is forthcoming, it will help to protect Yeltsin's flank against nationalist pressures for Russian intervention.

Warn Yeltsin of the danger of retaining the KGB.

Despite the victory of the democratic forces, the Soviet secret police—the KGB—remains in operation. In contrast with East European countries such as Hungary and Czechoslovakia, which dismantled their secret police, the Russian government has announced that it is retaining the KGB, albeit divided into two services and renamed the Ministry of Security and the Foreign Intelligence Service. Despite this new facade, its structure and personnel will be drawn primarily from that of its Soviet predecessor . . . tell Yeltsin that the retention of the KGB in any form is a profound mistake and represents a threat to Russia's fragile democracy. . . .

Insist that Yeltsin cease KGB operations against the United States.

U.S. intelligence officials have told The Heritage Foundation that the level of KGB operations in the U.S. has not decreased since the demise of the Soviet Union and has even increased in the area of military intelligence and defense technology. The same is true for operations conducted by the GRU, the military intelligence organization. Harry Brandon, head of the FBI's counter-intelligence service, recently confirmed that Russia is virtually alone among the republics of the former Soviet Union in continuing these operations. Most of the East European countries have ceased or greatly reduced their intelligence operations in the U.S., and some of these are actively cooperating with the West to reveal the identities of their former agents.

Bush should declare in the strongest terms that continued KGB operations in the U.S. and elsewhere are incompatible with Russia's desire to establish close relations with the U.S. This type of spying is unacceptable for a country receiving assistance from the West. Astonishingly, part of the Western aid given to the Russian government to support political and economic reform likely is being used to support KGB operations against the West. Yeltsin must be made to understand that once the American public becomes aware of the continuation of these KGB activities, its support for his government will be seriously undermined. Yeltsin must be firmly told that U.S. assistance for his government will cease unless he ends the KGB's Cold War operations against the West and dismantles its old spy networks. . . .

Urge Yeltsin to continue Russia's demilitarization.

The proportion of the Soviet economy devoted to defense production exceeded even the most radical estimates in the West. It is now clear that the Soviet economy was essentially a war economy with the preponderance of its industry devoted to defense production. The enormous Soviet military inventory produced by stupendous effort remains by far the world's largest.

Agreement has been reached among the former republics on the division of most of that inventory. Nevertheless, Russia's portion remains far in excess of its needs. The recently announced creation of a Russian army presents a good opportunity to restructure. Russian Defense Minister Pavel Grachev has announced plans for a force of 1.5 million troops, which is roughly one-third the size of the former Soviet military.

This means not only that Russia should cease manufacturing unneeded military equipment but also that it should restrict the deployments of those systems, such as ballistic missile-carrying submarines, which are most threatening to the U.S. and which are among the most difficult to control. Russia should not just deactivate these weapons but destroy them; the retention of such dangerous and unnecessary systems would signal that the break with the imperialist past is not yet complete. They also are costly to maintain and they only sour U.S.-Russian relations.

The Black Sea Fleet is an instructive example. Ownership and control of the former Soviet Black Sea Fleet is one of many areas of contention between Russia and Ukraine. The fleet is based in the Ukrainian port of Sevastopol but is manned largely by Russians. So far, there has been no agreement between Russia and Ukraine on how to divide the fleet.

Unfortunately, this dispute has become a symbol of nationalist feeling in both countries. Both sides forget, however, that neither Russia nor Ukraine has any need for a blue-water navy. Because it did not rely on maritime trade and faced no danger from invasion by sea, the Soviet Union had no need for an ocean-going navy. The Black Sea Fleet, along with the Pacific Fleet based in Vladivostok, the Northern Fleet in Murmansk, and the Baltic Fleet, was built as part of the enormous Soviet effort to achieve military superiority over the West and was designed as an offensive force to threaten Western interests and to disrupt its lines of communication.

If the Soviet Union had no legitimate need for a blue-water navy, certainly neither Ukraine nor Russia has one. Neither should want one. Andrei Kokoshin, Russia's Deputy Minister for Defense, stated on June 3 that Russia has not identified any enemies, "not even in the south," and that, contrary to the Soviet Union, Russian military doctrine and force deployments will be strictly defensive. This being the case, the naval requirements of both Russia and Ukraine are limited to coastal defense, and even these are quite modest. Thus, the current fight over the division of an unneeded instrument of imperial expansion is doubly absurd.

Secure Yeltsin's agreement to accelerate the pace of arms reductions, while avoiding the adversarial patterns that characterized U.S.-Soviet arms control negotiations.

The opportunity exists to cut significantly the arsenals of both the U.S. and Russia. The announcement that the two countries tentatively have agreed to further reduce the number of nuclear warheads in their arsenals from the Strategic Arms Reduction (START) Treaty's level of 8,500 to 4,700 by the end of the decade is evidence that the demolition of the Soviet regime has made possible rapid advances in mutual security. But the reduction in numbers itself provides little, if any, additional security, and has the possibility of actually harming it. Further reductions to the level of 2,000 to 2,500 warheads, as proposed by the Russian government, could in fact make the potential danger more acute. More important than overall numbers is the structure of the remaining forces. The Bush Administration is right to focus on those systems, such as Russia's multi-warhead SS-18 missiles, which have no function other than as first-strike weapons.

The Russian government has dragged its feet in discussions with the U.S. on reducing these systems. This is a result of its ill-considered attachment to erroneous arms control theories. Russia claims that it needs to retain some of these systems in order to balance the U.S. forces. This approach is profoundly mistaken and is a holdover from the Soviet era when arms control theorists raised balance into an absolute good, a consequence of abstract theories of stability and of equating Soviet threat and American defensive response. The U.S. is not a threat to Russia and does not need to be defended against, any more than Britain or Japan need to protect themselves against America. Bush must reject any Russian insistence on "equivalency," whether it results from misplaced pride or inertia from the Soviet era. He should explain that such an approach is neither necessary nor desirable and constitutes the biggest obstacle to an improvement in mutual security. . . .

Persuade Yeltsin to agree that the 1972 Anti-Ballistic Missile Treaty has lapsed.

With the Soviet Union no longer in existence, the ABM Treaty no longer is valid. It should not be revived. This is an opportunity for the U.S. and Russia to cooperate in advancing ballistic missile defense. In a televised speech on January 29, Yeltsin called for the U.S. and Russia to "create and jointly operate" a global defense system. The two governments already have taken the first step by

agreeing to establish a joint monitoring center to track the launch of ballistic missiles anywhere in the world. There now exists agreement between the two governments that at least some defenses are prudent as a hedge against an accidental, unauthorized, or light missile attack from any of an expanding number of ballistic missile states.

For this defense to be effective, it will have to go beyond the limits of the ABM Treaty. This can best be done through discussions with the Russian government. With the U.S. and Russia moving toward a more cooperative relationship, there need be no fear that such defenses will spark an arms race. There is no reason that limited defenses should be viewed as threatening by Moscow, any more than they would be by London or Ottawa. On the contrary, as was suggested in March by former Soviet Defense and Space Talks delegate Alexander Savelyev, strategic defense cooperation with America offers Russia an opportunity to protect itself against expanding threats at a time when it cannot bear the costs of such a defense itself.

Discuss with Yeltsin methods of accelerating the dismantling of the strategic nuclear systems remaining in Ukraine, Kazakhstan, and Belarus.

Although the transfer of tactical nuclear weapons to Russia from other areas of the former Soviet Union is virtually complete—to be followed by the weapons' destruction—there remain active strategic nuclear systems in the countries of Belarus, Ukraine, and Kazakhstan. Each of these countries has agreed to the eventual destruction of these systems but the projected timetables envision a very slow process stretching out over several years. There is no reason, however, to wait for such an extended period, especially as there is no guarantee that these countries will remain stable. Disabling these weapons would be relatively simple and could be accomplished very quickly.

None of these states has any legitimate need for these weapons, which in any case are supposed to be under the control of the joint Commonwealth of Independent States (CIS) command. The governments of these countries want the weapons to remain on their territories for the political status and negotiating leverage that they bring. The U.S., however, has an interest in the destruction of these weapons as soon as possible and should enlist the assistance of Russia in this endeavor, including encouraging Russia to announce cuts in its own strategic forces.

Persuade Yeltsin to rein in Russian arms sales, especially weapons of mass destruction and the technology associated with them.

In May, the five permanent members of the United Nations Security Council—the U.S., Russia, Britain, France, and China—signed an agreement limiting the sale or transfer of nuclear, biological, and chemical weapons technologies to the Middle East. Although this agreement has no enforcement mechanism, it can serve as a starting point for further U.S.-Russian cooperation on limiting arms sales.

This effort will not be easy. Currently, the U.S. is attempting to prevent a sale by Russia to India of rocket engines which can be used for ballistic missiles. Both countries claim that the intended use of these engines is for civilian space research, but they are applicable to military use. Bush should dispel a belief widespread in Moscow that these U.S. actions were motivated primarily by a desire to defend its own markets and emphasize to Yeltsin the U.S. determination to prevent other countries from duplicating Iraq's acquisition of advanced military technology.

A more difficult task is limiting Russian conventional arms sales, which have grown rapidly. Russia's tremendous need for hard currency, and its vast inventories of high-quality military equipment, have resulted in a flood of weapons to the Third World. Often, these are directly threatening to Western interests. Earlier this year Russia agreed to provide Iran with 3 *Kilo*-class submarines and training for their crews, in return for cash. As a result, Iran has acquired a dangerous capability to threaten shipping in the Persian Gulf and Arabian Sea and the ability to control the Strait of Hormuz, through which much of the world's oil supply must pass. Iranian purchases from Russia also include high-performance MiG-29 fighters, Su-24 fighter-bombers, and T-72 tanks. Some 500 Iranian pilots are being trained in Russia.

Although it is unrealistic to expect that the Russian government can be persuaded to eliminate all of its Third World arms sales, Bush should get Yeltsin to agree not to supply such countries as Iran that are likely to use these weapons against Western interests.

Encourage Yeltsin to withdraw Russian forces from the Baltic states of Estonia, Latvia, and Lithuania.

Although Russia has recognized the independence of the Baltic states, and although these newly independent countries are not part of the CIS, Moscow has not acted on their demands that former Soviet, now largely Russian, military forces be removed from their territory. . . .

Negotiations on this issue between the Russian government and the three Baltic governments have not gone well; Russian Defense Minister Pavel Grachev stated on May 31 that these troops will remain in place until after troop withdrawals from Germany are completed at the end of 1994.

These forces are a burdensome legacy of the forcible Soviet annexation of these countries in 1940 and have no legal or other right to remain. It is in Russia's interest to have good relations with the Baltic states, and it faces no threat from this region. The U.S. stood by the Baltic states during the half-century of Soviet rule; it has an obligation to ensure that their independence and sovereignty are fully restored. . . .

The most urgent task facing the Russian government is reversing the accelerating economic collapse inherited from the Soviet era. This can only be accomplished by a rapid transition from the existing state-owned, centrally directed economy to a market economy based on private property. The scope of the needed changes is staggering: writing and implementing new laws; creating new institutions such as a banking system; and dismantling the remnants of central planning. But by far the most important element is privatization of the state-owned economy, for without massive privatization there can be no market system. . . .

Encourage Yeltsin to move ahead rapidly and aggressively on privatization.

The greatest obstacle to privatization is not a shortage of expertise or the complexities of a rapid transition to a market economy, but delay. The delay of privatization is very dangerous and guarantees only continued economic decline. None of the economic reforms, from the freeing of prices to the breaking of the monopolies of state-owned enterprises, can work without extensive privatization of the state sector.

The U.S. and the West can play a valuable role in emboldening the reformers by insisting that Western assistance will be contingent on rapid and massive privatization. Bush should also tell Yeltsin that he intends to press the IMF to reverse its priorities and stress privatization and the development of the private sector.

The IMF has mandated privatization as one of its conditions for Western assistance, but this is only one target among many. Many of its other recommendations work against the creation of a private sector. For example, the IMF's insistence on raising Russia's astronomical taxes still further in order to balance the budget threatens to choke off the growth of the tiny private sector by further reducing profit margins or by forcing private businesses underground.

Declare that American and Western assistance will be directed to the private sector, not to the government.

Most Western assistance is heavily weighted toward government-to-government aid, the result of which will be to bolster the very bureaucracy and government control that economic reform should be directed at eliminating. The history of Western assistance to this area of the world is one of unrelieved waste and abuse. The West has pledged $24 billion in assistance, but this is unlikely to be more effective than the approximately $80 billion delivered or pledged to the Soviet regime by the West from September 1990 to January 1992. Far from improving Russia's economy, this massive infusion of aid has made matters worse. As much as half of it has ended up in Western bank accounts, much of it still controlled by former officials of the now-banned Communist Party. More important, Russia and the other newly independent countries of the former Soviet Union have been saddled with the burden of repaying these senseless loans, much as the new democracies of Eastern Europe struggle to repay the Western loans squandered by their communist predecessors.

If the U.S. and the West must provide financial assistance, it should be directed toward the Russian private sector. Assistance should be given only to enterprises which are fully privately owned and none at all to those which remain state-owned. This approach would support the emergence of new private businesses as well as bring additional incentives to the rapid privatization of the state-owned sector. Western assistance to the private sector should be distributed through private Russian financial institutions to the maximum extent possible, bypassing the state ones entirely. In this way, Western assistance would also promote the creation of a private financial sector, a key element in a market economy.

33.   A Strategy for Dealing with Russia

Bill Clinton

Today I want to discuss what America must do to secure democracy's triumph around the world, and most of all, in the former Soviet empire. No nation-

SOURCE: Bill Clinton delivered this speech to the Foreign Policy Association, New York, on April 1, 1992.

al security issue is more urgent, nowhere is our country's imperative more clear. I believe it is time for America to lead a global alliance for democracy as united and steadfast as the global alliance that defeated communism. If we don't take the lead, no one else can, and no one else will. As we proceed, we must keep in mind three realities.

First, the end of the Cold War does not mean the end of danger in the world. Even as we restructure our defenses, we must prepare for new threats. Where might these threats arise? From armed conflict within and among the former Soviet republics, four of which have nuclear weapons. From the spread of nuclear, chemical, and biological weapons. From regional tensions on the Korean Peninsula and in the Middle East. From terrorist attacks on Americans abroad. And from the growing intensity of ethnic rivalry and separatist violence, which could spill across borders in Yugoslavia and elsewhere. . . .

A second reality is that the irresistible power of ideas will shape the world in the Information Age. Television, cassette tapes and the fax machine helped ideas to pierce the Berlin Wall and bring it down. Look at the defining images of the past decade: Lech Walesa scaling the fence at the Lenin Shipyard; Vaclav Havel sounding the call for freedom at Wenceslas Square; Chinese students marching in Tienanmen Square; Nelson Mandela walking out of prison a free man; Boris Yeltsin standing defiantly atop a tank to face down the coup. These pictures speak of people willing to fight against all odds for their convictions, their freedom, and the right to control their own destiny.

This means that we are in a position to do more with less than at any time in our recent history. During the Cold War, we spent trillions to protect freedom where it was threatened. In this post Cold War era, the West can spend a fraction of that amount to nurture democracy where it never before existed.

America's challenge in this era is not to bear every burden, but to tip the balance. Only America has the global reach and influence to lead on the great issues confronting the world.

Third, and most important, none of this will be possible unless we restore America's economic strength. . . .

If we're not strong at home we can't lead the world we've done so much to make. In today's world, foreign and domestic policy are inseparable. But if we withdraw from the world, it will hurt us economically at home. We can't allow a false choice between domestic policy and foreign policy

to hurt our country and our economy. If the President fails in either responsibility, it is not just others who will suffer but the people of the United States above all. . . .

We need to respond forcefully to one of the greatest security challenges of our time, to help the people of the former Soviet bloc demilitarize their societies and build free political and economic institutions. We have a chance to engage the Russian people in the West for the first time in their history.

The stakes are high. The collapse of communism is not an isolated event; it's part of a worldwide march toward democracy whose outcome will shape the next century. For ourselves and for millions of people who seek to live in freedom and prosperity, this revolution must not fail.

I know it isn't popular today to call for foreign assistance of any kind. It's harder when Americans are hurting, as millions are today. But I believe it is deeply irresponsible to forgo this short term investment in our long term security. Being penny wise and pound foolish will cost us more in the long run in higher defense budgets and lost economic opportunities.

What does a democratic Russia mean to Americans? Lower defense spending. A reduced nuclear threat. A diminished risk of environmental disasters. Fewer arms exports and less proliferation. Access to Russia's vast resources through peaceful commerce. And, the creation of a major new market for American goods and services.

As I said at Georgetown last December,

We owe it to the people who defeated communism, the people who defeated the coup. And we owe it to ourselves. . . . Having won the Cold War, we must not now lose the peace.

Already, chaos has threatened to engulf Russia. Its old economy lies in ruins, staples remain scarce and lawless behavior is spreading. The immediate danger is not a resurgence of communism, but the emergence of an aggressively nationalistic regime that could menace the other republics and revive the old political and nuclear threats to the West.

Boris Yeltsin has embarked on a radical course of economic reform, freeing prices, selling off state properties and cutting wasteful public subsidies. Hopes for a democratic Russia ride on these efforts, which must produce positive results before economic deprivation wears down the people's patience.

I believe America needs to organize and lead a long-term western strategy of engagement for democracy. From Russia to Central Europe, from Ukraine to the Baltics, the U.S. and our allies need to speed the transition to democracy and capitalism by keeping our markets open to these countries' products, offering food and technical assistance, and helping them privatize key industries, convert military production to civilian uses, and employ weapons experts in peaceful pursuits.

Make no mistake: Our help should be strictly conditioned on an unswerving commitment by the republics to comprehensive economic reform and on continued reductions in the former Soviet nuclear arsenal.

Russia faces two economic challenges. The short-term challenge is to stabilize the economy and stem hyperinflation, so that Russia doesn't go the way of Weimar Germany. The long-term challenge is to build a market system from the ground up—to establish private property rights, create a banking system, and modernize its antiquated capital stock, which outside the defense sector lags behind world standards.

Russia is intrinsically a rich country. What it needs is not charity but trade and investment on a massive scale. What the major financial powers can do together is help the Russians help themselves. If we do, Russia's future holds the possibility of a stronger democracy rather than a resurgent dictatorship, and a new American market rather than a new American nightmare.

We should look at this assistance not as a bail out, but a bridge loan, much as a family gets from the bank when it buys a new house before selling their old house. I propose that the U.S. must take the lead in putting together a bridge loan to help Russia make the transition from its old system to its new economy.

We must have no illusions: The West cannot guarantee Russia's prosperity. Even with our help, the future of Russia and the other republics is un-certain. But we can give President Yeltsin's reforms and Russian democracy a fighting chance.

The West should establish a $6 billion fund to help stabilize the Russian ruble. Without the fund, the ruble will continue to lose its exchange value and inflation will continue to soar. America's share would be about $1 billion, in the form of a loan, not a gift. In return, Russian leaders have to agree to tough conditions. They must rein in public spending and stop excessive printing of money. A fund of this kind is like a net for acrobats. By building confidence, it reduces the chance it will ever be used. . . .

Finally, it is also crucial to give Russia some breathing space for servicing its external debts, at a time when it doesn't have the money to stabilize its currency or import goods.

Let me be clear: Our nation can afford this. This is not an exorbitant price to pay for a chance to create new American markets and anchor a revitalized Russia firmly in the democratic camp. The amount of money we need is available from defense and other foreign aid savings that the end of the Cold War makes possible. If Boris Yeltsin and his economic advisers stay the course, the chances are good that Russia will be in a position to pay us back in full by the latter part of the decade. Nevertheless, passing such aid will require an act of political will by the Congress and the President, and the kind of leadership from the White House we have not previously seen.

I also strongly support fulfilling the commitment America has made to our share of the IMF quota increase. Of a total increase of $60 billion, our share is 19 percent, or roughly $12 billion. But we are not talking about giving the $12 billion away. It is like a line of credit in a cooperative bank, and we earn interest on it. The quota increase was voted two years ago. It was necessary to help emerging democracies in Eastern Europe. It is all the more urgent now, with Ukraine, the Baltics, and other newly independent nations whose economic fate depends on it. Every other country in the IMF has agreed to pay their share, except the U.S. Why? Because our President has not taken the lead in persuading the Congress to authorize the necessary funds. We need a President who doesn't mind taking a little flak to seize this moment in history.

At the same time, we should encourage private American investment in the former Soviet Union. The newly independent republics, after all, are rich in human and natural resources. One day, they and Eastern Europe could be lucrative markets.

But Russia needs to do more than make the transition from state socialism to free markets. Constitutional democracy must take root firmly there as well. The popular movement for Russian democracy has been held together more by anti-communism than by a clear or common understanding of how to build a democratic society. Democracy remains an abstract and theoretical notion; there is an enormous deficit of knowledge in the former Soviet Union about the texture and dynamics of a free society.

No one on earth can fill that gap better than Americans. We need to make our engagement for Russian democracy a matter for people, not just governments. We need person-to-person contacts: a Democracy Corps, as Rep. Dave McCurdy has proposed, to send Americans over there; a crash program as others have proposed to bring tens of thousands of Russians and others here to learn how free institutions work; and a strong National Endowment for Democracy to lead the way in spreading American values. Promoting democracy is not just a task for the American government. For years, labor unions, universities, and volunteer organizations in this country have nurtured the democratic revolution around the world.

Without democratic institutions and values, economic reforms will not succeed. Our nation's greatest resource is ultimately not our dollars nor our technical expertise, but our values of pluralism and enterprise and freedom and the rule of law—and our centuries of experience in making those values work. In an era of fledgling democracies, those values can be our proudest export and our most effective tool of foreign policy.

Questions for Discussion

1. Is it in the U.S. national interest for Russia to "succeed"?

2. What kinds of policies might enable the United States to influence developments in Russia?

3. What are the pros and cons of extending large-scale economic assistance to Russia?

4. Why were the United States and Russia/Soviet Union adversaries in the past? Might these same reasons recur in the future?

5. What is Russia's importance to Europe?

6. Is a Russian-American defense pact feasible? What are the arguments, for and against?

Selected Bibliography

BREMENT, MARSHALL. *Reaching Out to Moscow: From Confrontation to Cooperation.* New York: Praeger, 1991.

GINBURGS, GEORGE, ALVIN Z. RUBINSTEIN, and OLES SMOLANSKY (Eds.). *Russia and America: From Rivalry to Reconciliation.* Armonk, NY: M.E. Sharpe, 1994.

HEWETT, ED A., and VICTOR H. WINSTON (Eds.). *Milestones in Glasnost and Perestroyka: Politics and People.* Washington, DC: Brookings, 1991.

HUBER, ROBERT T. *Soviet Perceptions of the U.S. Congress: The Impact of Superpower Relations.* Boulder: Westview, 1989.

HYLAND, WILLIAM G. *The Cold War Is Over.* New York: Times Books, 1990.

MARKS, JOHN, and IGOR BELIAEV (Eds.). *Common Ground on Terrorism: Soviet-American Cooperation Against the Politics of Terror.* London: Norton, 1991.

MORRISON, JOHN. *Boris Yeltsin.* London: Penguin, 1991.

SAVIGEAR, PETER. *Cold War or Détente in the 1980s: The International Politics of Soviet-American Relations.* New York: St. Martin's, 1988.

YANOV, ALEXANDER. *The Russian Challenge and the Year 2000.* New York: Basil Blackwell, 1987.

CHAPTER 11

The Middle East

U.S. foreign policy first became actively involved in the Middle East at the end of the Second World War, in response to a combination of British weakness and Soviet pressure on Turkey and Iran. Prior to that, in the late nineteenth and early twentieth centuries, America's interests in the region had been primarily missionary-related and educational, such as the establishment of the Syrian Protestant College in 1866 (which was developed into the American University in Beirut), and commercial, especially after 1920, with its focus on oil exploration in the Persian Gulf area. By 1940, U.S. relations with Saudi Arabia assumed considerable importance, resting on the preeminence of American oil companies in the Middle East's most important source of oil. Elsewhere in the region, between 1918 (when the Ottoman Empire collapsed and the modern system of nation-states such as Egypt, Syria, and Iraq took form) and 1945, Britain and France were the principal great powers influencing developments in the area.

A financially strapped Britain no longer able to sustain large-scale military deployments in the Middle East, a harassed Greece threatened by Communist subversion, and a relentless pressure by Moscow to extract territorial concessions from Turkey and Iran prompted the enunciation of the Truman Doctrine in March 1947 and the American military involvement in the eastern Mediterranean, heretofore the preserve of Britain and France. The United States undertook to guarantee the territorial integrity of Turkey and Iran against possible attack by the Soviet Union. Thus, its strategic involvement in the Middle East began with the purpose of containing the expansion of Soviet power; and this remained the driving force behind its foreign policy until the early 1990s when the Soviet Union was dissolved, ending Moscow's threat to U.S. interests in the Middle East.

U.S. policy's involvement in the Arab world deepened as a result of its support for the United Nations' partition of Palestine in November 1947 and recognition of Israel on May 15, 1948. Much has been made of President Harry S. Truman's de facto recognition of the new state of Israel minutes after the British mandate ended. But the Soviet Union on May 17 was the first country to extend de jure recognition and give the most significant assistance to Israel during its war of independence. Without the flow of arms, immigrants, and logistical assistance from the Soviet bloc, Israel would not have survived beyond infancy. From 1949 to 1967, the United States downgraded its Israeli relationship and courted Arab countries. Until 1968, Israel's weaponry was primarily French. Not until after the 1967 June War, in which Israel defeated Egypt, Syria, and Jordan, did the United States undertake to provide Israel with advanced weaponry in sizable quantities. That decision was largely the consequence of a massive rearming of the Arab states by the Soviet Union and of Moscow's growing projection of its own military power into the Arab world, that is, into Egypt, Syria, Iraq, Algeria, and Libya.

Throughout the 1949 to 1967 period, the United States sought to come to terms with Arab nationalism. Its decisionmaking on the Middle East was dominated by a pro-Arab and antiimperial outlook that considered Israel an annoyance and Britain and France colonial anachronisms, all to be avoided lest they embarrass Washington's courtship of the Arab world. But even Eisenhower's rescue of Egypt's Gamal Abdel Nasser in the fall of 1956, when Britain, France, and Israel combined, for different reasons, to topple him, failed to secure Nasser's friendship or that of any other radical Arab nationalist.

Tensions dogged U.S.-Egyptian relations, primarily because Nasser's aims were antithetical to Washington's. The Kennedy administration tried to demonstrate that the United States would not automatically support conservative Arab regimes against progressive ones, that it would provide economic assistance without regard for an Arab government's political system or foreign policy, and that it would steer clear of intra-Arab regional rivalries. But it could not ignore Nasser's Soviet-backed military intervention in the Yemeni civil war (1962–1967) which represented a major threat to Saudi Arabia. The importance of a special relationship with Saudi Arabia and access to Saudi oil, coupled with Moscow's role in Nasser's campaign in Yemen, impelled the United States to oppose Nasser's Yemeni campaign and antimonarchical policy. By late 1966, the U.S. National Security Council concluded that Moscow's involvement in Yemen and in the restiveness in the

British Protectorate of Aden, which became independent in 1968, reflected a policy aimed at undermining Western influence in the increasingly important Arabian Peninsula area and challenging NATO's general position in the Mediterranean region.

The overthrow of the pro-Western Hashemite monarchy of Iraq in July 1958 ushered in an era of poor relations between Iraq and Iran. As an ally of Iran's (until 1979), the United States found its relations with Iraq shifting from friendship to an antagonism that was further exacerbated by Iraq's ambitions in the Persian Gulf, where it opposed not only Iran but also Saudi Arabia.

With the June 1967 Arab-Israeli War, U.S.-Soviet rivalry in the Middle East intensified and transformed the Arab-Israeli conflict from a troublesome regional conflict into a dangerous one with global implications. It ended too quickly for Moscow to have intervened effectively, but the Soviet decision to reequip Egyptian and Syrian forces surprised Washington. Preoccupied in Vietnam, President Lyndon Johnson did not, unlike Eisenhower, pressure the Israelis to withdraw unilaterally. Different circumstances, the major Soviet military presence for one, entitled them, he believed, to hold on to bargaining chips for future negotiations. Moreover, to ensure that Israel retained its military edge over the Soviet-supplied Arab states and could deter any Syrian move against Jordan or Saudi Arabia, President Johnson opened the American arms tap. For the first time, the United States became Israel's prime source of modern weapons; its policy was to keep Israel strong and, hopefully, to maintain regional stability.

The October 1973 Arab-Israeli War brought some fundamental changes in U.S.

policy, which emerged with unanticipated prestige. Moscow had saved Egypt and Syria from military defeat and enabled them to garner a political triumph of sorts, yet no sooner had the fighting stopped than Egypt turned to Washington, not Moscow. Whereas in 1967 the Arab states had broken off diplomatic relations with the United States even though it had not aided Israel, in 1973 they restored diplomatic ties despite Washington's intervention in significant fashion on behalf of Israel. To strengthen the post-October War cease-fire and arrange a disengagement of forces in Sinai and on the Golan Heights, a conference was convened in Geneva on December 21, 1973, under the auspices of the UN secretary general, with the United States and the Soviet Union as co-chairmen. But the Geneva Conference, which Moscow viewed as a legitimation of its participation in the peace process, was adjourned less than forty-eight hours after it had convened, with Moscow clearly the odd capital out.

The American position in the Arab world was strengthened. Secretary of State Henry Kissinger fashioned, through his step-by-step diplomacy, disengagement agreements between Egypt and Israel and between Syria and Israel without Soviet participation, much to Moscow's annoyance. In the process, U.S. leaders modified some previously held policy assumptions, to wit, that although military power mattered a great deal, "Israeli strength alone, however, would not lead to a political settlement, as Johnson had hoped it would in 1967"; that détente between the United States and the Soviet Union would reduce the danger of superpower confrontations in regional conflicts; and that the key Arab regimes could not forge a common policy toward Israel. On the contrary, not only had

Egypt and Syria fought comparatively well, "they had also achieved surprise in the initial attack; the degree of Arab solidarity was impressive; the use of the oil weapon was well coordinated with the diplomatic and military moves; and the tone of restraint in private and public communications was a welcome contrast to 1967."[1]

New presidents often try to make their mark in the Middle East arena, which holds a continuing attraction for the American public. A major example of this occurred on October 1, 1977, when President Jimmy Carter initiated a joint statement with the Soviet Union, calling for a reconvening of the Geneva Conference without bothering to consult with the prospective regional participants. Within a week, facing a furor at home and abroad (neither Israel's Prime Minister Menachem Begin nor Egypt's President Anwar Sadat wanted to tackle a comprehensive settlement, for each preferred to focus on a step-by-step approach) Carter retreated. The incident had the unforeseen effect of prompting Sadat's dramatic decision to make his historic trip to Jerusalem on November 19, 1977, and the pursuit of a separate Egyptian-Israeli accord. Once again the Soviet Union was left outside the bargaining process.

President Carter's personal commitment and involvement made the difference. Lengthy but inconclusive Egyptian-Israeli talks were given an essential impetus when the leaders were invited to meet with Carter at Camp David, Maryland, in early September 1978. An agreement was reached, and the Egyptian-Israeli peace treaty was for-

---

[1] William B. Quandt, *Decade of Decisions: American Policy Toward the Arab-Israeli Conflict: 1967–1976.* Berkeley: University of California Press, 1977, p. 201.

mally signed on March 26, 1979. It has served to keep the two former antagonists in a state of cold peace and, thus far, has prevented another major Arab-Israeli war. (The peace process was given new impetus with the convening in late October 1991 of a conference in Madrid involving face-to-face talks between Israel and all the key Arab parties to the Arab-Israeli conflict, including, most prominently, Syria and the Palestinians. A result of the 1991 Gulf War, the discussions have been held intermittently ever since.)

At the end of the 1970s Washington had reasons to be gratified by the situation in the Arab-Israeli sector of the Middle East: Soviet influence was diminishing (in 1976, Sadat had ended all of Moscow's once formidable military presence in Egypt), the threat of a war that might trigger a superpower confrontation like that in October 1973 was remote, and the steps toward a comprehensive settlement of the Arab-Israeli conflict had been taken, without jeopardizing any U.S. interests.

In the Persian Gulf region, however, U.S. policy took a grievous blow when, in January 1979, the pro-U.S. regime of the Shah was toppled, and the Ayatollah Ruhollah Khomeini returned from exile and established an Islamic Republic. American-manned intelligence-gathering stations situated along the Soviet border were shut down, Iranian arms purchases from the United States ended, and Iran withdrew from the role of policeman for the West in the Gulf. Khomeini's anti-Americanism was accompanied by denunciations of and ideological pressure on the Arab monarchs of the Gulf. Relations between the United States and Iran assumed a sharp adversarial aspect, when, on November 4, 1979, Iranian militants seized the U.S. Embassy in Teheran and held 52 Americans hostage for 444 days.

With the Soviet invasion of Afghanistan in December 1979, Saudi Arabia's heightened vulnerability prompted President Carter to asseverate that the United States would come to the defense of any friendly power in the region threatened by aggression. U.S. influence among the Persian Gulf Arab leaderships, seriously damaged after the fall of the Shah, increased in the wake of Iraq's invasion of Iran in September 1980: fearful of Iran's Shiite revolutionary aspirations and of Iraq's growing military power and ambitions to dominate the oil of the region, the Sunni Arab leaders of Saudi Arabia and the mini-states of the Gulf drew closer to the United States.

The Iran-Iraq War dragged on for eight years. The United States tilted toward Iraq, but remained officially neutral. Fear that the price of oil would skyrocket, precipitating economic distress in the West, proved unwarranted and made an international effort to stop the fighting less urgent. Once it was clear that neither side could achieve victory on the battlefield, the great powers (the United States, the Soviet Union, France, and Britain, in particular) maneuvered for marginal advantage. Convinced that the Iranians were unlikely to prevail, they sold weapons to the oil-rich states (the USSR was Iran's main supplier), deployed a naval force to ensure the flow of oil from Saudi ports, and watched uneasily as the USSR under Gorbachev established diplomatic relations with Oman and the United Arab Emirates in 1985 and introduced a Soviet naval presence in the Gulf in October 1986. Eager to improve relations with the United States, Moscow joined with Washington in adopting UN Security Council Resolution 598 of July 20, 1987, which called for an immediate cease-fire and stipulated that otherwise "further steps" (the imposition of sanctions) would be taken to ensure compliance. However, the Iran-Iraq War raged on for another year, finally ending with a cease-fire on August 20, 1988.

In 1989 and 1990, the Bush administration courted Iraq with loans and transfers of high technology, believing that it could moderate Saddam Hussein's behavior. It took the Iraqi invasion of Kuwait on August 2, 1990 to dispel some of the illusions in the White House about the region. The consequent mobilization of an international coalition reversed Saddam Hussein's aggression and subjected Iraq to UN-supervised inspections in order to make sure that it is not secreting nuclear or nonconventional weapons of mass destruction. All of this demonstrates that the Persian Gulf is a special region; with two-thirds of the world's reserves of oil under its sands, it is the only nonindustrial area that is of crucial importance to the United States, Western Europe, and Japan.

In the 1990s, any formulation of America's strategy and future role in the Middle East must consider what the Gulf War revealed about U.S. foreign policy. First, the time is past when the president has a blank check to act unilaterally abroad in complex and difficult situations. Against a tough adversary who is not directly challenging vital U.S. interests, he must obtain support among the electorate and in the Congress. Second, there are serious financial and economic constraints on major military operations. As the Gulf War suggests, the president would require generous contributions from other concerned parties, who for various reasons were unable to defend their interests on their own. A third insight deriving from information that has come to light

since the Gulf War is the paucity of strategic thinking at the highest levels of the U.S. government. The Bush administration chose not to see what it did not want to believe. Whereas the Reagan administration's covert assistance to Iraq during the Iran-Iraq War could be justified strategically since an Iranian victory coming in tandem with the high tide of Ayatollah Khomeini's fundamentalist appeal might have shaken the foundations of the pro-Western oil-rich Arab regimes of the Gulf, the Bush White House pandered to Saddam Hussein long after the threat from Tehran had crested. It overlooked Saddam's bellicose speeches and military buildup (conventional and nuclear), and misinterpreted his intentions toward Kuwait. The doleful result was that Saddam Hussein was encouraged to believe that he could get away with just about anything in the region. Finally, there was nothing in the Bush policy to suggest a blueprint for promoting future stability and security.

Two assessments illustrate the range of proposals for a post-Gulf War U.S. policy toward the Middle East. James A. Phillips, Deputy Director of Foreign Policy Studies at The Heritage Foundation, argues that the end of the Soviet threat means that the United States "can treat access to Gulf oil as an economic question rather than a vital strategic interest" and that a diminished U.S. interest in fostering a comprehensive Arab-Israeli settlement might encourage regional actors to shoulder a greater responsibility for development in the area (Reading 34). Leon T. Hadar, an adjunct scholar at the Cato Institute, believes that a more effective U.S. policy would be one that seeks to do less, and that "by renewing military and diplomatic commitments, the United States would remove the incentives for Middle Eastern regimes to reform their

political and economic systems, to create
stable balance-of-power systems and viable
security arrangements, and to reach diplomatic solutions to their conflicts" (Reading
35).

To paraphrase Kierkegaard, policy for-

mulation is future-oriented, but it can only
be formulated looking backward. At the
heart of a U.S. strategy toward the Middle
East, there is a need to reappraise the validity of past assumptions and approaches.

34.   Rethinking U.S. Policy in the Middle East

James A. Phillips

The disappearance of the Soviet military threat removes the chief reason for Washington to worry
about continued American access to overseas oil.
Not only is the risk of a Moscow-led seizure of
strategic oil-rich regions such as the Persian Gulf
greatly reduced, if not eliminated, but the threat
that Moscow-controlled naval or air forces will interdict the flow of oil has practically disappeared.
Moreover, the likelihood of a lengthy conventional
war between the U.S. and the Soviet Union, the
worst case scenario which heightened the need for
assured access to oil, of course has declined to
almost zero.

No other potential American adversary has the
military strength to block long-term American access to vital oil resources. Regional crises such as
the 1978–1979 Iranian revolution or the 1980–1988
Iran-Iraq war indeed may trigger short-term oil supply interruptions and price hikes that could impose
economic costs on the U.S. The results, depending
on the economic policies taken by Washington,
could be higher inflation and slower economic
growth, but these would not severely threaten the
U.S. economy and could be corrected fairly quickly.

Although foreign oil imports account for over 40
percent of American oil consumption, only 1.8 million barrels of oil per day, or slightly more than 10
percent, come from the Persian Gulf. Vast oil re-

SOURCE: James A. Phillips. "Rethinking U.S. Policy in
the Middle East," *The Backgrounder*, no. 891, April 10,
1992, excerpts. Published by The Heritage Foundation.
Footnotes deleted. Reprinted with permission.

sources are available in Mexico. The creation of a
U.S.-Mexican free trade area would allow the U.S.
to expand and tap into these resources.

Market Protection.   The operation of a free market, moreover, would provide substantial protection in the event of an oil supply crisis. A shortfall
in available oil supplies would trigger higher oil
prices which would balance supply and demand.
Higher oil prices would increase oil supplies by
bringing high-cost oil into production in the U.S.
and elsewhere, while reducing oil demand by encouraging the development of more efficient technologies for using oil and boosting the development of such alternative energy sources as coal,
natural gas, and nuclear power. This, in fact, is
what happened in response to the oil crises of the
1970s. . . .

Although the U.S., as the world's largest oil im-
porter, has an economic interest in low world oil
prices, it has a security interest in high world oil
prices. High world oil prices would reduce American vulnerability to disruptions of foreign oil supplies by making the production of high-cost U.S. oil
commercially feasible and reducing U.S. dependence on imports of foreign oil that can be produced at low cost.

For energy security reasons it would not make
sense for the U.S. to go to war merely to lower the
price of oil. Such a policy only would make the
U.S. more vulnerable to oil supply disruptions in
the future by encouraging greater dependence on
imports of cheap foreign oil. Moreover, the poten-

tial economic advantages of fighting a war to lower oil prices could be lost if oil production or export facilities were damaged in the fighting.

Economic and Political Leverage.

What would warrant an American military response, however, would be the threat of a hostile power gaining hegemony over Persian Gulf oil. This would be unacceptable to America because it would allow that hostile power to use its control over two-thirds of the world's oil reserves to gain tremendous economic and political leverage over oil-importing states, including America.

More important, gaining control over Persian Gulf oil would give a hostile power enormous economic resources with which it could build a modern military machine and possibly a nuclear arsenal. The two chief regional threats, Iran and Iraq, are infused with radical anti-Western ideologies, Islamic fundamentalism and pan-Arab socialism, respectively. These ideologies have encouraged them to sponsor anti-western terrorism and have led them into violent confrontations with America in the past. Both have suffered humiliating military defeats in clashes with America—Iran in 1987–1988 when it attacked Kuwaiti oil tankers and Iraq in 1991 when it refused to withdraw from Kuwait.

Most disturbing, both have undertaken large-scale military buildups that include the acquisition of nuclear weapons. The enormous scale of Iraq's buildup was revealed in the Gulf War. Iran in 1990 launched a five-year $10 billion program to buy arms from China, North Korea, and the former Soviet republics. Iran already has bought 20 MiG-29 *Fulcrum* jet fighters and some Su-24 *Fencer* fighter bombers from Moscow and is shopping for T-72 tanks.

These buildups not only threaten American forces and America's friends in the region, particularly Israel and Saudi Arabia, but eventually could threaten America as well, if Iran or Iraq should acquire intercontinental ballistic missiles. America's principal strategic aim in the Persian Gulf should be to prevent the rise of a hostile hegemonic power that could turn the enormous oil wealth of the region against the U.S.

POST-COLD WAR PROSPECTS FOR ARAB-ISRAELI PEACE

The American victory in the Cold War and in the war against Iraq opened up what many Middle Eastern analysts characterized as a "window of opportunity" for Arab-Israeli negotiations. Radical Arab states received dramatic proof that they could not count on Moscow to support their policies or back them in a crisis. This not only weakened radical states that rejected peace negotiations with Israel, but reduced the feasibility of the Arab military option against Israel.

The prospects for peace were improved by Saudi Arabia's new assertiveness following Iraq's crushing military defeat. Saudi Arabia previously had been content to hew to the Arab consensus on foreign policy issues. But the defeat of Iraq, the weakness of Syria, the irrelevance of Libya, and the blunders of the increasingly isolated PLO left Saudi Arabia free to pursue a more independent foreign policy regarding the Arab-Israeli issue.

The war, moreover, gave the Saudis stronger incentives to help resolve the Palestinian problem, to demonstrate that the Saudis could do more for the Palestinians than Saddam could. Riyadh's disgust with the PLO's pro-Iraqi stance and the Gulf War's evisceration of Pan-Arabism gave the Saudis more latitude to elevate their own state interests over pan-Arab and Palestinian interests. For example, Saudi Arabia attended the multilateral round of peace talks held in Moscow on January 28-29, 1992, despite the refusal of Syria and the Palestinians to attend.

The Bush Administration tried to use the Gulf War as a springboard for diplomatic progress in the Arab-Israeli dispute. The Administration apparently was anxious to demonstrate that the war paid foreign policy dividends, despite Saddam's stubborn survival in power and the near certainty that, if he continues to survive, he again will threaten the region's peace. Secretary of State Baker made eight trips to the region to orchestrate the diplomatic process which began at Madrid last October 30. Bush, like his predecessors, had joined the quest for Arab-Israeli peace, something that Middle East scholar Martin Indyk perceptively calls "the Holy Grail of the American presidency."

Yet Washington's stake in a settlement of the Arab-Israeli conflict has diminished for three reasons.

First, America no longer has to worry that Moscow will exploit simmering tensions between Israel and the Arabs to expand Moscow's own influence in the region. Moscow seeks Western assistance in solving its economic problems and is unlikely to jeopardize this to make marginal gains in the Middle East. Yevgeny Primakov, then Soviet President Mikhail Gorbachev's chief Middle East adviser, noted on September 4, 1991, that "Middle East issues have retreated and do not now have a place in our current thinking."

Second, after the end of the Cold War there is little chance that an Arab-Israeli crisis could escalate into a superpower military confrontation. This, after all, is what made the thought of conflagration in the Middle East so terrifying. This worry is now gone. It is extremely unlikely that a democratic Russia will risk a war with America on behalf of Arab dictatorships that, in any event, are critical of Russia's political and economic reforms and its retrenchment. For example, Russia's relations with the PLO were strained severely by the PLO's support for the abortive August 1991 Soviet coup. The head of the PLO's Political Department, Faruq Qaddumi, applauded the coup and gushed, "We support the friendly Soviet Union in its new era."

Third, the risk that Arab-Israeli tensions will threaten the continued flow of Persian Gulf oil has been reduced by the deterioration of relations between the PLO and the oil-rich Arab Gulf states. For the foreseeable future, Saudi Arabia and Kuwait, stung by Palestinian support for Iraqi aggression, are extremely unlikely to launch an oil embargo against the U.S., their chief protector, as they did at the time of the 1973 Arab-Israeli war.

An Arab-Israeli settlement, of course, is an appropriate and laudable U.S. foreign policy goal. But too often . . . Washington acts as if Arab-Israeli peace is more important to America than it is to the parties involved. This leads astute negotiators on both sides to try to wring the maximum amount of concessions [from the U.S.] before seriously sitting down to negotiate with each other. [This] leads to constant U.S. interventions that encourage the Arab negotiators to cling to the hope that America eventually will force a settlement on Israel. This harms the prospects for a settlement because a lasting peace can only be attained by the agreement of the parties involved and cannot be imposed by an outside power.

RETHINKING AMERICA'S MIDDLE EAST POLICY

Although the Cold War is over and the superpower rivalry has abated, the Arab-Israeli conflict, inter-Arab rivalries, and Arab-Iranian tensions continue to roil the Middle East. The U.S. does not have the resources, will power, or imperial inclination—nor should it—to impose a Pax Americana on the Middle East that would suppress or resolve these destabilizing power struggles. The best that the U.S. can do is to work with the parties involved to reach a compromise negotiated settlement of outstanding issues wherever possible, and to maintain a favorable balance of power regardless of the state of negotiations.

To further American interests in the Middle East the . . . Administration should:

Deemphasize the U.S. role in the Arab-Israeli peace talks.

This will encourage the Arabs and Israelis to become accustomed to negotiating with each other, not with Washington. Although much is said about a "window of opportunity" for Middle East peace, it is more like a "keyhole of opportunity." Most of the parties were dragged to the negotiating table by Bush and Baker. The Middle East nations thus surely are motivated more by desire to avoid antagonizing Washington, the ascendant power in the region, than they are by a spirit of genuine reconciliation. . . .

Given the more pressing issues at hand in the former Soviet Union, in Europe, and in Iraq, the . . . Administration should not continue devoting such high-level attention to the torturously slow Arab-Israeli talks. . . .

Guard against the rise of a hostile hegemonic power in the Persian Gulf.

This should be done through military deterrence and security cooperation with Saudi Arabia and other friendly Persian Gulf states. America should continue as the dominant external military power in the region and the chief guarantor of the security of Saudi Arabia and the other conservative Arab states of the Gulf. America's goal should be the forging of a stable regional balance of power in which Persian Gulf oil continues to flow, unimpeded by regional conflict or the hostile policies of a regional hegemonic power. To assure this, the U.S. should:

1. **Maintain forces armed and equipped to project power rapidly from bases in the U.S. to the Persian Gulf,** even without the support of local allies. This requires the deployment of strong naval forces, including at least one aircraft carrier battle group, continuously in the Persian Gulf and Arabian Sea area, along with a quick reaction force of Marines, special forces units, and airborne troops. U.S. F-15 *Eagle* fighter-bombers should be rotated continually into Saudi or other air bases for joint training exercises. To move Army tank divisions rapidly in a crisis, the U.S. will have to continue investing in strategic airlift and sealift capabilities, and to preposition military supplies and equipment at depots and at sea near the Persian Gulf. The American military presence on the ground in conservative Arab Gulf states should be minimized to reduce the risk of a destabilizing anti-Western political backlash that Muslim fundamentalists could exploit.

2. **Deter and defend against Iraqi and Iranian aggression** through bilateral security arrangements with Saudi Arabia and other members of the Gulf Cooperation Council (GCC)—Bahrain, Kuwait, Oman, Qatar, and the United Arab Emirates. The U.S. should press the GCC states to increase their military cooperation with each other as well as with Washington. The U.S. should strengthen the armed forces of GCC countries by augmenting the number and expanding the scale of joint military exercises with them, assisting them with military training, prepositioning military supplies on their territory if possible and increasing joint military planning. U.S. arms sales should be considered if they make it easier for the U.S. to deploy forces by encouraging a compatible defense infrastructure and if they do not significantly threaten Israel.

By prepositioning military equipment in Gulf states, the U.S. can reduce the number of personnel it needs to keep in politically sensitive countries, while reducing the time needed to build up a military force to defend that country against external threats. The U.S. had planned to leave about one armored division's worth of tanks and heavy equipment in place near the King Khalid Military City in northern Saudi Arabia as a hedge against a future crisis. The Saudi government, however, has balked, fearful that American soldiers guarding the prepositioned stocks could give the appearance of the establishment of an American base. These prepositioned stocks perhaps could be shifted to nearby Bahrain or Qatar, or alternative arrangements could be worked out with the Saudis in which Riyadh would buy the equipment and guard it with Saudi personnel.

3. **Encourage the creation of a Saudi-Egyptian alliance** and the deployment of Egyptian troops along the Saudi-Iraqi and Kuwaiti-Iraqi borders. Egypt and Syria had agreed to provide the nucleus of an Arab peacekeeping force in the Persian Gulf under the terms of the March 6, 1991, Damascus Declaration, but Saudi Arabia and Kuwait grew ambivalent, preferring to rely on the U.S. for protection. Washington should seek to block Syrian participation in the defense of the Gulf states because Syria itself is a threat to regional stability. But an Egyptian military presence in the Gulf and close Saudi-Egyptian ties would bolster regional security and help strengthen the Egyptian economy through Saudi aid, trade, and investment. . . .

Reject a rapprochement with Iran until Tehran has stopped trying to export its Islamic revolution forcibly to its neighbors and halted its support of terrorism.

Washington should not permit its focus on containing Saddam Hussein's Iraq to obscure the continuing threat of Iran, which looms large on the Persian Gulf horizon as the dominant regional power. Although Iran may in the long term become a useful counterweight to Iraq, America should be in no rush to seek a rapprochement with Iran.

Washington should try to constrain Iran's military buildup by seeking the cooperation of China, North Korea, the Soviet successor states, and other arms exporters in withholding sales of destabilizing missile and nuclear technology. If these countries refuse to accept some sort of export controls on these dangerous technologies, then the U.S. should punish them by freezing them out of Arab-Israeli peace negotiations and other multilateral negotiations on regional problems. The U.S. should seek to isolate Iran and deprive it of Western aid, loans, and technology until Tehran has halted its support of terrorism and stopped trying to export its Islamic revolution forcibly to its neighbors.

Maintain close ties with Israel.

Although the end of the Cold War has reduced Israel's strategic value to the U.S. as a potential ally against Moscow, Israel remains an important and dependable friend in an unstable region. Israel can provide help to America in the form of intelligence, forward bases, and military cooperation against regional threats such as Iran, Iraq, Libya, and Syria. Israel also can assist the U.S. in fighting terrorism, in developing military technology, and in combatting drug trafficking in the Middle East.

The chief threat to Israeli security in the post-Cold War era is no longer an Arab conventional military threat but the prospect of proliferation of weapons of mass destruction and surface-to-surface missiles. To help Israel to blunt the threat of missile attack the U.S. should continue financial support for the joint U.S.-Israeli research and development program for the *Arrow* anti-tactical ballistic missile (ATBM) system, which will amount to 72 percent of the $270 million cost of the program from 1991 to 1995. Washington also should continue its annual military assistance of $1.8 billion to help Israel maintain its qualitative military edge over potential Arab adversaries.

To help Israel solve its festering economic problems, Washington should press Israel to adopt free market economic reforms such as reducing taxes, privatizing Israel's 160 state enterprises, selling land owned by the government, and deregulating Israel's economy.

Encourage the development of an informal working relationship between Saudi Arabia and Israel.

These two countries, which were simultaneously attacked by Iraqi *Scud* surface-to-surface missiles during the Gulf war, have an interest in shoring up a more stable regional status quo. Such cooperation could be critical to the success of a negotiated Arab-Israeli settlement. Since the defeat of Iraq, Riyadh has taken a more active and supportive role in the negotiations. A delegation of leaders from the American Jewish Congress visited Saudi Arabia in January 1992 at the invitation of the Saudi Ambassador to America, Prince Bandar Bin Sultan. Saudi Arabia also helped finance the costs of the multilateral round of the peace talks held in Moscow on January 28-29, 1992.

Urge Turkey to become the dominant model for political and economic development in the Middle East and Central Asia.

Turkey's modern brand of secular democracy and free market capitalism would be a stabilizing influence in the Middle East as well as in the former Soviet republics of Central Asia. To reward Turkey for its moderate pro-Western policies and strengthen the appeal of the Turkish model of political and economic development, the U.S. should:

1. Support Turkey's bid to join the European Community . . .
2. Grant Turkey $50 million to help finance scholarships for promising Central Asian Muslim students to study at universities in Turkey. This would strengthen the appeal of the Turkish model of development for future leaders and intellectuals of Central Asia . . .

CONCLUSION

The collapse of Soviet power and diminution of the Soviet threat to American interests in the Middle East should allow America to redefine its interest in protecting Persian Gulf oil. Since no power now has the military means to deny long-term Western access to Persian Gulf oil, the energy security problem now can be defined more as an economic than a strategic threat. This allows America, cushioned by the Strategic Petroleum Reserve, to make the free market, rather than the U.S. armed forces, the first line of defense against oil supply crises.

America will retain an interest, however, in keeping military forces in the vicinity of the Persian Gulf to prevent Iran or Iraq from establishing hegemony over Persian Gulf oil. America's goal should be to deny Iraq or Iran a monopoly over the enormous oil wealth of the Gulf, which they could use to build an arsenal that would make them much greater threats to U.S. security.

Long-Term Focus. The collapse of Soviet power also reduces the importance to America of pushing Arab-Israeli peace negotiations forward. Washington should continue its efforts to mediate such negotiations but should not sacrifice its ties to Israel or jeopardize Israeli security in an overeager attempt to accelerate negotiations. Real peace will require a solid Israeli-American relationship and only will be attained after years of arduous negotiations. Washington must focus on the long-term goal of peace rather than become obsessed with the short-term "peace process."

Compared with the Persian Gulf, the Arab-Israeli theater is a minor strategic sideshow from Washington's perspective. The U.S. therefore should be much more concerned about who controls Persian Gulf oil than about who controls the West Bank, Gaza Strip, and Golan Heights.

---

35. Pulling Back from Middle East Entanglements

Leon T. Hadar

The lessons of the Gulf War, particularly those of the diplomatic and military processes that led to the Iraqi invasion of Kuwait, are not found either at the "macro" level (e.g., the failure of Washington to prevent the breakdown of the balance in the gulf) or at the "micro" level (e.g., the wrong signals that the Bush administration supposedly sent to Saddam on the eve of the invasion).

SOURCE: Leon T. Hadar. "Extricating America from Its Middle Eastern Entanglements," Cato Institute *Policy Analysis*, no. 154, June 12, 1991, excerpts. Footnotes deleted. Reprinted with permission.

Those who raise such arguments imply that the United States can now help restore the balance in the gulf and develop "a military balance such that no hostile state could dominate the region." Placing limitations on local military capabilities, creating regional security arrangements and arms control agreements, and more effective micromanagement of Middle Eastern diplomacy will supposedly deter the next Middle Eastern "bully" from threatening its neighbors.

The problem is that the rise of Saddam as a local bully was largely the outcome of the same policies that the current grand strategists are advocating. They again assume that a neat formula can secure regional balance in the area with limited military or financial costs for the United States, thereby eliminating the need for another large-scale American intervention.

Until the 1979 Iranian Revolution, U.S. policy in the Persian Gulf was based on an attempt to establish a regional balance of power among Iran, Iraq, Saudi Arabia, and the other Arab oil states. In the early 1970s, while the United States was pursuing the Nixon Doctrine, American defense policy in the gulf rested on the twin towers of Iran and Saudi Arabia. The shah's Iran was expected to deter radical Iraq from realizing its aggressive intentions against Kuwait (a role played by Great Britain in the 1960s).

The costs to the United States and the American people were enormous. To help the shah and the Saudis build their military might, the Nixon administration encouraged a spiraling rise in the price of Middle Eastern oil. Increased costs led to the emergence of OPEC as an international economic power, to the traumatic oil and economic crises of the 1970s, and to the rise of the petro-military states of the region, which included Iraq and Libya in addition to Iran and Saudi Arabia.

Those developments, in turn, helped create a major Middle Eastern crisis, the 1973 Yom Kippur War, that produced new and very risky American military and diplomatic commitments. They also created the conditions for the anti-shah and anti-American backlash inside Iran that culminated in the 1979 revolution and the birth of the Iranian regional bully, whom Washington was asked to contain, and eventually the bloody Iran-Iraq War.

The decision to strengthen Iraq in order to deter Iran, and the policies that followed—especially the decision that U.S. naval vessels would escort reflagged Kuwaiti tankers during the Iran-Iraq War—are examples of Washington's balance-of-power games in the region.

Those policies were celebrated by the same analysts who later criticized the pro-Iraqi "tilt," who called for military action against Iraq, and who again advocate American restoration of regional balance. But the pro-Iraqi tilt was a natural outcome of the balance-of-power policies. Trying to co-opt Iraq into the pro-American regional system

and punishing Tehran made sense in the context of those policies. What was missing from the calculation was the realization that if the policies were pursued to their ultimate conclusion, they might eventually produce unpleasant results, such as the invasion of Kuwait, that would create extra costs for Washington.

THE REAL LESSONS OF THE GULF WAR

The lessons of the Gulf War are not that the United States needs to more "effectively" restore the regional balance or to more efficiently micromanage U.S. ties with the regional players. The real lessons are different: being part of the Middle Eastern kaleidoscope entails heavy costs, which are unpredictable and certainly cannot be calculated in advance, for all the players, especially those, like the United States, who invest the most in the game. It is impossible to keep the kaleidoscope's configuration in place for long after a move, such as the U.S. victory in the Gulf War. Any player finds after a while that a positive outcome in one configuration (for example, Iraq containing Iran) can become negative in another configuration (for example, a strengthened Iraq invading Kuwait), which necessitates a new move (for example, the Gulf War). Hence, the Middle Eastern game is never ending, and Washington is bound to encounter new entanglements and higher costs. As it cuts one head off the hydra, Washington will see several new ones spring forth. . . .

THE ILLUSION OF RELIABLE REGIONAL SURROGATES

Some suggest that an extensive U.S. military role can be avoided by creating a security arrangement in the gulf. Such an arrangement would combine military forces of the Arab gulf states and mercenary forces of Egypt (in exchange for Saudi financial aid for Egypt's bankrupted economy).

However, that security arrangement would be as stable as the shifting sands of Arabia and could actually create more long-term problems. The principal effect would be to foster the illusion in the United States and throughout the Arab world that

Washington can ensure the security of the region without a large-scale military presence merely by maintaining a naval presence and keeping some military equipment there.

There are several problems with such an updated application of the Nixon Doctrine. Not only are there questions about Egypt's military capacity to maintain the balance of power in the gulf against the military forces of Syria, Iran, and Iraq, but Saudi Arabia has never previously welcomed a high-profile Egyptian role. Indeed, historically the two have been regional rivals (for example, supporting opposing sides in the Yemen War in the 1960s). Also, Egypt and Iraq are traditional rival power centers in the Middle East. The Egyptians might therefore join the wolves lurking in the corner to divide the Iraqi corpse, a development that would be against Saudi interests.

Moreover, the optimistic expectation that the Saudis and other Arab gulf states will distinguish themselves in new generosity to Egypt (perhaps as part of a new Marshall Plan of economic development for the region, through which the wealthy oil states would help restructure the economies of the "have not" Arab states) reflects wishful thinking. The gulf states, especially Saudi Arabia and Kuwait, are experiencing a major financial crunch as a result of the high costs of the Gulf War and because their own economies need postwar reconstruction. For example, it has been reported that, for the first time, the Saudis are seeking a $3.5 billion three-year loan from international banks. The oil states will lack the resources to contribute large sums of money to support the Egyptian economy or to fund a major regional Marshall Plan. Those states, like other donors and financial institutions, also take a gloomy view of the socialized Egyptian economy.

Finally, the Saudis are aware that the Egyptian ally of today can become the rival of tomorrow and that the military machine they help build can turn against them. It is not inconceivable that the population explosion in Egypt and the inability of its government to feed its people could lead to the rise of a more radical regime in Cairo. The main target of that regime might become the well-to-do Arab ruling families of the gulf. The conservative gulf regimes will be understandably reluctant to risk using their own resources to create a new Frankenstein monster that one day might direct its resentment and frustration toward them. After all, the Saudis and Kuwaitis helped build Saddam's regime—with disastrous results.

PROSPECTS FOR A PERMANENT U.S. MILITARY PRESENCE

If Washington insists on maintaining a balance in the gulf that is favorable to the United States, no regional security arrangement will be able to substitute for American military forces in dealing with various contingencies, especially protection of the Arab gulf states. That mission could lead to more Pentagon spending and plans to improve U.S. "long-reach" military capabilities in the region. Such steps would certainly entail maintaining a rapid deployment capability and perhaps even continuing a peacetime presence of ground troops.

Such a development would go beyond the "over the horizon" type of U.S. presence currently envisioned. It would be more politically costly for the United States in terms of support at home, and it might actually undermine the legitimacy of traditional regimes in the gulf. One major outcome of the Gulf War, therefore, would not be the rise of a viable regional security organization but an increasing commitment of the United States to direct defense of Arab oil states, and a growing dependency of the latter on Washington.

Indeed, some U.S. officials are already suggesting that the administration will favor permanently stationing ground troops in Saudi Arabia and other gulf states as part of joint security arrangements with the Arab nations. As a first step, the Pentagon is planning to establish the forward headquarters of the U.S. Central Command in Bahrain. The American contingent would be of brigade size (about 3,000 troops), and its mission would include joint planning and training with Arab ground forces for responding to a military crisis. "Cheney feels and Powell feels that you have to leave something there," indicated one official, who hinted that agreements to station ground forces in the region will be signed with other countries in the region.

Moves in that direction were made during Cheney's visit to the gulf in early May.

American officials have expressed the hope that after the Gulf War, Washington's Arab allies will rely less on diplomacy and more on strong military deterrence. But with the removal of the Arab League as a forum for managing intra-Arab conflicts, the region's states lost another incentive for managing their own interests through a regional mechanism. They also lack both the military power and the political will to form an independent regional security structure. As a result of the war, the United States will become a more active player, an external balancer, that is drawn into the kaleidoscopic balance-of-power games of the region at growing military and diplomatic costs.

PUTTING THE ARMS CONTROL CART BEFORE THE POLITICAL HORSE

Encouraging regional arms control arrangements, especially on weapons of mass destruction, has even less chance of succeeding than does structuring regional defense pacts. Comprehensive approaches to regional arms control would have to encompass a large number of states with varying capabilities and motives—a most difficult prospect. Moreover, although arms control agreements reflect and at the same time contribute to changes in the political environment, they cannot substitute for those changes. If one assumes that the Middle East will continue to be a center of unpredictable political rivalry, it is probable that to secure their fragile margin of security, the region's states will continue to build their military machines, especially at a time when the sources of arms are not exactly drying up. The Gulf War has opened up a new cycle of regional military buildup, led by the champion of Middle Eastern arms control, the United States. . . .

THE PERVERSE EFFECTS OF AMERICAN ACTIVISM

The limited American power to affect Arab-Israeli relationships and the increasing irrelevancy of those relationships to American interests, should lead to a reassessment of the hyperactive American diplomatic approach toward Arab-Israeli peace. The activist approach has been based on a perverted assumption: Washington should pay the financial and diplomatic costs of helping Arabs and Israelis to stop killing each other, since by so doing they are supposedly doing more of a favor for the United States than for themselves.

That assumption derived from Washington's Middle Eastern policy paradigm, which assumed that unless Americans helped make peace between Israel and its Arab neighbors, there would be several unpleasant results. First, Washington, as a result of Arab resentments, would find it difficult to safeguard Western oil and strategic interests in the gulf. Second, the United States would endanger its moral commitment to Israel, since that state's security can be guaranteed in the long run only by recognition and acceptance by its neighbors. Finally, U.S. failure to secure peace would produce regional instability that would invite Soviet meddling and expansionism.

The end of the cold war has largely eliminated the third factor from the overall American calculation, although Washington will have to recognize the legitimate Soviet interests in Moscow's Middle Eastern geopolitical back yard and should not exclude the Soviets from regional diplomatic efforts. As noted, the Gulf War at least weakened, if not removed, the first factor: the linkage between the Arab-Israeli issue and American interests in the gulf.

Continued Israeli occupation of the West Bank and Gaza raises major questions about the second element in America's Middle Eastern paradigm: Washington's moral commitment to the Jewish state. American support and aid keep a repressive militant government and a bankrupt socialist economy in Jerusalem. If Israel wants to maintain American public support, which was based on the argument that Israel is a democratic nation and is different from the surrounding Arab authoritarian and dictatorial regimes, it will have no future choice (in its own interest) but to decouple itself from the occupied Arab territories, reach some modus vivendi with its Arab neighbors, and reform its political and economic systems. Then it could focus on its real challenge—the absorption of hundreds of thousands of Soviet-Jewish immigrants. Israel could become a major trading state, a kind of a Middle Eastern Singapore.

By perpetuating its Middle Eastern paradigm, Washington is actually removing incentives for diplomatic and economic changes on both the Israeli and the Arab sides. Washington's high-profile involvement in trying to bring peace between Arabs and Israelis creates the impression that the diplomatic stakes in solving the conflict are higher for Washington than for the regional adversaries— that it owes them diplomatic support or financial compensation if they are willing to make concessions. The United States also ends up a party to domestic political battles in the Middle East as Israelis and Arabs opposed to its moves begin to direct their frustration against Washington. Moreover, by creating the expectation that it can deliver a solution, the United States is bound to produce an eventual backlash when its commitments to each side are not fulfilled.

NEEDED: POLICY OF BENIGN NEGLECT

Washington should consider a new approach: an attitude of neglect toward the Palestinian-Israeli conflict, the kind of attitude it has adopted toward other regional conflicts such as that between India and Pakistan. That approach might actually persuade more Israelis and Palestinians that unless they move seriously to solve their conflict they will be the ones to bear the costs of their own intransigence.

The Palestinians will remain under Israeli control for the foreseeable future. Notwithstanding the usual solidarity rhetoric of their Arab brothers, the Palestinians and their problems will be marginalized regionally and internationally in the same way that the lack of a Kurdish homeland in the Middle East has gone unremedied.

Israel will retain the burden of occupation in the midst of a bloody communal conflict with the Palestinians, will lose the Western support it gained during the Gulf War, and will be unable to take care of its rising economic and social problems, particularly the absorption of Soviet-Jewish immigrants.

One main reason that American mediation between Egypt and Israel was successful in the late 1970s was that both Cairo and Jerusalem were willing from the outset, even without American intervention, to accept the land-for-peace formula as a basis for solving their conflict. Washington should be ready to help the Israelis and the Palestinians only when they are ready to help themselves, and then it should offer its services only as a mediator and an honest broker. In contrast to its conduct during the Egyptian-Israeli peace process, the United States should avoid either creating undue expectations about its ability to deliver a solution or making a commitment to pay the two sides for agreeing to settle their differences.

AMERICA'S NO-WIN STRATEGY

It is doubtful that Washington will soon adopt such a benign neglect approach to the Arab-Israeli conflict or a more disengaged policy toward the Middle East in general. The Gulf War weakened the forces in the foreign policy establishment who were interested in seeing the United States divert resources from its military and restructure its economy for more effective participation in international economic competition. The "splendid little war" played into the hands of members of the military-industrial complex who want to see Washington play the role of a global police officer and extend its military commitments in various parts of the globe, especially the Middle East. . . .

Since the victory in the Gulf War, Europe seems willing to accept American leadership in the region. However, as Washington faces increasing diplomatic and military problems in shaping security arrangements in the gulf and in maintaining the Israeli-Arab peace momentum, new acrimonies between the United States and Great Britain on the one hand and the rest of Europe (particularly the Mediterranean states—France, Italy, and Spain) on the other will resurface.

France would like to play a more independent security role in the region, perhaps as part of a new military undertaking of the Western European Union, which would put Paris in conflict with Washington and London, who want any European "out of area" security policy firmly anchored in an American-led NATO. Italy and Spain, with French support, have begun pushing their plan for establishment of a Conference on Security and Cooperation in the Mediterranean. . . .

Washington should welcome the possibility that France and the European Community will return to play a more active diplomatic and military role. And Washington should be prepared, if asked by all sides of the Arab-Israeli conflict, to offer its diplomatic services as an honest broker, while making it clear to both Arabs and Israelis that such a move will depend on their willingness to reach an agreement. Furthermore, it should be clearly understood that the United States will not be willing to incur major financial costs or to undertake military commitments in the region as part of a final peace agreement.

Similarly, the United States should be willing to help the gulf countries and other Middle Eastern states adopt free-market systems and establish free-trade areas. The American private sector can help Middle Eastern businesses help themselves by encouraging Western investment, improving marketing techniques, and providing training programs to facilitate entrepreneurial activity.

While democratic values may be alien to the political cultures of the Middle East, respect for the traditional market, the bazaar, is not. The expansion of islands of free enterprise in countries such as Egypt, Tunisia, and Jordan can strengthen the existing business community in those countries as well as the power of the young professional middle class. Those segments of society tend to be more westernized and pragmatic in their political orientation and could eventually serve as a counterweight to both the decaying military regimes and the rising fundamentalist groups. Even here, American expectations must be realistic; the effort, therefore, should be low key and modest in nature.

The United States should refrain from entering a new cycle of military commitment and diplomatic hyperactivity, which would lead political elites in the region to look to Washington to solve their domestic and political problems and to contain regional threats. By renewing military and diplomatic commitments, the United States would re-move the incentives for those regimes to reform their political and economic systems, to create stable balance-of-power systems and viable security arrangements, and to reach diplomatic solutions to their conflicts. Instead of becoming a symbol of political and economic freedom (a model to be imitated), the United States would be identified with repressive regimes and become a symbol of evil in the eyes of new, rising elites. Washington would also risk becoming a party to regional conflicts and being drawn into one military intervention after another.

Indeed, as the Bush administration learn[ed] in the aftermath of the Gulf War, a successful military operation did not produce a neat strategic solution to regional balance-of-power problems. Instead, it has created new dilemmas for American policy. Washington would like to see Saddam go, one official was quoted as saying, but "we have no desire to see Iraq splinter into its many constituent parts. And so it's tough to know what, if anything, to do in the current situation." Bush and his advisers discover[ed] that getting into the gulf crisis was easier than getting out. Typical of the problem is the anger expressed by one Iraqi exile leader who blames the United States for the chaos and destruction of the war and calls on Washington to invade Baghdad and impose democracy. If Washington refuses to take that step, he warns, "the Middle East will be worse than it was before the war in spite of the demise of Saddam Hussein." Moreover, "the Arabs will remember the war as having been simply about destroying Iraq," and there will be "a legacy of hate and bitterness" against the United States for generations to come.

Instead of letting itself be lured into such a morass, the United States should seize the opportunity provided by the end of the cold war and the completion of the Gulf War to replace its decaying Middle Eastern paradigm with a more cautious approach toward the region. Washington should maintain friendly relationships with Middle Eastern countries that share its values and should increase its economic ties with those who want to trade. But the United States cannot hope to impose stability on that fractious region or to solve its multifaceted problems.

Questions for Discussion

1. What are U.S. interests in the Middle East today? How have they changed over the past few decades?
2. Should the United States intervene to impose peace in the Middle East?
3. Should the United States have intervened on behalf of Kuwait in the 1990 Gulf crisis?
4. What are the linkages between the Arab-Israeli conflict and tensions in the Persian Gulf region?
5. What are some of America's main policy problems with respect to the Persian Gulf? With respect to the Arab-Israeli sector of the Middle East?
6. Should the United States sell large quantities of advanced weaponry to oil-rich Arab states?
7. What is the nature of the U.S.-Israeli relationship?
8. What are the similarities—and differences—in the policies advocated by James Phillips and Leon Hadar? Towards which one do you lean?

Selected Bibliography

ASPIN, LES, AND WILLIAM DICKINSON. *Defense for a New Era: Lessons of the Persian Gulf War*. New York: Brassey's, 1992.

COOLEY, JOHN K. *Payback: America's Long War in the Middle East*. New York: Brassey's, 1991.

EVELAND, WILBUR CRANE. *Ropes of Sand: America's Failure in the Middle East*. New York: W.W. Norton, 1980.

FREEDMAN, LAWRENCE, AND EFRAIM KARSH. *The Gulf Conflict 1990–1991*. Princeton: Princeton University Press, 1993.

HADAR, LEON T. *Quaqmire: America in the Middle East*. Washington, DC: Cato Institute, 1992.

QUANDT, WILLIAM B. *Decade of Decisions: American Policy Toward the Arab-Israeli Conflict: 1967–1976*. Berkeley: University of California Press, 1977.

———· *Peace Process: American Diplomacy and the Arab-Israeli Conflict Since 1967*. Washington, DC: The Brookings Institution, 1993.

SAFRAN, NADAV. *Israel: The Embattled Ally*. Cambridge: Harvard University Press, 1978.

SCHOENBAUM, DAVID. *The United States and Israel*. New York: Oxford University Press, 1993.

SPIEGEL, STEVEN. *The Other Arab-Israeli Conflict: Making America's Middle East Policy from Truman to Reagan*. Chicago: University of Chicago Press, 1985.

STOOKEY, ROBERT W. *America and the Arab States: An Uneasy Encounter*. New York: John Wiley, 1975.

TIMMERMAN, KENNETH R. *The Death Lobby: How the West Armed Iraq*. New York: Houghton Mifflin, 1991.

WILSON, EVAN M. *Decision on Palestine: How the U.S. Came to Recognize Israel*. Stanford: Hoover Institution Press, 1979.

YERGIN, DANIEL. *The Prize: The Epic Quest for Oil, Money, and Power*. New York: Simon and Schuster, 1991.

PART FIVE

ENHANCING SECURITY

CHAPTER 12

Coping with the Nuclear Genie

During the Cold War, the unifying theme among U.S. leaders and analysts of all political persuasions was the military threat posed by the Soviet Union, particularly its nuclear aspect. From September 1949 on, after the Soviet Union surprised the West by detonating its first atomic bomb a decade earlier than had been expected, disagreements revolved around what were Soviet capabilities and what were Soviet intentions. American fears of a possible all-out war were aggravated by the Moscow-encouraged aggression in Korea in 1950 and by the successful Soviet testing of a thermonuclear, or hydrogen, bomb in 1953, less than a year after the United States had done so. By the mid-1950s both sides had accelerated their nuclear buildups and, even more important, their development of the means of delivering such weapons of mass destruction against enemy targets. As the first to test an intercontinental ballistic missile (ICBM) successfully, in late August 1957, and to place a satellite, Sputnik I, in orbit around the earth, on October 4, 1957, Moscow seemed to be leading in the race to acquire a commanding advantage in the nuclear-missile sector of military power.

To keep defense spending from unduly escalating, President Dwight D. Eisenhower emphasized reliance on nuclear strikes to deter any possible Soviet attack, thus giving rise to the strategy of massive retaliation. Implicit was a warning to Moscow that an attack against the United States or its allies would be met by a full-scale nuclear response, and not, as in Korea, by a limited conventional one.

As always, compromises and accommodations affect the size and composition of a country's armed forces: no government can afford to defend against all the worst-case scenarios conjured up by military planners. For example, during the 1950s, U.S. Air Force Intelligence inflated the Soviet missile threat in order to justify greater expenditures on long-range bombers. When the Kennedy administration took office, it reevaluated these threat assessments and found them wildly inaccurate. Moreover, the so-called "missile gap," which Kennedy had alleged to exist during the 1960 election campaign, turned out to be nonexistent: in fact, the United States had an overwhelming advantage over the Soviet Union in deliverable nuclear warheads, 6000 to 300. This led Kennedy to stabilize the U.S. ICBM force at 1054, in the hope that the Soviet Union would slow down its ICBM buildup and deployment once it reached the U.S. levels. Actually, it was Nikita Khrushchev's desire to avoid substantially increasing military spending on strategic (ICBM) forces that prompted him to decide in the spring of 1962 to implant short- and intermediate-range missiles in Cuba. Not only would the success of this stratagem have enhanced Soviet prestige, punctured Chinese criticisms that Khrushchev was behaving timidly vis-à-vis U.S. imperialism, and demonstrated

Moscow's credibility as a patron, but "the force of some forty MRBM [medium-range ballistic missiles] and IRBM [intermediate-range ballistic missiles] launchers dispatched to Cuba would have narrowed in one quick stroke the actual margin of the U.S. advantage in strategic forces, for it would have had the effect, as Raymond Garthoff has pointed out, of transforming readily available missiles of 1100 to 2200-mile range into 'ersatz' intercontinental missiles. In terms of the Soviet Union's then-existing first-strike salvo capability against targets in the United States," this would have meant an increase of 80 percent.[1] (Note: At the time, MRBMs had a range of about 1100 miles; IRBMs, about 2400 miles. According to information later revealed by the Soviets, all the missiles in Cuba were then SS-4 MRBMs.) Khrushchev's failure triggered a massive increase in Soviet military spending.

By the mid-1960s, each superpower had the nuclear capacity to do unacceptable harm to the other, giving rise to a policy of deterrence known as mutual assured destruction (MAD). MAD meant that the previous U.S. reliance on massive retaliation had lost its credibility. Moreover, it was not politically, militarily, or morally a viable defense strategy for the United States. Accordingly, in 1967, Washington adapted MAD to include a policy of "flexible response" and "extended deterrence," the purpose of which was to commit the United States and its NATO allies to meeting any aggression initially at whatever level it was launched,

---

[1] Thomas W. Wolfe. *Soviet Power and Europe 1945–1970*. Baltimore: Johns Hopkins University Press, 1970, p. 98; and Raymond L. Garthoff, "The Meaning of the Missiles," *The Washington Quarterly*, vol. 5, no. 4, Autumn 1982, pp. 77–80, excerpts.

while retaining the flexibility to escalate the fighting in order to force the aggressor to withdraw. Nuclear buildups proceeded unchecked, as President Lyndon B. Johnson failed in his attempt to persuade Moscow to limit strategic (offensive) weapons and defensive systems. Soviet Premier Aleksei Kosygin later told him that the Kremlin could not believe that limiting defensive systems might actually enhance security. Not until the early 1970s were conditions ripe for an agreement to limit nuclear weapons.

On May 26, 1972, the first strategic arms limitation treaty (SALT) was signed in Moscow by President Richard M. Nixon and CPSU Secretary Leonid Brezhnev. It consisted of three agreements. The first is a treaty of unlimited duration on the limitation of anti-ballistic missile (ABM) systems. It prohibits the development of an ABM system, though originally permitting each side to protect its national capital and one ICBM silo launcher area; a protocol, added in 1974, formally restricted each side to only one ABM deployment. It is this treaty that became a source of continuing controversy after President Ronald Reagan's speech of March 23, 1983, proposing a departure from a policy "that relies solely on offensive retaliation for our security." The second agreement was a five-year interim accord, fixing Soviet ICBM and SLBM (submarine launched ballistic missiles) launchers at 2350 and American launchers at 1710, thus marking the first time in the nuclear era that the USSR and the United States had agreed to set up quantitative limits on their strategic delivery systems, that is, missiles capable of striking the other's homeland. Bombers were not covered in this agreement. The third agreement dealt with interpretations of technical issues such as radars, testing, and so on.

By 1992 several follow-up SALT or START (strategic arms reduction talks, the name adopted during the Reagan administration) agreements were reached. Under Soviet President Mikhail Gorbachev, and then under Russia's President Boris Yeltsin, Moscow agreed to sharp cuts in offensive weapons, so that by the year 2000 or earlier, the two sides will have reduced their strategic and tactical nuclear weapons to levels that existed in the mid-1960s. All of this is predicated on continuation of a government in Moscow dedicated to detente and reconciliation with the United States and on adequate verification of any agreements concluded.

Throughout history, every offensive weapon invariably occasioned a countervailing defense to offset it. Conversely, defensive systems have, over time, succumbed to new offensive systems. Technological innovation is the catalyst that has transformed the character of the battlefield. During the nuclear era, technology initially favored the development of offensive nuclear weapons. Some comparative yields may illustrate the destructiveness of nuclear weapons. The biggest conventional bomb dropped on Germany by Allied bombers in World War II contained the equivalent of 2 tons or 4400 pounds of TNT; the atomic bomb dropped on Hiroshima in August 1945 was a 20-kiloton bomb or one equivalent to 20,000 tons of TNT; and a one megaton hydrogen bomb is equivalent to the destructive power of one million tons of TNT. Perhaps even more significant than the destructiveness of these weapons have been the advances in delivery systems: the greater throw-weight or lifting power of the new missiles, increased accuracy and miniaturization of guidance systems, and new lightweight casings for the missiles. Moreover, a MIRVed (multiple independently targetable reentry vehicle) missile can carry from two up to ten nuclear warheads, each directed toward a different target. With the development and, in the late 1970s, mass production of cruise missiles, the offense seemed unchallenged. (Cruise missiles are small, subsonic, low-altitude, accurate, and maneuverable pilotless flying bombs, capable of carrying nuclear bombs to targets within a range of 2000 miles. They were used with great effectiveness against Iraq during the 1991 Gulf War.)

In the 1960s a ballistic missile defense (BMD) began to be deployed, but it was quite primitive and overshadowed by offensive weapons. Today ABMs, which are small missiles designed to intercept and destroy incoming nuclear-armed offensive missiles, remain expensive, unreliable, and potentially destabilizing, in that a determined move by any power to develop an effective BMD would act to stimulate an intensification of the arms race in both offensive and defensive weapons.

President Reagan's proposal of March 23, 1983 to embark "on a program to counter the awesome Soviet missile threat with measures that are defensive" was based on the premise that U.S. security would be enhanced if "we could intercept and destroy strategic ballistic missiles before they reached our own soil or that of our allies"; and that, though "a formidable, technical task," it was one that could, in time, perhaps decades down the road, be achieved. In brief, Reagan argued for trying to save lives, not avenge them. His strategic defense initiative (SDI), as it was called, was criticized for various reasons: it was expensive, of dubious technical feasibility, and destabilizing.

Moscow's opposition to SDI was immediate and intense. Under Gorbachev, it had several aims: to prevent the United States from effecting a technological breakthrough that could diminish the USSR's security and degrade its offensive capability; to avoid the diversion of scarce resources to a new and extremely costly phase of the arms race; to exploit the differences within NATO; and to exploit arms control to limit a possible U.S. military-technological advantage, as Moscow had done in the early 1970s when it used the SALT I treaty to freeze the U.S.'s ABM development. For their part, the Soviets had been working on a space-based defense system for more than 30 years, but it was nowhere good enough to threaten the U.S. ability to deliver offensive weapons against designated targets. The issue of a space-based defense against ICBMs never came to a head because Gorbachev was committed to a sweeping program of reform at home and détente abroad, and the last thing he wanted was a new arms race with the United States, especially one that would be extraordinarily costly. With improved U.S.-Soviet relations from 1986 on, SDI lost much of its immediacy for the Reagan administration. The end of the Cold War in the early 1990s brought a rethinking of U.S. defense priorities, including a need to reduce defense expenditures and devote more resources to domestic problems.

The most dangerous developments in the nuclear realm have been reversed, namely, an expanding arms race in the name of deterrence and nuclear forces deployed globally and kept at a high state of battle readiness. But the challenge is far from over. Sources of insecurity abound. The nuclear genie may be considered to be in the process of being house-broken, but not forced back into the bottle.

Les Aspin, the former Chairman of the House Armed Services Committee, now Secretary of Defense in the Clinton administration, has been in the vanguard of those who are rethinking U.S. security needs and the threats facing the country in the post-Cold War period. Of primary concern are the emerging nuclear threats such as proliferation of weapons to rogue regimes (Iraq, North Korea, Libya, to cite a few), accidental launches, and "loose nukes." Possible remedies are being explored (Reading 36). Now that the danger of nation-destroying nuclear war between the United States and the Soviet Union/Russia has passed, or at least significantly declined, the problems in the future inhere in the possible acquisition and use of nuclear weapons by irresponsible regimes or terrorist groups. The technology is no longer a secret. The main issues are how to control its use and regulate the behavior of nonnuclear states and states that have nuclear reactors but not weapons grade material.

Kathleen C. Bailey, Director of Arms Control Studies at National Security Research in Fairfax, Virginia, and author of *Doomsday Weapons in the Hands of Many*, examines the policies adopted by the United States and international organizations in an effort to prevent nuclear proliferation (Reading 37). Her focus is on preventing the acquisition of ballistic missiles, the assumption being that without the means of delivering nuclear weapons a would-be aggressor nation would be powerless to mount a credible threat. Accordingly, she looks at the record of the Missile Technology Control Regime (MTCR), established on April 16, 1987.

Paul L. Leventhal, president of the Nuclear Control Institute in Washington, D.C., believes that the proper focus must be on preventing "not the spread of nuclear weapons per se, but of the materials and technology essential to their manufacture."[2] Using Iraq's nuclear weapons program as a mini-case study, he argues that it is feasible as well as essential to ensure that no country is permitted to produce or use separated plutonium or highly enriched uranium, the material needed for nuclear weapons. It is lax enforcement of existing export controls and the power of nuclear industrial interests that call into question the seriousness of purpose of countries such as the United States, Germany, Britain, and France.

In the absence of authoritative, effective measures to prohibit or control the acquisition of missile technology or weapons grade nuclear material by potentially dangerous, anti-status quo regimes or groups, the United States has a responsibility to look to its safety and that of its allies. These uncertainties have revived the debate over the long-term costs and feasibility of Ronald Reagan's "star wars" proposal. Its latest variant focuses on the Strategic Defense Initiative Organization's (SDIO) proposed space-based weapon, known as Brilliant Pebbles, for the Global Protection Against Limited Strikes (GPALS) strategic defense system. The proposed system would consist of both earth- and space-based sensors and interceptors. In its early stage of conceptualization, it represents a major adaptation and contraction of Reagan's original proposal.

It entails hundreds of individual interceptors in orbit around the earth at relatively evenly spaced intervals. Each interceptor would be linked by communications to the others and to ground stations. In the event of a ballistic missile attack, each could be given a high degree of autonomy to detect and intercept missiles that enter its battle space. A set of deployed Brilliant Pebbles, referred to as a constellation, would be made up of several staggered rings orbiting at 400 kilometers above the earth, with several Brilliant Pebbles in each ring. The constellation could be deployed either to provide partial or complete global coverage for detection and interception of ballistic missiles on a continuous basis. Once enabled by human command, the Brilliant Pebbles interceptors could select their targets and divert from their orbits into the path of enemy missiles. The interceptors would carry no explosives, but the force of their high-speed collision is expected to destroy targets.[3]

Samuel Johnson's comment, "imagination should be disciplined by reality," is apt. Ultimately, the issue will be decided by what emerges from the scientific-engineering community's research and development. However, at present, the debate is highly political. Arguments in the struggle for public and Congressional support are being marshalled by advocates of going ahead who see it as an essential step toward ensuring U.S. security and opponents who see it as a squandering of scarce resources in the quest for the unrealizable goal of absolute security. Baker Spring, an analyst at The Heritage Foundation, contends that those who have opposed SDI from the very beginning continue to do so on the same old grounds, despite advances in technology

[2] Paul L. Leventhal, "Plugging the Leaks in Nuclear Export Controls: Why Bother?" *Orbis*, vol. 36, no. 2, Spring 1992, p. 174.

[3] U.S. General Accounting Office, "Strategic Defense Initiative: Estimates of Brilliant Pebbles' Effectiveness Are Based on Many Unproven Assumptions," March 27, 1992, GAO/NSIAD-92-91, p. 2.

and evidence that some kind of strategic defense against random attacks is feasible (Reading 38). Kosta Tsipis, Director of the Program in Science and Technology for International Security at MIT, argues that the United States did not need an ABM system in the past and that existing technology precludes the necessity for one now (Reading 39).

36.   From Deterrence to Denuking: Dealing with Proliferation in the 1990s

Les Aspin

The proliferation of nuclear weapons is now the chief security threat we face in the post-Soviet era. Proliferation of the technology has continued for the past 20 years, largely obscured by the shadow of the superpower competition. The extent of Saddam Hussein's nuclear ambitions, and near-success in achieving them, should be a wake-up call not just about Iraq but about other countries as well.

Today, in addition to the five acknowledged nuclear powers (U.S., the former Soviet Union, Great Britain, France and China), another four countries are believed to either have nuclear weapons or the ability to assemble them on short notice: Israel, India, Pakistan and South Africa.

Several more nations are now pursuing nuclear capabilities, or have done so in the past, including Iraq, North Korea, Libya, Iran, Argentina, Brazil and (according to some reports) Algeria. Iraq appears to have been within a year of acquiring a nuclear capability. North Korea is now within a similarly short distance. Additional countries, including Moamar Gadhafi's Libya, have had less success to date, but would very much like to have a nuclear bomb.

"Loose Nukes"

Of particular concern today is the impact that the breakup of the Soviet Union could have on prolif-

SOURCE: Les Aspin, "From Deterrence to Denuking: Dealing with Proliferation in the 1990s," February 18, 1992, pp. 4–14, 16, excerpts.

eration. At issue here is a set of problems that has come to be known collectively as "loose nukes."

The Soviet Union had nearly 30,000 nuclear weapons, of which about 10,000 were long-range strategic weapons and the remainder tactical weapons. The proliferation dangers of this stockpile are threefold.

The first concerns proliferation of nuclear weapons states. Strategic missiles are deployed today in Russia and three other republics. Belarus has on its territory a substantial force of 100 strategic weapons. Both Ukraine or Kazakhstan have well over 1,000 strategic nuclear weapons deployed on their territory. . . .

It is strongly in the U.S. interest that there be only one nuclear chain of command and that it be in experienced hands. More than one button, each controlling a portion of the present arsenal, would increase nuclear danger to the U.S. Even if we had good relations with the new nuclear nations, there would be an increased possibility of accidental or unauthorized launch.

Present trends are positive. All three republics have committed to eliminate the strategic weapons on its territory, Ukraine by the end of 1994, and Belarus and Kazakhstan by 1999. In the meantime, it has been agreed that control of the weapons will remain in Moscow. Nevertheless, relations between the republics are strained, and there remains a residual danger that strategic weapons will be employed as bargaining chips in inter-republic conflict.

The second, and most immediate, concern is the danger posed by the possibility that a weapon or fissile material for making a weapon will fall into the wrong hands. This chiefly arises with tactical weapons. The troubling equation is a simple one: bad morale in the armed forces equals reduced security equals greater risk of lost or stolen weapons. . . .

Third, there is the danger that the economic chaos of the former Soviet Union will drive its nuclear scientists into Third World nuclear programs, hastening the day when more members join the nuclear club. This is the so-called Brain Drain problem.

From whatever source, nuclear proliferation poses three distinct security challenges to the United States.

First, proliferators may threaten nuclear use to deter the United States and the international community from taking actions that are in our interests. The overwhelming performance of U.S. conventional forces in the war with Iraq was not lost on Third World nations. The Indian defense minister is reported to have responded when asked what lessons to draw from the Gulf War: "Don't fight the United States unless you have nuclear weapons."

The second security challenge arising from enlarging the club of nuclear nations is the high potential that the proliferators may lose control of their weapons, resulting in accidental or unauthorized use, or loss to third parties.

It is unlikely that the sophisticated command and control schemes of the United States or Russia, or even the more rudimentary system in China would be duplicated in a Third World nation conducting, perhaps clandestinely, a program to develop a bomb.

The third and perhaps most problematic security challenge arises from situations in which deterrence may not operate. Deterrence requires that adversaries be identified and that they behave rationally. These elements are present in the large majority of situations in which we might be militarily challenged in this new era, and we can therefore expect deterrence to work should those opponents have or acquire nuclear weapons. The absence of either one of these two factors, however,

could remove the fear of retaliation on which deterrence depends.

Candidates for such an event include a national leader who is not rational, a surrogate acting for a nation seeking to hide its responsibility, or a terrorist or other sub-national group that could expect to remain hidden and out of the reach of retaliation.

Unauthorized or Accidental Launch

The existence of strategic nuclear arsenals has always carried with it the possibility of accidental or unauthorized launch. The question here is how the enormous changes going on in the successor states to the Soviet Union affect the chances for either.

In fact, our concerns with these two possibilities have been reversed. The absence of superpower tensions and confrontations has reduced the chance for accidental launch. The changes that brought about a reduction in those tensions have also introduced a number of uncertainties. Those uncertainties increase the chance of unauthorized launch.

In the old threat era, concern centered on accidental launch in time of crisis. Nuclear forces are generally postured to "fail safe." That is, they are postured so that a failure of the control system does not result in a launch or detonation. The failure is safe. In time of crisis, when forces are put on a high state of alert, that shifts to "fail deadly." That is, control system failure can result in a launch. The failure is deadly.

During the Cold War, global competition, often through surrogates, provided crises and opportunities for confrontation. In today's world, it is difficult to write a plausible scenario for bringing the respective nuclear arsenals to full alert status, so the chances of accidental launch are accordingly reduced, and will remain so in the absence of a political reversal.

Unauthorized launch presents the opposite picture. In the days before the second modern Russian revolution, there was no question that iron-clad control was maintained over strategic weapons. There is no direct, specific evidence today that that control has lessened.

Today, however, the changes going on in the former Soviet Union have raised the possibility of civil strife or civil war. These would greatly increase the risk that a nuclear weapon would be used without authorization from higher political authority. Short-range tactical weapons present the larger threat, since many are not protected by permissive action links (PALs). Although tactical weapons launched from Russia could not reach the U.S. directly, the risk is that they could reach U.S. soil by airplane, ship or other means.

All Soviet strategic weapons are believed to have PALs, and so should pose less of a risk than tactical weapons. However, there are at least two scenarios where the control of strategic weapons could be compromised. The first is a conspiracy involving at least one person in the General Staff with access to the PAL launch codes, and one military officer with the ability to employ these codes to launch a strategic missile. Not enough is known about the command and control of Russian strategic forces to be sure exactly how many people would be required for such a conspiracy to succeed in launching a missile. If the right people (or from our perspective wrong people) got together, it is possible that only a very few would be needed.

The second scenario is a breakdown of order in the former Soviet Union and discipline in the armed forces. PALs do not protect against unauthorized launch indefinitely, but are designed to buy time for the weapon to be recovered. If a state of societal chaos or civil war develops in the former Soviet Union, the risks of losing control of a strategic missile for a sufficient period to allow its launch could grow enormously.

Under circumstances that obtain today, the possibility of an unauthorized launch of a strategic nuclear weapon—while still small—must be rated as greater in the post-Soviet world. In the event of widespread civil strife or civil war, neither of which can be ruled out, this risk would rise dramatically.

REDUCING NUCLEAR DANGER IN THE NEW ERA

The era of the classical superpower nuclear threat is passing. Deterrence is still a necessary response to the residual classical threat, but it is not adequate to deal with the full range of nuclear dangers we face in the post-Soviet era. Two characteristics of this new era are central to the discussion of reducing its nuclear dangers.

The first is that there is no analogue to deterrence as a nuclear policy in the new era. That is, no single policy or action will meet these diverse threats. It will be necessary to generate a package of responses.

The second is that the fundamental shift in our interests regarding nuclear weapons has undercut old notions of what constitutes appropriate responses from the political left and the political right. Responses to the new dangers will be found across the former political spectrum of nuclear policy.

I have made an attempt below to outline a program to produce such a package of responses. The program is tentative and intended to spur frank discussion of the requirements of this new era.

Directly Reducing Nuclear Threats

The first line of defense in the new nuclear era must be to devote much greater effort to the direct reduction of potentially undeterrable nuclear threats.

Stemming Proliferation   In the past, chemical weapons were considered the "poor man's nuke." Within the next decade, the poor man's nuke may be nukes. Nuclear weapons would likely be the only way a nation with inferior conventional forces could hope to counter our superiority. So it is in our supreme national interest to stem the spread of nuclear weapons, nuclear weapons technologies, and their associated delivery systems.

There are a number of steps we need to consider. These include: how to strengthen the International Atomic Energy Agency (IAEA), which is responsible for verifying compliance with the Non-Proliferation Treaty but simply does not have the authority or resources to do so; how to tighten export controls on sensitive technologies, an area where some of our allies have been sorely lacking; and how to improve our intelligence capabilities about emerging nuclear programs.

Table 1.   Nuclear Threats to the U.S.: Old versus New

The Old Threat	The New Threats
Single threat	Multiple threats
Known	Unknown
Soviet rational actor	Non-Soviet, non-rational, or both
Large-scale (intentional) attack	Small-scale, terrorist
Deterrable	Non-deterrable
Accidental	Unauthorized

Iraq is a perfect case study where efforts fell short in all these areas: Iraq signed the NPT in 1968, and was considered in full compliance with its safeguards agreement with the IAEA; it received much technical help from the West; and U.S. and Western intelligence seriously underestimated the extent of Saddam's nuclear program.

Changing global circumstances offer new possibilities for slowing or stopping nuclear proliferation in two important ways.

First, because we are no longer engaging in proxy wars or conflict with the former Soviet Union, proliferation does not have to take a back seat in our relations with Third World countries to broader geopolitical concerns.

Second, the possibility is much greater for cooperating with the Russians to stop proliferation. This can involve activities ranging from the sharing of intelligence, to promoting regional security in the Middle East and Southwest Asia, to combined efforts to physically destroy Third World nuclear facilities. The Soviet support of the Gulf War, and the United Nations' continued efforts to root out Iraq's nuclear, chemical and biological capabilities is a very encouraging sign that increased cooperation may be possible in the future.

Accidental/Unauthorized Launch   We should look for ways to cooperate with the former Soviet Union in a manner that advances our goals. One area already under discussion is joint activities to improve missile warning to reduce the chance of mistaken retaliation. Another would be to improve the technical means to help prevent accidental or unauthorized launch, including the placement of

PALs and post-launch destruct switches on all ballistic missiles. PALs are devices that require an additional code or step in the firing process before the individual weapon can be launched. Post-launch destruct switches are common in test missiles so they can be destroyed in the air if they go off course. Such devices could be used to destroy missiles in flight whose launch was unauthorized.

Congress expressed its support for such measures in the FY92 defense authorization bill. I am told that a report on the subject is forthcoming soon from a presidential panel headed by Ambassador Jeanne Kirkpatrick. The committee will be looking into these measures in detail over the coming months.

Loose Nukes   The immediate problem presented by "loose nukes" in the former Soviet Union has the potential to greatly accelerate the proliferation of nuclear weapons to more countries. If we mishandle this problem, it could create dangers that we will have to deal with for years to come.

Congress took an important step to deal with "loose nukes" when it approved recently the spending of $400 million from the FY92 defense budget to assist in disabling, dismantling and destroying Soviet nuclear weapons. To date, however, none of these funds has been spent, and no nuclear weapons have been disabled or dismantled under international supervision. A big reason for the slow pace over the last several months was that the Russians were poorly organized, and not prepared to identify where they needed help. That has now changed, and the U.S. technical working group had a productive meeting with their Russian counterparts just a few weeks ago. We now need to follow-up much more aggressively in addressing this problem.

Our goals are straightforward. If we met them all, the following situation would result within a short period: all Soviet tactical nuclear weapons would be either dismantled or in secure storage in Russia, awaiting dismantlement; the fissile material resulting from warhead dismantlement would be well-protected and safeguarded in secure storage; and Soviet nuclear scientists would not be producing new weapons, but working to dismantle the Soviet nuclear arsenal and clean up the environmental mess it created. Finally, strategic weapons will be consolidated in Russia and under the tight control of Russia and/or the Commonwealth of Independent States.

If these goals can be accomplished in their entirety, which will be extremely difficult, most of the serious and immediate risks associated with "loose nukes" in the former Soviet Union would be eliminated.

Defenses—Prescriptions of the Right

Defenses were once largely prescriptions of the right. The kind of nuclear threats emerging in this post-Soviet era have put defenses in a new light, and not just a defense against ballistic missiles. Many commentators have rightly pointed out that missiles are far from the only way to deliver a nuclear weapon.

Missile Defenses   The end of the Cold War has already had an important impact on U.S. policy in missile defenses—further adjustment will be needed. The role of missile defenses has shifted from trying to complicate a large-scale Soviet attack to protecting the United States from much smaller, but potentially undeterrable attacks, whether accidental, unauthorized, or by a future Third World nation with ICBMs.

The Administration took the first step by scaling back the Strategic Defense Initiative from "Phase I" to a smaller version called "Global Protection Against Limited Strikes," or GPALS.

Last year Congress further defined the type of defense needed for the future in the Missile Defense Act, part of the FY92 Defense Authorization bill. The Missile Defense Act requires the Secretary of Defense to develop for deployment a single-site ABM system consistent with the 1972 ABM Treaty, while at the same time engaging the Soviets in discussions on the possibility of modifying the treaty to allow more extensive defenses.

It appears increasingly likely that the Soviets, or now the Russians, will be amenable to reasonable clarifications and modifications of the ABM Treaty. Then-President Gorbachev announced the Soviet willingness to consider cooperative efforts in missile defense and early warning in his October 5, 1991 response to President Bush. Russian President Yeltsin went much further on January 29, 1992, by saying that "We are ready jointly to work out and subsequently to create and jointly operate a global system of defense in place of SDI."

Our future missile defense efforts should be guided by four precepts.

First, any ABM deployment beyond the 100 interceptors allowed by the ABM Treaty should be negotiated with Russia (and to the extent necessary with other successor states to the Soviet Union). If we were to go beyond the ABM Treaty unilaterally and thereby set back our relationship with Russia, it could encourage a return to the old Cold War relationship. If this were to happen, the nuclear threat to the United States could well rise instead of fall.

Second, the size of our defense should be scaled appropriately for the limited size of the threat, whether accidental, unauthorized or from a future Third World country. These threats require significantly smaller defenses than those previously considered to defend against a large-scale Soviet attack.

This suggests that both the extent of Third World missile proliferation and the structure of remaining Russian strategic forces will influence the appropriate size of the defense. Today, the largest unauthorized attack for which the GPALS is sized is the launch of all twenty SS-N-20 missiles from a Typhoon class submarine, a total of 200 warheads.

Down-loading SS-N-20 missiles from 10 to 5 warheads, for example, would reduce the size of the Typhoon threat by 50 percent, to 100 warheads. Further down-loading of both ICBMs and SLBMs would further reduce the size of the threat.

Third, our defense should not raise concerns about strategic stability. The problem here is that if forces are not inherently survivable, defenses can create what has been called the "leaky umbrella" problem of working better in a drizzle than a downpour—i.e., better against a ragged second-strike than a well-structured first-strike. This could increase incentives to attack first, in the event that there is a political reversal in our relations with an ensuing crisis.

The strategic stability of an offense-defense mix depends both on the size of offensive forces, and their survivability: if both sides' forces are highly survivable even without being defended, then there is little or no incentive to attack first to swamp the defense.

Fourth, any defense architecture we choose should be cost-effective compared to other defense schemes. With declining budgets for the foreseeable future, we can't afford to waste defense dollars. We need to make this cost comparison not only between alternative ABM deployment schemes, but also between funds spent on ABM defenses and funds spent on defending against other delivery means for nuclear weapons, such as low flying aircraft or ships.

Other Defenses   Defenses against nuclear weapons will involve much more than ballistic missile defenses, however. Included are also air defenses, our intelligence capabilities, and technology for detecting nuclear weapons with our customs and coastal defense.

We gave up on air defenses of the United States a long time ago. The reason was that nation-wide air defense against the potentially large Soviet threat was expensive and difficult, and all the more so when the Soviets acquired large numbers of ballistic missiles. The Soviets could suppress our air defenses with their ballistic missiles, and even more important, it made no strategic sense to spend many billions to defend ourselves against bombers and leave ourselves completely vulnerable to the much larger threat posed by Soviet ballistic missiles.

The same is now true in reverse: it makes no sense to spend many billions of dollars on an ABM system for the United States if we are going to leave ourselves vulnerable to other delivery vehicles that may be at least as accessible to Third World leaders. Congress's action to re-orient SDI to dealing with small potentially undeterrable threats makes good sense; we should now consider restructuring our air defense and other efforts in the same way.

Defending the United States against nuclear terrorism is extremely difficult. However, any attempt to smuggle a nuclear weapon into the U.S. would subject the would-be attacker to multiple chances to be discovered. We should devote more intelligence assets to this problem to give us the best possible chance to discover and foil such an attack in the future.

Detecting a smuggled nuclear weapon is analogous in some ways to fighting drug smuggling, with the fortunate difference that nuclear weapons are less widespread than are drugs. We need to begin thinking hard about methods of detection; nuclear weapons have emissions or "signatures" that drugs do not.

Deterrence-Era Policies—Prescriptions of the Left

In the deterrence era, there were four prescriptions of the left that ran against the prevailing grain—institution of a comprehensive test ban, an end to production of fissile material for bombs, removal of forward-based tactical weapons and renunciation of first use of nuclear weapons.

These proposals fared badly because there was a strong presumption that the U.S. needed to continue nuclear testing and the production of fissile materials and, most significantly, to hold out the possibility of first use of nuclear weapons.

There has been a fundamental shift in our security interests regarding nuclear weapons. In the deterrence era, we needed nuclear weapons to deter strategic attack on the United States and to deter an overwhelming conventional attack in Europe. In the post-deterrence era, the incentives are reversed. It would be in our interest to get rid of nuclear weapons.

In the deterrence era, the burden of proof was on anyone who wanted to shift away from policies supporting U.S. nuclear weapons. Today, the burden of proof is shifting toward those who want to maintain those policies in light of the changed world.

Therefore, opposition to the Comprehensive Test Ban, the further production of fissile materials for new weapons, the forward deployment of tactical nuclear weapons in Europe, and, above all, the threat of nuclear first use are up for reconsideration. . . .

Considering The Most Difficult Choice— Pre-emption

There is one final issue to deal with as we consider this new era. It is one on which we can anticipate widespread and strong disagreement. That issue is pre-emption. We must confront and work through together the prospect that force may be the only way in some instances to stop proliferation of nuclear weapons.

If future leaders like Saddam Hussein are intent on developing nuclear weapons, and have a relatively advanced economy to support that effort, the choice that is presented to us may be stark: use force to put a halt to the nuclear program, or welcome a new member to the nuclear club.

Everyone but the would-be new nuclear states agrees that proliferation should be stopped. Everyone does not agree that goal is worth the use of force.

The United States will have sufficient non-nuclear military forces in the future to employ force unilaterally against Third World proliferators. Employing force effectively, however, will be much more likely if the action is taken with international approval. This is a central lesson of the Gulf War.

There is at this moment no international consensus on the use of non-nuclear force for this purpose. No nation aside from the United States can effectively lead an effort to create such a consensus against proliferation. To do so will require a much more concerted effort to stop proliferation short of force, including the prior use of economic and political sanctions.

37.   Can Missile Proliferation Be Reversed?

Kathleen C. Bailey

In 1988, the Intermediate-range Nuclear Forces Treaty (INF) eliminated all U.S. and Soviet ground-launched missiles having a range of 500 to 5,500 km, and at that time many spoke as though this entire category of weaponry had been removed from the scene. But it had not. Today, just such intermediate-range ballistic missiles (IRBMs), bought or developed by a host of other states,

SOURCE: Kathleen C. Bailey, "Can Missile Proliferation Be Reversed?" *Orbis*, vol. 35, no. 1, Winter 1991, pp. 5, 8–14, excerpts. Footnotes deleted. Reprinted with permission of *Orbis: A Journal of World Affairs*, published by the Foreign Policy Research Institute.

threaten world stability [for example, Iraq, India, Brazil, Israel, South Africa, Syria, Egypt, Iran]. . . .

U.S. POLICIES TO CONTROL MISSILES

When it became apparent in the early 1980s that the widespread possession of ballistic missiles was a growing and potentially serious threat, the U.S. arms control community looked to the techniques developed to combat nuclear proliferation as a model for controlling this new proliferation. Specifically, because controlling the export of technology and materials critical to nuclear weapons production had proved quite effective in slowing the spread of nuclear weapons, the same tool of export control was adapted to fight missile proliferation.

At the time, the reasoning behind the choice of export controls was sound: most advanced missile technology was available primarily from the USSR and the seven Western economic partners (the United States, the United Kingdom, Canada, France, Japan, West Germany, and Italy). Although other countries produced components and technology pertinent to ballistic missile production, most did not export whole systems or provide the critical components. Little thought was given to China's potential for becoming a major supplier, much less to the notion of the lesser powers themselves becoming suppliers.

In 1985 and 1986, Washington worked with its six economic partners to develop an effective system of export controls. The product was named the Missile Technology Control Regime (MTCR), and was formally announced on April 16, 1987. The MTCR consists of a basic policy statement, a set of guidelines to limit the conditions under which missile technology may be transferred, an annex listing technologies to be controlled, and an informal mechanism by which the partners can share information about potential transfers.

The items controlled by the MTCR are divided into two categories. Category I items are complete rocket systems and unmanned air-vehicle systems capable of delivering a payload of 500 kg or more to a range of at least 300 km (three-fifths of the conventional lower limit for IRBMs). Production facilities and subsystems for such delivery vehicles are also contained in Category I. Category II contains a long list of items, including propulsion components, propellants, equipment for making propellants, guidance components, flight control systems, avionics, computers, and software.

The MTCR partners also agreed on some basic ground rules for export control. (1) All transfers would be considered on a case-by-case basis. (2) Governments would implement the guidelines through national legislation. (3) The exporting government would assume responsibility for taking all steps necessary to ensure that the item was put

only to its stated end-use. (4) The decision to export would remain the sole and sovereign judgment of the individual government.

Undoubtedly, the MTCR has succeeded in creating an awareness of the missile proliferation problem among Western suppliers, and it has provided a structure for export controls. But how well has the MTCR succeeded in its goal of stopping missile proliferation?

Those who helped shape the MTCR point to the failure of the Condor program of Argentina, Iraq, and Egypt, and say that it failed owing largely to an inability to import technology and equipment. Others, however, point to the intense bilateral pressure that Washington put on Argentina and Egypt as the main reason for the Condor's problems.

Nevertheless, whatever credit the MTCR may claim in the case of Condor, the problem of missile proliferation has unquestionably worsened since the inception of the MTCR. Saudi Arabia, Iraq, India, Israel, South Africa, and North Korea have all acquired or developed ballistic missiles with ranges in excess of 500 km. Iran, Pakistan, Argentina, Brazil, and perhaps other countries continue their efforts to acquire IRBMs. Thus, while the MTCR may be a valuable tool in slowing proliferation, it is incapable of stopping it.

THE PROBLEMS WITH MTCR

At present, MTCR is beset by at least five major problems. If these are not solved soon, more may arise in the future. In 1992, for example, European integration is to take place. If all countries in the European Community are not MTCR members by that time, the regime may be undermined badly. MTCR partners will be unable to impose special rules governing exports that differ from those of the Community. The following problems, however, are the major current ones.

1. MTCR is a nuclear nonproliferation tool. Because the MTCR derives from the nuclear nonproliferation regime, it is specifically designed to "control the transfer of equipment and technology that could contribute to *nuclear-capable* missiles." As the MTCR guidelines are written, a country that does not have the capability or intention to possess nuclear warheads is a suitable recipient of missile technology. Thus, technically, a country whose objective is to arm its missiles with chemical, biological, or conventional warheads is a suitable purchaser under the MTCR. Indeed, Chinese officials have pointed out, correctly, that China's export of intermediate-range CSS-2 ballistic missiles to Saudi Arabia would have been totally legitimate even if China had been a partner in the MTCR. They base this conclusion on the absence of any evidence suggesting Saudi Arabia is trying to obtain nuclear warheads.

2. The MTCR allows peaceful space cooperation. The MTCR is ". . . not designed to impede national space programs or international cooperation in such programs as long as such programs could not contribute to nuclear weapons delivery systems." France has used this statement as the basis for its decision to supply missile technology to countries that have legitimate space programs, as long as they are not known to possess nuclear warhead capability. France has noted that, under the MTCR rules, any decision to sell is a sovereign one, and it has argued that if it first determines that the end-use of the technology it sells will be for peaceful space programs, then the MTCR permits for such sales.

The United States counters by pointing out to its MTCR partners that there is a strong "presumption of denial" for Category I items: missiles and missile systems. It further stresses that the potential for nuclear proliferation is indicated when a country with significant nuclear facilities refuses to be party to a nuclear nonproliferation treaty. Washington also notes that the MTCR compels suppliers to take into consideration the capabilities and objectives of the missile and space programs of the recipient state. In the U.S. view, because space launch vehicles and ballistic missiles use the same technology, any space program is a potential military missile program.

The debate over the ability of MTCR partners to assist other states' space programs has put the MTCR at risk. In 1989, France offered to sell rocket motor technology to Brazil and India. It said that the end-use assurances offered by both recipients were sufficient, that the MTCR allows such cooperation, and that France has the sovereign right to sell if it wishes.

The United States responded that neither Brazil nor India participates in a nuclear nonproliferation treaty and that such a sale would destroy the MTCR. France put the space technology sales on hold, but the debate is likely to continue. There will be a motive to sell such technology as long as there is a demand for it by countries which want it for "peaceful space uses."

3. The MTCR is not a treaty or legal obligation. The MTCR relies on an understanding among the partners. In 1989, when legislation was introduced in the U.S. Congress to create sanctions against those caught in violation of MTCR guidelines, Bush administration officials objected. They pointed out that the MTCR is not a legally binding document, and that it recognizes the final decision on any export belongs to the sovereign partners individually. Washington cannot impose its will or its interpretation.

4. All suppliers are not in the MTCR. Several European states, Australia, and the USSR have signalled their intention to join the MTCR soon. Nevertheless, the MTCR does not and probably will not include some key suppliers. China is the obvious example. When, in August 1988, Washington asked China if it would adhere to the MTCR controls, Peking said no. Chinese officials give three basic reasons. (1) Politically, China could not afford to be viewed by developing countries as a member of a Western condominium designed to deprive them of technology. (2) The United States has made vast amounts of money from arms exports, including missile exports, and China should be able to do the same without interference from the United States. And (3) China was already showing restraint in its missile exports. . . .

5. The MTCR focuses on suppliers. The MTCR's weakest point, perhaps, is that it does nothing to dampen the motivations of states seeking ballistic missiles for military purposes. This is in stark contrast to the nuclear nonproliferation treaties, under which states proclaim their decisions to refrain from acquiring nuclear weapons. While this is no guarantee they are being truthful, the act of signing such a treaty creates a political barrier to proliferation. Another important attribute of the nuclear nonproliferation regime is the existence of safeguards, which are a technical means of verifying that specific nuclear materials and facilities are not being used for nonpeaceful purposes. By contrast, the MTCR is imposed on those without missile technology by those with missile technology. There has been no attempt to establish a voluntary, international, verifiable regime to limit the spread of missile technology.

TOWARD A NEW NONPROLIFERATION POLICY

The MTCR has been useful in slowing the pace of ballistic missile proliferation, but it is not enough. Its weaknesses are so serious that additional policies must be developed that address the motivations of states to acquire ballistic missiles for military uses. Four policy options exist, none of which will be easy to implement.

1. Close the "warhead loophole" in the MTCR. The MTCR should not be a simple extension of nuclear weapon nonproliferation policy. Agreement among partners should be sought to change the export controls of the MTCR to include any offensive military application of ballistic missile technology, whether the warhead is conventional, chemical, biological, or nuclear.

This policy option has a serious drawback: one change in the regime will open the floodgates to other potential changes. France, for example, might use the opportunity to seek greater leeway for supplying technology for peaceful space programs. Because this is a serious concern that should be addressed, the second policy option might be undertaken simultaneously.

2. Establish an international space agency. This option follows up on a Soviet suggestion that the United States agree to negotiate an international

space organization. The USSR has raised this idea in a number of contexts, including ballistic missile control, although it has not fleshed out the details of the proposal.

Washington should explore with Moscow whether an organization might be formed that would, in return for a state's signing an international INF treaty, provide space-related services, such as the design and construction of satellites, launchings, tracking and data analysis, and verification of treaties.

Such an offer of international assistance would probably appeal to many states with indigenous space efforts. These states wish to have access to communications and intelligence gathering, but are suffering from the immense financial burdens and from difficulties in getting pertinent technology. Already, verification by multinationally controlled satellites is being used. For example, West European defense and foreign ministers agreed in November 1989 to create a European satellite agency to verify a conventional arms agreement.

3. An international INF treaty. The Soviet-American Intermediate Nuclear Forces Treaty provides an attractive, practical model for an international treaty. It simply bans all ground-launched ballistic missiles with a range of 500-5,500 km.

Because the United States and the Soviet Union have already accepted the ban, they are in an ideal position to call upon other states to forswear such missiles. Traditionally, one of the problems with arms control measures, such as nuclear nonproliferation, has been a division of the world into "haves" and "have-nots." In the case of INF, the United States and the Soviet Union have already taken the steps that they would be asking developing states to take.

Of course, an international INF agreement would still allow countries to develop intercontinental ballistic missiles (with a range over 5,500 km). But the banning of IRBMs would probably stand in the way of developing ICBMs, both technically and financially. It would simply be hard to develop an ICBM without testing missiles of the IRBM range—which would be prohibited under the international INF agreement. And given the high risk of failure, few countries would be willing to go to the expense of developing ICBMs when they cannot test missiles in the IRBM range.

Another argument against an international INF agreement is the probability that U.S. allies, particularly France, would not like it and would not join. That may be true. However, an international INF agreement need not have French participation to be successful. The Nuclear Non-Proliferation Treaty, one of the most adhered-to arms control treaties, does not have French participation. Also, France may be increasingly motivated to participate in an international INF treaty, if it means getting rid of the Middle East IRBMs that may someday target Paris.

An important point to the idea of an international INF agreement is that it would be verifiable by the same means used to verify the Soviet-American INF: satellite verification, on-site inspection, and other methods. This is crucial to gaining participation by states that suspect or know their neighbors are acquiring IRBMs. Israel, Egypt, Syria, Iraq, and Iran, for example, are unlikely to accept restraint until they are convinced that all states in their region are willing to give up existing missiles as well as future missile development.

4. *Develop antiballistic missile programs.* Even if there were an international ban on INF-range ballistic missiles, some countries would still be threatened. In the Middle East, for example, enemy states are so close that missiles with ranges of less than 500 km pose a danger. Those states that agree to give up INF-range missiles should be offered assistance in developing short-range antitactical ballistic missiles (ATBMs).

Currently, the United States has a venture with Israel to develop an ATBM, called the Arrow Program. To attract other states to sign a pledge not to develop INF-range ballistic missiles, the United States and the Soviet Union should share ATBM technology with signatories of an international INF treaty.

No specialized ATBM has thus far been deployed. Efforts should be made to accelerate the program and make ATBM technology operational, so that it will be available as a means of discouraging worldwide ballistic missile proliferation. Until these systems are operational, programs similar to the U.S.-Israeli Arrow program should be generated for those who are willing to give up INF-range ballistic missiles, but who remain threatened.

CONCLUSION

The MTCR contains too many deficiencies to serve as the sole means of fighting ballistic missile proliferation. These deficiencies need to be rectified, and other tools employed.

One crucial issue that must be addressed is: How can states obtain access to the peaceful use of space without developing a ballistic missile capacity? One way is for the great powers to offer other states assistance with their space programs through an international organization—but only in return for a state's commitment not to develop ballistic missiles. Such a pledge could be made by adherence to an international treaty, based on the U.S.-Soviet Intermediate-range Nuclear Forces Treaty. The problems that remain, especially with short-range ballistic missiles below the INF range, could be addressed with programs to help states develop antitactical ballistic missiles.

38. MAD Dogs and Congressmen: Arguments against SDI are Impotent and Obsolete

Baker Spring

Congressional interest in missile defenses is likely to increase as uncertainty grows about control over 30,000 Soviet nuclear warheads.

It is therefore useful to review the criticisms that have been leveled at the strategic defense initiative (SDI) since the program's founding in March 1983. Because SDI undermines the key tenet of liberal foreign policy, the doctrine of mutual assured destruction (MAD), liberal criticism has been shrill. But the shrillness of the voices has only highlighted the distortions and scare tactics resorted to in the campaign to kill SDI.

In general, five criticisms have been leveled at the SDI program since its inception: it would be too expensive; it wouldn't provide 100 percent protection; it would create strategic instability and make nuclear war with the Soviet Union more likely; it would jeopardize U.S.-Soviet relations, particularly in the field of arms control; and it just was not technically feasible.

Each of these criticisms was of questionable validity in the mid-1980s, and subsequent events have shown them to be completely groundless.

CRITICISM #1: COST

The easiest way to terminate a defense program is to call it unaffordable, as supporters of the B-2 bomber program can attest. The "sticker shock" tactic has been resorted to with particular zeal by the opponents of SDI, who have put forth outrageous estimates of what it would cost to deploy an SDI system. Jimmy Carter's defense secretary, Harold Brown, warned in 1983, "The proposed defenses against nuclear attack, which could well

SOURCE: Baker Spring, "MAD Dogs and Congressmen: Arguments Against SDI Are Impotent and Obsolete," *Policy Review*, Fall 1991, pp. 79–81, excerpts. Reprinted by permission of the Heritage Foundation. All rights reserved.

become the first trillion-dollar defense system, would then constitute a nightmare rather than a hope we would leave to our children in the 21st century." "It would cost something like a trillion dollars to test and deploy weapons," claimed Democratic candidate Walter Mondale in a 1984 presidential debate. By 1985, Sovietologist Stephen Shenfield had doubled the number, maintaining in the *Bulletin of Atomic Scientists*: "The total cost of a Star Wars [SDI] system may eventually reach $2 trillion."

Technological advances and changes in the SDI architecture have brought down significantly the cost of deploying such defenses. The existing Pentagon proposal for deploying an SDI system, referred to as Global Protection Against Limited Strikes (G-PALS), is now estimated to cost about $42 billion, about 2 percent of Shenfield's estimate. This puts the cost of an SDI system within the same general category as other strategic systems. For example, the B-2 program is now estimated to cost about $65 billion; and while there are no firm estimates for the cost of the Midgetman missile system it will likely turn out to cost between $30 billion and $40 billion.

CRITICISM #2: THE NEED FOR A PERFECT DEFENSE

Perhaps the strangest criticism leveled at SDI is the assertion that no defense against missile attacks would be worth deploying unless it were virtually 100 percent effective against a large-scale Soviet nuclear strike. This straw-man argument is constructed to convince the public that there is no practical alternative to the doctrine of mutually assured destruction (MAD). It sets an artificially high standard for SDI, which SDI critics know would be impossible to meet. Harold Brown argued in a March 1983 *Washington Post* column: "If a single weapon can destroy a city of hundreds of thousands, only a perfect defense (which, moreover, works perfectly the first time) will suffice."

The standard set by Brown for deploying SDI would prevent the deployment of any U.S. weapons system. No weapons system will work perfectly every time. But what makes Brown's argument against SDI so disingenuous is the assertion that limited or imperfect defenses have no value. The Patriot system, which performed so well in the Persian Gulf War, did not provide a perfect defense. Still, nobody would argue today that U.S. forces and allies would have been better off if the Patriot had not been sent to Israel and Saudi Arabia because of its imperfections. The Senate vote this summer was a direct repudiation of Brown's criticism of SDI. The senators recognized that there is considerable value in protecting the United States and its allies against accidental or small-scale missile strikes.

CRITICISM #3: STRATEGIC INSTABILITY

Liberal critics of the SDI program have taken great pains to charge that the deployment of strategic defenses would increase strategic instability and therefore increase the risk of nuclear war. Editor John Tirman in a publication of the Union of Concerned Scientists made the connection between strategic stability and continued vulnerability explicit: "[A]n attempt by either super-power to protect its population or to develop counterforce weapons designed to attack the other's nuclear forces would be destabilizing. Either of these actions would erode the assured destruction capability of the adversary, undermining mutual deterrence by creating the possibility of a successful first strike."

It is important to remember that the liberal embrace of a strategy of mutual vulnerability underlies an ambitious arms control agenda. As Stanford physicists Sidney Drell and Wolfgang Panofsky wrote in the fall 1984 *Issues in Science and Technology*, "A further serious risk is that the effort to neutralize the effect of nuclear weapons by deploying nationwide missile defenses might make the use of such weapons appear to be more acceptable,

thereby deflecting efforts to reduce through negotiations the dangers and burdens of arms competition."

The liberal orthodoxy concerning nuclear vulnerability cannot stand up to scrutiny. No self-respecting society would ever purposely leave itself open to attack. But liberals have come to view such vulnerability as a necessity, subordinating American national security to the quest for improved relations with the Soviet Union. This is why arms control became such a critical element of the liberal agenda. As Drell and Panofsky candidly admitted, they want to use strategic vulnerability to force U.S.-Soviet cooperation. The implicit message is that the United States cannot be trusted to be a responsible power, and therefore MAD's constraints on U.S. foreign policy is a healthy thing.

But MAD itself is a destabilizing doctrine full of internal contradictions. First, purposeful vulnerability is an open invitation to the Soviet Union to build strategic missiles capable of destroying U.S. retaliatory forces, which is exactly what the Soviets did in the 1970s and 1980s. The U.S. inability to protect its retaliatory forces allowed the Soviet Union to devise a carefully designed plan for a first strike without worrying about the complications or uncertainties that U.S. strategic defenses would impose.

Second, liberal criticism of strategic defenses has been one-sided. The Soviet Union historically has spent about 50 percent of its strategic budget on defenses. As of now the Soviets have 2,800 strategic defense weapons. The U.S. has none. The Soviet Union has deployed an anti-ballistic missile (ABM) system around Moscow, fielded extensive air defenses, and possesses the world's most ambitious civil defense plan. All of these are designed to reduce Soviet vulnerability to nuclear attack.

Perhaps no episode better demonstrates the extent of the liberal double standard than the debate over whether the Soviet Union's phased-array radar near the town of Krasnoyarsk violates the 1972 Anti-Ballistic Missile (ABM) Treaty, which all but bans anti-missile defenses. Liberal Congressmen Bob Carr of Michigan, Thomas Downey of New York, and Jim Moody of Wisconsin reported after they visited the radar facility in September 1987:

". . . we judge it to be not a violation of the ABM Treaty at this time." Two years later Soviet Foreign Minister Eduard Shevardnadze stated: "[T]he construction of this [radar] station, equal in size to the Egyptian pyramids, constituted an open violation of the ABM Treaty." Even Soviet leaders feel compelled to admit what SDI critics seek to deny about Soviet intentions toward building strategic defenses.

Liberals seldom criticize these Soviet programs, which also undercut a policy of mutual vulnerability. Finally, SDI critics fail to explain how purposeful vulnerability, supposedly stabilizing in terms of a purposeful Soviet strike, would not be destabilizing in terms of an accidental or unauthorized Soviet strike or attacks from third countries.

CRITICISM #4: SOVIET OPPOSITION

SDI critics have taken at face value claims by the Soviets that they were unalterably opposed to U.S. deployment of anti-missile defenses. In essence, the Soviet Union threatened to balk at reducing offensive nuclear arsenals if the United States proceeded with SDI. Liberal critics of the SDI program then argued that SDI jeopardized the arms control process. As Senator Joseph Biden of Delaware stated in 1986: "The Soviets are in fact [through their opposition to SDI] expressing no more than the simple logic of arms control, which is that neither side, in its own interest, can agree to sharp reductions in offensive weaponry when faced with the prospect of defensive deployments by the other."

But the fact that these Soviet statements were part of a negotiating ploy, and not truly reflective of Soviet strategic thinking, sometimes put SDI critics in embarrassing positions. For example, after months of parroting Soviet statements that there would be no Intermediate-range Nuclear Forces (INF) Treaty unless SDI were curtailed, liberals were shame-faced when the Soviets announced in February 1987 that an INF Treaty could be concluded without resolution of the "SDI problem." The INF Treaty was signed later that year, while the SDI program continues to this day. SDI critics are now parroting the same type of statements by the Soviets concerning the implementation of the Strategic Arms Reduction Treaty (START).

But reductions in offensive nuclear arsenals are not incompatible with the deployment of non-threatening strategic defenses. In fact, much of the early discussion at the Defense and Space Talks (DST), which are the U.S.-Soviet negotiations concerning SDI, focused on when, not if, defensive deployments would take place. At the December 1987 Washington summit Soviet leader Mikhail Gorbachev agreed to a joint communique that stated it was the objective of both sides to set a period of time after which each could deploy strategic defenses, notwithstanding the restrictions of the ABM Treaty. The same communique committed both sides to proceeding expeditiously with negotiations to reduce offensive nuclear arsenals through START. The 1987 communique gives testimony to Soviet willingness to agree to both the deployment of strategic defenses and the reduction of strategic offensive arsenals, as long as the United States does not allow the Soviet Union to gain unilateral advantage. The SDI program has proved to be our strongest negotiating tool for arms control.

CRITICISM #5: A DEFENSE IS NOT FEASIBLE

The final argument SDI critics have resorted to in their attempts to kill the program is that a defense against ballistic missiles is not technically feasible. As Senator John Kerry of Massachusetts charged on the Senate floor in 1985: "We will never know [whether SDI will work], because among other things we could never test the system under realistic wartime conditions ahead of time." Also, an army of liberal scientists and engineers spent countless hours studying ways the Soviet Union could "easily" counter such defenses. The list of Soviet "countermeasures" was lengthy. It included using fast-burn missile boosters, deploying elaborate decoys, shooting down U.S. satellite systems, and increasing the strength of missile bodies to withstand laser attacks. The same scientists and engineers also produced an impressive list of things that they thought would go wrong with an

SDI system. They included computer failures, communications breakdowns, and false warnings of attacks from sensors.

The argument that it is not feasible to shoot down ballistic missiles in flight was itself shot down by the performance of the Patriot missile in the Persian Gulf War. Millions of Americans saw on television that anti-missile defenses work. It is important to note that the Patriot had only received limited testing as an anti-missile weapon and had never been used in actual combat prior to the Persian Gulf War.

SDI critics have since retreated from the assertion that it is impossible to shoot down at least shorter-range missiles under combat conditions. But they maintain that long-range strategic missiles are much more difficult to shoot down than Scuds, particularly when such missiles are coupled with Soviet countermeasures. What the critics do not say is that the G-PALS system plans include interceptors much more capable than the Patriot to counter strategic missiles. It includes three layers of defenses, where the Patriot afforded only one. Space-based interceptors called "Brilliant Pebbles" would stop incoming missiles in their boost phase before they released individual warheads. Another interceptor, called the Ground-Based Interceptor (GBI) would smash individual warheads outside the atmosphere. The final interceptor, called the Exoatmospheric/Endoatmospheric Interceptor, would have the capability to counter strategic warheads after they have re-entered the atmosphere and decoys have been stripped away. This layered defense will be very effective against missile strikes of up to 200 warheads regardless of what countermeasures the Soviets choose to incorporate into their missiles.

OLD ORTHODOXIES

Old orthodoxies die hard. Just this July, Senator Carl Levin, a member of the Armed Services Committee, attacked in a *Washington Post* op-ed the Nunn-Warner plan to deploy limited strategic defenses. He maintained that limited deployment should be scuttled because it would not protect the entire country, would not counter other threats such as "suitcases from nuclear terrorists," and that it would "plunge us into a new round of arms competition with the Soviets." It can be expected that critics of the SDI program will continue to argue that keeping America vulnerable to missile attacks is essential.

But it is an argument they are destined to lose. If for no other reason, the argument in opposition to strategic defenses will lose because it is the product of a liberal dream world, in which both the Soviet Union and the United States would jettison their national interests and even jeopardize their national security in the pursuit of better relations. It is a world where arms control is substituted for a rational and balanced security policy. It is a world in which accidents or miscalculations would never occur. Finally, it is a world where neither the U.S. nor the Soviet Union would face the threat of missile attacks from third countries. In short, the opposition to anti-missile defenses will have to succumb to the unbending forces of reality. The only question that remains is how much longer will it take.

39.   A Weapon without a Purpose

Kosta Tsipis

The political attractiveness of ballistic missile defenses continues undiminished in this country. Some U.S. conservatives still dream of a perfect defense that would let the United States destroy its adversaries with impunity, and they resent the loss of sovereignty that the prevailing doctrine of nuclear deterrence implies. This doctrine makes the security of the United States dependent on the good sense and realism of Soviet leaders, whose fear of certain U.S. retaliation would deter them from attacking the United States. The general public, meanwhile, filled with notions of the omnipotence of this nation's technology, would like to believe that American ingenuity could protect them from any threat—nuclear holocaust included. Apparently, Americans still yearn for the insular security the country enjoyed before the advent of nuclear explosives and ballistic missiles. The problem with such concepts of national security is that they have been, and remain, impossible.

That there is no rational reason to pursue ballistic-missile defenses is illustrated by the fact that ABM advocates have summoned up a non-event—the performance of the Patriot ground-based anti-ballistic missiles against Iraqi Scuds—to bolster their position. In his 1991 State of the Union message, President Bush, citing the "success" of the Patriots, called for support for a refocused Star Wars program "to provide protection from limited ballistic-missile strikes whatever their source." In February, Sen. Malcolm Wallop (R-Wyo.) wrote a *New York Times* op-ed piece ("Patriots' Point the Way") in which he advocated, as he has in the past, abrogating the ABM Treaty and proceeding full speed ahead in developing and deploying Star Wars. Meanwhile, congressional opponents of space-based defenses, including Rep. Les Aspin

SOURCE: Kosta Tsipis, "A Weapon Without a Purpose," *Technology Review*, November/December 1991, pp. 53–58, excerpts. Reprinted with permission from *Technology Review*, copyright 1991.

(D-Wisc.), are using the Scud threat to push for ground-based ABMs and derail the deployment of Star Wars' space-based systems.

How did the Patriots perform? Despite the well-publicized fireworks over Tel Aviv and Riyadh, it is difficult to say definitively. The damage Scud missiles visited upon Israel was not demonstrably different before and after Patriots were installed there. This could mean the Patriot is ineffective against terrorizing attacks on cities, but another interpretation is more appropriate. Because Iraq unsuccessfully modified the Scuds, most of these missiles disintegrated upon reentering the atmosphere. As a result, there were few if any intact Scuds for Patriots to hit, so the performance of the Patriots was not actually tested. At best, then, their performance is unknown. This is hardly cause for optimism regarding the performance of ground-based ABM systems and even less a reason to invest heavily in them.

If the Gulf War provides a lesson, it is the success of cruise missiles. A future stealthy cruise missile could carry half a ton of high explosives, essentially unobserved, with almost perfect accuracy, over hundreds of miles. This kind of weapon would be relatively easy for a nation such as Iraq to develop or purchase and would be a genuine military threat to U.S. bases abroad. The United States should be pursuing battlefield anti-aircraft defenses against such weapons, not ABM systems.

In fact, for the foreseeable future, the United States faces only one credible threat that an ABM system might conceivably counter: an accidental or unauthorized nuclear attack from the Soviet Union, China, or, in the more distant future, emerging nuclear nations. But to counter even this threat, there exists a far simpler and better answer than an ABM system, both technically and politically: a self-disarming mechanism, installed on the nuclear warheads of all ballistic missiles, that could be instructed via radio to incapacitate the weapons and prevent unwanted nuclear detonations.

A SYSTEM IN SEARCH OF A MISSION

The United States began searching for a way to shoot down ballistic missiles in the late 1950s after Sputnik showed that the Soviet Union could apparently deliver thermonuclear weapons across intercontinental distances. But while the U.S. ABM system went through several incarnations, none could protect civilians from nuclear attack. First came the Nike-Zeus, a land-based system consisting of two types of nuclear-tipped missiles and radars that could track a few targets at a time. This was followed by the somewhat more sophisticated Nike-X, with phased-array radars that could engage many incoming warheads at once, and armed with the swifter Sprint and Spartan missiles, the first with a range of 10 to 20 miles, the second with a range of 300 miles. All these systems—indeed, all ground-based ABM systems intended to protect cities—shared two fatal flaws. First, they were terribly unpopular because defending cities meant deploying nuclear missiles in their suburbs; the Sprint missiles, for example, were nuclear-tipped. Second, nuclear detonations above or in the atmosphere would blind their radars. In fact, a nuclear-tipped defensive missile system would blind itself in the first few seconds of an engagement.

Nevertheless, under political pressure from the right to pursue missile defenses, in September 1967 the Johnson administration announced its intention to develop the Sentinel, a thin ABM system designed to counter the lesser Chinese threat. When that system fell victim to public opposition, the Nixon administration renamed it Safeguard and changed its mission to protecting Minuteman missile silos—but without altering it technically. Indeed, one Safeguard site was completed in North Dakota in 1975, but it was immediately shut down because the limited protection it offered to the silos wasn't worth its high cost: $600 million in 1973 and $340 million the following year.

Undaunted by the deactivation of the Safeguard site, in 1978 ABM enthusiasts attempted to advance an ABM system called LoADS (Low Altitude Defense System), this time to protect MX missiles that would be shuttling among 24 shelters arranged around a racetrack-shaped roadway planned for the deserts of Utah and Nevada. When the people of these states, with support from Nevada's usually pro-military Republican Senator Paul Laxalt, rejected this multiple-shelter basing mode, ABM advocates realized that ground-based ABM systems would probably never garner the necessary congressional support. While the Pentagon's budget soared in the first years of the Reagan administration, funding for the defensive systems remained low.

Space was the obvious alternative for basing antiballistic-missile defenses. First, Sen. Wallop championed space-based lasers, but the Pentagon's Defense Science Board rejected the idea in 1981. Next, in 1982, came "High Frontier," a proposal to orbit thousands of rockets that could be fired against Soviet ballistic missiles outside the atmosphere. When an Air Force study found that idea technically flawed, it too quickly dissolved as a serious option. . . .

Within months, however, on March 23, 1983, President Reagan proposed his "Star Wars" program to render nuclear-tipped ballistic missiles "impotent and obsolete," thereby protecting the nation from Soviet nuclear weapons "just as a roof protects a family from rain." Politically and psychologically, it was ingenious. As documents of that period indicate, the proposal was intended to co-opt the anti-nuclear message of the arms-control community and assuage the fears of nuclear war that had prompted over half a million people to demonstrate against the Reagan administration nine months earlier in New York City. Moreover, its exotic, space-borne character appealed to the science-fiction-fed younger generation, while some voters were heartened to see the government summon U.S. technological ingenuity to protect them from the Soviet nuclear threat. Finally, Star Wars countered the sense of interdependence with the Soviet Union that mutual assured destruction and nuclear deterrence imposed on the United States.

The trouble was that Star Wars I, Reagan's original proposal, couldn't work and was unfathomably expensive. Two years before the president's speech, technical studies performed by the MIT Program in Science and Technology for International Security had shown that the laws of nature make space-based population defenses impossible.

Laser and neutral-particle beams would lack the necessary lethality to destroy rising ICBMs many hundreds of miles away, and inexpensive countermeasures could blunt their effectiveness. Study after study since then has reached the same conclusion: it is impossible to protect civilians against an opponent like the Soviet Union. Even the most sophisticated Star Wars defenses would be vulnerable to countermeasures that could be implemented at one-tenth the cost of the system itself.

History began repeating itself. Once it became clear that protecting cities was impossible, the Strategic Defense Initiative Organization (SDIO), the Pentagon agency created to run the Star Wars project, shifted ground. Star Wars II directed essentially the same technology to protecting missile silos, thereby supposedly enhancing deterrence, an admission that the pre-Reagan doctrine of mutual assured destruction was still the only viable way to protect the United States from nuclear attack.

However, the end of the Cold War has left even Star Wars II lacking a credible mission, as the probability of a deliberate nuclear attack against the United States by the Soviet Union or China is dwindling to that of attack by France or England. Thus SDIO has once again shifted the mission and name of the system originally proposed meant to protect cities. The new name is "Global Protection Against Limited Strikes" (GPALS), a space-based system that SDIO claims can deal with some post-Cold War threats but *not* with most short-range ballistic missiles like the Scud.

The events of the Gulf War added a politically resonant mission for ballistic-missile defenses. But does the threat from short-range tactical ballistic missiles, or any other threat for that matter, make an ABM system militarily relevant?

POST-COLD WAR THREATS

For at least the decade ahead, the United States might conceivably face any of five ballistic-missile threats.

- A current nuclear power could deliberately launch a nuclear attack.
- A near-nuclear nation—for example, India,

Pakistan, or South Africa—could acquire both nuclear warheads and the long-range ballistic missiles to deliver them and launch a deliberate nuclear attack.
- A terrorist group might acquire one or more nuclear explosives and use them against a U.S. city.
- An enemy might launch tactical ballistic missiles such as the Iraqi Scuds, either with nuclear or conventional warheads, against U.S. military bases or forces overseas.
- An unauthorized or accidental nuclear attack might emanate from the Soviet Union, China, or any other nuclear nation with ballistic missiles.

To begin with, not only is a deliberate Soviet or Chinese attack highly improbable now that the Cold War has ended, but the United States already has the proven means to prevent it. Deterrence worked through the darkest days of the Cold War; it will continue to work in the future. That implies the need for the United States to retain a secure retaliatory force of a few hundred nuclear weapons, but at the same time it obviates any need for ballistic-missile defenses. What's more, as the United States and the Soviet Union reduce their arsenals of multi-warhead land-based missiles, the need to enhance deterrence with an ABM defense for missile silos evaporates.

The same deterring mechanism that has kept Soviet and Chinese communists at bay can restrain newcomers to the nuclear club. No political leader would invite the obliteration of his or her country by attempting to destroy a U.S. city. Self-preservation and self-interest, the sturdy underpinnings of deterrence, are concerns that no national leader can ignore.

Still, Iraq's use of Scud missiles against Saudi Arabia and Israel has prompted some to assert that deterrence may not always dissuade new nuclear powers. For example, Rep. Aspin observed in April that "Saddam Hussein wasn't deterred. He faced virtual destruction of his nation, yet he still used ballistic missiles against U.S. forces and our friends." The flaw in this argument is that deterrence applies only to weapons of mass destruction, not to conventional weapons, whether delivered by plane or missile. Directing a Scud against Tel Aviv to provoke Israel into war has little in common with a nuclear-armed missile aimed at New York—the threat we are concerned with here—or even Tel Aviv. In fact, Saddam Hussein *was* deterred from using weapons of mass destruction. Although Iraq possesses chemical weapons, the assurance of retaliation in kind apparently stopped it from wielding them either against U.S. troops in the battlefield or our allies' urban centers in the region.

An ABM system, no matter how effective, can't counter the third threat, a terrorist nuclear attack, because the nuclear weapons wouldn't be delivered by a ballistic missile. A terrorist group that procured or manufactured a nuclear explosive would attempt to carry it clandestinely into the United States by means—such as boat, plane, or truck—that no antiballistic missile could intercept. Furthermore, even if a stateless terrorist group had a ballistic missile, it would be highly unlikely to use it against the United States because the attack could be traced to the country of launch, which then would face nuclear retaliation. Deterrence would apply in this case as well.

We come to the fourth threat—tactical short-range ballistic missiles with ranges up to 1,000 kilometers wielded against U.S. allies around the world or U.S. military forces abroad. This is a two-part question because the threat from such missiles carrying conventional warheads is fundamentally different from that of nuclear-tipped missiles.

Tactical ballistic missiles with conventional warheads are not accurate enough to be militarily significant. Even with sophisticated and expensive guidance systems, a tactical ballistic missile with a 1,000 kilometer range can only come within 60 to 100 meters of a target. Even armed with a half-ton of high explosives, such a weapon has little probability of destroying a bridge, communications center, runway, or aircraft shelter.

Still, conventionally armed missiles are effective "terror weapons" when aimed at cities. From the German V-2 missile attacks on London in World War II to the missiles used in the Iran-Iraq war and the Gulf War, these weapons have terrorized civilians. Partially effective ground-based defenses against such attacks may become more feasible as the technology advances. But since this type of attack can't reach the United States, should U.S. taxpayers pay for protecting allied cities from it?

A tactical ballistic missile with a nuclear warhead could destroy military targets such as airfields or communications and transportation nodes, but the 1987 INF Treaty between the United States and the Soviet Union has banned such intermediate-range nuclear weapons from the arsenals of the two nations. And although new nuclear countries could develop these weapons, it is doubtful they would use them against U.S. forces, given the ability of the United States to respond devastatingly.

In any case, defenses against nuclear tactical ballistic missiles would be technically difficult. Ground-based defenses would face the same problem that defeated the ABM systems of the 1960s and 1970s: a nuclear detonation preceding the main attack could blind their radars. And GPALS' reach isn't low enough to knock out tactical ballistic missiles, which barely leave the atmosphere. SDIO director Henry Cooper has testified that the system's "brilliant pebbles"—orbiting self-contained missiles that would detect and attack ballistic missiles on their own—couldn't hit missiles at altitudes below 100 kilometers.

One can conclude that the United States needs no further defense against tactical ballistic missiles: conventional warheads aren't a significant military threat; nuclear warheads, if ever built, wouldn't be used against U.S. forces abroad for fear of retaliation. Thus to invoke the threat from such missiles as justification for pouring money into theater defenses is simply irrational.

THE ACCIDENT THREAT

That brings us to the last threat, and the one that merits the most careful consideration. Even after successful negotiations to reduce their strategic nuclear arsenals, both the United States and the Soviet Union will each retain between 6,000 and 9,000 intercontinental nuclear weapons through the end of the century and perhaps beyond; 4,900 of them on either side will be ballistic-missile warheads. Even if negotiations lead to further reductions, it is doubtful that either nation will reduce its arsenal to under 1,000 warheads in the foreseeable future.

Yet even as the number of nuclear weapons and the probability of their deliberate use declines, the risk of either an accidental or an unauthorized launch of strategic missiles remains. In an accident, a launch crew is convinced it has a valid order to act when in fact none has been issued. A missile launch is unauthorized if the crew acts without a command from the proper national authorities.

These two scenarios demand proportionately more attention as the prospects of a deliberate nuclear exchange diminish. Bomber-delivered nuclear weapons can be recalled or intercepted hours after their dispatch, but neither ballistic missiles nor long-range nuclear cruise missiles are recallable. Remote though it may be, the possibility of an unsanctioned launch of one or more nuclear delivery vehicles is real and presents the only danger of a nuclear attack on the United States.

The probability of a peacetime accidental launch of a U.S. or Soviet land-based missile is very small, but it can increase somewhat during practice exercises. And during a deepening crisis, when controls are relaxed and launch crews are under enormous stress, an accidental launch of one or more such weapons is not unthinkable.

An accidental ballistic-missile launch from a submarine is even more probable, whether during peacetime or a crisis. This is primarily because central authorities have no physical control over submarine-launched ballistic missiles. The probability that an entire submarine crew could misinterpret a message as an authorization to launch its missiles is, no doubt, minute during peacetime, but it, too, can be amplified by the uncertainty and tension brought on by a crisis. Because Soviet and U.S. ballistic-missile submarines each carry nearly 200 nuclear warheads, any system to protect the United States from an accident would have to be able to intercept this many warheads arriving in a brief period of time, in a narrow corridor of space, and from any point on the compass.

As for unauthorized attacks, elaborate launch procedures for both land-based silos and submarines are designed to thwart but do not eliminate cases where, for instance, a rogue commander might persuade the officers and crew to launch. Over-zealous, psychotic, treacherous, or (espe-

cially in the case of the present-day Soviet Union) parochial launch controllers in some renegade region could attempt an unauthorized launch during peacetime, a crisis, or even negotiations aimed at ending a war. Again, the probability of such an episode is higher in a crisis and for submarines.

There are two conceivable ways to avoid the catastrophe of accidental or unauthorized launches of nuclear ballistic missiles.

The first is an ABM system, based either on the ground or in space, that shoots missiles down as they approach the United States. In January 1988, Sen. Sam Nunn (D-Ga.), chair of the Armed Services Committee, suggested that the United States redirect SDI research toward developing a limited shield against a potential accidental or unauthorized ballistic-missile launch. His proposed "accidental launch protection system" (ALPS) would use land-based—as opposed to Star Wars' space-based—high acceleration interceptor missiles to destroy a few warheads as they reenter the atmosphere. At the end of July 1991, the Senate voted 60-39 to fund essentially this proposal.

While no current interceptor missiles could stop a reentry vehicle, two under development are prime candidates for Sen. Nunn's system—the Exoatmospheric Reentry Interceptor System (ERIS) and the High Endoatmospheric Defense Interceptor (HEDI). Both weapons are relatively short-range; consequently, many of them would have to be deployed to cover the entire perimeter of the nation, given that submarine-launched nuclear warheads could come from the Pacific, Gulf of Mexico, Arctic, or Atlantic basins, and a ballistic-missile attack from the Soviet Union or China would come from the north. Depending on how widely some 200 sophisticated reentry vehicles could spread, Sen. Nunn's idea could require as many as several thousand ground-based interceptors. For now, the Senate has authorized 100 interceptors to be deployed by 1996. Ironically, it wants to base them at the old Safeguard site in North Dakota.

Not only would the ALPS deployment require renegotiating and probably drastically changing the ABM Treaty, but it also could arrest or reverse efforts to reduce the nuclear arsenals of the superpowers. The Soviet Union could perceive an ABM deployment in the United States as a threat to *its* nuclear deterrent and might then proceed to build more warheads to ensure that its weapons could penetrate U.S. defenses.

Nor could such a system assuredly shoot down every rogue warhead aimed at the United States. The system would be especially vulnerable to low-flying, submarine-launched ballistic missiles and cruise missiles launched close to U.S. shores.

For its part, SDIO has proposed assigning defenses against accidental or unauthorized nuclear attacks to the GPALS system of about a thousand of the so-called brilliant pebbles. However, such a system would offer little protection for two reasons. First, the brilliant pebbles would have to be turned off during peacetime to avoid attacking civilian space launches. Since an accidental or unauthorized launch can't be foreseen, it could occur while GPALS was on non-alert status. Second, only a few brilliant pebbles would be in range of an accidental or unauthorized launch at any time. At best, they could intercept only a fraction of the rogue weapons released by, say, a submarine. And, as with the ALPS proposal, deploying GPALS would destroy the ABM Treaty, an eventuality some Star Wars supporters might welcome but one most people would oppose. Finally, SDIO estimates the cost of GPALS to be about $40 billion, but estimates by independent experts put it at twice that price.

Thus neither ground-based nor space-based ballistic missile defenses can deal effectively with the threat of an accidental or unauthorized attack against the United States. Fortunately, a sound alternative exists.

A FAIL-SAFE SOLUTION

The difficulties of erecting an effective antiballistic-missile system to counter this last type of threat have prompted the emergence of another solution: simple self-destruct devices installed on all ballistic missiles of all nations. Just as NASA safety officers can, and often do, destroy civilian space launches that go awry, so can ballistic missiles carrying nuclear weapons be destroyed remotely.

This approach has two requirements—one technical, one diplomatic. The first is that an opponent couldn't exploit the self-destruct system to blunt an intended nuclear attack. The second is that all nations with nuclear ballistic missiles adopt such self-destruct mechanisms.

Several schemes have been proposed for fulfilling the technical requirement. A ballistic missile is armed at the end of its boost phase by an on-board computer that ascertains it is on the right trajectory. A coded destruct command beamed from one or more safety-control centers in each nation would either prevent the arming process in accidental or unauthorized missiles or incapacitate the warheads in some other way.

There have been numerous suggestions, some simple, some complex, on how to prevent an opponent from intercepting or duplicating the destruct command during an intended attack. A recent research report of MIT's Program in Science and Technology for International Security describes how this can be accomplished by using randomly generated numbers and encrypted codes to initiate the self-destruct procedure. One approach is to have the missile computer and the computer at the ground control center generate a secret destruct code at exactly the same time and to change the code every few minutes. When the missile is launched, a signal automatically notifies the control center. If the launch is unwanted, the safety control center sends the destruct code to the missile via satellite. The nuclear weapons on the missile disarm when the codes on the missile computer and from the safety control center match.

Admittedly, this effective and safe approach raises several technical issues, but all are solvable. For example, where would the receiver of the destruct signal be located? It could be on the missile itself, giving the safety-control center only a few hundred seconds to incapacitate an unwanted launch, or it could be on the individual reentry vehicles, which would allow 15 minutes or more. But putting the receiver on missiles would be relatively simple and inexpensive, while placing it on reentry vehicles would require lengthy and expensive modification of existing reentry vehicles—they would have to be reconfigured and retested extensively unless the self-destruct mechanisms maintained the vehicle's current physical parameters, such as center of gravity and moments of inertia.

Another technical question would be the exact means to incapacitate the warheads. Detonating the nuclear weapon in outer space would generate a giant electromagnetic pulse that would play havoc with satellites and electronics on the ground; detonating the conventional high explosives in the warhead would spread plutonium in outer space. To merely incapacitate the arming or fusing mechanisms could cause intense plutonium contamination at the point of impact.

Not long before his latest Senate proposal to install a ground-based ABM system, Sen. Nunn had suggested that a self-destruct system for ballistic missiles with nuclear warheads be seriously studied, and, indeed, careful investigation of these issues is in order. The advantages are clear-cut: such a system would assure that *every* warhead in an accidental or unauthorized nuclear attack could be prevented from reaching its target, avoid the political and arms-control complications that would result from violating or abrogating the ABM Treaty, and save tens of billions of dollars by abandoning the irrational pursuit of ballistic-missile defenses of all kinds, ground-based or of the Star Wars variety.

So far at least, no military or government officials have raised objections to a self-destruct system for ballistic missiles. The technology for this solution exists; diplomatic negotiation to adopt it is the rational next step.

Questions for Discussion

1. How did U.S. nuclear strategy evolve?
2. What is SDI? How has it evolved since 1983?
3. Do fears of proliferation warrant a thin "star wars" deployment?
4. How effective an organization has the MTCR been?
5. What options are open to the United States in its aim of curtailing nuclear proliferation?
6. What are the arguments for and against the development of a space-based strategic defense system?
7. Is proliferation a threat to the United States?

Selected Bibliography

ADELMAN, KENNETH. *The Great Universal Embrace*. New York: Simon & Schuster, 1989.

BERKOWITZ, BRUCE D. *Calculated Risks: A Century of Arms Control, Why It Has Failed, and How It Can Be Made to Work*. New York: Simon & Schuster, 1988.

BROAD, WILLIAM J. *Teller's War*. New York: Simon & Schuster, 1992.

BRODIE, BERNARD (Ed.). *The Absolute Weapon*. New York: Harcourt, Brace, 1946.

FISCHER, DAVID. *Stopping the Spread of Nuclear Weapons: The Past and the Prospects*. New York: Routledge, 1992.

FLOURNOY, MICHELE A. *Nuclear Weapons after the Cold War: Guidelines for U.S. Policy*. New York: HarperCollins, 1993.

GLYNN, PATRICK. *Closing Pandora's Box: Arms Races, Arms Control and the History of the Cold War*. New York: Basic Books, 1992.

JERVIS, ROBERT. *The Meaning of the Nuclear Revolution: Statecraft and the Prospect of Armageddon*. Ithaca: Cornell University Press, 1989.

KULL, STEVEN. *Minds at War: Nuclear Reality and the Inner Conflicts of Defense Policymakers.* New York: Basic Books, 1989.

LAKOFF, SANFORD, and HERBERT S. YORK. *A Shield in Space? Technology, Politics and the Strategic Defense Initiative.* Berkeley: University of California Press, 1990.

NOLAN, JANNE E. *Guardians of the Arsenal: The Politics of Nuclear Strategy.* New York: Basic Books, 1989.

TALBOTT, STROBE. *Deadly Gambits: The Reagan Administration and the Stalemate in Nuclear Arms Control.* New York: Vintage, 1985.

ZUCHERMAN, LORD SOLLY. *Star Wars in a Nuclear World.* London: William Kimber, 1986.

CHAPTER 13

Is the United Nations Still Mankind's Last Best Hope for Peace?

In the closing days of World War II, the enthusiasm of the Western powers for a new international organization to replace the defunct League of Nations led to the establishment of the United Nations (UN) in April 1945. As one of the founders, and because of its enormous power and prestige, the United States was thrust into a position of instant leadership. The organization, however, became quickly polarized, as the Cold War increasingly touched all aspects of world politics. From the very first session of the UN Security Council in January 1946, when the USSR was severely criticized for its failure to withdraw Soviet troops from Iran in accordance with the 1942 agreement among Iran, Britain, and the USSR, Washington and Moscow emerged as prime adversaries.

U.S. assumptions about the UN proved to be overly optimistic. Washington had assumed that the five permanent members of the Security Council, namely, the leaders of the wartime coalition against Germany and Japan (the United States, the USSR, Britain, France, and China), would continue to work together to preserve the peace. Instead, the UN scene was permeated by antagonism between the Western countries and the Soviet bloc. Also, being *the* great power in 1945, the United States expected that its views would predominate in the Security Council, the General Assembly, and other ancillary bodies of the UN. But by the early 1960s, the mushrooming membership of newly independent Third World countries began to play an active political role that had not been envisaged by the UN's founding fathers and that often conflicted with U.S. interests and preferences.

In the 1970s and 1980s, U.S. policymakers grew disenchanted with the UN, seeing it as an arena of conflict in which the Soviet Union often found a congenial coalition of Third World states prepared to criticize, thwart, and undermine U.S. interests. Washington believed that the goals for which the UN was created were being distorted, and that a double-standard reflected the strong undercurrent of anti-Americanism. The issues of contention varied from year to year, but the United States discerned certain harmful trends.

First, the UN General Assembly was radicalized. As a result of decolonization, more than 100 new nations acquired membership in the UN; in UN specialized agencies such as UNESCO (United Nations Educational, Scientific, and Cultural Organization), the International Labor Organization, and the International Atomic Energy Agency; and in regional economic commissions such as ECAFE (Economic Commission for Asia and the Far East). Third World blocs such as the Arab League and the Organization of African Unity (OAU) combined to outvote the Western countries and pass resolutions the effect of which would have been to mandate a shift of influence and resources from the West to the Third World. For example, the General Assembly espoused a New International Economic Order (NIEO) and at special sessions of UNCTAD (United Nations Conference on Trade and Development) pressed for trade concessions, easy loans, and debt rescheduling. On politically charged issues, such as the Arab-Israeli conflict, support for national self-determination, and opposition to "imperialism" (the term used to criticize American actions), it adopted highly partisan resolutions, as often to accommodate the preference of some bloc or other as to intensify pressure on the wealthier countries for economic concessions. For example, in 1975 the General Assembly's pro-Palestine Liberation Organization (PLO) position led it to adopt a resolution equating Zionism with "racism and racial discrimination." The effect was a heightening of anti-UN feelings in the United States. (This resolution was revoked in the fall of 1991.)

Second, Washington believed that the General Assembly's resolutions pressuring the West to contribute more to the development of less developed countries (LDCs) were heavily influenced by Soviet criticisms of imperialism and Western colonialism, and that its approach toward disarmament was unbalanced, since it was rarely objective in apportioning responsibility for the global arms race.

Third, successive U.S. administrations reacted to the UN's politicization and ever-expanding budget with calls for reform and with a growing alienation. As the largest single contributor to the United Nations, the United States pays 25 percent of the regular budget and 30 percent of peacekeeping costs. It has accused the UN Secretariat, and some of the specialized agencies, of mismanagement, wasteful programs, and top heavy salaries for permanent staff. After giving one year's notice, the Reagan administration withdrew from UNESCO on January 1, 1985, charging the organization with "an endemic hostility toward the institutions of a free society—particularly those that protect a free press, free markets and, above all, individual human rights. UNESCO's mismanagement also continues, and approximately 80 percent of its $374 million biennial budget is still spent at its Paris headquarters, leaving only 20 percent to be spent elsewhere."[1] Although unreconciled to UNESCO, the United States, has been encouraged by the UN budgetary committee's adoption of a system of consensus building in reaching final decisions, which in effect grants major contributors a veto over major increases in the budget.

Finally, the UN was ineffective in fulfilling its primary responsibility to promote international peace and security. Until the turnabout in U.S.-Soviet relations in the late 1980s and the development of détente, it was unable to end major conflicts in Vietnam, Afghanistan, Angola, Ethiopia, Cambodia, and Nicaragua. However, as foreign scholars have noted, the United States itself was partially responsible for undermining the UN's authority, for example, in the mid-1980s defying "the ruling of the International Court of Justice that assistance to the Nicaraguan Contras was contrary to international law" and vetoing "a Security Council resolution which merely drew attention to that judgment (although the US herself invoked the jurisdiction of the ICJ in the Iran hostage crisis in 1979)."[2]

---

[1] From the text of the U.S. government's statement of withdrawal, as published in *The New York Times*, December 20, 1984.

[2] Evan Luard, "The Contemporary Role of the United Nations," in Adam Roberts and Benedict Kingsbury (Eds.), *United Nations, Divided World*. Oxford, UK: Clarendon Press, 1988, p. 219.

Most of these U.S. criticisms were significantly moderated when Soviet policy toward the United Nations changed under Mikhail Gorbachev. As the East-West rivalry was replaced by widening cooperation, the diplomatic relationship between the United States and the Soviet Union altered beyond the most optimistic expectations of earlier interludes of détente. Gorbachev set the reconciliation in the UN in motion on September 17, 1987, when in a major article in *Pravda* he proposed the wider use of UN peacekeeping forces "in disengaging the troops of warring sides, and observing ceasefire and armistice agreements." His plan entailed greater use of the permanent members of the UN Security Council to guarantee regional security; cooperation in "uprooting international terrorism"; and more frequent recourse to the International Court of Justice "for consultative conclusions on international law disputes." On October 15, his sweeping proposals for revitalization of UN functions—not just in the area of peacekeeping—gained credibility when the Soviet government announced that it was paying its $225 million debt to the UN, of which $197 million was for peacekeeping operations and $28 million for the regular budget. With this sharp policy reversal, Gorbachev enhanced Soviet prestige and highlighted U.S. arrears to the UN. His commitment to a strengthened UN was demonstrated by the cooperative role of the USSR during the Gulf crisis. On August 2, 1990, Iraq's invasion and annexation of Kuwait prompted condemnation by a series of Security Council resolutions and the formation of a powerful multinational military force in Saudi Arabia under the leadership of the United States.

During the Gulf crisis (August 1990–March 1991), the UN worked as its creators had envisaged. After years of ineptitude and Cold War cleavages that exposed an unwillingness to condemn Third World aggressors, it reclaimed a major role in world affairs. From the beginning the Security Council, particularly the five permanent members, took the lead in isolating and defeating Iraq. The Arab League and the nonaligned movement were hopelessly divided and without resources to act.

Edward C. Luck and Toby Trister Gati, president and senior vice president for policy studies, respectively, of the United Nations Association of the USA, discern in the international community's determination to reverse Iraq's aggression a new opportunity for the UN to function as a collective security organization in the manner originally intended in the UN Charter (Reading 40). Their aim is to promote collective security through the United Nations. They discuss the policy implications of the UN's role in the Gulf crisis, the changes that are needed to help the UN function more effectively, and the special responsibility devolving on the United States.

Advocates of collective security, however, often underestimate the constraints imposed by a country's pursuit of its own national interest. No foreign policy option is more often mentioned then collective security—and none is more misunderstood or less frequently implemented. Quite simply, collective security stipulates that in the event of an aggression against one member of the international community all other members will immediately coalesce against the aggressor. It assumes that all states will be able to agree on who is the aggressor; that they will band together, irrespective of ideology, race, religion, economics, or ethnicity, in the common interest; and that such coalitions will disband, once an aggression has been thwarted. Further, it assumes a readiness to subsume one's own national interests, whatever they may be in regard to the country held to be an aggressor, to the general will of the international community.

Conceivably, the United Nations could become the foundation of a U.S. policy based on the principle of collective security. But in the UN, the collective decisionmaking on issues of peace and security is vested in the Security Council, particularly the five permanent members; and only as long as they are in agreement is a "collective" response to aggression possible. From 1945 to 1990 there had been no such concord among the permanent members. To assume that henceforth they will act collectively in all circumstances affecting international peace and security requires a wild leap of faith, a belief that the period we are entering heralds "an end to politics," an end to competitive interests that might divide the Big Five. Moreover, there are the other 183 UN members to consider. Most of them were left out of the process that led up to the decision to use force against Iraq. That is not a model of how a system of collective security is supposed to operate.

There are also reasons to believe that the United States is a problematic partisan of collective security. For one, it has not been a leader on the crucial issue of financing UN peacekeeping operations. Indeed, the United States is more than $800 million in arrears to the UN. It has not evinced any interest in establishing a reserve fund to help underwrite peacekeeping operations, for example, by offering to apply the cost of one B-2 bomber (about $2 billion), if others make comparable contributions. If the United States wants the UN to be the main instrument for preserving the peace, then it

must become a reliable and generous contributor whose financial commitments set the standard. Otherwise, the means will invariably fall short of the ends. Conflict containment in Bosnia, Cambodia, Lebanon, Cyprus, the Western Sahara, Angola, and elsewhere depends on greatly expanded financial commitments. For another, the United States has not been willing to bring problems affecting its national interests before the Security Council. The past cannot serve as a pattern for the future; the United States was quick to use the UN to isolate Cuba, but not to discuss its own intervention in Vietnam or unilateral use of force against Panama in December 1989.

On January 31, 1992, the UN Security Council held its first summit meeting, in which 13 of the 15 members were represented by heads of state or government. The summit was convened to affirm their pledge to strengthen the UN's peacemaking role and capacity for "preventive diplomacy." The members of the Security Council called on UN Secretary General Boutros Boutros-Ghali to draft proposals for revitalizing provisions in the UN Charter that had long lain dormant because of the ideological polarization of the UN during the Cold War. However, they were not specific about providing the Security Council either with a body of troops readily available for crisis-management or with financial means to undertake extensive operations. Although they agreed that "the United Nations Secretary General has a crucial role to play," the Security Council and the Secretary General were at loggerheads over how to proceed: whereas the United States, France, and Britain pressed for expansion of UN peacekeeping resources in Yugoslavia, Secretary General Boutros-Ghali demurred, arguing against the involvement of UN forces in "a new

Vietnam" at a time when UN resources were needed in Africa, particularly in Somalia, where more than one million people were at risk from famine.[3]

On September 21, 1992, in his address to the UN General Assembly, President Bush called for "enhanced peacekeeping capabilities" and transformation of the UN's institutions, but he did not propose new ways to finance expanded UN operations or offer to set aside U.S. forces for the UN's use (Reading 41). Two months later, responding to the worsening crisis in Somalia, he decided to commit U.S. troops to ensure that food was delivered to the needy. The UN

Security Council quickly gave the operation its imprimatur and called on member states to place their troops under U.S. leadership. Bush acted out of humanitarian concern to avert starvation. The UN Secretary General believes that to make "a secure environment for humanitarian operations" in Somalia, pursuant to UN Security Council resolution of December 3, 1992, the U.S.-led troops must disarm the warring clans. This conflict of interpretations needs to be resolved.

The United States needs to decide what kind of a United Nations it wants. Does the UN Charter's mandate extend to the melioration of ethnic strife and famine relief? How are such activities to be financed? How much authority is the UN to have? How do these issues bear on the determination of the U.S. national interest?

[3] Patrick E. Tyler, "U.N. Chief's Dispute with Council Boils Over," *The New York Times*, July 31, 1992, p. A9.

40.   Whose Collective Security?
Edward C. Luck and Toby Trister Gati

The founders of the United Nations (UN) had it right, but it took 45 years and the end of the Cold War to prove it: given the proper international environment, the entire global community can mobilize a collective response to aggression through the UN. The international community was determined to oust Iraq from Kuwait by diplomatic, political, economic, and, finally, by military means, but it was, in the end, a Security Council authorization to use force—even if it was not a "UN force" itself—that provided the mandate to the 28 nations allied with the United States to undertake the Persian Gulf War. After the ceasefire agreement was signed, the UN returned to center stage to carry out that

SOURCE: Edward C. Luck and Toby Trister Gati, "Whose Collective Security?", *The Washington Quarterly*, vol. 15, no. 2, Spring 1992, pp. 43–56, excerpts. Reprinted by permission of the MIT Press, Cambridge, Massachusetts.

agreement's disarmament provisions, especially the dismantling of Iraq's nuclear, chemical, biological, and ballistic missile capabilities, its restrictions on the sale of Iraqi oil and the use of funds for humanitarian purposes, and its procedures for returning properties taken during the occupation of Kuwait.

The UN's founders had hardly intended, however, that one member state should play such a dominant role in marshaling the world's military might and that in doing so it should ignore the collective security mechanisms outlined under chapter VII of the UN Charter. Moreover, they would have been shocked to witness the collapse of the Soviet Union just when the possibility of U.S.–Soviet cooperation in defense of peace—for four decades the dream of every supporter of a more activist UN—seemed within reach.

If the original vision of the United Nations has new life, then, there are also many unanswered questions about the shape of future international security arrangements. Indeed, by turning to the United Nations as a critical component of its Gulf strategy, the United States brought to the surface both the hopes and the fears surrounding any discussion of collective security. If today's transformed international environment raises the hope that the collective might of the international community can protect the weak against the strong, as originally intended in the UN Charter, it also raises concerns that the strong will seek to impose their vision of world order on the weak, without regard for the principles of national sovereignty and non-interference in domestic affairs also enshrined in the UN Charter. The ambivalence of many states toward a stronger UN is now coupled with apprehension about a pax Americana, even a UN-centered one, without a Soviet counterweight.

If collective security has a future, it is not yet clear what it will look like. Americans are far from eager to assume the role of global policeman, but neither are U.S. political leaders ready to suggest putting even part of U.S. military forces under an international or UN command. Other countries have similar concerns. During the Persian Gulf War, national leaders of the major contributing states hailed the new era in international relations, but none expressed a willingness to cede authority to the UN so that it might implement existing provisions of the charter regulating the use of force. The detailed structures for implementing collective security outlined in the UN Charter need to be reviewed in light of the changing international security environment of the world after the Cold and Persian Gulf wars. For if a "new world order" is to be created, a way must be found to strengthen the institutional capability for responding to global threats to the peace.

Here, the role of the United States is crucial. It is the only country with the combination of political, economic, and military strength necessary to defend the interests of smaller countries against powerful neighbors. At the same time, as seen in the Gulf, preponderant military power cannot always be brought to bear without the active support, both political and increasingly financial, of other states

in the international community. Not every crisis will rivet U.S. attention as did the Iraqi invasion of Kuwait or call for a massive U.S.-led response. But if the United States does not take the lead, then who will? In a world characterized by repeated outbreaks of low-level fighting between neighboring states and disregard for the welfare of civilian populations caught in the cross fire, by mistreatment of ethnic or national minorities, and by large-scale human rights violations, the greatest threat to international stability may be a situation in which everyone knows something should be done but no one wants to take the lead.

It is at this point that "the system" should take over—a system of collective responsibility that would engage the international community in tasks ranging from preventive diplomacy, to economic sanctions, and to joint military action as needed to maintain international peace and stability. The UN Charter provides for such a system and it is the purpose of this paper to consider ways in which its collective security provisions can be strengthened and reinvigorated to take advantage of exciting new possibilities in the post-cold war world.

National decision makers in many parts of the world, not least in Washington, D.C., are rediscovering the potential utility of the range of coercive actions permitted the UN Security Council under the charter's chapter VII, with its 13 articles detailing the possibilities for a concerted multilateral response to threats to international peace and security. There is no lack of authority or tools, as amply demonstrated in the diplomatic, economic, and military efforts to expel the Iraqi invaders from Kuwait. But this was a highly unusual situation that provides no clear precedent for the future. If the UN's full potential as an instrument of collective security is to be realized, four clusters of questions need to be addressed with some urgency:

- Who should have the authority to decide when to invoke the charter's collective security provisions, or more precisely, which countries should be represented on the Security Council and how should it take its decisions?
- Who should be authorized to oversee the implementation of sanctions and the use of force once these steps have been mandated by the council?

• When should the UN decide to become involved in a local conflict and when should it leave this burden to regional organizations or to the parties themselves?
• Who pays the bill when the UN is asked to serve as world policeman and how are the funds to be raised?

The UN Charter speaks to all of these concerns to some extent, of course, but fuzzy answers that seemed acceptable in the days when the UN was usually left sitting on the sidelines are inadequate as the organization enters the center ring of international security politics for the first time. In the days ahead, these provisions are likely to be tested as never before.

WHO DECIDES?

It is clearly the Security Council—the subject of all 13 articles of chapter VII—that has full and unrivaled responsibility for determining when and how collective security steps will be undertaken. Only the council has the authority under international law to make decisions that are binding on all member states. So with the new-found cooperative spirit among the five permanent members—none has cast a veto on a substantive issue in almost two years—has come increasing discussion among the whole UN membership about the composition of the council itself. The more active and assertive the council becomes, the more the 150-plus member states not on the council will mutter about decisions it makes in their name but without their input.

The Persian Gulf War was a striking case in point. Although initially there was widespread excitement in the UN about the close collaboration of the five permanent members of the Security Council, over time the disenfranchised expressed growing apprehensions. They included both developing countries, concerned about their exclusion from UN decision making, and leading developed countries like Germany and Japan, which were expected to shoulder much of the cost of the UN-authorized operations but were largely excluded from key decision-making sessions. Simply put, during the Gulf crisis most UN members were left out of the process of consultation and deliberation that led up to the resolution authorizing the use of force. Even the 10 elected, nonpermanent members of the Security Council professed frustration that the permanent five met alone under U.S. leadership to design security policy and then presented them with a fait accompli to be voted up or down. For the rest— more than nine-tenths of the UN's total membership—the system seemingly afforded no say at all. They were not involved in the consultations, and their assent was unnecessary according to the charter even on decisions that could bind their actions.

This is particularly galling to the larger states in the developing world that exert enormous influence over events in their regions and in the General Assembly yet have no comparable input into UN security policy. Because it is in the developing world, after all, that the UN again and again becomes involved, developing countries large and small are uneasy about the way future decisions on critical war and peace issues may be resolved at the UN. The fact that U.S. power is no longer counterbalanced by another superpower only heightens these concerns. Paradoxically, the renewed emphasis on consensus in UN decision making has resulted not only in a less acrimonious process but also in suspicions in some developing countries of a more subtle, behind-the-scenes dominance by the United States. Even the low-key, restrained U.S. stance in the selection of a new secretary general in the fall of 1991 was at first misinterpreted by some of the smaller countries as a U.S. device for getting its way without having to express its preferences publicly.

Even some American allies, who once complained that the United States failed to use the UN, now fret that it may use the world body too much, turning it into a mere instrument of U.S. foreign policy. On the other hand, if the middle and smaller powers seek to make the UN a mechanism for constraining U.S. power, then trouble could lie ahead. The UN cannot succeed without strong, constructive U.S. leadership, while the United States needs the UN to manage and promote a fair international division of labor and burden-sharing arrangements on security as well as development issues. The Security Council could not work under

Cold War conditions, but sustaining a balance of interests in a post–Cold War world in which the United States is the only remaining superpower will also be a challenging proposition for all concerned.

The larger economic powers in the industrialized world do not fear UN encroachment on their domestic order, but, like many developing countries, they too resent their exclusion from decision-making circles. Because they are assessed substantial amounts for UN operations that the Security Council authorizes and they are obliged to suspend economic relations when the council imposes sanctions, UN enforcement actions have real consequences for them. Accustomed to being part of the inner circle that makes decisions in other areas of international policy-making, some of the Group of Seven (G–7) economic powers complain that this is tantamount to "taxation without representation." Japan has been especially vocal in recent years in insisting it should be part of the Security Council circle; Germany has also begun to voice similar concerns. Certainly if key economic powers like Japan and Germany showed a greater willingness to participate directly in peacekeeping and enforcement operations, as the British and French did in Desert Storm, it would enhance their claims for permanent Security Council seats. . . .

WHO ENFORCES THE PEACE?

The war with Iraq displayed both the strengths and the weaknesses of the UN system of collective security for all the world to see. The UN itself proved to be a remarkably good forum for rallying an international political response to naked aggression, yet when it came to using force, the carefully laid out provisions in chapter VII of the UN Charter were never invoked. The UN's authority was proclaimed everywhere—including most vividly in the U.S. Senate—up to the point of authorizing the use of force, and again the UN came front and center in the effort to clean up the mess left by Desert Storm. But the world body seemed to fade once again into irrelevance when the fighting was in progress.

There were, of course, good reasons for this pattern: after all, the evolution of international relations has not yet reached the point at which most nations are ready to accept international command of their forces in combat. And there is reason to question whether a UN command could have prosecuted the war as efficiently as the coalition and with as little loss of life among allied troops. But there were political costs to excluding the world body completely, including a loss of credibility both for the United Nations and for the concept of a "new world order."

Clearly, the international community is still improvising rather than institutionalizing mechanisms for dealing with regional crises. The mobilization of a global consensus was possible in the Persian Gulf not only because the Iraqi actions were so egregious but also because the United States was willing to take the lead politically, diplomatically, and militarily (although not financially). Future crises may follow a similar pattern, but many states feel that eventually the role of world policeman should rightly belong to the world community as a whole rather than to any one country—no matter how strong—and that authority and responsibility should be shared more equitably among all nations. A number of recent opinion polls, moreover, have shown that the U.S. public is not eager to have the United States play the role of global policeman and would far prefer to send the UN's blue helmets to handle regional crises rather than the U.S. Marines. Whether this represents a growing confidence in the UN, a desire to have other countries carry more of the burden, or a new isolationist spirit remains to be seen.

For all its shortcomings, no one has been able to advance a more credible plan than the UN Charter for carrying out collective security. Moving beyond "pacific settlement of disputes" under chapter VI of the charter to enforcement actions under chapter VII, however, has put the UN into largely uncharted territory. The Kuwaiti crisis of 1990 led to a highly improvised application of the collective security *principles* in the UN Charter, while the charter's *provisions* for UN enforcement of security

(Military Staff Committee, UN troops, UN command) were circumvented.

Whether the UN collective security structures envisioned almost half a century ago, with the various peacekeeping mechanisms that have evolved since, can be reshaped to make the UN a potent agent for international security—and whether the major powers have sufficient commitment to making them work—is an open question. The resistance of major military powers to consideration of a unified or UN command and the general reluctance of member states to negotiate "special agreements" for standby forces under article 43 of the charter bespeak the difficulties involved.

Article 43 goes to the heart of the matter because the UN at present has no forces automatically at its disposal and must appeal to the members to volunteer forces even for noncombatant peacekeeping missions. This sometimes results in significant delays in responding to urgent crises, reducing the world body's credibility as a potential deterrent to would-be aggressors. In a long-forgotten passage of the 1945 UN Participation Act, which defined U.S. relations with the new United Nations organization, Congress acknowledges that article 43 agreements, should they be concluded between the United States and the UN, could well turn the command of those U.S. forces over to the Security Council and thus possibly to non-American officers. This might be seen today by many Americans as ceding too much of the president's authority as commander-in-chief to a multilateral body. Certainly, in an operation as large and risky as Desert Storm, to do so would seem unrealistic, although it would be less so in more limited operations of less strategic importance to the United States.

It should not be forgotten, however, that the United States would retain a veto in the Security Council over the commitment of any UN forces. There are no precedents, moreover, so it would be quite possible to consider negotiating article 43 agreements with the UN that would stipulate that the standby forces would be put at the UN's disposal only under conditions and circumstances specifically agreed to by the president and/or Congress,

and only with their consent. In other words, the United States could designate certain units, and perhaps give them special training for participation in prospective UN collective security operations, without committing them to the UN in advance.

This topic remains controversial, but we believe it is time for the United States to open quiet consultations with the other permanent members of the Security Council about the possibility of all five nations negotiating simultaneous article 43 agreements with the UN. As the countries protected by the veto, as well as by their nuclear deterrents, the five are best positioned to open this new chapter in collective security. The size of the designated forces need not be enormous, but they should fit the needs of rapid deployment and force projection missions. Logistical support, communications, and intelligence capabilities should be shared with the UN whenever possible. Although it might take some time to negotiate such agreements, as well as to get all five permanent members on board, the very suggestion that these major military powers were consulting on how to bring force to bear under the UN umbrella should in itself serve as a powerful deterrent to potential aggressors, especially after the experience of the Persian Gulf War.

Other UN member states should also be encouraged to negotiate standby agreements. Because these countries would not be able to veto the deployment of their article 43 forces by the UN, it was suggested at a UNA-USA meeting in Moscow in spring 1991 that these countries be given the right to determine whether or not their forces would take part in a particular enforcement operation. This would provide them with essentially the same assurances that possession of the veto gives the five permanent members, while making it possible for them to prepare for future enforcement operations.

A second key building block of the UN collective security system was meant to be the Military Staff Committee, consisting of the chiefs of staff of the five permanent members or their representatives. Again, the elaborate article 47 provisions regarding its operation were largely set aside during the cold war era. In the buildup to the Persian Gulf War, the committee met once at a relatively high level, chiefly to scare the Iraqis by showing the determination of the major powers, but no real efforts have ever been made to create a unified command structure under UN auspices. Should article 43 forces ever come into existence, command and control questions—and the role of the Military Staff Committee—would take on greater urgency.

In the meantime, the committee could undertake more modest, but important, roles to test the prospects for cooperation and to prove its utility. Its first task under the charter, "to advise and assist" the Security Council on military matters, makes considerable sense, especially if the UN's security role is to expand in the future. It has been said that war is too important to be left to the generals, but surely questions of how to maintain the peace should not solely be the preserve of diplomats unaided by the best professional military advice the military has to offer. Among the questions on which the Military Staff Committee is to proffer advice is "the regulation of armaments, and possible disarmament." In the case of Iraqi disarmament, the UN is taking unprecedented steps to disarm a major military machine. As the whole body more and more approaches arms control and disarmament as an integral component of peacemaking and peacekeeping efforts specific to regional conflicts, the technical expertise of military specialists will be increasingly important to its work, as has been the case in Iraq. Activating the Military Staff Committee to aid in these tasks, in other words, need not represent a commitment to, nor even a step toward, multilateral command and control of national forces—something the charter says would "be worked out subsequently" in any case. If the committee had been functioning fully prior to Iraq's invasion of Kuwait, it might have been helpful in several ways. First, its very activity might have been a useful deterrent, suggesting the possibility of a broad-based international response to Iraq's aggression. Second, the charter states that the committee shall be responsible under the Security Council for the "strategic direction of UN forces." This could have included, first, sorting out the general division of labor among the various national contingents deployed in the Gulf theater

and, second, laying out overall military and strategic objectives in the Gulf operation, possibly including limits on the use of force against largely civilian targets. Even modest results from general consultations on these subjects could have proven beneficial politically, particularly in the uncertain months leading up to the commencement of hostilities. Third, a little-noticed clause in article 47 speaks of the establishment of "regional subcommittees," to which local UN member states would presumably send military representatives. This might have proven a politically acceptable way to expand the commitment of the moderate Arab states and others in the coalition with less political arm-twisting by the United States and less need for these Arab leaders to defend their cooperation with the United States to skeptical domestic advisers.

WHEN SHOULD THE UN INTERVENE?

With increasing opportunities for UN intervention has come a growing need to choose when UN involvement is most appropriate and a renewed debate about where national sovereignty ends and international responsibilities begin. The UN Charter gives the Security Council considerable freedom to "determine the existence of any threat to the peace, breach of the peace, or act of aggression . . . and to decide what measures shall be taken" (chapter VII, article 39). And, under article 99, the secretary general is authorized to bring to the attention of the Security Council those items that "in his opinion" may threaten international peace and security.

Although the preamble lays out a series of principles and purposes that sound universal, the remainder of the charter describes a decision-making structure that is highly political and selective. In practical terms, then, most of the responsibility for deciding when, where, and how these sweeping principles will be applied rests with the members of the Security Council. Theirs necessarily must be a subjective rather than an objective judgment. Thus, council members chose to respond vigorously to the Iraqi invasion of Kuwait, but they showed no inclination to get involved in the strife in Liberia, Ethiopia, or the Sudan that raged at the same time. To some observers, this selectivity undermines the credibility and integrity of the institution as a global peacekeeper, but to others it is a sensible bow to reality in view of the UN's limited capabilities and capacity for influencing events. A keen sense of when to get involved and when to stay out, moreover, helped to sustain the organization through such politically difficult times as the Cold War.

In the past, Soviet–U.S. tensions—reflected in the penchant of the two states to use their vetoes—ensured that the UN would get involved in relatively few crises. Today, the unprecedented cooperation among the permanent members, as well as their more narrowly defined interests in the developing world, could provide—in fact already has provided—a much wider menu of problem areas calling for UN attention. With the UN's continuing physical and financial limitations, however, this growth of tempting opportunities calls for a corresponding sense of restraint and for selectivity.

Will it simply be, as many smaller nations complain, that the UN will get involved only when the interests of the five permanent members are demonstrably involved (Kuwait being a case in point) but when none of them can or wants to handle the situation unilaterally? In that case, how will the security interests of developing countries that are not deemed strategically important get addressed? There is a growing danger, for instance, that conflicts in Africa will be essentially excluded from the map of Security Council interests. Over time, it may be useful to try to develop generally applicable rules of intervention regarding when the collective security provisions of chapter VII should be invoked. For example, specific kinds of events, threats, or situations might automatically trigger Security Council action, such as the possibility that weapons of mass destruction might be used in a regional dispute, clear evidence of genocide, a huge flow of refugees that threatens to destabilize neighboring countries, massive human rights violations, the overthrow of democratically elected governments, or flagrant violation of earlier Security Council decisions. Not one of these questions has a simple answer, but each is worth grappling with if the concept of a new world order is to be based on

sustainable and broadly credible political and legal norms.

The increasing demand for UN security services, especially in internal or transnational conflicts, has also raised pointed questions about the capacity of the organization to deal with so many security problems simultaneously. Some of these questions deal with the personal time, talents, and priorities of the secretary general, who cannot be everywhere at once, while others deal with the organization, staffing, and communications capabilities of the UN Secretariat for overseeing so many far-flung operations. These issues are especially timely at a point when restructuring the secretariat is being given serious attention by the member states, and a new secretary general, well-versed in international diplomacy, seeks to put his stamp on the organization. The old question of the relationship between the UN and regional organizations takes on a renewed urgency under these conditions.

The UN Charter does not assume that the Security Council will address all security problems or that it will necessarily be the first recourse in case of threats to international peace and security. Article 52, in fact, calls on member states to "make every effort to achieve pacific settlement of local disputes through . . . regional arrangements or by . . . regional agencies before referring them to the Security Council." Chapter VIII, probably the least explored territory in the charter, addresses the possibilities for coordinating the efforts of regional bodies and the Security Council aimed at both peaceful resolution and enforcement of council decisions.

Such coordination of global and regional action might have been a politically, and perhaps militarily, attractive option in the Gulf crisis, especially given the symbolic importance of bringing Arab states into the coalition. Unfortunately, in the Middle East as in other areas of strategic importance, adequate regional partners for the UN do not yet exist. In the past, when regional organizations were weak and divided or where a superpower had a clear interest, the venue for action more often than not was the Security Council. Where regional organizations exist, as in Africa, Latin America, or Europe, the track record of regional–global cooperation has been mixed at best. The recent crises in Haiti and Yugoslavia, on the other hand, engendered a greater degree of cooperation between the UN and regional organizations in dealing with stubborn local conflicts. Developing a fuller global–regional partnership would also help address the endemic problem of alienation among developing countries within the UN security structure.

One of the most fundamental questions facing the UN today is whether principles of collective security—and other global norms—apply to individuals and groups within states or only to relations between member states themselves. If the latter, then nations could be allowed to do to their own people what international norms do not permit them to do to other nations. On the other hand, if the international community can tell states how they should treat their own populations, how are these verdicts to be enforced? Many still feel reluctant to condemn the violation of human rights or disregard for basic human needs when these result from internal political breakdown or civil war. It is only in recent years that the international community has come to accept the idea that certain domestic policies (e.g., apartheid, genocide, and other massive human rights violations) should not be tolerated by the community of civilized nations. Yet the Security Council remains cautious about labeling even gross rights violations within established borders as "threats to international peace and security" requiring chapter VII action, at least beyond economic or arms transfer sanctions in especially egregious and persistent cases.

The aftermath of the Kuwait crisis dramatically raised these issues in a way that was distinctly unwelcome to many governments. The intervention by the Western powers to create "safe havens" to protect Iraq's Kurds and other minority groups from their government, for example, may have set a precedent with far-reaching consequences for traditional notions of state sovereignty. Recent suggestions by the French that international law recognize a "duty to intervene" in cases where a government's actions are creating a humanitarian catastrophe has set off alarm bells in a number of capitals, especially in the developing world.

With refugee crises around the globe and famine present or looming in parts of Africa, this controversy will not go away. Many governments assert that the "duty" concept is a dagger directed at them, threatening to formally reduce their sovereignty and affording the great powers, through the Security Council or worse yet unilaterally, an excuse to intervene in domestic conflicts. The dilemma posed by the conflict between government claims to sovereignty and human claims to survival will almost certainly become one of the major issues of international law and security in the 1990s.

WHO WILL PAY THE BILL?

There has clearly been no "peace dividend" for the UN peacekeeping, arms monitoring, and collective security budgets. The more these services are demanded by the international community, the higher the costs to the world body. Once a small fraction of UN spending, with the launching of the Cambodia operation the costs of peacekeeping operations alone may soon exceed the whole regular budget of the United Nations. Although puny compared to the costs of national defense or of local conflicts prevented or contained, these expenditures loom very large in UN eyes. If the UN begins to undertake collective security operations directly, then its expenses will multiply many times. Operation Desert Storm, for example, cost 10 times as much as the annual outlays of the entire UN system, including all of the specialized agencies. Even a more modest collective security operation would be very expensive by UN standards.

These new demands come at an awkward time for the UN, which is still struggling to overcome the painful effects of massive U.S. financial withholdings during the mid-1980s and of smaller delinquencies by other member states. The United States has begun to pay off its arrearages, but they still exceed $500 million (or one-half of the UN's regular annual budget), of which more than $100 million (as of October 1991) is owed to peacekeeping alone. The United States is clearly a lot more ready to enunciate a new world order than to help pay for it. And although the Russians are clearly supportive of the principles of the UN Charter and supportive of recognizing the right of the international community to intervene, they may not be able to contribute even their assessed dues on time, much less extra for new peacekeeping operations in the next few years.

Although separate assessments are made for most new peacekeeping operations, the prospects for successfully completing new assignments are inevitably affected by the overall financial health of the institution. The most obvious problem has been the virtual elimination of the UN's modest reserve funds, leaving no discretionary funds that could cover the start-up costs for a new operation until the hat can be passed around the member states for longer-term support. Subsequent delays in payments from major donors, like the United States, tend to compound the problem. There is a built-in nine-month mechanical delay in the payment of U.S. regular dues, which are due each January but paid at the earliest when the next U.S. fiscal year begins in October. And U.S. funding for peacekeeping operations is particularly problematic when new operations, unanticipated by the federal budget cycle or the agreement to reduce the budget deficit, are begun. Although the United States cannot solve the UN's financial problems alone, it could at least set a good example for others.

When the United States and other major contributors are unable to come up with the funds in a timely fashion, the ability of the UN to maintain peacekeepers in operation is dependent largely on the willingness of countries contributing troops to wait for compensation or on emergency supplemental support by a few states. When it was time to dispatch UN observers to the Iraq–Iran front following the UN-brokered armistice, for example, there were no funds to get them there until a member state agreed to make an extraordinary payment. More recently, the efforts of the UN Special Commission to ferret out Iraqi weapons of mass destruction were hampered by the lack of adequate transportation and logistical support from member states, which otherwise professed keen interest in the operation. Many months after the operation had begun and had proved its extraordinary value, still

no funds had been appropriated by the UN member states to fund it.

The issue of financing looms even larger when one moves from peacekeeping to enforcement actions. Although Operation Desert Storm demonstrated a clear U.S. willingness to provide military leadership and troops for collective action, a central aim of U.S. foreign policy was to share the financial burdens more broadly. The Bush administration appears to have persuaded its coalition partners to pay more than $48 billion in cash and other contributions toward an estimated $60 billion in war costs, with additional Saudi Arabian payments likely. In future crises, however, the countries that foot the bill may be unwilling to allow the United States the degree of military and political control it had in the Persian Gulf and may link issues of financing to greater participation in strategic decision making. The UN, of course, can offer a forum both for sorting out the division of labor in carrying out such operations and for developing a formula for sharing the financial burden.

Another endemic problem has been the separation of substantive and budgetary decision making within the UN. Under the charter, the Security Council has authority over the former and the General Assembly over the latter. This anomaly in the UN's structure—a bit reminiscent of Washington's system of checks and balances but more clumsy in practice—could cause serious difficulties down the road, especially if the resentment of the council's prerogatives grows among those countries excluded from its deliberations. Haggling between the council and assembly over the size and cost of the Namibian operation delayed the deployment of the peacekeeping forces and almost jeopardized the success of their mission. Japanese officials have complained that their minor role in the decision-making process for the UN-brokered peace agreement in Cambodia, which looms as the largest, riskiest, and most complex security mission ever undertaken by the UN, has not been commensurate with the financial burden Japan will be expected to carry in the implementation of the agreement.

There have been many creative suggestions for producing a larger and steadier flow of income for

UN peace and security operations, which often cannot be anticipated in the regular budget cycle. These proposals have ranged from a tax or assessment on international commerce or on arms sales, to a renewal of the UN's reserve fund, to shifting U.S. contributions from the State Department to the Defense Department budget. Rebuilding the reserves should be the first priority, especially as the United States begins to pay its arrearages. Although it might be unwieldy in practice, the concept of an international levy on arms transfers is very appealing because the greater the volume of weapons proliferation, the greater the funds available to the UN to contain the consequences of their use. The possible establishment of a UN arms trade registry might provide a data base for such an undertaking. Developing countries, which depend on arms supplies from the major arms producing countries, are likely to have strong objections to such a system, however, because it would let countries with indigenous arms manufacturing capabilities off scot-free. Whether or not this is the best approach, clearly some kind of regular financing mechanism is needed, given the increasing number and importance of UN efforts at both enforcement and peacekeeping. Anything approaching a "new world order" cannot be obtained on a shoestring, especially an ad hoc one.

CONCLUSION

Global threats to the United States have receded, perhaps creating a false sense of security. Regional instabilities, many based on ethnic hatreds and thwarted national aspirations, are multiplying at an alarming rate. Certainly the United States cannot resolve all of them with the use of force, nor should it aspire to do so. Multilateral crisis management, peacekeeping, and collective security should be as fundamental to the defense of U.S. national security interests in the 1990s as participation in the North Atlantic Treaty Organization (NATO) has been during the past 45 years. The threats we face are different today and so should be the mix of responses.

If the White House and Congress are serious about a new world order, they should begin by putting their own house in order. A first step would be to put some real money and political capital behind their lofty rhetoric. Just as the U.S. government mobilized an international coalition against Iraq, so, too, it can energize international diplomacy to develop at least a rudimentary collective security system based on broader consultations, modest commitments of forces to the UN, and financial burden sharing.

Certainly there is the risk of failure. But the unprecedented opportunities to build new security structures that are present today will not last forever. Untapped potential is wasted potential. Without U.S. leadership in forging a new collective security system based on the UN Charter, the only alternatives when the next bully comes along will be another large-scale commitment of U.S. troops or letting an aggression go unpunished. Surely the political and security risks of either of these outcomes are greater than those inherent in a determined effort to bring the UN Charter back to life.

41.   Defining the U.S. Commitment to the United Nations

George Bush

With the cold war's end, I believe we have a unique opportunity to go beyond artificial divisions of a first, second, and third world to forge instead a genuine global community of free and sovereign nations; a community built on respect for principle, of peaceful settlements of disputes, fundamental human rights, and the twin pillars of freedom, democracy and free markets.

Already the United Nations, especially the Security Council, has done much to fulfill its original mission and to build this global community. U.N. leadership has been critical in resolving conflicts and brokering peace the entire world over. But securing democracy and securing the peace in the century ahead will be no simple task. Imperial communism may have been vanquished, but that does not end the challenges of our age, challenges that must be overcome if we are finally to end the divisions between East and West, North and South that fuel strife and strain and conflict and war.

As we support the historic growth of democracy around the world, I believe the community of nations and the United Nations face three critical, interrelated challenges as we enter the 21st century.

First, we face the political challenge of keeping today's peace and preventing tomorrow's wars. As we see daily in Bosnia and Somalia and Cambodia, everywhere conflict claims innocent lives, the need for enhanced peacekeeping capabilities has never been greater, the conflicts we must deal with more intractable, the costs of conflict higher.

Second, we face the strategic challenge of the proliferation of weapons of mass destruction, truly the fastest growing security challenge to international peace and order.

SOURCE: George Bush, President of the United States (1989–1993), Address to the United Nations General Assembly, September 21, 1992, *Weekly Compilation of Presidential Documents*, vol. 28, no. 39, September 28, 1992, pp. 1697–1699.

And third, we face the common economic challenge of promoting prosperity for all, of strengthening an open, growth-oriented free market international economic order while safeguarding the environment.

Meeting these challenges will require us to strengthen our collective engagement. It will require us to transform our collective institutions. And above all, it will require that each of us look seriously at our own governments and how we conduct our international affairs. We too must change our institutions and our practices if we are to make a new world of the promise of today, if we're to secure a 21st century peace.

With you today, I would like to discuss these three challenges: peacekeeping, proliferation, and prosperity. And I'd like to use this opportunity to begin to sketch how I believe the international community can work together to meet these three challenges and how the United States is changing its institutions and policies to catalyze this effort.

Let me begin with peacekeeping. The United Nations has a long and distinguished history of peacekeeping and humanitarian relief. From Cyprus and Lebanon to Cambodia and Croatia, the blue beret has become a symbol of hope amid all that hostility, and the U.N. has long played a central role in preventing conflicts from turning into wars. Strengthened peacekeeping capabilities can help buttress these diplomatic efforts.

But as much as the United Nations has done, it can do much more. Peacekeepers are stretched to the limit while demands for their services increase by the day. The need for monitoring and preventive peacekeeping, putting people on the ground before the fighting starts, may become especially critical in volatile regions. This is especially the case because of the rapid and turbulent change that continues to shake Eastern Europe and Eurasia.

Across the lands that once were imprisoned behind an Iron Curtain, peoples are reasserting their historical identities that were frozen in communism's catacomb. Where this is taking place in a democratic manner with tolerance and civility and respect for fundamental human rights and freedoms, this new democratic nationalism is all to the good. But unfortunately, we need only look to the bloody battles raging in places such as the former Yugoslavia to see the dangers of ethnic violence. This is the greatest threat to the democratic peace we hope to build with Eastern Europe, with Russia and Eurasia, even more so than economic deprivation.

We fully support the efforts of NATO and CSCE and WEU, the C.I.S. and other competent regional organizations to develop peacekeeping capabilities. We are convinced that enhanced U.N. capabilities, however, are a necessary complement to these regional efforts, not just in Europe and Eurasia but across the globe.

I welcome the Secretary-General's call for a new agenda to strengthen the United Nations' ability to prevent, contain, and resolve conflict across the globe. And today, I call upon all members to join me in taking bold steps to advance that agenda. I, therefore, will be discussing with my colleagues the merits of a special meeting of the U.N. Security Council to discuss the Secretary-General's proposals and to develop concrete responses in five key areas:

One, robust peacekeeping requires men and equipment that only member states can provide. Nations should develop and train military units for possible peacekeeping operations and humanitarian relief. And these forces must be available on short notice at the request of the Security Council and with the approval, of course, of the governments providing them.

Two, if multinational units are to work together, they must train together. Many nations, for example, Fiji, Norway, Canada, and Finland, have a long history of peacekeeping. And we can all tap into that experience as we train for expanded operations. Effective multinational action will also require coordinated command-and-control and interoperability of both equipment and communications. Multinational planning, training, field exercises will be needed. These efforts should link up with regional organizations.

Three, we also need to provide adequate logistical support for peacekeeping and humanitarian operations. Member states should designate stockpiles of resources necessary to meet humanitarian emergencies including famines, floods, civil disturbances. This will save valuable time in a crisis.

Four, we will need to develop planning, crisis management, and intelligence capabilities for peacekeeping and humanitarian operations.

And five, we must ensure adequate, equitable financing for U.N. and associated peacekeeping efforts.

As I said, we must change our national institutions if we are to change our international relations. So let me assure you: The United States is ready to do its part to strengthen world peace by strengthening international peacekeeping.

For decades, the American military has served as a stabilizing presence around the globe. I want to draw on our extensive experience in winning wars and keeping the peace to support U.N. peacekeeping. I have directed the United States Secretary of Defense to place a new emphasis on peacekeeping. Because of peacekeeping's growing importance as a mission for the United States military we will emphasize training of combat, engineering, and logistical units for the full range of peacekeeping and humanitarian activities.

We will work with the United Nations to best employ our considerable lift, logistics, communications, and intelligence capabilities to support peacekeeping operations. We will offer our capabilities for joint simulations and peacekeeping exercises to strengthen our ability to undertake joint peacekeeping operations. There is room for all countries, large and small, and I hope all will play a part.

Member states, as always, must retain the final decision on the use of their troops, of course. But we must develop our ability to coordinate peacekeeping efforts so that we can mobilize quickly when a threat to peace arises or when people in need look to the world for help.

I have further directed the establishment of a permanent peacekeeping curriculum in U.S. military schools. Training plainly is key. The United States is prepared to make available our bases and facilities for multinational training and field exercises. One such base nearby with facilities is Fort Dix. America used these bases to win the cold war, and today, with that war over, they can help build a lasting peace.

The United States is willing to provide our military expertise to the United Nations to help the U.N. strengthen its planning and operations for peacekeeping. We will also broaden American support for monitoring, verification, reconnaissance,

and other requirements of U.N. peacekeeping or humanitarian assistance operations.

And finally, the United States will review how we fund peacekeeping and explore new ways to ensure adequate American financial support for U.N. peacekeeping and U.N. humanitarian activities. I do believe that we must think differently about how we ensure and pay for our security in this new era. . . .

Questions for Discussion

1. Is the United Nations in the U.S. national interest?

2. What contributions has the UN made to U.S. security?

3. Has the United States always been a staunch supporter of the UN?

4. What, in Washington's view, have been the UN's shortcomings in the past? What are they today?

5. What effect did the end of the Cold War have on U.S. policy in the UN?

6. What problems does the United States face in its attempt to enhance the UN's importance?

7. What criteria are relevant for an assessment of the effectiveness of the UN?

8. Was the UN's humanitarian intervention is Somalia in the U.S. national interest?

Selected Bibliography

FINGER, SEYMOUR M. *Your Man at the U.N.: People, Politics and Bureaucracy in Making Foreign Policy.* New York: New York University Press, 1980.

FRANCK, THOMAS M. *Nation Against Nation: What Happened to the U.N. Dream and What the U.S. Can Do About It.* New York: Oxford University Press, 1985.

GATI, TOBY TRISTER (Ed.). *The U.S., the U.N. and the Management of Global Change.* New York: New York University Press, 1983.

GERSON, ALLAN. *The Kirkpatrick Mission: Diplomacy Without Apology: America at the United Nations, 1981–1985.* New York: Free Press, 1988.

LEE, JOHN M., et. al. *To Unite Our Strength: Enhancing the United Nations Peace and Security System.* Lanham, MD: University Press of America, 1992.

MOYNIHAN, DANIEL PATRICK, WITH SUZANNE WEAVER. *A Dangerous Place.* Boston: Little, Brown, 1978.

RIKHYE, INDAR JIT. *The Theory and Practice of Peacekeeping.* New York: St. Martin's, 1984.

ROBERTS, ADAM, AND BENEDICT KINGSBURY (EDS.). *United Nations, Divided World: The UN's Role in International Relations.* New York: Oxford University Press, 1988.

URQUHART, BRIAN. *A Life in Peace and War.* New York: Harper and Row, 1987.

VAN DEN HAAG, ERNEST, AND JOHN P. CONRAD. *The U.N.: In or Out?* New York: Plenum Publishing, 1987.

WILLIAMS, DOUGLAS. *The Specialized Agencies and the United Nations: The System in Crisis.* New York: St. Martin's, 1987.

PART SIX

A STRATEGY FOR THE YEAR 2000 AND BEYOND

CHAPTER 14

What Should the United States Do?

For the third time in this century the United States must fashion a national strategy to accord with a drastically changed international system. At the end of the First World War, Woodrow Wilson failed to engage the United States in the management of European and international affairs, and the result was a new world war. After the Second World War, Harry Truman responded to the clear and present danger from an imperialist Soviet Union by adopting a policy of containment. Although enormously costly, containment proved an effective and flexible strategy. Over the course of more than four decades, it prevented a major war, enabled Western Europe and Japan to rebuild and assume leading roles in world affairs, and eventually led to the West's prevailing over the East.

In the 1990s, the United States finds itself at another watershed: the Cold War is over; the Soviet Union has been dismantled, inadvertently by the very leaders who sought to reform it; communism has been discredited and deprived of a central authority capable of manipulating captive minions; and American military power is being rapidly reduced, albeit not fast enough for some, but well before the purposes it is supposed to serve in the future have been adequately discussed or determined. Driven by domestic considerations, U.S. foreign policy is being confined to an ever-narrowing circle of options.

As we move into the post-Cold War period, the United States, although the world's most powerful country, finds its influence limited. A straitened economic condition circumscribes the political leverage that should be the concomitant of a military superpower. Thus Japan shelters under the protective U.S. nuclear umbrella and defers to U.S. wishes on extra-Asian matters such as the Gulf War, but can resist making compromises on key trade issues. Germany's precipitate initiative on the break-away Yugoslav republics of Croatia and Slovenia was taken with little regard for Washington's wishes, and it dragged the European Community into a position that foreclosed the possibility, however remote, of a political solution. In the Middle East, the United States has little to show politically as a result of its overwhelming victory in the Gulf War: in the Persian Gulf region, arms sales go on as usual, as the Saudis and Kuwaitis use financial carrots to induce the United States to sell sophisticated weaponry in return for continued moderate oil prices; Iraq remains unfinished business; and the Kurdish problem, far from being resolved, is downplayed. Only in the Arab-Israeli sector has the United States scored diplomatic points, but these hardly seem appropriate recompense for the costs and dashed expectations that resulted from the use of force against Iraq in 1991.

The restructuring of U.S. foreign policy will take time. No comprehensive, fully-integrated strategy can be expected in the short term, if only because of the absence of an overriding threat. Rather, the quest for a coherent strategy will evolve in a piecemeal, erratic, often contradictory fashion. What the United States may want to do in foreign policy will inevitably be constrained by the growing demands of domestic needs and budgetary pressures. The constraints have been consistently emphasized by eminent specialists: enormous budget deficits, balance of payments deficits, declining investment, low productivity growth, aging and obsolescing infrastructure, and a work force that is failing to keep pace in education and innovation with leading competitors. According to two close observers of America's economic plight,

> The awkward but enduring fact is that, taken together, the claims of our various national interests and global obligations will far outrun our available resources to sustain or defend them. As the full implications of being the world's largest debtor dawn on us *and* on the rest of the world, the gap between our interests and our capacities will become larger, more obvious, and more painful. As Eisenhower sought to teach us, military and economic security over time depend on each other; countries that lose control of their economic destinies lose control over their foreign policies.[1]

This assessment by Peter G. Peterson, a former U.S. secretary of commerce and present chairman of The Blackstone Group, a private investment bank, and James K. Sebenius, an associate professor at Harvard University's John F. Kennedy School of Government, clearly identifies some of the key economic problems and difficult choices that need to be faced by America's leadership (Reading 42).

[1] Peter G. Peterson and James K. Sebenius, "The Primacy of the Domestic Agenda," in Graham Allison and Gregory F. Treverton (Eds.). *Rethinking America's Security: Beyond Cold War to New World Order.* New York: W.W. Norton, 1992, p. 61.

The Center for Defense Information, a Washington-based research organization committed to an affordable defense and a minimalist foreign policy, focuses on the changes that it maintains should be made in U.S. defense policy and proposes a major reduction in costly overseas bases and commitments (Reading 43). It contends that U.S. security does not require the stationing and deployment abroad of "more than a million American military personnel and civilian Pentagon employees," and that in the post-Cold War world the United States should be able to "reduce its annual military budget to two-thirds or less of its present size" [about $290 billion in 1991–1992].

The economic and military proposals noted above go beyond what President Bill Clinton seems prepared to embrace, although it is too early in his administration to judge. He is sympathetic in spirit to sweeping reforms in economic and defense policies, and in a major foreign policy speech delivered on August 13, 1992, he sounded a call for change, but did so against a background of continuities in the internationalist orientation that has dominated U.S. foreign policy since the end of the Second World War:

> Global change is inexorable. And can work to our advantage or to our disadvantage, depending on what we do. The currency of national strength in this new era will be denominated not only in ships and tanks and planes, but in diplomas and patents and paychecks. My first foreign policy priority will be to restore America's economic vitality. I have laid out a strategy to raise our people's skill levels, boost productivity, spur innovation and investment, reduce the national debt, and make us the world's strongest trading partner. I will elevate economics in foreign policy, create an economic security council similar to the National Security

Council, and change the culture in the State Department so that economics is no longer a poor cousin to old school diplomacy. . . .

The second imperative of Presidential leadership in this new era is to reinforce the powerful global movement toward democracy and market economies. Our strategic interest and our moral values are both rooted in this goal. . . . Growing market economies expand individual opportunity and social tolerance. . . .

My administration will stand up for democracy. We will offer international assistance to emerging fragile democracies in the former Soviet Union, and Eastern Europe, and create a democratic core to help them develop free institutions. We will keep the pressure on South Africa until the day of true democracy has dawned. . . .

We can never forget this essential fact: power is the basis for successful diplomacy. And military power has always been fundamental in international relationships. So a President must provide the American people with a clear explanation of our enduring security interests, and a new estimate of the threats we are likely to face in the post cold war era. . . .

Today there are two wrongheaded and dangerous approaches to adjusting our defenses for this new era. One . . . talks of strategic change, but basically, simply shrinks the existing cold war force structure. Continuation of this policy runs the risk of weakening the two elements that were absolutely critical to our victory in the Gulf: our superbly trained and motivated personnel and our world class weapons technology.

At the same time, there are those, some in my party, who see defense cuts as largely a piggybank to fund domestic wish lists, with our defense structures and missions as a mere afterthought rather than a starting premise. This policy would also weaken our technological superiority, and the quality and morale of our superb personnel. . . .

We must start with a fresh assessment of the new dangers that could threaten our interests and potentially require the use of force, including the risk of new threats from former Soviet republics should democracy fail, especially before all the nuclear weapons had been dismantled; the spread of weapons of mass destruction, historic tensions in various regions, especially the Korean peninsula and the Middle East; and the related risks of terrorist attacks; and the growing intensity of ethnic, fundamentalist, and separatist violence, as we have seen in Yugoslavia and elsewhere, that can spill across borders and engulf other nations.

The mission of containing an expansionist Soviet Union has disappeared, but an enduring mission remains. To maintain nuclear deterrence even as we reduce nuclear arsenals. To reassure our friends and allies and discourage potential adversaries. To pursue our interests when possible through strengthened institutions of collective security. To preserve freedom on the high seas and protect our global economic interest. And to provide the superior technology and forces that are the ultimate guarantor of liberty. . . .

My administration will make security and savings compatible. It will reduce forces, but maintain a credible presence in Europe and Asia. We will stand up for our interests, but we will share burdens, where possible, through multilateral efforts to secure the peace, such as NATO, and a new voluntary UN rapid deployment force. In Bosnia, Somalia, Cambodia, and other torn areas of the world, multilateral action holds promise as never before, and the UN deserves full and appropriate contributions from all the major powers.

It is time for our friends to bear more of the burden.

By contrast, the foreign policy agenda prepared by The Heritage Foundation offers the essentials of a different strategic outlook (Reading 44). Rejecting both isolationism and policies "that risk the lives of Americans for such purposes as territorial aggrandizement, imperial adventure, or missionary crusading—even for such lofty purposes as the spread of democracy," it espouses a kind of minimalist internationalism that is not far removed from the proposals of the Center for Defense Information. In comparing the various recommendations noted above, the reader is cautioned to keep in mind that "the devil is in the detail," it is in the specific proposals for particular policy issues that one may discern fundamental differences in philosophical and political outlook.

The open-ended commitments of the Cold War era are not possible in the acentric post-Cold War world. On vital issues of mutual defense, cooperate with allies and friends; on all matters of general concern, discuss, bargain, and seek consensus; but on marginal matters that do not involve the core interests of the United States, permit our allies and friends to find their own way. In the uncertain strategic environment emerging in Africa, Central Asia, the Middle East, Eastern Europe, and the Balkans, the quest for tactical advantages has little long-term logic. One need not be an isolationist to accept that there are limits to what a nation's foreign policy can achieve. In the determination of policy choices, purposes need to be weighed against the power available, and commitments need to be disciplined by considerations of cost. Two opposing conceptions—isolationism and internationalism—help define two very different strategic approaches (Reading 45).

42.   Ostrichism and the Choiceless Society

Peter G. Peterson and James K. Sebenius

America has demonstrated a debilitating incapacity to face and make the kind of hard trade-offs needed for progress on this expanded national security agenda. We have become a "voiceless" society, substituting denial and rhetoric for meaningful action. We tolerate that which we declare resoundingly to be "intolerable"; we are passive in the face of "imperatives" that are universally described as "compelling."

One might recall how a Roman historian complained about the decadence of his time: the citizens of Rome, he wrote, "can neither bear their ills nor their cures." In short, these are not merely economic and social policy failures; they are major political failures. Let me illustrate this proposition with examples from the areas of energy policy as well as the linked questions of deficits, investments, and entitlements.

A DANGEROUS, CHOICELESS ENERGY POLICY

Many experts are saying today that oil will go down below $15 a barrel, given overproduction at a time of declining demand. In my view, this is an overly simplistic and short-term picture. Now that some stability has been restored in the Persian Gulf, and now that Kuwait and Saudi Arabia have had to expend so much of their financial reserves, incen-

SOURCE: Peter G. Peterson and James K. Sebenius, "The Primacy of the Domestic Agenda," in Graham Allison and Gregory F. Treverton (Eds.). Rethinking America's Security: Beyond Cold War to New World Order. New York: W.W. Norton & Company, 1992, pp. 70–77. Reprinted by permission of W.W. Norton & Company, Inc. Copyright © 1992 by The American Assembly.

tives for finding ways to cut production and raise prices are already growing.

This is particularly significant in light of the drift of U.S. policy toward ever more oil consumption, ever less production, and ever more dependence on imported oil. Let me offer a very brief history. When the Organization of Petroleum Exporting Countries (OPEC) overplayed its hand in 1979 and sharply raised prices, the U.S. temporarily decreased its oil consumption and domestic oil production rose. But the decrease in consumption was over by 1983—ironically just as many Americans were convinced that they were entering a period of painless national prosperity. U.S. oil consumption has since risen by 12 percent. And the good news about increased domestic energy production was over by 1985. Between 1985 and 1989 U.S. production declined by 12 percent, and it was expected to decline another 4 or 5 percent in 1991. From net crude oil imports of about 4 million barrels a day in the mid-1980s, our oil deficit has lately been increasing; it exceeded 7 million barrels a day in 1990.

The warning signs are clear. The U.S. now depends on oil imports for about half its needs. In 1987 Persian Gulf producers accounted for only 6 percent of U.S. oil imports. In 1991 they were supplying 28 percent and could reach 50 percent by 1995. Moreover, increased U.S. imports have accounted for more than half of the growth of OPEC exports. Thus, however unwittingly, the United States has been a principal force in restoring the basis for a potentially resurgent OPEC, and the likely decline—or even reversal—in Soviet oil exports only magnifies this danger.

Projections indicate that U.S. oil imports will rise to perhaps 10 million barrels by 1995. At $20–25 per barrel, such an increase would add about $15–20 billion to our annual trade deficit. By 1995, at the level of $20–25 per barrel, our oil deficit *alone* would be $75–90 billion—approaching the size of the entire U.S. trade deficit in 1991. (Even with oil at $15 per barrel, these trade deficit effects would be massive.) And to this we must add the new melancholy dimension that our foreign debt service will increasingly overwhelm our overseas investment income, adding ever-increasing amounts to our current account deficit.

The U.S. has been lethargic in devising ways to reduce its oil gluttony. In Europe and Japan, governments have raised the price of oil to the consumer and have continued to invest both in more efficient energy use and in different energy sources. As a result, they will be able to keep increases in oil imports under some degree of control during the next decade. France now gets over 70 percent of its electrical power from nuclear energy, and it has set a goal of 100 percent by 1995. Its nuclear industry has had no major safety problems so far, enabling the French to avoid some of the worst effects of fossil fuel generating plants.

Japan—which has no oil of its own to speak of—has nonetheless managed to render itself less vulnerable to the economic consequences of rising oil prices. Japan has done a much better job than we have in terms of energy conservation and efficiency. Aside from the obvious lower consumption of energy in automobiles, the Japanese get 2.5 times more manufacturing output per unit of energy than we get in the United States, and 2.4 times the real output with the same amount of energy as in 1977. Through conservation, efficiency, and increasing of nuclear capacity, Japan is today scarcely more dependent on imported oil than the United States is, when viewed in GNP terms. The American bill for imported oil now stands at about 1.1 percent of our GNP. Japan's bill is almost identical—and down by two-thirds from past levels. What's more, because Japan has such a large trade and current account surplus, it can much more readily absorb whatever oil price increases may lie down the road.

The U.S. faces a choice. On the one hand, we can eschew any meaningful action to bring national oil consumption more in line with national energy production. And when our children ask us why we saddled them with vast debt obligations to our overseas creditors, we will have to tell them: "Despite the fact that in 1990 our national appetite for oil was far out of proportion to our population or our productivity—in 1990, with less than 5 percent of the world's population, the U.S. consumed fully one-quarter of the world's oil output, including *one-tenth just for our automobiles*—we deemed any reduction on your behalf to be too great a sacrifice for us to make." Or, better: "We left the outcome up to the free choice of the American consumer and, too bad, you lost!"

Clearly, we will be unable to tell our children that our appetite for imported fuel was good for their health, for the air they breathe, for the climate in which they live, or, indeed, for their economy. Other industrial democracies have confronted similarly difficult political problems and have made real choices instead of the cost-free "choices" we persist in making. Why not the United States? We could, in my view, work out a farsighted energy policy that would increase our productive use of energy, improve the environment, avert the risk of crisis being imposed by foreign energy producers (whether through a sudden cutoff or a "slow bleed"), and do much to minimize our trade and budgetary deficits.

A main component of such a policy should be an energy consumption tax, or at least a tax on petroleum products, such as a sales tax on gasoline of 25 to 50 cents a gallon that would be phased in over several years. A primary benefit and purpose of such a policy would be to reduce the federal deficit. But a significant gasoline tax would lower the volume of the trade deficit in oil by restraining total U.S. oil consumption. Indirectly it would help to lower the dollar trade deficit by boosting national savings and bringing down world oil prices. This last effect is important. While fearing OPEC's power to push up prices, Americans have seldom understood that the U.S., as the world's largest oil consumer, possesses sufficient buying power to pull down prices, if only we care to use it. With an energy tax, we could at least try to do just that—playing the OPEC game in reverse. A farsighted energy policy would also go much further in encouraging conservation of petroleum and the development of clean energy sources. Here, we should consider not only the risks of dependence on imports and the dangers of a swollen foreign debt, but also the growing national consensus that fossil fuels pose serious environmental hazards, possibly including the greenhouse effect.

Gasoline taxes could raise at least $25 billion and perhaps as much as $40 to $50 billion more yearly in new federal revenue. They could cut our oil import deficit by perhaps $5 to $15 billion yearly, and would still leave us with by far the lowest heating oil and gasoline prices of any major Western nation. Even with an added U.S. gasoline tax of 50 cents a gallon, Americans would still be paying only 40 percent of what consumers pay in other leading industrialized countries, where the average gasoline tax is about $2. During the 1990 U.S. budget "crisis," it was considered a major political triumph that Washington settled on a paltry 5 cents per gallon gas tax. Contrast that to the recent German imposition of an additional 50 cent per gallon tax to pay for their efforts to rebuild East Germany. Eschewing conscious, meaningful choice, we have come to regard cheap gasoline as yet another entitlement.

"CHOICELESS" POLICIES ON DEFICITS, INVESTMENT, AND ENTITLEMENTS

Solving the budget deficit in the United States has never received the serious political attention it deserves. In the wake of the Gulf War, it has become virtually impossible to attract focused attention to this crucial problem at all. Yet the red ink continued to spill forth from Washington as we headed toward a record federal deficit in the range of $300 billion in 1991.

The deficit is likely to remain very high regardless of the exact number. One might well ask: why is this the case, in view of the supposedly "Draconian" efforts to reduce the deficit we have read about? Well, the dirty little secret is we did not do very much about the *big spending items* that have been ballooning out of sight. These include, of course, the vast entitlement programs for the elderly, and other transfer payment programs for the relatively well off. To give you some historical perspective, if you look back twenty-five years, the entitlement programs have *increased* by 6.1 percent of the GNP. Just the *increase* alone is larger than our entire defense budget.

On these issues, as with energy conservation and so many others relating to our real national security, we are refusing to face the problem head-on and make the necessary choices. We have become the "choiceless society," a label inspired by the American poet Peter Viereck who captured something of the national preference with the plea to "suspend me in the choiceless now." One might ask: don't Americans know better? Don't we know that savings and investment are the fuel of productivity and competitiveness? Don't we know that if the Japanese economy invests two and a half times per capita what we put into capital investment, and installs ten times the number of industrial robots per capita as we have in our manufacturing systems, that Japan will be more competitive? Don't we know that education, R & D, and technologically sophisticated investments are required to reverse our lost lead in critical fundamental technologies? Don't we know, living in a society where the phrase "crumbling public infrastructure" has become the ultimate redundancy, that if the Japanese invest ten times what we do in public infrastructure per capita, it is they and not we who will have not just bullet trains, but magnetic-levitation trains running at even higher speed and even more efficiently? And if we Americans know all this, what does it say about the courage of our convictions? Everyone agrees that America has a crying need for public and private *investment*, in both physical and human capital. Indeed, our *rhetorical* investment "imperatives" enjoy a uniquely bipartisan consensus of support that extends from education of the workforce, to infrastructure, to R & D. Everyone agrees except on one brute question: where do we get the *resources* for this consensus investment agenda?

To invest, there must be savings—ours or those of more thrifty people elsewhere. Unfortunately, our largely consumption based deficits constitute negative savings. Counting the S&L bailout and the illusory social security "surpluses," we now face deficits that, incredibly, could average over $300 billion annually between 1991 and 1995. From 1985 through 1989, with federal borrowing wiping out over half of all private sector savings, the U.S. net savings rate fell to 2.2 percent of GNP, less than *one-third* the equivalent rate for the rest of the industrial world.

There were few visible effects of the 1980s "deficit decade" largely because savers from abroad "bailed us out"—even if it did mean borrowing nearly a trillion dollars from them. During the 1990s, however, the two biggest "surplus savers" of the Western world, Japan and Germany, will be less ready lenders. Japan's available savings pool will continue to shrink, as a rapidly aging population saves less, and as the Japanese invest more at home, and spend ever more on consumer goods (both at U.S. urging). Likewise, German savings are now flowing toward the reconstruction of Eastern Europe and the Soviet Union. And reconstruction of the war-ravaged Middle East will be yet another major capital claimant: some estimate that bill will amount to over $100 billion dollars.

As we seek to cut deficits and fund investments, the hard choice between "less spending" and "more taxes" will continue to be interpreted by politicians as a false dichotomy—when our third option is more borrowing. And borrow more we will to fund our deficits. These deficits will increasingly be driven by non-means tested entitlements—benefits passed out regardless of financial need—which have ballooned from $27 billion in 1965 to $472 billion in 1990 and continue to spiral. In addition to current budget deficits, the "pay-as-you-go" financing of our vast entitlement edifice has created *unfunded liabilities* that almost certainly exceed $10 trillion, a hidden debt of $100,000 for every American worker that will be borne by our children.

Our national interest is best served by programs that direct public resources toward *investment* and *youth*—not toward consumption and age. Perversely, we squeeze the former each year, while the latter are Gramm-Rudman "exempt" from cuts and protected with automatic cost-of-living allowances (COLAs). Americans under age eighteen have the highest poverty rate of any age bracket, yet in recent years have received only $1 per capita in federal benefits for every $11 going to Americans over age sixty-five (who have the lowest poverty rate, when all benefits are included as income). From subsidies to rich farmers to free medical care for old millionaires, we have massive "welfare for the well off."

The structural aspects of our entitlements must be put on the table. Setting aside interest costs (a genuinely uncontrollable 16 percent of the budget) and "discretionary expenditures" (which should be raised to the extent they represent genuine public investment), *non-means tested entitlements virtually constitute half of everything left over in the federal budget.* Most of the rest, national defense, is already projected to fall to 4.8 percent of GNP by 1995—the lowest level over the entire postwar era—and the Iraqi adventure reminds us there are clear limits. This latter point bears elaboration. It is commonly felt that spending a dollar less on defense will free up a dollar for "social programs." In reality, there is a complex four-way trade-off among defense, private investment, private consumption, and the various forms of nondefense government spending.

To ensure that the right redirection of resources toward investment is made, we should move from age based to need based transfer payment programs by progressive taxation of benefits, gradual reduction in COLAs for the nonpoor, lower initial benefit levels for upper-income retirees, gradually increasing retirement ages, and increased cost sharing for health benefits. For upper-income beneficiaries like myself, above some threshold, such as an annual income of $50,000, an additional sliding-scale rate of up to 100 percent should be used to tax away the full value of benefits in excess of total contributions plus interest; there should be no more "welfare for the well off." When the Japanese government recognized in 1986 that their versions of these programs were unfair to the young and the cost of its public retirement system was quickly rising to unaffordable heights, it made a clear choice and reduced average future benefit levels by roughly 20 percent. Choicelessly, however, we say it is "politically impossible" to change entitlements. Tomorrow, we may have to relearn—quickly and painfully—the true meaning of impossibility.

The "Reagan Revolution" was no revolution in terms of the largest social entitlement programs; it merely ratified and preserved them, while paying for them not with taxes but with debt and hidden inflation. Tax increases such as the gasoline tax I discussed above must play a role in a *real* revolution. But such taxes will provide only a short-term stopgap solution. Without structural entitlement reform, but with greater longevity, earlier retirement, low birth rates, and medical hyperinflation, the cost of our federal entitlements system could climb by a colossal 11.5 percentage points of GNP between 1991 and the year 2025, necessitating a tax of 20 to 40 percent of worker payrolls to pay for it. Even if the public consensus were suddenly to shift to allow such an unsustainable level of new taxes, these increased revenues would at best simply cover entitlement cost increases—leaving nothing to meet the needs of the new "imperative" investment agenda in other crucial areas such as education, R & D, and infrastructure, which lie at the heart of what I believe are our real national security interests. Here, too, our rhetoric overwhelms reality. We may say that regaining our competitiveness is "essential" to our economic security, but we ignore the awkward question: what are we willing to give up to get it back?

It is said that our current deficit debacle is a tragic political gridlock, between those who want high spending and those who want low taxes. In fact, no one is truly choosing and both sides are getting just what they want: *high spending* and *low taxes.* Judged by our actions, what we really want is to protect *ourselves*—at the expense of our children.

43.   Downsizing America's Overseas Role

There are at least 10 good reasons why the U.S. should begin gradually to reduce its foreign military involvements, close down its costly foreign bases, and withdraw and demobilize all U.S. troops in foreign countries by the year 2000.

Reason 1: U.S. Military Forces Based in Foreign Countries Do Not Contribute to the Defense of the U.S.   There is no national consensus about what constitutes the "vital interests" of the U.S. There is also no consensus about how to protect them. Interests change with time and politics, but most people would agree that America does not have interests everywhere in the world and that some interests matter more than others.

According to General Wallace Nutting, former Commander-in-Chief of the U.S. Readiness Command, "We today do not have a single soldier, airman, or sailor solely dedicated to the security mission within the United States." In fact, about 70 percent of America's annual military spending and most of its military forces—even those based in the U.S.—are intended to further U.S. capabilities for fighting nonnuclear, "conventional" wars in foreign countries.

Many things said to be vital interests cost more to defend than they are worth. While America's industries, living standards, and military power remain all too dependent upon oil, *any hardship suffered by the U.S. from losing access to Persian Gulf oil or from an increase in the price of oil seems negligible when compared with the devastating costs of war.*

Persian Gulf oil is much less important to the U.S. than it is to Europe and Japan. Japan imports 99 percent of the oil it consumes, 70 percent coming from Gulf countries. The U.S., on the other hand, imports 46 percent of the oil it uses. Only 24 percent of U.S. oil imports and 8.5 percent of total U.S. energy supplies come from the Persian

SOURCE: Center for Defense Information, "The U.S. as the World's Policeman?" *The Defense Monitor*, vol. XX, no. 1, 1991, pp. 2–7, excerpts. Reprinted with the permission of the Center for Defense Information.

Gulf. Iraqi and Kuwaiti oil together account for just 7.5 percent of all U.S. oil imports.

A country willing to spend almost $300 Billion each year for its military certainly could endure the far smaller economic costs of a cutoff of the supply of less than a quarter of its foreign oil. If the U.S. spent only half as much money on domestic energy conservation and diversification efforts as it does on military forces to fight for oil, the nation would be far more secure in terms of energy resources.

Interests that were defined in the context of the Cold War—particularly containment of communism—are now overdue for reevaluation. *Those interests precious enough to be deemed "vital interests" should have a direct, immediate, and substantial connection with America's physical survival.* First and foremost the U.S. should defend its own territory and the immediate approaches to its territory.

Reason 2: The U.S. Is Not Bound By Treaties to Use Its Military Forces to Defend Other Countries   Two hundred years ago George Washington admonished his countrymen to "steer clear of permanent alliances." Thomas Jefferson spoke of "peace, commerce, and honest friendship with all nations, entangling alliances with none." For most of America's history their advice was heeded. Since World War II, however, the U.S. has signed military treaties with 43 countries.

Nevertheless, *not one U.S. defense treaty with other countries commits America to military action in the event of an attack on its treaty partners. Nor does any treaty require the U.S. to station its armed forces on another country's territory.*

The North Atlantic Treaty, signed in 1949, states that an attack against one or more alliance member "shall be considered an attack against them all." Each alliance member, however, retains the right to decide "individually and in concert with the other parties *such action as it deems necessary* [emphasis added], including the use of armed force."

The original U.S.-Japan Security Treaty, signed in 1951, stated that "the U.S. is presently willing to maintain forces in and about Japan," but "in the expectation, however, that Japan will itself increasingly assume responsibility for its own defense against direct and indirect aggression." Similarly, the revised treaty in effect today does not commit a single U.S. soldier, sailor, airman, or Marine to defend Japan.

America always has possessed the freedom to bring home its military forces in foreign countries whenever it chooses. It need not secure the blessing or permission of host governments or enter into drawn-out negotiations before closing obsolete bases and withdrawing troops.

Reason 3: The World Has Changed Significantly

The existing U.S. military force structure, with its forward deployment of troops and weapons in foreign countries and waters, was designed to meet the perceived threats of a very different world. Over the past few years some startling changes have taken place.

Communism in Eastern Europe has collapsed. East and West Germany have united. As a military organization the Warsaw Pact is defunct. . . .

Just how much the world has changed is perhaps most evident in Germany's agreement to pay the Soviet Union several Billion dollars a year to subsidize—until they depart—the 600,000 Soviet troops and dependents remaining in what used to be East Germany. In Asia, meanwhile, the Soviet Union may return several islands to Japan which it has occupied since World War II. Relations between North and South Korea are improving to the point where federation before the end of the century seems possible.

In today's world *national power has become more complex. It is defined as much by economic, social, and political components as by military power.* Today military power generally is less practical, less usable, and less translatable into political or economic advantage. Increasingly, economic leadership is the true measure of a nation's strength. While governments in the Soviet Union, Europe, and Japan appear to have recognized this, U.S. officials lag behind.

America can ill afford to continue to postpone putting its economic house in order. It needs an economy that is innovative, that is dynamic, and

that is doing the kinds of things people now see Japan doing. If the economic challenge goes unmet, then our security is threatened. The American way of life can be endangered by economic weakness just as surely as by a Soviet attack. In fact, *economic vulnerability now is a much greater threat to the U.S. than Soviet aggression.*

Reason 4: Other Countries Are Capable of Providing Their Own Defenses

The countries hosting U.S. troops are more than capable of providing for themselves whatever military forces they deem necessary. Europe and Japan have long since recovered from the ravages of World War II. If anything, the ongoing U.S. military subsidy only acts as an incentive for host countries to be militarily weak, perpetuates a dependent relationship, and suggests that the security of these countries means more to the U.S. than it does to them.

Today the European members of the NATO military alliance have a collective gross national product (GNP) greater than that of the U.S. and at least two times greater than that of the Soviet Union. Yet *America spends more on NATO defenses than the other 15 alliance members combined.*

America's European NATO allies collectively have more than 3 million active-duty troops drawn from a combined population of almost 400 million. If needed, between them there are 87 million males aged 15–49 available for military service. Excluding Britain and Iceland, neither of which has compulsory military service, about 2.6 million males in the remaining 12 European NATO countries reach draft age annually.

Beyond questions of manpower sufficiency, France, Britain, Germany, and Italy—powerful industrial countries that are among the world's 10 leading exporters of weapons—are capable of manufacturing in mass quantity all of the weapons necessary to satisfy their own security requirements. France and Britain also possess sizable stocks of nuclear weapons.

Germany, the world's leading exporter of goods, hosted 240,000 U.S. troops before President Bush reassigned some units to the Persian Gulf. Yet a unified Germany has a population of 78 million and a military force that currently numbers almost

600,000 troops (to be reduced to 370,000 troops by the end of 1994). If needed, Germany now has 17 million males aged 15–49 available for military service. Every year about 418,000 German males reach military age.

Japan, although it faces no military threats, hosted 47,000 U.S. troops before President Bush ordered some of the Marines in Okinawa to the Persian Gulf. It is the world's second-ranking economic power with a GNP of $2.8 Trillion. It has a population of almost 124 million and more than 27 million males aged 15–49 available for military service. About a million Japanese males reach draft age annually.

South Korea remains host to 41,000 U.S. troops even though the Pentagon admitted in testimony to Congress that "South Korean forces are capable of defending themselves against any threat from the North that does not involve either the Soviet Union or the People's Republic of China." South Korea's population of 43 million is twice that of North Korea. Its economy is 10 times larger. It has more than 8 million males aged 15–49 available for military service. Every year about 445,000 South Korean males reach military age.

The Philippines, confronting only internal threats from the rebel New People's Army . . . has a population of 66 million, of which more than 11 million are males aged 15–49 available for military service. About 685,000 Filipino males reach draft age yearly.

Reason 5: The World Does Not Need the U.S. to Be Global Policeman The Bush Administration maintains that American troops must remain in allied countries as their security blanket, preparing not only to meet every known threat and enemy, but also to meet the "unforeseeable," and as yet unidentified, threats and enemies that may or may not materialize in the future. It cautions that the U.S. must guard against a possible reversal of policy in the Soviet Union and serve as a stabilizing force in the face of potential "volatility" and "turbulence" from ethnic, nationality, and religious conflicts and separatist movements. . . .

With the November 1990 signing of the Conventional Forces in Europe (CFE) Treaty, the Soviet

Union has agreed to destroy tens of thousands of its tanks, armored combat vehicles, artillery weapons, and combat aircraft. In the future *the U.S. may have as much as 2 years warning in which to dispatch military forces to Europe in the unlikely event that the Soviet military decided to prepare to fight its way through Eastern Europe to attack Western Europe.*

Many uncertainties and potential instabilities in the world are either peripheral or irrelevant to U.S. security and thus do not warrant American military involvement. If Romania and Hungary were to go to war over the disputed territory of Transylvania, for example, or if hostilities between Croatia and Serbia were to lead to civil war in Yugoslavia, in neither case would vital American interests be threatened.

The U.N. Security Council, with its multinational peace-keeping forces, or the strengthened dispute resolution mechanisms of the Conference on Security and Cooperation in Europe (CSCE), including the newly-established Center for the Prevention of Conflict, are better suited to intervene in such situations than are U.S. troops.

Increasingly, the leading concerns of nations in Western Europe are drugs, unemployment, environmental degradation, and the potential mass immigration of people from Eastern Europe and elsewhere—hardly problems that can be prevented or resolved with U.S. military forces. *Military might is a blunt instrument good at destroying things and killing people, but not at resolving complex political, ethnic, religious, and historical disputes.*

It is not in America's interest to be the world's "911 number." If the U.S. withdraws its forward-based military forces, the world is not going to come apart and America's security is not going to suffer. Since the peak years of the 1960s when it had bases in or special access arrangements with more than 60 countries, the U.S. has pulled military forces out of a number of countries. In no case has this led to a lasting decline in security.

Reason 6: Military Forces in the U.S. Can Respond Quickly to Crises Anywhere in the World At one time the U.S. needed bases abroad in order to supply coal, food, water, and supplies to Navy ships and their crews. In the early years of the Cold War it needed airfields for American nuclear bombers that lacked sufficient range to reach the Soviet Union from bases in the U.S. But today, while foreign bases may continue to be convenient to the U.S. in some cases, they are not vital to American security.

With in-flight refueling, modern U.S. Air Force strategic bombers can reach targets anywhere in the world within hours. Intercontinental ballistic missiles (ICBMs) can devastate the Soviet Union within half an hour. "Over-the-horizon" satellite communications have greatly diminished the need for radio relay stations.

The U.S. Navy has underway 56 replenishment ships to supply warships in distant waters with fuel, ammunition, and other stores. It has 41 maintenance logistics ships to provide repairs when necessary. Nuclear propulsion, by increasing the global reach of ships and submarines, has decreased the importance to the U.S. of having naval refueling facilities in other countries.

In the future there are likely to be increasingly fewer instances in which it would be in American interests to intervene militarily in foreign countries. But if deemed necessary, the U.S. can quickly dispatch armed forces to any place in the world from bases in California, North Carolina, and many other American locations. *There is no military requirement to have U.S. troops and weapons in place in foreign countries.*

Modern long-range transport aircraft, aerial refueling tankers, and strategic sealift ships have largely eliminated the need for overseas staging facilities. Currently the U.S. Air Force has 110 C-5 and 250 C-141 long-range cargo aircraft. It plans to build 120 new C-17 cargo aircraft. It has 591 KC-135 tanker aircraft for in-flight refueling. The U.S. Navy has 69 active sealift ships.

For additional air- and sealift the U.S. can rely on 504 commercial aircraft in its Civil Reserve Air Fleet, 242 reserve ships (93 Ready Reserve Force ships and 149 National Defense Reserve Fleet ships), and 318 U.S.-flag and effectively U.S.-controlled ships. . . .

The U.S. airlifted more personnel and equipment in the first 3 weeks of the Persian Gulf buildup than it moved in the first 3 months of the Korean War. By the sixth week the U.S. already had moved by air the equivalent of what was delivered during the entire 65 weeks of the 1948–49 Berlin Airlift.

Reason 7: Military Forces Do Not Assure Economic Access and Political Influence   Some argue that it is in the interest of the U.S. to keep military forces abroad because their presence in foreign countries enhances America's "status," guarantees the U.S. a voice in the affairs of the host countries, and reassures American companies conducting business in other countries. Total two-way American trade with Europe exceeds $200 Billion annually, with East Asia $300 Billion.

Having military forces abroad however, contributes little if anything to America's economic access and political influence around the world. On the contrary, *by continuing to relieve major economic competitors such as Germany and Japan of the military burden of providing their own defenses, the U.S. weakens its own security by placing unnecessary strains on its economy.*

At the present the U.S. still has the largest economy in the world. By virtue of this fact, it will have economic access, troops or no troops. As for providing security for businesses, a recent survey of multinational corporations operating in the Philippines revealed that the presence of American military bases ranked only tenth in their decision to invest there.

There is little recent evidence that having U.S. military forces in foreign countries translates into political influence. During the 1973 Yom Kippur war in the Middle East the U.S. was denied access to facilities and airspace over Western Europe in order to resupply Israel with weapons. In the early 1980s America's European allies refused to accede to Reagan Administration wishes that construction of a natural gas pipeline to the Soviet Union be stopped.

After the 1985 hijacking of the Achille Lauro cruise ship, Italian and American troops squared off against each other over the issue of custody of suspected terrorist Muhammad Abbas. European governments denied overflight rights for the Reagan Administration's bombing of Libya in 1986. Throughout the 1980s the Europeans also disagreed with U.S. policies toward Central America.

In the future it would be unwise for the U.S. to rely on its military power to influence other countries, whether friends or adversaries. America's foreign military bases increasingly are a drain on, rather than a contributor to, its national power. *It is in the interest of the U.S. to remain actively involved in the world's affairs, but primarily through economic and diplomatic efforts with much less reliance on military strength.*

Reason 8: U.S. Military Forces Are Not Needed to Deter German and Japanese Rearmament The reason for stationing U.S. military forces in Europe and in Asia sometimes has been expressed as follows: "to keep the Soviets out, the Americans in, and the Germans and Japanese down." Pointing to the last objective, some argue that withdrawing U.S. military forces would leave "power vacuums" that would encourage former World War II villains Germany and Japan to rearm even more than they already have, making neighboring countries apprehensive and resulting in regional instability.

Even while American troops have been stationed on their soil both countries, with U.S. encouragement, have amassed powerful militaries. Continuing to keep U.S. troops in Germany and Japan will not prevent these countries from exercising their sovereign right to further add to their armed forces if they so choose. On the other hand, it should be recognized that *German and Japanese citizens today have thoroughly rejected militarism and aggression.*

For the foreseeable future, battles involving Germany and Japan and other countries will remain in the global marketplace. What possible advantage could these economic juggernauts acquire through military means that cannot be satisfied without loss of blood through their powerful economies? . . .

Reason 9: U.S. Forces Are Wearing Out Their Welcome Anti-American sentiment is on the rise

in many of the places where U.S. military forces are stationed. The State Department recently cautioned Americans in the Philippines about "possible imminent terrorist bombing" by rebel guerrillas. Similarly, in South Korea the continued presence of U.S. forces has strengthened opposition groups and placed Americans at risk.

In Germany, many citizens have demanded reductions in destructive military training on their country's land and in its airspace. U.S. and other NATO forces already have been forced to limit the amount of realistic training they conduct to minimize citizen complaints regarding noise, environmental damage, and safety.

Support for U.S. bases and forces has declined in other countries as well. *Increasingly, American military forces abroad are regarded as an infringement upon sovereignty. They have outlived their usefulness and overstayed their welcome.*

Some host governments, given the choice, would prefer that the U.S. military remain in their countries. Through money spent and foreign nationals employed, American bases are a boon to host country economies. In addition, base rights agreements often entail quid pro quo transactions in the form of economic and military aid. . . .

When they leave, numerous enterprises, including apartments, bars, restaurants, and brothels, will be affected. But *the purpose of the U.S. military should be to defend the U.S., not to stimulate the economies of other countries.*

Reason 10: Withdrawing and Demobilizing U.S. Forces Will Save Tens of Billions of Dollars It costs more to operate military bases in expensive environments like Europe and Japan than in the U.S. As the value of the dollar drops, maintaining foreign bases becomes even more expensive. A dollar, worth 3.5 German marks in 1987, today is worth only 1.6 marks. *Withdrawing and demobilizing American military personnel and civilian Pentagon employees stationed in Europe and in Asia would go a long way toward resolving America's budget problems.*

In 1988 the U.S. spent $3.5 Billion to construct and repair bases in foreign countries, $2.7 Billion to employ 120,000 foreign nationals, $1.3 Billion for overseas cost-of-living differentials and supplements, $12.5 Billion for base operation support costs, and $500 million for financing currency fluctuations.

With their supermarkets, shopping malls, split-level homes, swimming pools, schools, day care centers, bowling alleys, barber shops, bars, and barbeque pits, America's foreign bases could be Anytown, USA. As such, they are enormously expensive to sustain. It costs the Pentagon about a Billion dollars alone each year to operate 271 schools for 150,000 American children at foreign bases in 19 countries.

In 1988 the Pentagon spent $1.3 Billion on travel costs for permanent change-of-station moves to foreign bases. Every month that year the Pentagon flew about 12,000 U.S. troops and 10,000 dependents between the U.S. and Germany. It costs American taxpayers about $4,000 for the Pentagon to relocate an enlisted soldier and family to Germany. It costs $13,000 to relocate an officer.

Every year the Pentagon transports 750 million pounds of household effects to foreign bases at a cost of about half a Billion dollars. In accordance with the so-called "buy American" rule, it stocks overseas commissaries and PXs with American-made goods at a cost of about $250 million annually. To pet owners, the Pentagon supplies 432,000 cases of cat and dog food. It provides American-brewed Miller, Coors, and Budweiser to soldiers stationed in beer-rich Germany.

In 1989 the Army shipped almost 50,000 cars to Europe at a cost of $1,000 per car—the shipping cost sometimes exceeding the value of the car. The total amount spent on delivering service members' cars equaled what was spent on transporting ammunition!

WHITHER THE U.S.?

The Pentagon's "forward defense" strategy of stationing U.S. military forces in foreign countries and in distant waters is now obsolete. America far too long has borne the burden of defending other countries that now are more than capable of defending themselves.

The U.S. has a choice. It can adapt to a changing world and begin drastically to reduce its military burdens by closing its foreign military bases and bringing troops home. We can choose to pay greater attention to crucial non-military determinants of the nation's security—social, political, economic and environmental components. Or the U.S. can further strain its economy and weaken its security by continuing and expanding its role as the world's policeman.

44.   A Conservative Conspectus

Conservative policies won the Cold War. Americans now will tend to look to conservatives for policies to lead the nation into the new era. The anti-communism and anti-Sovietism of conservatives sprang from a set of values and principles that in part predate, and in part have been shaped and influenced by, the Cold War experience. Conserva-

SOURCE: The Staff of The Heritage Foundation, "Making the World Safe for America: A U.S. Foreign Policy Blueprint," Washington, D.C.: April 1992, pp. 5-9; 11-24, excerpts. Reprinted with permission of The Heritage Foundation, Washington, DC.

tives first should look inward to these precepts to formulate a policy for the post-Cold War world. . . .

While the spread of democracy and free markets virtually by definition is in America's interests, the question that arises is the means by which America will advance democracy. Unless American interests are involved directly, these means almost without exception will be economic and diplomatic. While altruism surely is a noble instinct for individuals, governments are established solely to protect the interests of their own citizens. American resources, and lives, should be committed abroad sparingly and with the nation's interests in mind, no matter how noble the cause. . . .

America is not and should not be in the business of sending its armies abroad to benefit others when no American interests are at stake. America should not impose economic sanctions on a foreign country exclusively to help others if doing so hurts Americans. And it should not use taxpayers' money to promote foreign aid projects unless it can prove that these projects benefit U.S. strategic or economic interests. Americans are a generous people and may at times wish to extend charity through the auspices of their government. But as a rule, charity is a job best left to private individuals and private organizations.

Good Government is Limited Government. In the 20th century, as before, big government is the greatest threat to liberty. This has clear implications for American foreign policy. An overly ambitious foreign policy, particularly when it leads to military entanglement, poses domestic dangers because it fosters big government. Indeed, today's mammoth federal government is the product not so much of the New Deal but of the massive power assembled in Washington to wage World War II and the Cold War.

The huge Pentagon, of course, has preserved America's freedom; but it also legitimizes the vast centralization of power required to run the huge domestic programs started by Lyndon Johnson and Richard Nixon. Thus, while conservatives accepted the large Pentagon needed to wage the Cold War, [with the end of the Soviet threat] conservatives would welcome a dramatically smaller Pentagon and State Department. . . .

Power Still Matters. In a world of sovereign states, conflicts of interest will continue to arise. In this sense, conservatives are realists. They do not believe that there is immanent consensus in the international system on which to found a new world order. To the extent there is order, it will be enforced by states with predominant power and influence. Power will continue to be exercised through the traditional tools of statecraft, including diplomatic negotiation, economic incentives and sanctions, and ultimately military force. To maintain control of its destiny and defend its interests,

America will need the will and ability to exercise power in all its forms. . . .

Foreign Aid Is Not Charity. Internationally, as at home, the most efficient and deserving form of welfare is that which assists those willing to work hard to help themselves. Except for rare cases of disaster when outright charity is called for, foreign assistance should be tailored to help individuals and nations to better themselves by encouraging private enterprise and investment. Massive handouts to foreign governments and government-to-government loans are not legitimate uses of American taxpayers' money. They also strengthen the size and power of governments in recipient nations, burden these nations with debt, and hamper economic growth. When assistance is given, it should be predicated on such measures as trade liberalization, deregulation, lower taxes, and other measures that spur economic growth, expand economic liberty, encourage investment, and ultimately allow these countries to prosper. This then creates new markets for American exports and new sources for American imports.

GIVE NO NATION OR ORGANIZATION A VETO OVER AMERICAN ACTIONS

Sovereignty is the greatest guarantee of Americans' freedom. No institution, including the United Nations, should be given a veto over the sovereign decisions of the U.S. government, nor should U.N. approval be required for actions, military or otherwise, deemed in America's national interests. The defense of American liberty is justification enough. . . .

HISTORY COUNSELS COMMITMENT

Conservatives take their lesson from history. If there is a single overriding lesson for America from the history of this century it is this: America cannot ignore the affairs of the world and remain safe. After World War I, America learned the price of isolation. The country avoided the same mistake after World War II. America also learned from its mistakes in Vietnam and Lebanon that when the nation does become involved militarily in other states, the American military must be allowed to fight to win. . . .

Conservative principles must be applied collectively, with one tempering another. Together they constitute a general approach to America's role in the world, founded in the defense of America's vital interests, a faith in liberty, a devotion to basic American values and Western civilization, and a belief in the principles of limited government, free markets, and individual self-reliance.

In assessing concrete policy in a changing world, it is necessary first to identify the specific threats to each of America's interests, and to use conservative principles as a guide for devising strategies and policies for defending America against these threats.

INTEREST #1: PROTECT AMERICA'S TERRITORY AND AIRSPACE.

THREAT: Long-range Missiles Armed with Nuclear Weapons.

While the former Soviet Republics, now members of the Commonwealth of Independent States (CIS), promise to keep nuclear weapons under central control, Belarus, Kazahkstan, Russia, and Ukraine have nuclear weapons capable of obliterating much of America in about half an hour. During the Cold War, the main threat to America had been a deliberate Soviet nuclear attack. The main threat now is of an accidental or unauthorized attack as political and military powers fragment in the former Soviet Union. Meanwhile, the former Soviet arsenal to this day continues to be modernized, and again would become a threat in the event of a reactionary coup in Moscow. . . .

U.S. Action

With proliferation of missile technology an increasing threat to America, deployment of anti-missile weapons now should be America's top defense priority. While America has the offensive nuclear weapons capacity today to respond in kind to any attack, it has no ability to defend itself in the event

of an accidental or unauthorized attack, or an irrational attack by an unstable dictator.

Deploying an effective defense against a limited missile attack will require allowing the 1972 Anti-Ballistic Missile Treaty to lapse, now that America's treaty partner, the Soviet Union, no longer exists. The U.S. then could negotiate a new treaty permitting ground- and space-based defenses against limited attacks. Whether or not agreement is reached, the U.S. should deploy about 750 interceptors at six to eight sites across America, 1,000 space-based interceptors, and space-based sensors. Preferably the U.S. and Russia will cooperate on this program. The U.S. should begin deploying this system in 1996 and pursue a bold research and development program to deploy such advanced Strategic Defense Initiative (SDI) systems as particle beams when they are ready in the next century. . . .

INTEREST #2: PREVENT A MAJOR POWER THREAT TO EUROPE, ASIA, OR THE PERSIAN GULF.

THREAT: Short-term Revived Soviet Threat.

Even as its economy collapsed in 1991, the former Soviet Union outproduced all NATO members combined in major weapons systems, including tanks, artillery, armored troop carriers, and short- and long-range missiles. Even in its current weakened state, the ex-Soviet military far outclasses any other potential adversary except the U.S. If the ex-Soviet military were to come under the control of reactionary forces, it could become an expansionist threat within the borders of the former Soviet Union, and even outside those borders in Eastern Europe and elsewhere along the ex-Soviet periphery.

U.S. Action

While decreasing, the possibility of a revived threat from the CIS warrants a U.S. policy to ensure that the Soviet Union, or anything like it, is never put back together again. The goal of the U.S. should not be to guarantee a regional balance of power in the territory of the former Soviet Union—to prevent a democratic Russia, for example, from gaining pre-eminence in the region—but to encourage democracy and free markets in Russia and other republics as alternatives to totalitarianism and authoritarianism. While the U.S. can have only limited control over events in the former Soviet Union, it can strengthen the stability of elected governments committed to democratic and free market reforms, particularly in Russia and Ukraine. . . .

THREAT: Eventual Rise of Another Hostile Major Power in Europe.

Throughout this century, Berlin and Moscow have been the centers of expansionist, revisionist discontent in Europe, leading to two World Wars and a Cold War. With Germany reunited and America withdrawing the bulk of its military forces from Europe, Germany will be a question mark in the eyes of many Europeans until it demonstrates over time its commitment to democratic institutions and common security with its neighbors. Over the longer term, Russia, too, has the population and resources to threaten its neighbors.

U.S. Action

With the last of the totalitarian threats to Europe now disappearing and no other on the horizon, America's military involvement in Europe can be cut drastically. If the former Soviet threat continues to collapse, the U.S. need have no more than about 25,000 to 50,000 troops in Europe. In the meantime, however, somewhat higher levels of U.S. troops could be maintained for a few years if the situation in the former Soviet Union remains uncertain. As a sign of America's commitment, these troops would deter the type of hegemonic forces, in Germany or Russia, that eventually could upset the European balance and jeopardize America's interests. The U.S. troops in Europe thus would be mostly air and naval forces.

Given America's enduring interests in Europe and the price which America has paid this century to protect them, America should remain closely involved in European affairs, albeit as a mainly offshore power, to convey the will and ability to protect its European interests. . . .

America then will have to follow a two-track policy, accepting the necessity, and advantages, of European integration, yet at the same time seeking avenues to maintain its own influence over European affairs. Toward these ends, the U.S. should:

1. Not impede European integration, including defense and foreign policy integration. The European Community (EC) agreements signed at Maastricht last December 10 include the incorporation of the West European Union (WEU) as a military arm of the EC and set the objective of a common EC foreign policy. While the U.S. should not endorse a common EC foreign and defense policy, it should not view the EC and WEU as rivals to NATO. Particularly with the U.S. withdrawing most of its forces from Europe, it will be the EC and WEU which must anchor Germany in a common security structure, a role up to now played by NATO. A strong EC, moreover, will help Europe take the lead in resolving issues that do not affect U.S. security directly, like the war between Croatia and Serbia. . . .

2. Remain politically involved in Europe through NATO and the Conference on Security and Cooperation in Europe. The North Atlantic Treaty Organization should remain in place as a sign of America's enduring interest in European affairs. However, with the continuing decline of NATO's main *raison d' etre*, the Soviet threat, NATO inevitably will shrivel as a working military organization. The character of the alliance will change. The regular military exercises and day-to-day cooperation that characterized a tight alliance with hundreds of thousands of troops stationed in close proximity on each other's territory will disappear. Each of NATO's armies will be stationed for the most part on its home country's territory. Even those stationed abroad will have dual assignments (for the Europeans this will be the West European Union, destined to become the military arm of the EC). NATO's forces occasionally will engage in joint exercises, much as Americans sometimes train with

the Association of South East Asian Nations (ASEAN) or Australia. NATO's joint military command should, and probably will, remain in place for the time being. . . .

THREAT: Rise of a Hegemonic Power or Renewed Military Competition in Asia.

In Asia, only Japan now has the economic and technological capability to build the nuclear and power projection forces to threaten East Asia. While this is very unlikely absent a major shock of some sort, such as a trade war or global depression, Japan, like Germany, for the first time since World War II will be less dependent on America for its self-defense needs if the former Soviet threat continues to recede.

Much more so than Germany's neighbors in Europe, Japan's neighbors undoubtedly will be nervous about a former enemy again unfettered. Unlike in Europe, there is no emerging "community" to take over the stabilizing role of the U.S. and no community to absorb and tame Japan as the EC and WEU do with Germany. If Japan begins to feel insecure in the face, for example, of a nuclear-armed North Korea or saber-rattling China; or if Japan decides to rearm, sparking a reaction among its neighbors, U.S. interests could be jeopardized. Trade could be disrupted in a region that now accounts for more than 50 percent of U.S. trade. More serious would be a regional arms buildup, perhaps leading to nuclear proliferation and conflict.

Over the longer term, China could pose a threat to East Asia, as could India, which already has demonstrated imperial behavior against its neighbors. Today, however, China and India lack the economic or technological capability to mount any but local military threats or to build a modern and technologically advanced military.

U.S. Action

Given the stabilizing effect of the U.S. military in East Asia—reassuring Japan, obviating the need for powerful Japanese forces, and thus reassuring the former victims of Japanese aggression—America should keep strong naval forces in and near the region. These forces should include the current aircraft carrier battle group based in Yokosuka, Japan, and four carrier groups based on the U.S. West coast; this basing structure keeps at least two carrier groups always available for quick deployment. Close U.S. defense ties with Japan are needed to help prevent Japanese rearmament. Thus the U.S. should continue to conduct joint exercises and military planning with Japan, and continue to station U.S. military forces there, albeit at reduced levels, as long as Japan is willing to share the costs. The U.S. also should continue cooperating closely with the six Southeast Asian nations comprising ASEAN, which are important trading partners and potential staging areas for U.S. forces in the region.

America's China policy is up for re-evaluation since the most important reason for maintaining special ties to Beijing has been to balance Soviet power in the region. China's arms dealing with Iran and Libya bears close watching. For the most part, though, China is a military threat only in the distant future, if then. America and the rest of the West will be in a race to open China, economically and politically, before it develops the economic capacity to be a major regional superpower.

America's strategy in this regard should be to pry China open, rather than to isolate it. . . .

THREAT: Eventual Rise of a Hostile Hegemonic Power in the Persian Gulf.

The Persian Gulf, which contains two-thirds of the world's oil reserves, would give a hostile power enormous economic resources to build a modern military machine and, possibly, a nuclear arsenal. The two chief regional threats, Iran and Iraq, are infused with radical anti-Western ideologies, Islamic fundamentalism, or pan-Arab socialism. . . .

Both, too, have undertaken large-scale military buildups which include, it is widely assumed, attempts to acquire nuclear weapons. These buildups not only threaten American forces and America's friends in the region, particularly Israel and Saudi Arabia, but eventually could threaten the U.S. if Iran and Iraq acquired intercontinental ballistic missiles. The principal strategic aim of the U.S. in the Persian Gulf should be to prevent the rise of a hostile hegemonic power that could turn the enormous oil wealth of the region against the U.S.

U.S. Action

To guard against the rise of such a hostile hegemonic power in the Persian Gulf, the U.S. should remain the dominant external military power in the region and the chief guarantor of the security of Saudi Arabia and the other conservative Arab states of the Gulf. The U.S. goal should be the forging of a stable regional balance of power in which Persian Gulf oil continues to flow, unimpeded by regional conflict or the hostile policies of a regional hegemonic power. To assure this, the U.S. should:

1. Maintain forces armed and equipped to project power rapidly from the U.S. to the Persian Gulf, even without the support of local allies. This requires the deployment of a strong naval force in the region, including at least one aircraft carrier battle group continuously in the Persian Gulf area, along with a quick reaction force of Marines. U.S. F-15 *Eagle* fighter-bombers should be rotated into Saudi or other air bases continually for joint training exercises. . . .

2. Strengthen military cooperation with conservative Arab Gulf states. To increase the ability of Saudi Arabia, Kuwait and other conservative Arab Gulf states to resist Iranian and Iraqi aggression, Washington should increase the number and scale of joint military exercises with these countries, assist them with military training, stockpile military supplies on their territory if possible, and increase joint military planning. The U.S. should consider arms sales to these countries if the arms in question do not threaten Israel's security.

3. Contain the Iraqi threat. To reduce Iraq's threat to Persian Gulf stability, the U.S. should try to oust Saddam Hussein, who likely will seek vengeance against the U.S. and its allies as long as he survives. Because the Iraqi opposition is weak and divided, the chief threat to Saddam's power is the Iraqi army. The U.S. should encour-

age the Iraqi army to overthrow Saddam, by maintaining U.N.-sponsored political and economic sanctions and steadily increasing political, economic, and military support to the Iraqi opposition, especially the Kurds. Regardless of who is in power in Baghdad, the U.S. should seek systematically to destroy Iraq's ability to build and deploy weapons of mass destruction. . . .

INTEREST #3: ACCESS TO RESOURCES AND FREEDOM OF THE SEAS

THREAT: Uncertainty of Supply . . .

The decline of the Soviet military threat removes the chief reason for worrying about continued U.S. access to oil, strategic minerals, and other resources vital to U.S. security. Not only is the risk of a Soviet seizure of strategic resource-rich regions, such as Persian Gulf oil fields and South African minerals, greatly reduced, if not eliminated, but the threat that Soviet naval or air forces will interdict the flow of oil or strategic materials such as chromium, cobalt, or manganese has all but ended. Moreover, the likelihood of a lengthy conventional war between the U.S. and the Soviet Union, the worst-case scenario which motivated the buildup of strategic mineral stockpiles, has declined to almost zero. . . .

U.S. Action

The U.S. should rely on the market to safeguard its access to strategic resources over the long term. Higher prices for imported resources may impose economic costs in the form of inflation, slower economic growth, and balance of payments effects, but higher prices also help to improve U.S. resource security by encouraging an increase in domestic supplies and reduction in demand. . . .

Although the U.S. could ride out most oil crises with little economic damage, a major crisis in the Persian Gulf that resulted in the loss of its roughly 15 million barrels per day of oil production, about 25 percent of total world oil production, temporarily would wreak havoc in the world economy.

Although this scenario is unlikely, the U.S. should hedge against the unknown and maintain strong military forces in the Persian Gulf region to help deter another Saddam Hussein-type lunge for oil. The use of military force should be considered only as a last resort. In the long run, America's first line of defense against resource shortages is the free market, not the armed forces. . . .

INTEREST #4: FREE TRADE

THREAT: Protectionism, Trade Wars, Trading Blocs.

The disruption of free trade is the only non-military threat to America's vital interests around the world. Protectionism and ensuing trade wars can decrease American living standards and even trigger worldwide depression. This in turn can lead to military conflict as trading blocs begin to grab for new markets and access to resources. The two great threats to free trade would be a protectionist European Community and a Japan even more protectionist than it already is.

U.S. Action

The protectionist threats from the European Community and Japan are arising at just the time when the U.S. is losing its main source of leverage over the EC and Japan—their need for American military protection against the Soviet Union. The U.S. will have to develop other means of leverage against the EC and Japan if it is to force them to keep their markets open. This leverage cannot take the form of what is called "industrial policy" or "planned trade" or other forms of U.S. protectionism. These bureaucratic schemes inevitably fail because they hurt American consumers and producers enormously and thus weaken the American economy. Developing effective alternative means of applying pressure is a high priority task for the U.S.

America's best weapon is free trade itself. America should seek free trade agreements around the world, including with the entire Western hemisphere, Eastern Europe, and Russia and the emerging states of the CIS. This will help cushion the U.S. if the EC and Japan turn more protectionist. . . .

OTHER SECURITY COMMITMENTS

Outside of its commitments to NATO and Japan, the cornerstones of America's containment policy, America during the past four decades has accepted other explicit or tacit commitments that inevitably will be reevaluated in light of the Cold War's end. The three most important of these are the defense of Israel, the Republic of China on Taiwan, and the Republic of Korea.

In each instance, the case remains that the commitment serves U.S. interests, although in no case is this argument as strong as it was during the Cold War.

Even today, however, a successful aggression by North Korea against South Korea, or mainland China against the Republic of China on Taiwan, would affect U.S. interests in the region. In either case, Japan would feel threatened by the outcome, and could well begin to rearm. This could lead to the instability and arms racing that America most fears in the region.

In Israel's case, the country remains a stable, democratic, and reliable friend, almost surely available if needed as a staging area for U.S. forces in a critical area of the world. Unlike the vulnerable regimes of such allies as Saudi Arabia and Kuwait, America can be sure that Israel will remain strongly pro-American. As the region's leading military power, Israel's own capabilities balance Syria and other regional powers that could pose threats to U.S. interests.

Beyond strictly strategic concerns, America must ask itself if it can afford to abandon these friends of past decades which still face serious threats to their security, knowing that to do so might invite wars against them—wars that they could lose. It is one thing to balk at taking on new obligations, such as Armenia, Poland, Ukraine, or others now seeking American protection. It is another thing to abandon existing friends knowing that their fate could be uncertain. Maintaining these commitments for a time is the best hope of deterring war, and ultimately of convincing these countries' enemies that their best option is the peaceful settlement of differences.

America's commitment, of course, is not in perpetuity. It continually must be reevaluated to make absolutely certain that its serves America's interests. So far, and for the near term, America has an interest in keeping Israel, South Korea, and Taiwan strong and secure. Thus, America still must supply Israel with weapons and military aid to defend itself. At the same time, America firmly should press Israel to adopt the market reforms needed to strengthen the Israeli economy and reduce Israel's economic reliance on the U.S. As America seeks to broker a lasting Middle East peace, it should try to achieve a negotiated settlement that leaves Israel with defensible borders.

In the case of Taiwan, security means that the U.S. must abide by its obligations under the 1979 Taiwan Relations Act. As such, the U.S. should sell modern weapons and military technology to Taipei. These have allowed Taiwan to build a strong indigenous defense industry, including production of advanced fighter aircraft, frigates, and other ships.

South Korea's security requires that America's 40,000 troops remain stationed in that country to deter attack from North Korea. It also requires military cooperation, such as the "Team Spirit" annual joint U.S.-South Korean military exercises. The U.S. should sell South Korea advanced anti-missile defense systems, such as the Theater High Altitude Area Defense System, as they become available later in the decade.

45. In Search of a Foreign Policy for America

Alvin Z. Rubinstein

The disappearance of a defining ideological enemy, combined with hard times at home, has spawned a new isolationist impulse. This impulse comes for the most part from professional anti-communists who no longer feel impelled to save the world from communism; now they seek to save America. What this means is as varied as the proponents, who are a mixed lot. The isolationist rhetoric is not limited to the radical right. It is also to be found on the radical left, where the conspiratorial bent and apolitical pseudo-moralizing of a Noam Chomsky resembles that of a Patrick Buchanan. Fellow-travellers in zealotry, they desire to isolate America from the world, and in the process to transform it in their own authoritarian ideological image. Both men advocate extremist positions that are more apposite than opposite. As with most ideologues, their

SOURCE: Alvin Z. Rubinstein, "In Search of a Foreign Policy," *Society*, vol. 29, no. 6, September/October 1992, pp. 9–14, excerpts. Reprinted with permission by Transaction.

views are as close as the two ends that complete a circle.

Isolationists want to reverse five decades of involvement in world affairs. They play on economic distress to restructure America's foreign policy agenda. Wrapping themselves in the mantle of patriotism and concern for the working man, they call attention to "America First." According to Patrick Buchanan "what we need is a new nationalism, a new patriotism, a new foreign policy that puts America first, and, not only first, but second and third as well." . . .

The isolationists may talk about jobs, but what they want is a change in the orientation of American foreign policy. Patrick Buchanan has little expertise, and perhaps even less interest in economic policy. He rails against Bush for considering a tax increase in order to endear himself to the Reaganauts of the Republican Party's ultra-right, where there is money to finance his campaign and a surrogate ideology for the communist threat. Buchanan has no blueprint for the economy, and none is apt to be forthcoming. Rather, his aim is an assault on the internationalism of the past fifty years.

The tension between isolationism and internationalism is as old as the republic. Washington's injunction against "entangling alliances" and John Quincy Adam's declaration that America "goes not abroad, in search of monsters to destroy" contrasts with Woodrow Wilson's espousal of self-determination and a world made safe for democracy and John F. Kennedy's call, "My fellow citizens of the world, ask not what America will do for you, but what together we can do for the freedom of man." One strand of thought is one of constraint, caution, and a sense of limited capabilities befitting a nation with no serious threats to its security; the other is one of self-confidence, sweeping vision, and optimism which mirrors the nation's strength and status in the world. These conceptions have coexisted throughout the nineteenth and twentieth centuries. They were never mutually exclusive, but were adapted by American leaders to suit the circumstances of the time.

Thus, even in the heyday of twentieth-century isolationism in the 1920s, when Calvin Coolidge proclaimed, "The chief business of the American people is business" and disdained involvement in European affairs and the League of Nations, the United States pursued a blatantly interventionist policy—military and economic—in Central America, toyed with empire in the Philippines, and intrigued for position in an economically vulnerable China. His "isolationism" went hand-in-hand with assertive nationalism abroad.

In the late 1930s, "America Firsters" were against any involvement in the struggle against Nazism. Their proponents were ethnically diverse, but included a heavy representation of Germans and of Irish whose anti-British animus was intensified by their anti-Roosevelt and anti-New Deal attitudes. The America First Committee, established in the fall of 1940 when Britain stood alone against Nazi Germany, was against any aid to Britain and in favor or strict neutrality; in the circumstances of the time, this was effectively a pro-Nazi bias. Those of this ilk were swept aside by Pearl Harbor.

In the period after the Second World War, the Republican Party was dominated by its internationalist wing, led first by Thomas Dewey, then Dwight Eisenhower, Richard Nixon, and Ronald Reagan. Whatever their conservative impulses at home, they were committed to a foreign policy that assumed the preeminent role in the struggle against Soviet expansionism, opposed communism, favored containment, and engineered the integration of a democratic Japan and Germany into an international system that was shaped by Western ideas and Western institutions, under the leadership of the United States.

It is this essentially bipartisan legacy that is under challenge from Buchanan and others on the fringe right. Is the electorate on the threshold of a major realignment? Two circumstances, at once systemic and psychological, distinguish the 1990s from the earlier period and work to Buchanan's advantage. First, in the 1930s, the Depression, as John Lukacs put it in *Outgrowing Democracy*, "at its worst amounted to a crisis of confidence in the financial institutions of the nation. It did not amount to a crisis of confidence in the political institutions of the republic."

However, in the 1990s, should the recession prove to be a prelude to prolonged economic decline, the crisis of confidence could bring a turn to populist, nativist, ethnocentric politics. Second, the end of the cold war has ushered in a multipolar world, very different from any we have ever known. Neither the Republicans nor the Democrats have discussed this new political world with the electorate. The "new world order" Bush conjured up at the end of the Persian Gulf War has become a neglected phrase to which substance was never given.

Enter Patrick Buchanan and a congeries of well endowed think tanks promoting the isolationist line. . . . The totality of their activism conveys an illusion of importance. In time, we shall be able to assess their impact on the thinking and politics of the American electorate. For the moment, Buchanan provides name recognition and an intellectual argument that challenges long accepted foreign policy assumptions. In contrast to the right of the 1930s led by Father Charles Coughlin, which fell by the wayside in 1941 when America took up arms against an aggressive Japan and Germany and then went on to stand guard willingly and generously against a powerful, threatening Soviet Union, the right of 1992 strikes a more responsive chord with main-street America. So far, it alone has offered sweeping solutions to the foreign policy dilemmas and difficulties facing the United States. Even though rejected by the majority of Republican voters, the issues they purport to address do require attention. Thus far, neither of the two major political parties has been prepared to face up to them with any degree of consistency or conviction.

Buchanan's proposals are simplistic but appealing: bring home the troops, end foreign aid, curb illegal immigration, be tough in trade negotiations (in his words, stop being "trade wimps"), do not let the special interests (his mannered code word for Jews and pro-Israel groups) dictate United States policy, forget Russia, look first and only to the interests and welfare of the United States, and so on. Proposals with an appealing ring, they have a strong bite. But we are used to such things from Patrick Buchanan, a political pit bull whose pugnacity and mastery of the telling phrase made him a star speech writer in the Nixon and Reagan administrations. Political brawling is not political leadership. "No tax increases" and "bring the boys home" are not proposals for making America competitive, richer, or more secure. Buchanan, like the radical isolationist fringe he epitomizes, does not think constructively; he has no prescription to offer for what ails the economy and foreign policy, only slogans. He is a political crank not a viable candidate.

Certain basics seem to elude Buchanan's new isolationists. The United States has always been "America First." Its leadership, whether under Coolidge, Roosevelt, Truman, Eisenhower, Nixon, Carter, or Reagan, has always acted to promote what it believed to be "the national interest." Inevitably, there have been differences over how to put this admittedly general concept into operation. It has always been thus. Each generation has had to reinterpret the meaning of democracy, of liberty,

vital interests, and freedom. Foreign policy is no different. Every country seeks to promote its national security and its national welfare, and it is the purpose of foreign policy as well as defense policy to advance and secure these goals. Buchanan has trouble understanding all this. Unhinged by a world without communism to fight, he has taken to hawking anti-Semitism, prompting even William F. Buckley to take him to task in *The National Review*. . . .

Specifically, what then is to be done? Now that containment has outlived its purpose, what strategy should the United States adopt? Before such a new strategy can be devised, the prime threat must be defined. Problems abound, regional and functional, but there is no one overriding threat capable of mobilizing domestic support for a shared purpose in defense of vital national interests. Hence the ingenuous plausibility of the isolationists' demand for a return of all troops and an end to what Buchanan has derisively called "messianic global baloney."

Secretary of Defense Dick Cheney has tacitly acknowledged the difficulty of defending against an array of as yet uncrystallized threats. His call for "prudent retrenchment" seeks to retain a broad capability to deal with possible problems deriving from such things as instability on the Eurasian land mass, proliferation of unconventional weapons, and the activities of "rogue states." Basically, he is playing for time, hoping to keep the formidable, highly professional military capability largely intact. This is not unreasonable, at least until we know more about the fate of Russia's nuclear forces and its groping toward a democratic system and market economy; the outcome of the lingering threat from Saddam Hussein and other "rogue" forces in the Middle East; the extent to which European integration transforms not only the economic character of Europe but also its centuries-old pattern of rivalries and wars; and numerous related pitfalls of the emerging multipolar world. However, if the president cannot provide a compelling rationale for sustaining a large military establishment, a congress overwhelmed by domestic priorities and pressures will not be satisfied with minimal cuts. Calls for heftier "peace dividends" from the end of the cold war could well wreak havoc with orderly force reductions. In the absence of strategic vision and a firm hand in the White House, influential congressional leaders may use their political leverage to preserve their pork barrel goodies irrespective of the impact it might have on the·military's capability.

For the time being, a salutary foreign policy would be limited responses to regional and functional issues. These should be designed to help us through the interim uncertainty of the early post-cold war period in a way that builds on past relationships and present reconciliations; and they should embody certain criteria. First the policy must be affordable. As the recent war in the Persian Gulf showed, the United States can no longer assume the financial burden of major peace-preserving operations alone; it must rely on allies and major beneficiaries to share the costs. At a time of chronic budget deficits in the range of 400 billion dollars a year, the United States cannot continue to spend 150 billion dollars a year on the defense of financially well-off allies in East Asia and Western Europe.

Second, the policies must attract popular support. The American people need to be convinced that continued heavy engagement abroad is in the national interest. And in this instance what is good for the United States is good for the international community as well. The prevention of war between nations, the encouragement of regional stability, and the fostering of trade and economic development are objectives that redound to the benefit of the United States and that responsible leaders in the world should embrace in their own interests. A good deal of this can be achieved through an enhanced role for the United Nations Security Council—and at a far lesser cost to the United States Treasury—but this would require "new thinking" by the president and not attachment to the old ways.

Third, there must be mutual benefit. What is good for America must also be good for foreign partners. There must be a shared sense of purpose between the parties. But it must also be recognized that any partnership, whether between governments or between commercial enterprises, entails some specialization of function, within the overall framework in which the mutual benefits are to be realized.

Buchanan is right to recognize nationalism as the prevalent force in the post-cold war world. However, his proposed retreat into isolationism reflects a xenophobic and dog-bite-dog view of the world. Its inevitable consequence would be renewed arms races and recrudescence of past animosities, and the unfettered anarchy in the international system that gave rise to the Second World War. With no vision for the future, he views Japan-bashing through the prism of the past.

Unfortunately, President Bush's visit to Japan in December 1991 was not too different. Driven more by self-interest than the national interest, he failed to break new ground for solutions to the long-term problems besetting U.S.-Japanese relations. Trade issues are obviously a problem and important to negotiate, though their main solution lies probably with changes that must occur in the United States, not with Japan. What is crucial—and thus far this has been ignored by the Bush administration—is the future of the U.S.-Japanese security relationship. By its very nature this relationship is asymmetrical. There is nothing unusual in this, most durable alliances are.

In this instance, the United States has the military capabilities for a credible deterrent policy that ensures Japan's security and obviates its having to undertake a large and costly defense buildup; the U.S. Navy assures the flow of Japan's imports and exports across secure sea lines of communication. Japan, on the other hand, provides vital air and naval facilities for the forward deployment of American power, as well as substantial forces for the defense of its home islands. But now that the cold war is over and Russia does not pose the global threat the Soviet Union once did, the United States has little need for Japanese bases. Japan, however, wants the American military presence to continue, because it harbors historic suspicions of Russia.

Well and good. The time has come to update the post-1945 security relationship that served the United States and Japan so well in the past. In the 1990s, the United States can no longer afford to subsidize the defense of Japan, or of South Korea. The cost alone of maintaining and modernizing a carrier task force group, which is what the United States has kept on permanent station in the northeast Asian theater of operations, runs more than 20 billion dollars a year. This amount represents about one half of the current trade deficit with Japan. Some significant adjustment is in order. Japan must shoulder the primary burden of the costs associated with its defense by U.S. forces. For its part, the United States can ensure regional stability and the expansion of commerce in East Asia provided the costs do not exceed the gains from a free trade system. A fair sharing of the defense burden is an effective antidote to protectionist fever.

As in any partnership, changes are periodically required to safeguard the interests of both partners. Japan has the financial means to remove a major source of the divisiveness in its relations with the United States. Its own vital interests should make it receptive to a restructured partnership with the United States. Why Bush has not taken steps to revise cost sharing in our strategic-military relationship with Japan is a question in search of an answer. . . .

Russia's current "time of troubles" is a challenge and an opportunity for the United States. Timely, limited, clearly focused help is in the American national interest very simply because a non-expansionist, inner-directed Russia that is trying to develop a market economy and open its society is a potential partner, not only in commerce but also in foreign affairs. Investing in Russia now, with all its possible negative outcomes, is admittedly a speculative enterprise. Leaving aside consideration of the limits of American assistance, certain kinds of help are well within its means and could prove cost effective. Having spent several trillion dollars in waging a cold war for forty-five years, the United States can surely justify gambling several billion a year for five to ten years to promote the liberalization and democratization of Russian institutions and the development of a less threatening Russia, which remains very much a nuclear super-power. The United States can take steps to accelerate the dismantling of Russia's nuclear weapons and en-

sure that the country's economic decline will not tempt its nuclear specialists to sell their military expertise to radical regimes in the third world. In concert with Western Europe, the United States can cooperate with the republics of the former Soviet Union to work for the environmental protection of all of us.

Nuclear power plants in the territory of what is now the Commonwealth of Independent States (formerly the Soviet Union) are in extremely poor condition. With inadequate safeguards, maintenance problems that have been deferred far too long, and personnel demoralized by neglect and bureaucratism, these nuclear reactors are potential Chernobyls. Establishing special teams to help the Russians cope with their nuclear problems is a prudent investment in our own welfare and a step toward finding functional and mutually advantageous ways of working with our former adversary. Such interdependency is anathema to the Buchananite ideology.

More ambitious, and far more uncertain, are moves to help Russia develop a market-oriented economy. The United States government could provide loan guarantees to American firms entering into joint enterprises in the Commonwealth of Independent States. Agriculture, food processing, mineral extraction, and oil production are some of the obvious targets for American investment. Of course, the problems in helping the Russians (and other ethnic republics) to help themselves are enormous. The Russians have little understanding of business culture; currency convertibility is prerequisite to significant investment entailing a 6 to 10 billion dollar stabilization fund; the weakening of the centralized control system has spawned multiplying and competitive centers of local power, making business arrangements highly unstable; corruption is endemic; the transportation system is experiencing serious breakdowns in various regions; and ethnic strife is an ever-present and spreading threat.

All these factors complicate decisions of how much capital and technology the United States, and the West as a whole, should commit to the transformation of a seriously, but not mortally, weakened Russia. Martin Malia, a life-long deflator of roseate scholarly assessments of Soviet "social-ism" and an unflinching pessimist regarding Russia's chances of recovery in the decades ahead, deplores "the lack of a positive Western response" to Boris Yeltsin's possibly impossible efforts to return Russia to Europe and create a stable society. Writing in the *New Republic* in February 1992, he states:

> What we will have for at least one more year, therefore, will be an emergency executive government trying, from one crisis and improvisation to another, to navigate its way out of what is the most appalling national collapse in history. . . . For the task in Russia now is difficult beyond anything the privileged West has ever known. Not only must a modern society be built out of the unprecedented wreckage of the late Soviet economy and polity, but this building must be done by a population that until 1991 was molded and deformed by the Leninist lie. As the matter was put, on the day the Union died, by one longtime Party member who always knew the system was a fraud: 'And we must now try to produce good out of all that evil.'

Of course, involvement in Russia's future carries certain risks. But the greater risk may lie in doing nothing at all. Had Buchanan been an advisor in 1492 to Ferdinand and Isabella of Spain, he would undoubtedly have pooh-poohed investment in Christopher Columbus. Looking backward, fantasizing the return of an era that had its own warts, troubles, and dilemmas, and offering slogans in place of solutions is as dangerous and unpromising a political course for the United States as it is for Russia.

American foreign policy is at a crossroads. Choices need to be made, the consequences of which for the future of our country could be momentous. Many may dispute the premises and preferences implicit in these options for two of our most pressing foreign policy problems. These issues demand serious and sustained discussion. Japan and Russia are only two of the topics that comprise the American agenda for the next century. Germany and NATO, trade and foreign aid, Israel and Iraq, human rights and ethnic separatism, proliferation of unconventional weapons and arms sales, defense spending and national purpose, these are the issues that should be the focus of a national debate.

Isolationist evangelism is no basis for United States foreign policy. It never has been. Buchanan has raised issues he is unwilling to discuss and incapable of solving. Those who seek a popular mandate for guiding the country in the years ahead do, however, have an obligation to undertake precisely this kind of review.

Questions for Discussion

1. What are U.S. foreign policy goals in a post-Cold War world?

2. How would you rank order the purposes to which U.S. policy should be committed? Do you find any contradictions between the purposes you have identified?

3. How do these objectives differ from those that were pursued during the period of the Cold War?

4. Is the promotion of democracy around the world a core policy objective? Should force be used toward this end?

5. What specific foreign policy objectives do you feel this administration has tended thus far to neglect?

6. What can be done to bring U.S. economic capabilities in line with U.S. foreign policy aims abroad?

Selected Bibliography

ATTALI, JACQUES. *Millenium: Winners and Losers in the Coming World Order.* New York: Times Books, 1991.

BOOTH, KEN (Ed.). *New Thinking About Strategy and International Security.* New York: Harper Collins, 1991.

BRANDON, HENRY (Ed.). *In Search of a New World Order: The Future of U.S.-European Relations.* Washington, DC: The Brookings Institution, 1992.

CHACE, JAMES. *The Consequences of the Peace.* New York: Oxford University Press, 1992.

GARTEN, JEFFREY E. *A Cold Peace: America, Japan, Germany, and the Struggle for Supremacy.* New York: Times Books/Random House, 1992.

KAPSTEIN, ETHAN B. *The Political Economy of National Security: A Global Perspective.* Columbia, SC: University of South Carolina Press, 1992.

KENNEDY, PAUL. *Preparing for the 21st Century.* New York: Random House, 1993.

LUTTWAK, EDWARD. *Strategy: The Logic of War and Peace.* Cambridge: Harvard University Press, 1987.

NIXON, RICHARD. *Seize the Moment: America's Challenge in a One-Superpower World.* New York: Simon & Schuster, 1992.

REICH, ROBERT B. *The Work of Nations: Preparing Ourselves for 21st Century Capitalism.* New York: Knopf, 1991.

ROMM, JOSEPH J. *The Once and Future Superpower: How to Restore America's Economic, Energy and Environmental Security.* New York: William Morrow, 1992.

THUROW, LESTER. *Head to Head: The Coming Economic Battle Among Japan, Europe, and America.* New York: William Morrow, 1992.

TUCKER, ROBERT W., and DAVID C. HENDRICKSON. *The Imperial Temptation: The New World Order and America's Purpose.* New York: Council on Foreign Relations Press, 1991.

WEIGLEY, RUSSELL F. *The Age of Battles.* Bloomington, Ind.: Indiana University Press, 1991.